D1590898

**My
Silver
Planet**

Hopkins Studies in Modernism
Douglas Mao, *Series Editor*

My Silver Planet

A Secret History

of Poetry and Kitsch

Daniel Tiffany

Johns Hopkins University Press
Baltimore

This book has been brought to publication with the generous
assistance of Dornsife College of Letters, Arts, and Sciences,
University of Southern California.

Johns Hopkins University Press
2715 North Charles Street
Baltimore, Maryland 21218-4363
www.press.jhu.edu

Library of Congress Cataloging-in-Publication Data

Tiffany, Daniel.
    My silver planet : a secret history of poetry and kitsch / Daniel
Tiffany.
        pages cm. — (Hopkins Studies in Modernism)
    Includes bibliographical references and index.
    ISBN-13: 978-1-4214-1145-3 (hardcover : acid-free paper)—ISBN-13:
978-1-4214-1146-0 (electronic) — ISBN-10: 1-4214-1145-8 (hardcover :
acid-free paper) — ISBN-10: 1-4214-1146-6 (electronic)
    1. Poetry—History and criticism.   2. Kitsch—In
literature.   3. Banality (Philosophy) in literature.   I. Title.
    PN1126.T55 2013

    809.1—dc23   2013010184

A catalog record for this book is available from the British Library.

*Special discounts are available for bulk purchases of this book. For
more information, please contact Special Sales at 410-516-6936 or
specialsales@press.jhu.edu.*

Johns Hopkins University Press uses environmentally friendly book
materials, including recycled text paper that is composed of at least
30 percent post-consumer waste, whenever possible.

Contents

My
Silver
Planet

1 Arresting Poetry

Kitsch, Totality, Expression

Unpopular Pop

Once upon a time, long before it had been reduced to a synonym for mediocrity in the arts, the term "kitsch" functioned as a lightning rod in debates about mass culture and the fate of modernism confronting the rise of fascism in Europe in the 1920s and 1930s. For a word now applied quite casually to trivial and spurious things, "kitsch" has a surprising history of provoking alarm and extreme reactions: Hermann Broch called kitsch "the element of evil in the value system of art."[1] Theodor Adorno refers to kitsch as "poison" and, drawing upon the German etymology of the term, as "artistic trash."[2] Clement Greenberg later refers to the "looting" and "traps" associated with kitsch, to its criminal aspect.[3] In these same essays, the "evil" of kitsch acquires an array of sinister qualities: it is said to be at once parasitic, mechanical, and pornographic; a "decorative cult" and a "parody of catharsis."[4] These attributions—always linked to a presumption of complicit, indulgent pleasure—acquire specific and sometimes contradictory historical contours in Broch's and Greenberg's assertions about the correlation of kitsch and fascism.[5] In addition, noting the presumed affinities between the mimeticism of kitsch and homosexuality, Andrew Hewitt claims that kitsch "marks the aesthetic meeting point of homosexuality and fascism for the contemporary cultural imagination."[6]

The focal point of these accusations, the term "kitsch" was introduced into art criticism by modernist writers to identify (and condemn) productions of mass culture. Things characterized as kitsch, the original doctrine asserts, are derivative, sentimental, trivial, stereotypical, and therefore contrary to the values of true art. Kitsch is an object of complacent and harmless gratification, yet it bears an indelible moral stain: it flourishes in the shadow of its bad name. The discourse of kitsch thus acknowledges an important new source of aesthetic pleasure, even as it sponsors frequently vicious attacks on such pleasure. This ambivalence is reinforced by the fact that kitsch has never been embraced as an aesthetic category by any particular collective or subcultural formation (unlike, for example, the gay community's adoption of camp). Kitsch survives without a halo of collective identification—without belonging, it seems, to any group. In addition, the fugitive aspect of the term now appears to have been overtaken by a vague sense that its orientation toward popular culture is outdated: the very idea of kitsch may be an anachronism. If relations between elite and popular cultures are now changing in fundamental ways, then perhaps the category of kitsch is irrelevant, moribund.

For all of these reasons, kitsch continues to evoke, despite the apparent simplicity and innocence of its pleasures, a sense of ambivalence and polarization; the concept seems to be in perpetual flux, lacking clear definition, unsteady. As a result, the exact meaning of kitsch remains elusive in fundamental ways: it is commonly confused with camp and occasionally even with art itself. Theories about where and when kitsch originated are usually inexact and unconvincing; answers to the question of whether kitsch has a basic affinity with one art or medium have shifted erratically over time. Today, kitsch tends to be associated primarily with visual or material culture, yet the inaugural essays on the subject in the 1920s and 1930s identify poetry as a crucial matrix for the development of kitsch.

Modernist definitions of kitsch refer (as I will explain in subsequent chapters) to various canonical and noncanonical poets as a way of illustrating the features of kitsch and its wider cultural significance. Embedded in the essays I cited earlier is the idea that the cultural history of elite poetry, especially its relation to everyday language—to the vernacular—offers a crucial framework for understanding kitsch as an index of tensions (and transactions) between elite and popular cultures. Kitsch is therefore confusing and even incoherent today in part because its true history remains a secret history: a genealogy—reaching back to the early eighteenth century—in which poetry stands at the very source. Tracing this lineage, our assumptions about kitsch as a category of material culture will be called into question by viewing it through the matrix of poetry and poetics, even as the face of modern poetry will begin to look rather strange, and perhaps even disturbing, when it is seen from the perspective of kitsch.

The vehemence of the modernist campaign against kitsch demonstrates that, beneath the current associations with mediocrity and harmless pleasure, kitsch has always functioned as an irresistible locus of moral and aesthetic taboos: triviality, hedonism, fakery, but also—somewhat incoherently—homosexuality and fascism. Unresolved in the wake of high modernism, the anxiety about the pleasures (and dangers) of kitsch continues to assert itself in forceful, though perhaps less absolute, ways. If radicalism in the arts implies—at least in part—reorienting the viewer towards whatever appears to be vacuous, trifling, indulgent, or worthless, then kitsch still marks an elusive frontier: to equate art and kitsch, or to deliberately produce kitsch as if it were art, flirts even now with artistic suicide, with the self-destruction of art.

Kitsch in its original formulations is said to be the antithesis of "true" art—what Greenberg calls "synthetic art."[7] More bluntly, he states, "Kitsch is vicarious experience and faked sensations. . . . Kitsch is the epitome of all that is spurious."[8] Broch declares simply, "Kitsch represents falsehood (it is often so defined, and rightly so)."[9] For certain modernists, the spurious nature of kitsch is inseparable from its mimeticism (which Greenberg calls a "surplus of realism"), in contrast to modernist abstraction.[10] Whatever the terms of comparison (between kitsch and "true" art), the basic attitude towards kitsch adopted by the modernists who defined it is riddled with condescension. It is crucial, however, to emphasize that the term "kitsch" has been used historically by only a restricted segment of society, the intelligentsia. What the elite calls "kitsch" may in fact conform to the basic criteria of "art" for many people. Thus the person who consumes and enjoys kitsch is never "the person who uses the word 'kitsch.'"[11] From a sociological perspective, then, kitsch is an aesthetic category suspended between those who control its public name (to destructive ends) and those for whom it has no name (or who prefer not to use its public name), between those who refer to it with contempt and those who enjoy it without irony, reservation, or shame. This polarized structure reinforces the fundamental terms of misidentification and uncertainty surrounding kitsch: Is it art or not? But also, is it true or false, authentic or fake? Kitsch is thus not simply a particular kind of artifact but an artifact imagined and judged in divergent ways by communities in conflict with one another.

Identifying the formal and stylistic features of kitsch is a treacherous task (in part because of its proximity to camp). Although the work of classification and definition is essential to establishing the exact contours of poetic kitsch, formal analysis must be supplemented, I have been suggesting, by efforts to understand the term "kitsch" as designating not simply a particular kind of artifact, but a distinctive *relation* to artifacts (which can indeed influence their design and production): a relation that is consistently negative, derogatory, paranoid. The perspectival aspect of kitsch thus implies that its artifacts cannot be identified solely by their place in the history of material production (as symptoms, for example, of modern industrial culture). Taking this relational factor into account, one must conclude that certain elemental properties of kitsch are determined not simply by economics or a chronology of production—though these are certainly germane—but by distinctive patterns and disruptions in the history of taste.

Seemingly impervious to re-evaluation, the aesthetic ideology of kitsch combines childish pleasures (a regression to infantile gratification) with an affinity for social formations of disdain and polarization. The attribution of kitsch is determined by habits of alienation and paranoia that suppress correspondences between the subject and certain contemptible artifacts (in contrast to the logic of identification determining the experience of camp, which shares some of its objects with kitsch). Accordingly, Eve Kosofsky Sedgwick explains,

> Unlike kitsch-attribution, then, camp-recognition doesn't ask, "What kind of debased creature could possibly be the right audience for this spectacle?" Instead, it says *what if*: What if the audience for this were exactly *me*? . . . Unlike kitsch-*attribution*, the sensibility of camp-*recognition* always sees that it is dealing in reader relations and in projective fantasy . . . it acknowledges (unlike kitsch) that its perceptions are necessarily also creations.[12]

The negative attribution of kitsch is uninflected, without irony or critical self-consciousness. At the same time, because kitsch is always an object of disdain as well as affection, it is never simple (or simply benign), as convention suggests. Rather, kitsch is indeed a toy, a mere prop, but it is also unsettling, subversive: a treacherous bauble. In contrast, then, to the identificatory appeal of camp, the alternating configuration of kitsch supports a notion of trifling negativity, of shallow subversion.

Missing Verses

A trivial version of the abject, mustering forces of repulsion and attraction, kitsch harbors within itself its own taboo, a paranoid relation replicating the basic economy of modernist definitions of kitsch. The paranoid object targeted by kitsch—its very own demon—reveals itself through a comprehensive but implicit erasure of *poetry* from the symptomology of kitsch. All of the original theorists of kitsch in the 1920s and 1930s emphasized poetry, as I indicated a moment ago, in their efforts to map out the new aesthetic category, citing particular poets or poems and drawing significant comparisons between poetic kitsch and its counterparts in other media (architecture, painting, music). Within a generation or two, however, attention to poetry and poetics had completely vanished from serious discussion about kitsch. Not a single book in the revisionary studies of kitsch that began to appear in the late 1960s (with contributions in the 1980s by Danilo Kis, Svetlana Boym, and Celeste Olalquiaga) even mentions the example of poetry—an omission silently marking the garbled assimilation of kitsch to the category of camp but also replicating the paranoid exclusion of kitsch from the precincts of art.[13]

Precipitated perhaps by the explosive emergence of pop art in the 1960s, the phenomenology of kitsch appears to have drifted towards a new criterion of palpability and objecthood—contingent on the expulsion of language—in which poetry became an unrecognizable emblem of the abject nature of kitsch. Although the poetry of the New York school absorbed and elaborated the formal stratagems of pop art in significant ways (as I will demonstrate in subsequent chapters), it remained isolated from the contaminating *value* of kitsch. The curious neutrality, or immunity, of poetry in this context testifies to its veiled participation in transactions between kitsch and other formations of the abject—and to poetry's singular role in the secret history of kitsch.

The disappearance of poetry from the contemporary discourse of kitsch evokes the repressed nature of kitsch in general, but it also points dialectically to the scandalous role poetry once played in the genesis of kitsch. Adumbrating a poetics of missing things, Broch inadvertently discloses the recursive nature of this secret history when he asserts that kitsch is "lodged like a foreign body in the overall system of art": a live burial that is all the more insidious, he notes, because it can be difficult to distinguish between system and anti-system, between art and kitsch.[14] The unstable identity of modern kitsch (is it art or kitsch?) replicates turmoil of earlier scandals enveloping certain eighteenth-century poetic forgeries (by James Macpherson, Thomas Chatterton, and others). The process of authentication was frequently inhibited (as in the case of the Ossian forgeries) by the problem of a missing manuscript. In the latest disappearance of verse from the land-scape of popular culture, poetic language has once again gone missing from the misty borderlands of imposture.

Anticipating the formula of kitsch, dubious poetic "reliques" began to appear in the "ecstatic" archive of certain exclusive, highly cultivated, ho-mosocial circles (the Walpole Set, the Shenstone Set) in the 1750s: artifacts expressing the ambiguity of the sexual and social profiles of these cliques—what Sedgwick calls "the epistemology of the closet." Counterfeit texts, nursery rhymes, fake ballads, and Gothic verse thereby became poetic screens of queer identity (a paradigm foreshadowed by the reviled figure of "the poetaster").[15] The analogy between fraudulent texts and inscrutable sexual personae shows itself in the usage of the word "imposture," which refers at once to deviant textual and social practices. The tentative elabora-tion of queer personae in the eighteenth century thus resonated with the uncertainty about authorship and diction in the public theater of poetic imposture.

Insofar as poetry functions—in its belated and provisional absence from the discourse on the subject—as a lost relic of the abject paradise of kitsch, the homologies between kitsch and various formations of social and sexual obscurity reveal themselves through the anamorphosis of poetry. That is to say, disclosing—and restoring—poetry's place in the secret history of kitsch, establishes a basis for deciphering, for example, the promiscuous and formulaic correspondences (in the cultural imaginary) between fascism and a queer poetics of kitsch. Putting poetry to work in the service of kitsch (or vice versa) has the advantage as well of disclosing poetry's historical, yet largely unacknowledged, expulsion from the once-emergent bourgeois category of "literature" in the eighteenth century: an anguished and inter-minable event that doubles as the prehistory of kitsch. The etiolated, Au-gustan poetics of Gray, Goldsmith, and Shenstone assimilated the thrilling vulgarity of Gothic verse and the dubious border ballads, in opposition to the middling sensibility of the new supergenre, literature.

To write critically at this point in time about kitsch involves, as the fore-going observations suggest, a deliberate appropriation—and transvaluation —of the term "kitsch." The most pragmatic verbal evidence of such a trans-formation would be a shift in the *usage* of the word "kitsch": the prospect, for example, of using it as a transitive (or intransitive) verb applied to poems, authors, historical periods (in a manner resembling the deliberate shift in usage of the term "queer"). It may be instructive and revealing to *kitsch* particular poems and texts, especially works (such as Ezra Pound's *Cantos*) that appear to be vigorously opposed to kitsch in principle.

The insights to be gained from reconstructing and elaborating the concept of kitsch according to the criteria I have outlined above will emerge not by focusing on its most obvious referent—visual and material culture—but by attending to what has gone missing from the discourse of kitsch: poetry and poetics. In this regard, *My Silver Planet* is not a book about kitsch in general, or even about kitsch and visual culture, but about kitsch and poetry. To that end, I do not seek to directly accommodate poetry to existing insights about material culture or to make poetry comply with received models of kitsch as it pertains to material culture. Rather, it is my intention to develop a specifically poetological orientation towards kitsch that will trouble our reception and understanding of poetry written since the eighteenth century, not to mention our presumptions about the nature of kitsch in material culture.

Investigating the aborted relations between poetry and kitsch—thereby testing the possibility that the concept of kitsch may be truly moribund—will afford unexpected glimpses of the end of popular culture as a viable concept (as a domain of culture contingent on elite culture's condemnation of its artifacts and values). Acknowledging the interdependence of elite culture and the adversarial potential of popular culture inevitably engages Peter Bürger's conception of the historical avant-garde as a movement integrating art and life, vanguardism and populism.[16] From this perspective, kitsch may eventually be regarded not as the nemesis of the avant-garde (in Greenberg's formulation) but as a baffling mutation of Dada, a development marking the collapse of the iconic—and unstable—opposition between avant-garde and kitsch.

Bogus

The inaugural modernist essays on kitsch I cited earlier rest on two basic premises: first, kitsch is irremediably false—it is fake art—and, second, its roots are to be found in the ideology of Romanticism (an assertion that is fundamentally flawed in its chronology and its designations, since the aesthetic methods and fantasies leading to kitsch were first sponsored by neoclassicism in the eighteenth century). None of these essays explains, though, why *poetry* should be regarded as a primary model for the proliferation of spurious artifacts associated with popular culture, nor do they offer any concrete historical basis for linking fraudulence (the essential feature of kitsch) directly to the poems cited as examples of kitsch.

What, then, are the missing links between poetry and popularity, poetry and commodification, poetry and fraudulence? In the broadest sense, solutions to the riddles surrounding poetic kitsch remain embedded in the transformation of English poetic diction in the eighteenth century, a process reflecting changes in literacy and print culture, in the literary marketplace, and in the colonial conditions of anglophony: a process renewing the creative turmoil of English as a *synthetic* language. These changes paralleled the controversial assimilation of everyday language—of vernacular speech—into the diction of poetry written by the educated classes. Ultimately, these developments were comparable in their transformative effects on the poetic tradition to the revival and appropriation of classical languages. The reviled and misunderstood category of kitsch remains, in fact, the most controversial legacy of elite poetry's incorporation of the poetic vernacular, a legacy echoed and renewed by modernist denunciations of kitsch in material culture.

If lyric poetry in English fell asleep, as some claim, in the eighteenth century, it certainly experienced some rather strange dreams during its imaginative slumber: dreams of an uncanny idiom for poetry, at once familiar and alien, youthful and archaic, common and obscure—a language resisting the purified diction of "polite letters." Indeed, while lyric poetry slumbered, the British reading public became infatuated with archaic ballads that yielded a new constellation of "distressed" genres of poetry: nursery rhymes, made-up folksongs and bardic fragments, melodramas, peasant poetry, Gothic verse—not to mention the enduring subgenre of the pet epitaph! Many of these pseudo-vernacular genres of poetry made a powerful impact on certain elite poets of the period, combining to produce a "vicious" amalgam of archaic and "prettified" vocabularies (which eventually became the substance of poetic kitsch).

In the most precise historical terms, the correlation of poetry and fraudulence identified by modernist theorists of kitsch can be traced to the eighteenth century's affinity for—and contamination by—poems that are quite literally *counterfeit*. This affinity remained an essential feature of canonical Romantic poetry as well (along with its illegitimate twin, Gothic verse), yet it took root initially in neoclassical concerns about imposture and poetic diction. As a category of specious artifacts—a pretender to art—kitsch thus first acquired its association with fakery through a series of momentous and controversial literary forgeries, culminating in the scandals generated by Macpherson's invention of the Ossian fragments and Chatterton's fabrication of the Rowley manuscripts (in the mid-eighteenth century). The "distressed genre" of the counterfeit folk poem made available not only a popular palette of eccentric and even spurious poetic diction but a new poetic commodity. In Susan Stewart's articulation, "distressed genres are close to kitsch objects, artifacts of exaggerated surface and collective experience."[17] Kitsch first found its bearings during what Dwight Macdonald calls "the golden age of literary hanky-panky."[18]

Other basic tenets of kitsch theory (in addition to the specificity of its medium and its chronology) call for closer scrutiny as well. Greenberg, for example, adds to Broch's Romantic genealogy the presumption that kitsch is inseparable from modern industrial culture (though Greenberg also subscribes—incoherently—to Broch's genealogy). A quick glance at both of these sources dispels this supposition: Broch's paradigm of a Romantic genealogy and Greenberg's notion of kitsch feeding off "mature culture" both presume that kitsch does *not*, in fact, derive from vernacular or industrial culture but functions rather as a parasitic phenomenon, a medium replicating and adapting the productions of high culture.[19] Greenberg describes kitsch artifacts as "simulacra of genuine culture."[20] The history of the ballad revival in British poetry, especially the preoccupation with forgery, tells us that this influence can run in the opposite direction as well: fake lyrics sometimes shape and even transform canonical poetry. Kitsch thus provides a crucial bridge between high and low cultures, a premise that is rooted in a poetological model of kitsch.

The thesis that the earliest symptoms of kitsch—its basic DNA—emerge well before the development of Romanticism or the Industrial Revolution has an important bearing as well on presumptions about the geographical, or nationalistic, complexion of kitsch. At first glance, kitsch appears—from the national identity of most of the theorists writing about it (except Greenberg)—to be distinctly Germanic in its cultural physiognomy. However, it was not until the late eighteenth century that Germany inherited from Britain its preoccupation with folk culture, ballad composition, and poetic "reliques." (Johann Gottfried von Herder, for example, did not publish his essay on the bardic, and mostly counterfeit, fragments of Ossian—usually considered to be the catalyst for German interest in the *Volkslieder*—until 1773.)[21] Romanticism in both its German and British formations helped to elaborate, to be sure, the archetype of poetic kitsch, yet the histories of antiquarianism and imposture tell us that kitsch really began with the ballad revival in Britain during the first two decades of the eighteenth century.

The aesthetic category of kitsch thus first emerged with the introduction of vernacular idioms—whether fabricated or genuine—into the diction of elite poetry: an aberration in neoclassical poetics that would eventually transform the language of poetry in English.

In addition to revising our understanding of the broader cultural significance of certain developments in the history of poetry (and literature), a poetological approach to kitsch offers an opportunity for exposing the historical and theoretical correspondences between the simultaneous emergence of modern aesthetic theory (Kant, Schiller, Hegel) and the recurring incidents of poetic forgery that lock into place the basic criteria of poetic kitsch. From this perspective, the modernist polemic antagonizing the relation between avant-garde art and kitsch finds expression as well in a philosophical critique (by Georges Bataille, Paul de Man, and others) seeking to highlight a schism between an authentic model of the aesthetic (said to be buried in the prose of Kant) and the unmarked, historical development of a fraudulent "aesthetic ideology" (said to be initiated by Schiller).[22] Peter Bürger as well, refining this model, finds in the aesthetics of Kant and Schiller a theoretical reflection of the autonomy of art, against which the avant-garde would eventually revolt.[23]

The Kantian (and ostensibly materialist) theorization of aesthetics was quickly displaced, according to this narrative, by aesthetic *ideology*, which cultivates the artistic blasphemies of autonomy, idealization, and metaphysicality (said to be the cardinal features of "beauty").[24] More precisely, according to de Man, the idealist orientation of aesthetic ideology sustains a "genealogy which allows for a lineage that is supposed to lead from Kant, by way of Schiller and Coleridge, to decadent formalism and aestheticism."[25] Kitsch, it may be inferred, would be the final term in the evolution of aesthetic ideology. Hence this genealogy produces "a misunderstanding of the category of the aesthetic, . . . overestimating the apparent frivolity of the aesthetic and, hence, its vulnerability to moral censure."[26] The "frivolity" of a spurious model of the aesthetic leads ultimately, in de Man's view, to the aestheticization of politics—that is, to fascism.[27]

A template for de Man's neo-modernist critique of aesthetic "frivolity"—exposing the duplicity of his parallel investment in "poetics"—can be found in Bataille's nihilist program of "base materialism," which targets poetry in particular as an emblem of "emasculated" aestheticism: "servile idealism rests precisely in this will to poetic agitation . . . a completely unhappy desire to turn to upper spiritual regions."[28] Thus Bataille declares, "I can say that from now on it is impossible to retreat and hide in the 'wonderland' of Poetry without being publicly condemned as a coward."[29] The legacy of Bataille's trivialization (and demonization) of poetry—viewing it as an emblem of kitsch—can be found in the writings of later avant-garde apologists such as Serge Guibault and Benjamin Buchloh.[30] In this context, poetry, kitsch, and aesthetic ideology become targets of a positivist critique of false consciousness (and fraudulent artifacts). The most important—and least assimilable—inference of this critique is that aesthetic ideology (the fraudulent and usurping twin of a genuinely critical aesthetics), which finds expression in the spurious "wonderland of poetry," has never been about anything but kitsch. All our thinking about traditional art has really been about kitsch.

Thinking poetically about kitsch inevitably steers one, more precisely, towards the principal terms of aesthetic theory (especially beauty) in the eighteenth century, since the banality of kitsch is often intertwined with formulaic—even compulsory—models of beauty: Broch, for example, calls kitsch "a new religion of beauty."[31] The correlation of banality and beauty is perplexing, however, since (as Broch's thesis suggests) kitsch involves not merely the purification of beauty (i.e., the suppression of all qualities other than beauty) but exaggerated and even delusional regard for beauty. Elaine Scarry offers an especially promising solution to the riddling compound of banality and excessive beauty. She argues that beauty compels what she calls "replication," thereby situating beauty (structurally) between the deliria of sexual reproduction and technical reproducibility.[32] More importantly, beauty can sustain, Scarry contends, infinite sequences, or chains, of replication, which may extend irresistibly to "all the pockets of the world."[33] The seriality of beauty thus makes it susceptible to a "contagion of imitation"— to excess—revealing a basic structural affinity between beauty and the reproducibility of mass culture.[34] Kitsch marks a historical development in which the reproducibility of beauty becomes its most salient feature.

In poetry, beauty—as a quality defined by reproducibility, rarefaction, and excess—cannot be isolated from the material texture of diction: the replication of certain words, phrases, and verbal constructions that evoke the genre of poetry. Insofar as beauty is a matter of replication, or seriality, in poetry, then, kitsch is grounded, as I will discuss at length in subsequent chapters, in the verbal substance of poetic diction. Thus, whether one views poetic kitsch as barbarous or exquisite, as a verbal spectacle to be suppressed in English poetry or as the essence of poetic language (in contrast to prose), kitsch is the direct outgrowth of a heightened and restricted vocabulary associated specifically with poetry, a recursive genre designed to elicit certain generalized poetic *effects* (which places it at odds with the category of literature per se). Viewed in this way, kitsch exemplifies Poe's doctrine of poetic but calculated "composition," curtailing the functions of representation, communication, and meaningfulness while preserving the mechanism of replication in order to amplify a poetic regime of *special effects* and to expose the grounds of modern melodrama.[35] Poetic kitsch thus reveals its affinity for what Sianne Ngai calls verbal "gimmickry"—of writing backwards, for example—a temptation that marks a submerged correspondence between kitsch and certain "procedures" of the contemporary avant-garde.[36]

The orchestration of effects pertains, it must be emphasized, directly to the question of *audience*, of mass culture. Understood in this way, kitsch in poetry traffics in aesthetic hyperbole, counterfeiting poetry in a language that defies particularity yet captivates its audience: a hyperaesthetic formula radiating the common estrangement of "poetry." From a corresponding angle, poetic kitsch may be described as *poetry in drag*: not cross-dressing but something akin to female female-impersonation or male male-impersonation, a cosmetic distilling of lyrical expression, a poetic doll. Kitsch in poetry thus enacts in material and syntactic terms a poetic melodrama, exposing at once the intrinsic falsehood of poetic diction and the adulterated essence of poetry.

Twice Made

It is crucial to bear in mind that the idiosyncrasy of kitsch—the rarefaction of its materials—is sustained by, and indeed expresses fundamentally, the imitative and reflexive logic of the poetic tradition (and the nature of tradition in general). At the same time, kitsch functions, as I mentioned earlier, as a bridge between elite and vernacular cultures. Kitsch thus subscribes to Deleuze and Guattari's conception of a "minor literature": "only the possibility of setting up a minor practice of major literature from within allows one to define popular literature."[37] Lodged, as Broch asserts, "like a foreign body in the overall system of art," kitsch converts the exalted phrases of the poetic tradition into the abject substance of automation and monotony: the quintessence of poetry. It is precisely the passivity and insularity of poetic kitsch (its ability to domesticate and neutralize even the most grotesque stylistic flourishes) that identify it as a powerful engine of

simulation and conservation. Ezra Pound disparagingly called this phenomenon the "corpse language" of poetic diction.[38]

In its most rarefied and, at the same time, least distinctive aspect—an
art without qualities—the reproducibility and immobility of poetic kitsch
may succeed in *arresting poetry*, in removing poetic language from external
influence, from the continuous stream of historical incident.[39] Under these
conditions, the domain of poetic diction functions both aesthetically and
socially as a closed system of resonance and feedback, allowing for the possibility of collective experience—a way of modeling social and ephemeral
totalities—based on the reverberation of shared conditions. The echoing
diction of poetic kitsch thus acts primarily not as mode of representation
but as an insular and ambient medium of expression—confiding not the
interior secrets of individuals but the hidden grievances of collective social
formations. Marking the future horizon of kitsch, Keats refers to the reflective, totalizing substance of his poetry as "my silver planet."[40]

At the level of poetic form, the mechanism of reproducibility becomes
manifest in the dizzying effects of the *refrain*, which arrests and compels
poetry through repetition. Serving as a touchstone of the "cult of simplicity" engulfing the archaic ballad—an ornament of reproducibility—the vernacular refrain was widely adopted by neoclassical poets, an event marking
in retrospect the importance of the ballad revival to the poetics of kitsch.

In its ability to captivate—and to bring poetry to a standstill—poetic
kitsch operates in the mindless realm of the stereotype, the verbal cliché.
Gordon Teskey contends that the language of certain kinds of poetry is
"twice made": poetic diction, steeped in borrowed language, produces "an
oscillating, delirious effect: one of images and shadows from earlier poems
being preserved only so long as they have been cancelled."[41] Poetic kitsch,
in turn, heightens the "delirium" to which Teskey refers, evolving into a
hyperlyrical artifact so profoundly alienated from canonical sources that
it functions as a cultural cipher in the no-man's-land between lyrical and
anti-lyrical traditions of poetry. The markers of individuality dissolve, even
as the echolalia of an artificial, common language becomes an expressive
matrix for cultural, and even political, cohesion: the horizon of ephemeral
and potentially subversive totalities.

Yet the very idea of totality seems irredeemable, poisonous. Following
the rise of totalitarian societies (fascist and communist) in the 1930s—and,
later, the impact of French Marxist theories of difference in the 1960s—the
concept of *totality* has been equated with repression, delusional solidarity,

and false consciousness. In political discourse, the idea of totality is as disreputable as the category of kitsch in the realm of aesthetics—and the two
are linked in the public mind. Greenberg condemned kitsch as "totalitarian"
in 1939, aligning it with fascism and with Soviet communism.[42] The historical affinity of the terms supports an array of theoretical correspondences:
both kitsch and totality are condemned for privileging the operations of
synthesis, generalization, and replication. Kitsch and totality are said to be
equally *synthetic* (fabricated, but also combinatory, residual) in their ontolo-
gies. What is more, the suppression of the critical category of *diction* (as the
dimension of poetic language most closely associated with propaganda and
indoctrination) resonates with the corresponding censures of kitsch and
totality.

The social totalities sustained momentarily by the language of poetic
kitsch subscribe to the discredited legacy of Marxist theorizations of totality (the flip side of kitsch's insidious relation to totalitarian culture).
Though speculative and utopian in its orientation, the concept of totality
is, as Georg Lukács contends, indispensable to representing and motivating
revolution.[43] Thus, while the aesthetic significance of the "twice made," of
arresting poetry via the immobility of kitsch, is ostensibly conservative, its
political implications are less unambiguous. The reverberating social totality of kitsch might, for example, serve as a platform of revolutionary will
for communities stripped of their capacities for self-recognition, cohesion,
and activism. Like the craze or the fad, however, the totalities sustained by
kitsch are transient, ephemeral.

The collective dimension of kitsch—its potential role in helping to real-
ize new forms of totality—may also, as Walter Benjamin suggests, be inseparable from efforts to address the loss of historical experience—the basis
of tradition—in modern culture.[44] In this sense, Benjamin's correlation of
kitsch and authentic experience is diametrically opposed—as is the orientation of the present study—to the customary view of kitsch as that which
obscures or prevents genuine experience. According to this logic, the most
authentic practices and knowledges can only be obtained through *synthetic*
production of experience, precisely because this operation rejects any trace
of essential *nature* within the sphere of the human. Only that which is entirely artificial—such as the artificial paradise of a fleeting totality—can be
faithful to the unprecedented relations of human society.

Returning to a more narrowly poetic framework, kitsch is directly implicated in T. S. Eliot's so-called thesis of minority, a model of the poetic canon

in which the diction of minor poets sustains—by its absence of originality or invention—the main features of the poetic tradition.[45] The minor stance of a poet such as Dryden depends, according to Eliot, on his role in shaping "a language possible for mediocrity."[46] Cultivating the diction of mediocrity, Dryden becomes influential "by reason of his precise degree of inferiority."[47] By this measure, kitsch stands not on the margins of poetic tradition but at its core. What remains occluded—and susceptible to revision—in Eliot's thesis is the poetic substance of what he calls "inferiority" and "minority." Is it possible that the substance of poetic minority may disclose the conditions of poetry's vital antagonism to the criteria of "literature"?—its verbal resistance to the bourgeois affinities of literature—which in turn becomes the basis of poetry's harmonic relation (via kitsch) to mass culture? Kitsch may indeed offer an unprecedented reconciliation—overstepping the middle ground of literature—between elite and vernacular traditions.

Insofar as kitsch may be understood as the purest form of minor poetry, saturated with the highest concentration of poetic "capital" preserved by the tradition, the properties of mediocrity and inferiority serve as points of access to a verbal unconscious of the English poetic tradition but also, as I indicated earlier, to the reverberations of collective experience. It is precisely the reproducibility of poetic kitsch, along with its role as carrier of subliminal values and motives, that helps to clarify how kitsch in poetry may be related to the condition of mass culture. For if the aesthetic category of kitsch enables mass culture by arresting poetry, it must be possible to explain how poetic kitsch participates in the subliminal domain of mass experience, even if it is not reproduced or exchanged in a direct material sense on a mass scale. The collective experience of language itself—its synthesis of disparate voices, its drive towards impersonality—may be viewed as a verbal prototype, a native paradigm, of mass culture. Would it not therefore be possible to identify verbal artifacts whose elements (the stuttering repertoire of poetic diction) lend themselves to commodification and mass consumption? Does poetic kitsch offer a paradigm for mass intuition—through a common, synthetic language—for commodification without exchange: pop without popularity, subliminal pop, cult pop, private pop? Does poetry make it possible to be *inside* pop?

In the twentieth century, Andy Warhol's use of the terms "pop" and "plastic"—still veiled by the inattention of most art criticism on the subject —suggests that the New York poets whose work resonated with his revolutionary ideas and practice were fabricating a kind of poetic kitsch combining a deadpan "purity of diction" with the arcana of a visible underworld: a pop cryptonymy, a fusion of kitsch and avant-garde, a reproductive poetry rivaling the commodities of the marketplace and thus susceptible, as Walter Benjamin claimed of Baudelaire's poetry, to allegorical readings of capital. The new "plastic" poetry of the New York school (inspired by the revival of Dada in the 1950s) was often composed through collaboration, sampling, automatic writing, assumed identities, and outright forgery. Sociologically, the "New Realism" (as pop art was first dubbed in the early 1960s) emerged from a shifting, queer coterie, from "community's evil twin."[48] This "textual coterie" became the basis of a fugitive and partial totality—a model of "relational aesthetics"—achieved through the "silvering" effects (monotony, seriality, delirium) associated with Warhol's Factory.[49]

Mass Ornament

The qualities associated with poetic kitsch—triviality, generality, reproducibility, fraudulence—appear to contradict (as its detractors emphatically contend) the ideology of modernism (though it is not difficult to find significant pockets of kitsch in the canonical texts of poetic modernism). Immune to formal innovation yet cultivating a diction that both mimics and disfigures ordinary language (a synthetic vernacular), kitsch—like its progenitor, the traditional ballad—fails to represent accurately either the external world or subjective experience. Representation is secondary to its expressive priorities. Indeed, the flight from representation, which nevertheless allows for the persistence of reproducibility, is one of the seminal features, according to Deleuze and Guattari, of minor literature: "language stops being representative to move toward its extremities or limits."[50] Contrary, however, to assumptions that kitsch is the epitome of *self*-expression, kitsch in poetry works from the outside in, occupying a fictive interior with false feelings and specious phrases.

The lyric subject becomes through verbal imposture, through kitsch, an expression of inscrutable social and economic conditions. In its essence, kitsch is a mode of repetitive *expression* renouncing (like the authorless ballad) both physical and psychological verisimilitude, resisting the dogmas of exteriority *and* interiority. Viewed in this way, the poetics of kitsch lends itself to the aesthetic (and social) function of allegory. Accordingly, to begin to understand the allure and significance of kitsch, one must adopt a model of expression that is not disabled by the impersonality and the superficiality of kitsch or by its lack of originality. Kitsch, as Broch contends, follows a

Luciferian swerve from cosmos to cosmetics, yet its cosmetic properties also express conditions of the social cosmos that have been deliberately veiled or disguised.[51] In his essay "On Lyric Poetry and Society," Adorno contends that only poetry disfigured by artifice and falsification (by "false glitter") can disclose the actual conditions of "social antagonism."[52] The cosmetic nature of poetic kitsch presumes, moreover, an experience of *surface reading*, or *distant reading*—and the need to theorize the aesthetic surface, especially poetic surface, in terms of reception.[53]

Illustrating Kracauer's theory of the "mass ornament," whatever kitsch expresses defies its glittering surface, the spectacle of its formulaic diction —though these elements become the irresistible triggers of a social trance, at once banal and apocalyptic. "In pure externality, the audience encounters itself," Kracauer contends, "its own reality is revealed in the fragmented sequence of splendid sense-impressions."[54] What readers discover in the worn-out phrases, the artificial language—and the banality—of poetic kitsch is a reverberation of their own social being in historical conditions that would otherwise remain unheard, invisible. Mindlessly consuming the poetic "capital" of one's native tongue may be narcissistic, but "it is not," according to John Guillory, "the pleasure of the individual's recognition of his or her individuality; rather, it takes the form of identification with a social body expressed or embodied in the common possession of writer and reader, a common language."[55] The distressed genre of kitsch reveals to listeners and readers their own distress in a historical echo chamber of borrowed language. Glimpsing the apocalyptic face of kitsch, Adorno muses, "What art used to be, kitsch may become in the future. Kitsch may be a correction to the decomposing trend in art, perhaps it is even the true progress of art."[56] To gauge the future of Adorno's conjecture about the synthesizing (and synthetic) powers of kitsch, one must start by scrutinizing more carefully the history of its occluded relations with poetry.

2 Poetic Diction and the Substance of Kitsch

Dreams, Mottos, Gossip

References to the polemical history of kitsch are not uncommon in debates about popular culture, yet even the most astute contemporary observers usually overlook, as I have already noted, a central feature of the inaugural theorizations of kitsch: *poetry* is identified in the foundational essays on the subject as an important exemplum and genealogical source of kitsch. Robert Musil, for example, in his essay of 1923, "Schwarze Magie" ("Black Magic"), responds to the question "What is Kitsch?" by mocking the work of "poet X," who is at once a "popular hack" and a "bad Expressionist."[1] Later, in a more influential essay of 1933, Hermann Broch develops his theory of kitsch in reference to the poetry of Novalis, Joseph Eichendorff, Stefan George, and Mallarmé.[2] Even more prominently (in an American context), Clement Greenberg's essay of 1939 initiates—in the first paragraph —its polemical formulation of kitsch by drawing a contrast between the modernist poetry of T. S. Eliot and the lyrics of Tin Pan Alley (as well as the work of a poet named Eddie Guest, who published a poem a day for more than thirty years in the *Detroit Free Press*).[3] In addition, Greenberg, like Broch, points to Romantic poetry (Keats, in this case) as a progenitor of modern kitsch.[4] Though one may challenge—as I will do in this chapter— presumptions that the origins of kitsch are to be found in the Romantic sensibility, one must nevertheless acknowledge these critics' attentiveness to poetry as a primary medium of kitsch.

Certainly, it is not surprising that Musil and Broch (along with Walter Benjamin, as we will discover in a moment) approach kitsch as a verbal phenomenon, since they were themselves literary critics and theorists as well as authors of literary texts. Greenberg, we should recall, was an aspiring poet and literary critic when he published his essay on kitsch at the age of thirty—with little or no training in art history. As a result of these critics' literary orientation, the inaugural essays on kitsch offer grounds for assigning to poetry a significant place in the genealogy of kitsch, yet this orientation no longer shapes our presumptions on the subject today. It would be unthinkable now to claim, for example, that the problem of kitsch can be traced to certain notorious events in the history of poetry. From the perspective of poetry, however, there are those—starting with Wordsworth in his preface to the *Lyrical Ballads* and culminating in the orthodoxies of Imagism—who would assert that the fate of poetry since the neoclassical revival of archaic and demotic traditions has been frivolously and dangerously entangled with the problem of kitsch. Because the values of kitsch and of elite poetry (even the most progressive and innovative kinds) remain deeply polarized, however, it is impossible to say how such charges, were they found to have some merit, might affect our understanding of kitsch or of modern poetry. Kitsch and poetry are not on speaking terms these days. No charge more damaging can be brought against a poem, especially one subscribing to the tenets of modernism, than to describe it as *kitsch*. Yet it is precisely for this reason that the anathematic nature of kitsch can be revealed only by excavating its forgotten relationship to poetry—a disclosure that will yield important insights about the place and function of poetry in contemporary society.

The taboo against comparing kitsch and "serious" poetry—or finding some benefit in the correlation—has not, however, always been observed. In one of the earliest essays on kitsch—certainly the first to appreciate its dialectical appeal—Benjamin not only traces the genealogy of kitsch to the unfashionable dream life of a poet but develops his meditation on kitsch by returning repeatedly to the question of poetry. More precisely, he activates the verbal figurine of kitsch by referring (in the first sentence of his text) to the dream of the blue flower (the epitome of poetic artifice) suffered by Heinrich von Ofterdingen (the medieval poet-protagonist of Novalis' eponymous novel): "One cannot truly dream of the blue flower any more. He who wakes up today as Heinrich von Ofterdingen must have overslept."[5] Casting von Ofterdingen in the role of a proto-Surrealist poet, Benjamin offers an assessment of the slumbering liaison of kitsch and poetry: the *Traumkitsch* (dream kitsch) of Surrealism spells the end of poetry—it replaces it. He claims, "Louis Aragon reports how the mania to dream spread throughout Paris. The young people believed that they had found a secret to poetry—in reality they brought an end to poetry."[6] Poets heeding the methods of Surrealism, Benjamin concludes, need only dream to do their work. At the same time, "dreams are now a pathway to the banal," Benjamin declares. "The side which things present to dreams is kitsch"—also the side of an object grabbed awkwardly by a child, he notes.[7] The peculiar practice of making "dream kitsch" occupies a place once filled by poetry's oneiric language, a means of disclosing—after poetry's example—the secret life of everyday things. Poetry turns to "mottos" and "gossip" as a way of recovering the debris of historical experience—to the "worlds of childhood," to worlds revealed through nursery rhymes in the genealogy of poetic kitsch.[8]

The "dream energies" of past eras (which may help to rescue the present from oblivion) invade the present, according to Benjamin, through the detritus of fashion and, even more potently, through the aesthetic "blemishes" of kitsch (which include silly "maxims" about laziness and boredom, along with a book of poems entitled *Répétitions* by Paul Eluard).[9] Benjamin states, "The collective dream energy has taken refuge with redoubled vehemence in the mute, impenetrable nebula of fashion, where the understanding cannot follow."[10] What is more, kitsch must not be regarded as antithetical to modernism, since Benjamin—alone among his modernist peers—equates kitsch and avant-garde (in the form of Surrealism). For Benjamin (as for Adorno), poetry mediates the relation between kitsch and Surrealism in a way that destabilizes the antithesis (advanced by Greenberg) between kitsch and avant-garde. Reactivating poetry's relation to kitsch therefore exposes the premises of a new formulation of the avant-garde, a model anticipating Peter Bürger's characterization of the historical avant-garde as a movement seeking to integrate art into "the praxis of life."[11]

Benjamin's sympathetic revelation of correspondences between "dream kitsch" and vanguard poetry was, of course, an anomaly among modernists adhering to the priorities of formalism. Yet the modernist attack on mass culture did not, in the years following its original formulation, go unanswered. Shaped by the Frankfurt School's attention to popular culture, a furious critique on several fronts (ideology, semiotics, identity politics) has steadily undermined the polarization of high and low cultures. Poetry's place in these crucial developments remains, however, uncertain and marginalized, a lapse that can be addressed in part by exposing the dialectical features of kitsch, especially its reciprocal relation to high culture (a two-way exchange first cultivated deliberately by neoclassical poets).

Modernism's forgotten (and ambivalent) references to poetry as a possible framework for understanding the banality of everyday art suggest that the concept of kitsch still has the power to ignite controversy—especially concerning poetry's guarded susceptibility to the value system of kitsch. Standing apart from the ongoing desublimation of visual art into visual *culture*, modern poetry, despite the recent valorization of techniques such as appropriation (sampling existing texts), has only begun to assimilate the values intrinsic to the discourse of kitsch: triviality, mediocrity, sentimentality, lack of originality. Both the first and second generations of New York school poets may indeed have updated the diction of the conversation poem, dispersed it through collaboration, and dared to make verse from scraps of trivia and everyday experience, but their poems are not now lauded, nor are they viewed as significant, because they are held to be derivative, superficial, commonplace, or popular (though they may be all of these things).

Poetry's stubborn resistance to acknowledging and incorporating the values of kitsch requires it to ignore the tentative orientation towards poetry and poetics already outlined by modernist definitions of kitsch. And contemporary scholarship exerts little or no pressure on poets to think about the problem of kitsch. Poetry's role in shaping the origins of kitsch has been, as I indicated earlier, almost entirely ignored by later generations of kitsch theorists. (Matei Călinescu does, to his credit, briefly consider the properties of poetic kitsch in his book on modernism.)[12] At the same time, poetry's disappearance from the discourse of kitsch stems almost certainly from shifting models of reception, audience, and mass culture within the ideology of poetic modernism—not to mention anxious speculation about the fate of "literature" in contemporary society—which have had the effect of alienating poetry in public opinion from mass culture.

The shadowy relations between kitsch and poetry are inescapably and ruinously dialectical: even as increasingly stringent forms of modernism enable poetry's apparent immunity to kitsch, poetry itself becomes—for many intellectuals and even some poets—the veiled essence of kitsch. One witnesses the baffling ritual of major poets repudiating poetry: Laura Riding, for example, abandoning poetry for its truthlessness (its spurious nature), or Marianne Moore's famous denunciation ("I, too, dislike it") motivated by her equation of poetry with "all this fiddle."[13] Poetry may disappear from the discourse of kitsch, but the specter of kitsch eventually devours the reputation of lyric poetry—and indeed of all poetry (according to its detractors). By condemning kitsch to the realm of the abject—and by concealing poetry's hidden ties to this forbidden realm—modernism inadvertently lays a snare for itself, a rationale for the equation of poetry and kitsch. And the fate of these two polarized terms ends up being intertwined in the public imagination.

What appears to be a dereliction of poetry's role in contemporary accounts of kitsch may stem, however, from a curious lapse in the inaugural essays of Benjamin, Musil, Broch, and Greenberg. In each case, one finds assertions—however misguided their historical and literary coordinates may be—about the significance of Romantic poetry for a general model of kitsch, supplemented by comparisons between authentic and degraded modes of verse within the poetic tradition. Yet one searches these essays in vain for an explanation of how a linguistic phenomenon with apparently little or no relation to mass culture (eighteenth-century poetry), and one preceding significantly the historical emergence of kitsch in modern industrial culture, could legitimately serve as a model for theorizing the ubiquity and banality of industrial artifacts in popular culture. In what ways do the conditions of Romantic (or, to be more accurate, neoclassical) poetry prefigure the copycat mentality and the sensationalism, or triviality, of popular culture? How is the logic of kitsch encrypted in the origins of modern poetry? The inaugural formulations of kitsch, although they assert the relevance of poetry to kitsch and popular culture, do not provide answers to these questions. In this sense, the curious silences riddling the foundation of kitsch turn into gaping holes in succeeding generations of kitsch theory: poetry vanishes from the map of popular culture in part because its atavistic relation to kitsch can no longer be traced or illuminated.

If, following the transformative and irreversible advances in assessing and understanding popular culture in the last half century, the concept of kitsch retains some utility as an index of relations between aesthetic judgment and social values, its full significance (and its history) will remain partially veiled as long as we remain ignorant of its seminal but forgotten relations to poetry. My aim, accordingly, is to recover the specific conditions, or events, in the history of poetry that could account for the puzzling modernist assertions of poetry's significance for kitsch. Identifying how certain poetic events anticipate and model the general properties of kitsch will establish a basis for expanding the conversation about poetry and kitsch initiated, but also foreclosed, by modernist formulations of kitsch. Such an investigation will inevitably trouble certain basic assumptions, as I have indicated, about modern poetry's susceptibility to the values of kitsch and about the significance of these affinities for our understanding of kitsch in general (especially in its relation to the ideology of camp). The prospect of disclosing these affinities promises to set in motion a revision of the basic parameters of kitsch as it pertains to material culture, to revise the aesthetics of kitsch in the image of poetry—that is, to produce a *poetics* of kitsch.

Chatter and Virtuosity

Disclosing the relevance of poetry for our understanding of kitsch—and vice versa—must inevitably occur as a confrontation between values associated with modernism (formal integrity, originality, concreteness, authenticity) and a set of values that inevitably appear, through the filter of modernist ideology, to be contemptible if not perverse. Baudelaire's declaration of his poetic intention to "invent a cliché" (*créer un poncif*) at once defies and legitimates the triviality and mimeticism associated with kitsch.[14] Such an act necessarily incorporates into the making of an artifact its own reception —since clichés come into being only through the social circulation of frozen verbal phrases. Baudelaire's embrace of the poetic cliché also helps to explain why Benjamin would choose lyric poetry—and Baudelaire's poetry in particular—as a primary vehicle for his critique of consumer capitalism in his later writings. In his commentary on Baudelaire, which resonates with his observations on Surrealism and kitsch, Benjamin notes Baudelaire's reference to "the creation of a cliché" and declares, "In this he saw the condition of every future poet."[15] Assessing the relation between the immobility of the cliché—a means of arresting poetry—and a conception of social totality dependent on popular culture (a totality that is both partial and ephemeral) will be one of the principal theoretical tasks at hand in renovating the concept of kitsch.

The verbal cliché finds its aesthetic counterpart in poetic kitsch. As in the experience of the cliché, "cognitive reflection," according to Anton Zijderveld, is "lethal to kitsch."[16] The repetition of clichés, which Zijderveld calls "a substitute for stuttering," produces a language resistant to meaning and change: the scant meaning of a cliché gives priority to its social function, allowing it to serve as an expression, an index, of hidden social forces.[17] The mechanism of verbal clichés can be seen as corresponding in ways to the operation of advertising jingles, but also to the deployment of commonplace phrases (developing the phraseology of poetic diction) and, at a formal level, to the device of the poetic refrain. In addition, Zijderveld remarks, when expressions turn into clichés, "time freezes"; history comes to a standstill in a phrase: "like a magic formula it is unalterable."[18] Zijderveld thus describes clichés as "linguistic fossils" and, in an observation with some significance for poetic practice, notes that "clichés can be collected like stamps."[19] One can moreover become a kind of genius of clichés, "a virtuoso in chatter"—a remark recalling Baudelaire's contention that "inventing clichés" is akin to "genius."[20]

Any attempt to outline a poetics of kitsch must begin by acknowledging that, as a result of modernist inhibitions or forgetfulness, we simply have no idea how to identify precisely something called poetic kitsch. Though it seems to employ a familiar repertoire of images and to traffic in certain sentiments, kitsch in poetry seems to be a genre without distinct verbal qualities—indeed, "without qualities" (to echo the title of Musil's great novel). We are uncertain about what constitutes kitsch in poetry: Is it or isn't it? This uncertainty can be demonstrated quite easily by offering a primer, so to speak, of examples, antecedents, and variants of poetic kitsch (fragments of kitsch drawn—for the sake of brevity—from poems evoking in their entirety the physiognomy of kitsch). Take a moment or two to appraise, if you will, the specimens I have assembled below (names of poets withheld in order to eliminate prejudicial factors in the reader's judgment!).

Frail golden flowers that perish at a breath,
Flickering points of honey-coloured flame,
From sunset gardens of the moon you came,
Pale flowers of passion . . . delicate flowers of death . . .

———

I dreamed I moved among the Elysian fields,
In converse with sweet women long since dead;
And out of blossoms which that meadow yields
I wove a garland for your living head

———

The apparition of these faces in the crowd:
Petals, on a wet, black bough.

———

See! the white moone sheens onne hie;
Whyterre ys mie true loves shroude;
Whyterre yanne the mornynge skie,
    Mie love ys dedde,
    Gon to hys deathe-bedde,
    Al under the wyllowe tree.

———

Here she lies, a pretty bud,
Lately made of flesh and blood;
Who as soon fell fast asleep
As her little eyes did peep.

———

Dash'd by the wood-nymph's beauty, so he burn'd;
Then, lighting on the printless verdure, turn'd
To the swoon'd serpent, and with languid arm,
Delicate, put to proof the lythe Cadusean charm.

———

Kmart
Taco Bell
KFC
Staples
J. Crew

Kmart
KFC
Kmart
Taco Bell

Kmart
KFC
Kmart

———

White flower,
Flower of wax, of jade, of unstreaked agate;
Flower with surfaces of ice,
With shadows faintly crimson

———

Bereft of rune-gates.
Smoke is on the plaster,
Scarred the shower-burghs,
Shorn and shattered,
By eld under-eaten.

———

Porgy, I'se yo' woman now,
I is, I is!

An' I ain't never goin' nowhere 'less you shares de fun.
Dere's no wrinkle on my brow.

———

But all the time
I'se been a-climbin' on,
And reachin' landin's,
And turnin' corners,
And sometimes goin' in the dark
Where there ain't been no light.

———

So looks Anthea when in bed she lies,
O'ercome or half betrayed by tiffanies:
Like to a twilight, or that simpering dawn
That roses show when misted o'er with lawn.

———

Now the storm begins to lower,
(Haste, the loom of heel prepare,)
Iron-sleet of arrowy shower
Hurtles in the darkened air

———

O my kitten a kitten,
And oh! my kitten, my deary,
Such a sweet pap as this
There is not far nor neary.

———

I hoped that he would love me,
And he has kissed my mouth,
But I am like a stricken bird
That cannot reach the south

———

First, my Motorola
Then my Frette
Then my Sonia Rykiel
Then my Bulgari
Then my Asprey
Then my Cartier
Then my Kohler
Then my Brightsmile

Then my Cetaphil
Then my Braun
Then my Brightsmile
Then my Kohler
Then my Cetaphil
Then my Bliss
Then my Apple
Then my Kashi
Then my Maytag
Then my Silk
Then my Pom

———

Mourn, all ye little gods of love, whose darts
Have lost their wonted power of piercing hearts;
Lay by the gilded quiver and the bow,
The useless toys can do no mischief now.

We know poetic kitsch when we see it, but we also lack a critical vocabulary for articulating the basis of such judgments. There are no specific, verbal criteria in place—much less a general theory—to identify the particular features of poetic kitsch or to settle a dispute about it. This critical vacuum does not, however, disable the intuitive markers—based perhaps on usage—of what constitutes kitsch in poetry. The fact that our intuitive judgments about poetic kitsch may be based in our sense of the spectrum of *usage* rather than familiarity with a particular poet or poetic tradition tells us something important about kitsch in poetry: poetic kitsch takes root in verbal connotation, in expressive values acquired through, or against, common usage. Kitsch in poetry exercises certain social powers of language, revealing historical bonds of collective identity, which suspend, or supersede, the domain of the personal.

Let's return, however, to my sampling of test cases to sort out what features might allow us to say what is kitsch and what is not. I have not given the names of the authors of these fragments (although some are easily identifiable), since poetic kitsch is authorless in a way that is distinct from the use of the signature *Anon* throughout much of poetry's history. In this sense, kitsch in poetry turns out to be deeply and perversely rooted in the poetic tradition, which explains the historical reach of my little field guide, ranging from the early seventeenth century to the present moment.

Many of these passages are by canonical poets—all composed originally in English—including certain influential literary forgeries, though some examples (produced by sampling or appropriation) will perhaps not immediately be acknowledged as part of the tradition of poetry in English, or indeed as conforming to our intuitive assessments of poetic kitsch.

My decision to omit examples of ironized or calculated kitsch in poetry reflects my views concerning the complex relations of kitsch (even its most insipid or trivial forms) to the poetic tradition. This orientation is in keeping with Broch's basic understanding of kitsch as a pretender lodged in the system of art, but also as a *Luciferian* phenomenon: "a disastrous fall from the cosmic heights to kitsch"—from high art to aesthetic failure.[21] The idea that kitsch, as Roland Barthes contends, "implies a recognition of high aesthetic values" (and unwitting failure) suggests that even the most vulgar form of kitsch is haunted, quite literally, by the example and achievements of fine art.[22] From this perspective, the notion of "high kitsch"—whether folkloric, academic, or avant-garde—is no longer contradictory, since all kitsch is saturated with "cultural capital." In fact, if kitsch, in the strictest sense, is an alienated possession of elite culture, then all kitsch may be described as high kitsch. Reactivating the concept of kitsch thus promises, as I have already indicated, to reveal its primary function as a bridge between elite and vernacular cultures (rather than as simply an emblem of low culture). Frequently, the volatile concentrations of "linguistic capital" in poetic kitsch reveal the contested boundaries of ethnic or class identities, along with the effects of verbal and cultural translation.[23]

Phraseology

The earliest critical recognition of what we may call poetic kitsch can be found in a review written in 1810 by Francis Jeffrey (the founder of the *Edinburgh Review*) of Walter Scott's lengthy ballad *The Lady of the Lake*. (Broch later identified Scott's "antique" ballads as examples of kitsch, echoing the essential insight of Jeffrey's formative reception of Scott.)[24] Examining the modern phenomenon of "very popular poetry" (exemplified by fashionable imitations of archaic ballads), in contrast to poetry that appeals to more "refined taste," Jeffries observes,

> We know no way in which we could so shortly describe the poetry that pleases
> the multitude, and displeases the select few, as by saying that it consists of all
> the most known and most brilliant parts of the most celebrated authors—of a

splendid and unmeaning accumulation of those images and phrases which had long charmed every reader in the works of their original inventors.[25]

Jeffrey here acknowledges that "popular poetry" consists of passages purloined from the poetic tradition and, by implication, that popular poetry (kitsch) differs from serious poetry not in its verbal substance but in what he calls the "arrangement" and reception of materials borrowed from the tradition.

Astonishingly, Jeffrey concludes—in the earliest judgment of the merits of kitsch—that the difference between popular and "refined" poetry is not to be found in the verbal substance of poem: "It is not, then, because the ornaments of popular poetry are deficient in intrinsic worth and beauty that they are slighted by the critical reader, but because he at once recognizes them to be stolen, and perceives that they are arranged without taste or congruity."[26] Though the "beauties" of popular poetry may be stolen and displayed in bad taste (in a manner offending the refined reader), their "intrinsic worth" is equal to that found in the canonical sources from which they have been appropriated: popular poetry shares its basic materials with elite poetry, indicating a continuous and dynamic relation between the two. Jeffrey thus produces a complex model of the inherent beauty and censorious reception of kitsch, acknowledging the social corruption of authentic pleasure at its root: "Our associations with all this class of expressions, which have become trite only in consequence of their intrinsic excellence, now suggest to us no ideas but those of schoolboy imbecility and childish affectation."[27] Kitsch, he contends, is an irresistible byproduct—an adulterated residue—of elite culture.

One cannot emphasize too strongly the fundamental difference between Jeffrey's assessment of the qualities of poetic kitsch and the judgments we have inherited from modernist definitions of kitsch: acknowledging the "childish affectation" of kitsch, he nevertheless defends its intrinsic beauty. Measured by the ancient criterion of pleasure, he contends, popular poetry can claim—despite its illegitimate complexion—a value commensurate with poetry appealing to more restricted tastes (a model rooted in the reader's reception). And the higher concentrations of pleasure in kitsch (fortified by repetition) account for its greater social resonance and diffusion. In addition, the social dimension of kitsch cannot be isolated from the fact that Jeffrey's defense of it appeared in the colonial context of Scottish nationalism, the same context from which the "distressed genre" of the ballad (the subject of Jeffrey's review) had emerged nearly a hundred years earlier.

Returning once more to the little treasury of verse I have assembled here, one must ask again: what particular verbal qualities do *all* these examples of poetic kitsch share? One notices certain themes recurring: erotic or passionate love, death and encounters with the dead, spirituality, suffering, martial conflict, rhapsodic experiences of nature. Yet none of these themes, common as they may be, is sufficient to ensure the identity of kitsch in poetry. One also notices immediately the recurrence of certain images or tropes—a distinctive iconography—among these poems: flowers, naked bodies, twilight, dawn, airy phenomena (clouds, mist), pale colors, mythological creatures, precious materials (gold, silver), shadows, darkness. Some of these tropes (such as darkness or flowers, or even the phenomenon of color itself) might serve as subtle, reflexive emblems of poetic kitsch, yet none of these tropes, however much they may share with familiar modes of kitsch in other media, are either necessary or sufficient criteria for identifying kitsch in *poetry*. The same may be said about the possibility of defining poetic kitsch by its prosody (though jingling rhymes be as common as rhinestones).

The consistent iconography and themes of these verse fragments therefore fail to establish (despite their appeal and their correlation with kitsch in other media) a foundation for poetic kitsch because they are not sufficiently *verbal* in a material and structural sense. One must be able to identify certain specific verbal properties consistent with *all* of these samples to establish the grounds—a working definition—for poetic kitsch. Looking beyond the criteria of image, theme, or prosody, one can only conclude that kitsch in poetry is determined primarily by its *diction* and, more precisely, by what we call *poetic diction*.

Diction is an ancient and durable critical concept, first defined by Aristotle and revised many times since antiquity at crucial junctures in literary history (by Dante, Dryden, Samuel Johnson, Wordsworth, Coleridge, T. S. Eliot, Laura Riding, and so on). In the broadest sense, which extends beyond the confines of literature, diction pertains to the control of syntax, word order, orthography, and, most importantly, word choice or vocabulary—elements often associated in a literary sense with the question of *style*. Strictly speaking, however, "style" would be the narrower term (though we often use it as a synonym for diction), as Donald Davie explains: "there is no Miltonic diction in Milton; there is only Milton's style."[28] Miltonic *diction* is to be found in the works of his followers, a criterion revealing the deliberate and replicative nature of poetic diction.

Diction in poetry is determined by its antecedents in verse, by a particular (and often contested) model of colloquial speech, and by the possible incorporation of syntactical irregularities and vocabularies alien to the existing terrain of poetic diction. From these disparate sources, a distinctive (and frequently polemical) diction is synthesized, often involving the deliberate suppression of certain registers of language. At the same time, there are major poets, and minor ones, whose vocabularies are so variegated that their writing disables the problematic of diction. (The casual dissolution of boundaries, it must be emphasized, is not equivalent to calculated transgression and deliberate impurities.) Diction is therefore useful as a critical concept only to poetry that cultivates, rejects, or deliberately violates specific vocabularies, syntactic signatures, and tonal effects. Poetic diction—whatever its qualities—always results, Davie contends, from "an act of will, of contrivance and perseverance."[29]

The elements of diction combine to produce certain tonal qualities in language, which become objects of the faculty of taste—and, thereby, of powerful social delineations. As a result, different poems appeal to diverse tastes, depending on the kind of diction they cultivate—that is, poems are judged from various perspectives as being in good taste or bad. Diction is always a matter of particularity, determined either by policing or relaxing the boundaries of specific vocabularies and syntactic constructions—a matter of judgment acutely relevant, I would point out, to the production and evaluation of poetic forgery. Whether through closure or transgression, exclusion or transmission (and sometimes through translation), the tenor of a particular diction is always determined at its borders.

Amplifying the social resonance of diction, poetic kitsch exploits a dimension of language that is especially susceptible to commodification (advertising, propaganda, social media), a verbal platform susceptible to both calculation and enchantment. By harnessing language for indiscriminate ends, whether virtuous or indecent, poetic kitsch is at once worldly and naïve, amoral and seductive. Kitsch in poetry thus restages the ancient and insidious alignment of *poesis* and rhetoric, a coupling that isolates poetry from its other potential suitors: prophecy, history, and philosophy.

Emphasizing the rhetorical function of kitsch helps to account for its subliminal effects, just as, conversely, it reveals the importance of diction to the subliminal impact of rhetoric. Even more importantly, the framework of rhetoric offers a way of assessing the collective aspect of the language of kitsch—its adumbration of social totality—as Fredric Jameson suggests in distinguishing between rhetoric and style:

Rhetoric is an older and essentially pre-capitalist mode of literary organization; it is a collective or class phenomenon in that it serves as a means of assimilating the speech of individuals to some suprapersonal oratorical paradigm, to some non- or preindividualistic standard of the *beau parler*, of high style and fine writing. . . . Style on the other hand is a middle-class phenomenon, and reflects the increasing atomization of middle-class life.[30]

Especially germane to poetic kitsch—and contrary to received notions about mass culture—is the inference that "high style" could be a collective phenomenon, "a means of assimilating the speech of individuals to some suprapersonal . . . paradigm"—to a quixotic social totality.

Poetic kitsch shows no interest, as I have already noted, in describing either physical or psychological worlds with accuracy, authenticity, or originality. The authority of poetic kitsch lies not in its powers of representation, which are in fact extremely weak, but in its capacity to *express* through its artificial phraseology an impersonal, social "substance" concealed by ideology. In essence, what kitsch expresses lies beyond personal experience. Hence, kitsch in poetry strives to be conventional and formulaic in a manner revealing its expressive affinities with the aesthetic and social functions of allegory. What is at stake finally—to borrow Benjamin's famous trope for the manifestation of pop art—is the decay of the poem's *aura* of originality. The loss of originality would allow poetry to become—via the traits of its reproducibility—the impersonal and allegorical expression of millions of souls: a mass ornament.

The vicissitudes of poetic diction in English verse have been tied since the beginning of the eighteenth century to deliberate efforts to identify and regulate a vernacular core of poetry in English, but also to incorporate everyday language into elite poetry. Following the integration of vernacular writing (in English) into school curricula in Britain in the mid-eighteenth century, which sparked controversies about the place of common language in poetry, the "substance" of poetic diction became a recognizable verbal marker (along with meter) of the difference between poetry and prose: a way of preserving the cultural value of poetry.[31] At the same time, the integration of demotic language into the poetic tradition could occur, according to certain elite poets who sought to defend the "peculiar language" of poetry, by "importing" native archaic sources (including dialect)—a mode of recuperation resulting in verbal textures that are at once familiar and obscure. In this historical context, the inclination of elite poets to reinforce but also to supplement poetic diction (from native and even counterfeit sources) placed them at odds with the emerging category of "literature," which aimed to subdue the verbal and cultural distinctions of poetry.[32]

Momentous changes occurred, as many scholars have documented, in the realm of letters during the eighteenth century, changes that placed in question the basic verbal criteria of poetry.[33] More specifically, the pre-eminence of poetry as the *only* legitimate classical genre (even drama was written mostly in verse) was challenged in fundamental ways by the intro-duction of vernacular writing into school curricula and by the gradual devel-opment of a vernacular canon (in English), which included for the first time the nebulous genre of prose fiction.[34] As a consequence, since the language of prose was understood to be more colloquial than that of poetry, and less dependent on ancient sources, a new supergenre—called "literature"— emerged to encompass and moderate divergent levels of diction. The devel-oping institution of literature thus imposed a common disciplinary standard of diction on genres ranging from poetry and drama to prose fiction and essays (a genre initially included within the domain of literature—of "polite letters").[35]

As the new supergenre of literature inculcated the values of bourgeois assimilation (its diction situated midway between the heightened language of poetry and "unimproved" common speech), the insular diction of poetry came under increasing pressure to move toward the middle ground of po-lite letters (with its domestic—and domesticated—language). In accordance with the democratizing regime of literature, a polemical school of poetry appeared in the latter part of the eighteenth century that sought to make poetic language more prosaic, to reject the "gaudiness and inane phrase-ology" of poetic diction.[36] Correspondingly, this new "literary" school of poets (for whom Wordsworth's preface to the *Lyrical Ballads* was a kind of manifesto) advocated a new "purity" of diction grounded in "the language of conversation"—a language, however, "purified indeed from what appear to be its real defects."[37] What made the writing of these renegade poets "lit-erary" was precisely its anti-poetic stance, its prosaic qualities.

The disputed territory of poetic diction was thus a principal site of the great genre wars of the eighteenth century. The antagonism between elite poetry and the burgeoning supergenre of literature also disclosed, how-ever, the grounds for an unlikely affinity between poetry and the emergent domain of popular culture. Linked by independent commitments to insular-ity, convention, and reproducibility, this peculiar alliance resisted the aspi-

rational system of polite letters—that is, the encroachment of the bourgeois
category of literature.

The concept of diction was central to debates about poetry and poetics throughout the eighteenth and nineteenth centuries, yet the values and
problems of diction were largely eclipsed by the rise of modernism and
its preoccupations with form, innovation, and historical discontinuity. This
displacement can be explained in part by the fact that diction does not ordinarily extend to questions of poetic form, though certain forms (sonnet, vil-
lanelle, sestina) may become auratic icons of poetic value—forms of kitsch
prosody—allowing them to function, like diction itself, as indices of taste
and social stratification. The forms of the sonnet or the sestina radiate poetic "special effects" reminiscent of kitsch, as do certain formal innovations
of modernism—when shock effect becomes mechanical and rhapsodic.

The suppression, in the context of modernism, of a poetic system oriented towards questions of diction also helps to explain the withering of a
critical vocabulary adequate to the values of poetic kitsch—and the curious
disappearance of poetry itself from the discourse of kitsch. This constellation of lacunae comprehends (as I indicated in the previous chapter) the
political concept of totality. The suppression of kitsch in the context of
modernism has thus been accompanied by the suspension of those critical
concepts and vocabularies (such as diction and totality) that might have illuminated the properties of kitsch as something other than an obstacle to
modernist experimentation.

Only with increasing attention to textual practices such as appropriation
and sampling, which deploy and disclose the subliminal, social aspects of
diction (pertaining to the fabrication of aesthetic and political totalities), has
vanguard poetic practice begun to acknowledge and reactivate the problem
of diction. Though the term "diction" has not yet entered contemporary
debates about Conceptualism in poetry (and its preoccupation with "unoriginal writing"), the "fate of Echo" (as Craig Dworkin defines the prospect
of Conceptual Writing) has certainly evolved with a particular flamboyance
in the history of poetic kitsch.[38] (This is not terribly surprising, since Echo
is, after all, a very pretty nymph . . .) Unlike the impoverished, and even
dehistoricized, creature summoned by Dworkin, however, kitsch offers
an adorable Echo of the poetic tradition (perhaps even a notion of Echo
as tradition)—a silhouette that is perhaps a little too beguiling, yet always
probing unlikely chambers of class identity.

Under the regime of modernist ideology, the rarefaction of poetic diction (the substance of kitsch) has nevertheless remained essential to the propagation of conventional lyric. The lyric tradition is infused with a redundant, idiosyncratic vocabulary that cannot easily be distinguished from the verbal substance of kitsch. The modernist polemic against kitsch has therefore yielded a residual—and infelicitous—equation of lyric poetry and kitsch, of refinement and vulgarity. Equally disorienting, in a demonstration of the hegemonic thrust of modernist ideology, vanguard experimentation with diction today (via sampling and appropriation) is often portrayed by contemporary critics as an extension of modernist formalism—though the critical vocabulary of formalism is ill suited to identifying or describing the social resonance of borrowed dictions.[39] If anything, recent experiments with diction (a few of which appear in my primer of poetic kitsch) appear not to be observing the protocols of modernism but, rather, toying inadvertently with the poetics of kitsch. Conceptual Writing, gimmickry, and monotony are, it turns out, quite compatible.

Viewing the practice of sampling in modernist texts as a symptom of *formalism* bears directly on the vanished criterion of diction. Citation (or translation) in the *Cantos* or *The Waste Land*, for example, contribute less to the poetic *form* of these texts than they do to the range of diction encompassed by these poems. Although citation and appropriation are implicated in paratactic forms of modernist poetry (collage and montage, for example), these sampling practices do not function primarily as innovations in form. Rather, they operate as devices that involve verbal archaism (epitomized by the medievalism of the pre-Raphaelites or by fin-de-siècle orientalism, such as Fitzgerald's *Rubaiyat*). Pound's poetic personae, for example—a translational practice essential to modernist poetics—allow him to smuggle into his poetic texts varieties of diction (often archaic or markedly "poetic") that defy his own modernist principles. These verbal personae—clandestine reservoirs of poetic diction—are directly related to the citational means by which Pound elaborates the diction of the *Cantos*.

Morbid Animation

The problematic of diction becomes most visible in the history of English poetry when the naturalized standard of diction falls prey, so to speak, to the influence of external or archaic sources, whether it be Italian or French models during the sixteenth century, classical languages in the seventeenth and eighteen centuries, archaic (and sometimes invented) native sources in the eighteenth and nineteenth centuries, or nonliterary and technical vocabularies in the twentieth century. Poets and critics of various persuasions seek either to promote or to condemn such transactions. Even the most extravagant or grotesque verbal novelties, however, may ultimately be assimilated and sublimated within an expanded poetic diction, resulting in verbal textures—such as kitsch—that are at once eccentric and formulaic, barbarous and familiar, deviant and conventional, flamboyant and decorous.

Classical definitions of poetic diction call for a hybrid medium rooted in the vernacular. To avoid the "drab" style (unalloyed common speech), Aristotle states that poetic diction requires a "blend" of familiar and unfamiliar elements. "Ornamental" or "enigmatic" words mix with colloquial phrasing to produce a compound idiom.[40] Variants of the poetic vernacular thus presume a *synthetic* medium capable of mimicking common speech, but one that becomes susceptible to disparate traditions. The diction of poems written in dialect by Langston Hughes, for example, or sung by a blues musician such as Memphis Minnie, may resemble that of minstrel songs or a lyric in *Porgy and Bess*, and even of caricatures written in *blackface* in Pound's cantos or John Berryman's "dream songs." Folk traditions of poetry can thus be illuminated by a theory of "synthetic vernaculars" and, ultimately, by the counterfeit nature of kitsch.[41]

The artifice of blackface minstrelsy (employed by poets across the racial spectrum) may indeed be related—via the genealogy of poetic kitsch—to the so-called ballad scandals, the forged minstrelsy, of the eighteenth century. Indeed, the problem of fake or synthetic poetry associated with minstrelsy returns us to the correlation of fraudulence and poetics implicit in the inaugural modernist definitions of kitsch. For the idea that kitsch is counterfeit art can be traced, as I indicated earlier, to the neoclassical production of spurious epics and ballads, including the invention of durable relic-genres (such as the nursery rhyme and the poetic melodrama). Starting with Lady Wardlaw's forgery (or remediation) of the Scottish ballad "Hardyknute" in 1719 and followed by a veritable deluge of spurious texts in the 1760s, the Gothic impulse in verse (sustained by a rhetoric of morbid animation) shadowed the development of pre-Romantic poetry: the spectacular forgeries of Ossian, the bogus scholarship of Mother Goose, Thomas Percy's "improved" *Reliques of Ancient English Poetry*, Thomas Chatterton's factory of distressed (and fashionable) incunabula, William Henry Ireland's sprawling manufacture of "lost" plays by Shakespeare.[42]

Buried in this avalanche of counterfeit texts, one discovers a prototype of poetic kitsch, the Gothic melodrama. First imported from revolutionary France, the *melodrâme* imposed (in a manner anticipating spoken word performance in contemporary culture) a separation of speech and music—a dislocation of lyric—where poetry *alternates* with incidental music. In poetic melodrama, the alienated elements of lyric reinforce one another to the point of excess and irrelevance. The earliest known example of a *melodrâme* is a "Pygmalion" written by the young Jean-Jacques Rousseau in 1762.[43] Smartly furnished with antique figures and topical themes of imposture and social sublimation, Rousseau's poetical toy anticipates the Gothic tale of the Frankenstein monster, which may in turn be read as a symbolic narrative of the counterfeit "creature" gone astray, bent upon the destruction of its master: an allegory of the forged materials of kitsch (a monster of borrowed language) and their fatal appeal to modern poetry. Assembling a catalog of aborted subgenres to fill out the genealogy of kitsch, one might also note that the apostrophes and epitaphs composed by Frankenstein's monster (with which he taunts his maker) could be counted among the belated pseudo-genres of poetic kitsch.

Since the origins of poetic kitsch can be traced to eighteenth-century forgeries, restorations, and imitations of traditional ballads, one could, as I suggested earlier, identify it as one of the "crimes of writing" surveyed by Susan Stewart.[44] Yet to place kitsch, according to Stewart's model, at the intersection of literature and legal definitions of intellectual property, or at the intersection of literature and the "forging" of history (as Ian Haywood's model would require), inevitably diffuses, or suppresses, its poetic significance.[45] Such divergences from the specifically poetic scandal of kitsch can be rectified by placing kitsch, as I suggested earlier, at the junction of *rhetoric* and *poesis*—a context that foregrounds the ancient and controversial relation between the calculated orchestration of verbal enchantment (rhetoric) and its creative expression (poetry).

Reading kitsch into the polarized relation between poetry and rhetoric lends coherence to the qualities of its divergent sources: the eighteenth-century rhetorical practice of the commonplace book and the spectacular diction (exemplified by forgery) of Gothic verse. Rooted in the classicism of the early modern period, the book of "commonplaces," or verbal topoi, functioned as a compositional tool in which quotations from classical (and, later, vernacular) sources were recorded and memorized as the basis of a normative style of writing. Closely associated with the compositional method of eighteenth-century poetry, the commonplace book provided "a means of both consuming and producing texts" and, hence, functioned as a crucial device in the accumulation of the clichés and ornaments of poetic diction.[46] Rejected, ostensibly, as a method of composition by Romantic poets, the normalizing procedures of the commonplace book nevertheless played a central role in assimilating the extravagant verbal textures of Gothic verse to a new archive—oriented more broadly towards mass culture—of poetic diction. In this regard, the trivializing redundancy of poetic kitsch finds a methodological paradigm in the routine of the commonplace book, which domesticates the barbarous diction of Gothic verse and forged balladry.

The cumulative scandals of Gothic forgery and the residual influence of the commonplace book ultimately converged—or collided—in a vehement debate over "poetic diction" in the preface (along with other accessory texts) to the *Lyrical Ballads* in 1802. Wordsworth's vituperative sketch and denunciation of the diverse temptations of poetic diction ("a motley masquerade of tricks, quaintnesses, hieroglyphics, and enigmas") may be regarded as echoing, but also reorienting, neoclassical anxieties about "Gothicke" diction (soon to be vigorously challenged by Jeffrey) and as condemning the finicky accessories of Augustan poetry: a prototype of the modernist aversion to kitsch.[47]

One could also claim, however, that the first symptoms of the problematic of kitsch appear considerably earlier in an age troubled, like the eighteenth century, by the importation of archaic materials and their effect on the native store of poetic diction. For it is among the Cavalier poets of the seventeenth century (who refashioned English—with a controversial taste for dainty and trifling things—after the examples of Latin and Greek) where one discovers the first tropes depicting the phenomenon of poetic *mediation*, an idea central to the problems of imitation, restoration, and indeed to forgery. Robert Herrick in particular appears to be intrigued by various translucent media (such as the luxurious and diaphanous "tiffany"— a gauzy, linen veil) through which the world, especially nature and erotic objects, appears to be essentially ornamental and even illusory.[48]

The atmospheric properties of these tropes became more fully developed in Gothic verse (likewise concerned with the problem of mediation), where one discovers a whole range of meteoric, phenomenalistic, and ephemeral objects of perception, including Coleridge's hallucinatory "spectres" and Keats's dainty "silver proxy" (a figure of moonlight as both perceptual medium and aesthetic artifact).[49] All of these ambiguous and immaterial objects function as tropes of derealization, of the evolving concept of aesthetic experience, but also, in their most hyperbolic forms, as totalizing emblems of kitsch: a topos Keats calls, as I noted earlier, "my silver planet."[50]

A later development of the poetics of mediation and forgery (likewise concerned with the impact of foreign languages on poetic diction) occurs with the modernist "translations" and incorporations of Chinese, Anglo-Saxon, and Provençal texts (modernist variations of archaic "minstrelsy"). The twentieth-century traffic in poetic diction places the methods and resources of kitsch in perilous proximity, one should note, to the emerging practice of the poetic avant-garde.

Poetic diction modulates the sensuous currency of language (word choice, spelling, word order) in order to produce an expressive halo, a reverberating abyss of aesthetic and social history. Yet the substance of poetic diction must also be understood in a related sense as establishing the vice of *cosmetic materialism*. Indeed, the cosmetic nature of kitsch invites us to think in terms of sham materialism, or sheer materialism: an orientation, a signature, marking the enigma of the surface. The disappearance of poetry from conversations about kitsch—and the question of diction from modern poetics—can thus be seen as exposing the operation of paranoia: the expulsion of verbal materials from kitsch, even as kitsch comes to define the scandal of cosmetic verse. Under these conditions, modern poetry falls prey to formations of the abject, mastered by the thing it forbids and expels, by a delirious substance it cannot acknowledge.

3 Miscreant
Dialectics and the Persistence of the Commonplace

Doppelgänger

Modernist definitions frequently identify kitsch as the antithesis of art (or, in Clement Greenberg's case, of the avant-garde), yet they also acknowledge a genealogical relation between art and kitsch. Hermann Broch, for example, discussing the artistic (or poetic) antecedents of kitsch, declares, "There are moments when the child becomes so like its mother that one cannot differentiate them."[1] Here, Broch describes kitsch as a direct descendant of art. In addition, the idea that kitsch becomes so much like art that the two cannot be differentiated recalls Francis Jeffrey's judgment concerning the ostensibly divergent "beauties" of vulgar and refined poetries: "the qualities in a poem that give the most pleasure to the refined and fastidious critic are, in substance, we believe, the very same that delight the most injudicious of its admirers."[2] Jeffrey and Broch both stress the uncanny similarities between art and kitsch, yet Broch warns the reader not to view kitsch as merely derivative or imitative, stressing instead its insidious autonomy: "Kitsch is certainly not 'bad art'; it forms its own closed system, which is lodged like a foreign body in the overall system of art."[3] Hence Broch views kitsch as dependent on art—a genealogical descendant of it—yet also somehow independent of it. Kitsch bears an uncanny resemblance to art yet operates according to an autonomous "system" which undermines the values of art. Contrasting the destructive effects of internal and external threats—of kitsch and propaganda—to art, Broch states, "The enemy within, however, is more dangerous than these attacks from outside; every system is dialectically capable of developing its own anti-system and is indeed compelled to do so. The danger is all the greater when at first glance the system and the anti-system appear to be identical."[4] What makes it difficult to distinguish art from kitsch, system from anti-system—according to both Jeffrey and Broch—is the shared "substance" of beauty: a quality susceptible to infinite and indiscriminate replication.[5]

If one accepts the premise that kitsch emerges historically from a schism dividing art into system and anti-system, then it becomes evident that the principal thesis of this book—that kitsch originates with poetry—will have a significant bearing on the question of how and when the crisis in art leading to the emergence of kitsch occurs. That is to say, if kitsch emerges from a crisis in the development of art (preceding the rise of industrial culture), and kitsch originates more precisely with poetry, then one must search for evidence of a schism or rupture specifically within the history of poetry, in order to explain the emergence of the anti-system of kitsch.

The question of poetry's priority in the genealogy of kitsch bears directly on the larger question of whether kitsch should be regarded as a product of industrial capitalism, as Marxist analysis requires (a view supporting a fundamental correlation between kitsch and material culture), or whether kitsch, as Broch claims, must be understood essentially as "a *specific* product of Romanticism" (a view, however misguided in its historical coordinates, supporting the idea that kitsch arises from a crisis in poetry prior to the rise of industrial culture).[6] These two positions can be reconciled by acknowledging the *influence* of industrial culture on the manifestations of kitsch, but if kitsch originates specifically with poetry—and with the conditions of the ballad revival in the eighteenth century in particular—then one cannot adequately explain the sources of kitsch by focusing solely on the rise of industrial capitalism and consumption in relation to the arts in general.

The search for the poetic origins of kitsch must involve, as I indicated in the previous chapter, attention to the problem of diction. In his essays on the antagonism between "literary" poetry (epitomized by Wordsworth's project) and the verbal "masquerade" of popular ballads, it was Jeffrey who first identified poetic diction as the appropriate framework for discussing "very popular poetry": a kind of verse signaling, moreover, the emergence of a poetic anti-system, a lyric antibody to "literature." Jeffrey thus established the earliest criteria for assessing the manifestations of kitsch arising in tandem, but also at odds with, the phenomenon of "polite"—that is, *literary*—poetry. His essays in the *Edinburgh Review* in the first two decades of the nineteenth century indicate that the schism in poetry leading to the emergence of kitsch had begun to develop a hundred years earlier in concert with various experiments in poetic diction. These developments in the early eighteenth century were responding at once, as I have already indicated, to the increasing influence of literary antiquarianism and to the introduction of vernacular sources—principally prose—into school curricula and "literary" culture. These contradictory developments led, on one hand, to the emergence of the category of literature and, on the other, to provisional formations of mass culture, anchored initially in the medium of print amid the "genre wars" between poetry and literature.

Careful examination of these historical developments reveals that the schism underlying the emergence of kitsch occurred not between literature and popular culture as we know it today but between the residual genre of poetry and the emergent supergenre of literature. A recalcitrant but also renegade school of poetry—the precursor of kitsch—assembled a fossilized language from archaic diction and a radicalized vernacular to avoid the middle ground of "polite conversation"—the purity of diction—cultivated polemically by the new school of *literary* poets (Wordsworth and his followers). In this bitter and melancholy contest, it was a refractory and militant form of poeticism that exposed a dialectical affinity between traditional poetry and incipient forms of mass culture, becoming the hyperbolically poetic anti-system to the middling, bourgeois system of literature.

In the essay of Jeffrey's that I cited earlier, containing the earliest definitions of poetic kitsch (in a review of Walter Scott's ballad, *The Lady of the Lake*), Jeffrey argues that his thesis regarding the common substance of beauty shared by vulgar and refined poetries can be confirmed by attending to "the history and effects of what may be called *Poetical diction* in general, or even of such particular phrases and epithets as have been indebted to their beauty for too great a notoriety."[7] Here, Jeffrey's reference to diction as the key to understanding the nature of poetic kitsch acknowledges the contradictory judgments called forth by the "phrases and epithets" of poetic diction. No longer able to recognize the "intrinsic excellence" of such expressions—and allowing their beauty to become a source of "notoriety"— we see only the "imbecility and childish affectation" of kitsch: "we look upon them merely as the common, hired, and tawdry trappings of all those who wish to put on, for the hour, the masquerade habit of poetry."[8] As evidence of the garbled legacy of kitsch, Jeffrey reminds the cultivated reader of "the vivifying spirit of strength and animation" in Scott's poetry even as he acknowledges the heterogeneity of its diction:

With regard to diction and imagery, too, it is quite obvious that Mr. Scott has not aimed at writing either in a very pure or a very consistent style. He seems to have been anxious only to strike, and to be easily and universally understood, and, for this purpose, to have culled the most glittering and conspicuous expressions of the most popular authors, and to have interwoven them in splendid confusion with his own nervous diction and irregular verification.[9]

The great popularity of Scott's poetry, which Jeffrey views as a sign of its intrinsic merit, can be attributed then to a combination of "nervous diction" (an allusion perhaps to agitation), its preoccupation with poetic effects ("anxious only to strike"), and to the accessibility granted to the "animation" of these qualities.[10]

Synthetic Vernaculars

Jeffrey's observations about poetic diction often serve, I want to emphasize, as a way of theorizing about the anomalous features of "popular poetry" (Scott, Byron, and Keats are his favorites)—about kitsch. One should note that discussion about the character and formulation of poetic diction—reaching back to Aristotle—frequently addresses the question of popular poetry and therefore serves as a prehistory of the problem of kitsch in poetry. Jeffrey's emphasis on the impurity—the "splendid confusion"—of Scott's diction in his evaluation of popular poetry offers a good example of this concordance.

In Aristotle's discussion of diction (*lexis*)—understood as a function of vocabulary—he states, "Diction is at its clearest when composed of words in everyday use, but then it is commonplace. . . . An impressive diction, on the other hand, one that escapes the ordinary, results from the use of strange words, by which I mean foreign words, metaphors, expanded words, and whatever departs from normal usage."[11] To avoid the extremes of the "drab" and the enigmatic, Aristotle explains, "what is needed, therefore, is a blend, so to speak, of these ingredients, since the unfamiliar element . . . will save the diction from being drab and commonplace, while the colloquial element will ensure its clarity."[12] Thus poetic diction is a synthetic language, so to speak, founded on the vernacular yet mixing the familiar and the unfamiliar, the drab and the ornamental, the colloquial and the enigmatic.

One cannot help but note the similarity between the classical formulation of poetic diction as a compound of materials and the heterogeneity of Scott's "nervous" yet popular poetry, composing "a diction tinged successfully with the careless richness of Shakespeare, the harshness and the antique simplicity of the old romances, the loneliness of vulgar ballads and anecdotes, and the sentimental glitter of the most modern poetry—passing from the borders of the ludicrous to those of the sublime."[13] Jeffrey here describes a poetic language accessible to a mass audience, combining simplicity, vulgarity, archaism, sublimity, and the "sentimental glitter" of modern phrasing.

Following Aristotle's definition, variations of the concept of a *synthetic vernacular*—a common language synthesized from disparate elements and therefore alienated from common usage—have figured prominently in discussions of poetic diction. For example, Dante's seminal (and unfinished) essay on language and poetry, *De vulgari eloquentia*, addresses the problem of diction by elaborating the advantages of writing in the vernacular— in one's native tongue, instead of Latin. At the same time, the title of his treatise, *Eloquence in the Vulgar Tongue*, conveys the crucial idea of a synthetic language combining vulgarity and refinement, the ordinary and the extraordinary. According to Dante, "vernacular language is that which we learn without any formal instruction," yet he is careful to explain that the vernacular—as a medium for poetry—"has left its scent in every city but made its home in none."[14] The vernacular is "common to all yet owned by none," a medium "tempered by the combination of opposites": a language that is at once "womanish" and "brutally harsh," belonging to no place and spoken, in effect, by no one.[15] Ultimately, Dante describes the vernacular as a "homeless stranger."[16] In Italian, Dante uses the term *peregrinatur*— wanderer, vagabond—suggesting that the poetic vernacular is not merely homeless but outside the bounds of ordinary usage: a *miscreant* language.

The problem of poetic diction in the English tradition received, as I indicated earlier, its most polemical exposition—after a century of controversy—in Wordsworth's appendices to the *Lyrical Ballads* (especially the revised preface of the 1802 edition). The polarization of views is epitomized by his articulation of the first programmatic stance *against* poetic diction (exemplified at once, in his view, by Thomas Gray's insularity and by the new barbarism of Gothic verse). Wordsworth's provocative stance (and his poetry) then became targets of Jeffrey's defense of poetic "animation": volatile and tender feelings, echoing a notable irregularity of diction and reliance on borrowed sources.

The preface to the *Lyrical Ballads* (and the controversies surrounding it) is in fact a culmination of experiments and disputes about diction reaching back to the middle of the eighteenth century. Stepping back even further, although Wordsworth addresses a range of issues pertaining to the immediate historical debate, he also inevitably conveys and revises the terms of a longer, episodic conversation about poetic diction reaching back to the early seventeenth century. He does so in order to reinforce the values of the "plainer and more emphatic language" (newly tied to "literature") that he deems appropriate for poetry.[17] Wordsworth's contrast between the "inane phraseology" of poetic diction and the "real language of men" echoes —and eludes—the categories of diction established in the earliest commentaries about English poetry.[18] Ben Jonson, for example, contrasts "a verse as smooth, as soft, as cream;/In which there is no torrent, nor scarce stream" with a verse in which one finds "nothing but what is rough and broken."[19] In these assessments, one discovers the polemical basis of Wordsworth's antipathy to diction that is *either* quaint or rude, trivial or barbarous. Of the first kind of poet, Jonson remarks, "Women's poets they are called: as you have women's tailors. . . . They are cream-bowl, or but puddle deep"; and of the latter kind, "They would not have it run without rubs, as if that style were more strong and manly, that struck the ear with a kind of unevenness."[20] Though the commentary becomes more partisan (a seventeenth-century preface to Cleveland's poetry contrasts "strenuous masculine style" with "enervous effeminate froth"), Jonson, Dryden, and, later, Samuel Johnson call for a blend of the strong and the smooth.[21]

The basic framework of this polemic about poetic diction clearly recalls the Aristotelian model of a synthetic vernacular combining disparate elements: familiar and unfamiliar, colloquial and exotic, drab and ornamental, rough and smooth. At the same time, the potentially "vicious" nature of either type of diction (rough or smooth) is often attributed in the English tradition to the incorporation of foreign sources, to the effects of *translation*. Dryden, for example, commenting on the strength of Jonson's diction, remarks, "Perhaps, too, he did a little too much Romanize our tongue, leaving the words which he translated almost as much Latin as he found them: wherein, though he learnedly followed their language, he did not enough comply with the idiom of ours."[22]

Infatuation with the foreign and the unfamiliar could also, by contrast, extenuate and corrupt the delicacy of tone prized by the Cavalier poets. Herrick, and even a poet like Abraham Cowley (usually associated with the robust style of the Metaphysical poets), produced collections of *Anacreontiques*, described by Samuel Johnson as "paraphrastical translations of some little poems, which pass, however justly, under the name of Anacreon."[23] These dubious translations yield "songs dedicated," Johnson explains, "to festivity and gaiety, in which even the morality is voluptuous."[24] Recalling Ben Jonson's comparison of "women's poets" to "women's tailors," Douglas Bush finds in Herrick's diction "the feminine particularity of a dressmaker . . . the phrases are a succession of delicate or delicately mock-heroic paradoxes which turn a woman into a dainty rogue in porcelain, and one whose roguishness is not limited to her costume."[25]

The "intermixture of tongues" (as Coleridge calls it) can therefore produce either the Romanized diction of Jonson's hybrid tongue or the delicate but "rogue" phrasing of Herrick's songs.[26] In both cases, impurities of diction result from excessive exposure to foreign languages—impurities scorned by "literary" poets. Some have even claimed (including Coleridge) that the origins of bad taste—of poetic kitsch—may be found in the chimerical diction produced by a classical education.[27] But that is only part of the story.

Poetry vs. Literature

I want to return to the rift between poetry and literature, to the genre wars of the eighteenth century, to controversies about poetic diction, in order to examine more closely the texts in which these debates occurred. By the time Wordsworth published his manifesto calling for a poetry based on "a language near to the language of real men," the historical commentary on poetic diction—or types of diction—had evolved into a ferocious debate about the distinguishing features of poetry itself (in contrast to prose)—about the "essence" of poetic language.[28] Although the matrix of vernacular language could be construed in a variety of ways (as preserved in archaic ballads or the language of "rustics," or synthesized in "polite conversation"—as Wordsworth liked to think), one must acknowledge, as John Guillory notes, that these conflicts about the substance of poetic diction (which would dilate the spectrum of language available to English poetry) represent a struggle to define the nature of the vernacular: "it is only vernacular writing that has the power to bring into existence the category of 'literature' in the specific sense of poetry, novels, plays, and so on."[29] In addition, the contemporaneous development of a model of Standard English guaranteed the value of writing associated with the category of literature, which in turn became the ultimate measure of usage (as the examples of usage in the *OED* attest). Hence, as Guillory explains, "Purity of diction [a marker of the literary indifference of the languages of poetry and prose] requires the participation of nearly all writing genres in the forging of a standard vernacular, in other words, a linguistically homogeneous bourgeois public sphere."[30] Poetry could become part of literature only by renouncing its peculiar language. In reaction, however, to literary homogenization, certain poets sought to develop an alternative model of the vernacular: a language that is impure and "impolite" in its diction.

Wordsworth was not the first poet, as we have seen, to make a distinction between "vicious" diction and the qualities of the "plain style," but he was the first to advocate a programmatic rejection of poetic diction: "there will also be found in these volumes little of what is usually called poetic diction; I have taken as much pains to avoid it as others ordinarily take to produce it."[31] He goes to considerable lengths in the preface (supplemented by a separate appendix on the subject of poetic diction in 1802) to explain the basis of the "adulterated phraseology" of poetic diction, condemning its "abuses" and "corruptions," its "wanton deviation from good sense and nature," its "extravagant and absurd language," its "gross and violent stimulants."[32] Ultimately, he explains, poets "became proud of a language which they themselves invented and which was uttered only by themselves."[33] He condemns in particular the formulaic nature of "phrases and figures of speech which from father to son have long been regarded as the common inheritance of Poets . . . and which have been foolishly repeated by bad Poets."[34] As a result, "the taste of men was gradually perverted; and this language was received as a natural language."[35]

Wordsworth, it seems, wished to replace one "natural" language with another. And he was not alone in ridiculing the "quaintnesses, hieroglyphics and enigmas" of poetic diction.[36] The growing prestige of vernacular writing, along with the controversies surrounding the distinction between poetry and prose, had already begun to cast doubt on the integrity of poetic language. Coleridge, too—though in a manner far less doctrinaire than Wordsworth—shows no hesitation in condemning "the unmeaning repetition, habitual phrases and other blank counters" of poetic diction; he, too, appears to reject "the false and showy splendours" of the poet's inheritance.[37] Yet Wordsworth radicalized his campaign against poetic diction—a step Coleridge was unwilling to take—by *equating* the languages of poetry and prose: "there neither is, nor can be, any essential difference between the language of Prose and metrical composition."[38] Stripped of the "foreign

splendor" of poetic diction, the language of poetry becomes, in Wordsworth's conception, nearly identical to prose or indeed to polite conversation.[39] At the level of diction, the two are indistinguishable.

The lone material distinction between poetry and prose depends, according to Wordsworth, on the "charm" of meter "superadded" to natural
language: "the only strict antithesis to Prose is Metre."[40] Hence the specifically poetic character of Wordsworth's writing is achieved, he claims, solely
"by fitting to metrical arrangement a selection of the real language of men
in a state of vivid sensation."[41] By implication, without meter—and without
the "gross and violent stimulants" of poetic diction—poetry would no longer possess any distinctive verbal properties: poetry could not be identified
by the qualities of its language. This formulation, one must acknowledge,
is so restrictive that it would deny the name of poetry to the bulk of post-
metrical, colloquial "poetry" written in the twentieth century.

Wordsworth's emphasis on "vivid sensation" preserves, however, a
means of distinguishing poetry from prose without reference to any characteristic properties of language (besides meter)—a way of defining poetry
that would become crucial to the integrity of modern poetry advancing the
elimination of poetic diction (and eventually meter as well). When Wordsworth declares, "all good Poetry is the spontaneous overflow of feeling,"
he implies (deliberately or not) that poetry can exist, in essence, solely as
a state of feeling in the poet and in the reader—without possessing any
distinctive or consistent verbal traits.[42] According to Jean-Pierre Mileur, the
Wordsworth of the preface argues that "one is not a poet by virtue of actually having written poetry but by virtue of an essential disposition of the
self."[43] Under such conditions, poetry persists not as a particular verbal formation but as a state of heightened sensibility. Without the disorienting
matrix of poetic diction, the language of poetry (in a material sense) can
be distinguished from prose only in the most feeble terms, thereby forcing
the essence of poetry to retreat from the page to the sensibility of the poet.
Guillory declares, "In the absence of poetic diction, the distinction between
poetry and prose must be maintained elsewhere, as an assertion of the difference embodied in the poetic sensibility."[44] Poetry is poetry not because it
may be distinguished from prose in any material sense but because it somehow expresses—in ways extrinsic to its verbal properties—the sensibility of
the poet. Wordsworth, like many others (including his principal adversary,
Francis Jeffrey), equates poetry with passion, yet his erasure of distinctions
between the languages of poetry and prose—his willingness to demateriai-

ize poetry, to force its withdrawal into the sensibility of the poet—reveals the fundamental importance of poetic diction to the verbal identity and viability of poetry.

Challenges in the eighteenth century to the verbal integrity of poetry, culminating in Wordsworth's attack on poetic diction, provoked reactions from poets and critics reasserting the "peculiarity" of poetic language—an orientation essential to the emergence of poetic kitsch. Robert Heron, for example, a critic whom Wordsworth paraphrases approvingly in the preface, rejects Wordsworth's equation of the languages of prose, poetry, and conversation: "the purposes of poetry are therefore most successfully accomplished when its sentiments and images are conveyed in appropriated language and measures, distinct from those of prose."[45] One should note here the stress on "appropriated" language. Coleridge, as well, despite his avowed distaste for "artificial phrases" and "pseudo-poesy," defies (and mocks the particular phrasing of) Wordsworth's equation of poetry and prose: "there may be, is and ought to be, an essential difference between the language of prose and of metrical composition."[46] Regarding his own poetic practice, Coleridge states simply, "I write in metre because I am about to use a language different from that of prose."[47]

Defending the idea of a language suitable only to poetry, Coleridge's position resembles—though it is free of condescension and the ugliest forms of class bias—the views of Jeffrey, who condemns "Mr. Wordsworth's open violation of the established laws of poetry" and his repudiation of "expressions which have been sanctified by the use of famous writers, or which bear the stamp of a simple or venerable antiquity."[48] Jeffrey's defense of poetic language is directly linked, one must emphasize, to his focus on poetic diction in his formulations of "popular poetry": a defense of what can later be identified—with radically different class connotations—as kitsch in poetry.

Romantic apologies for the idiosyncratic but also formulaic nature of poetic language echo a line of defense that arose midway through the eighteenth century in response to the increasing popularity of prose and shifting views about generic distinctions. Oliver Goldsmith, for example, anticipating the terms of Wordsworth's polemic, declares in 1765 (the year he is said to have produced—anonymously—the first edition of Mother Goose), "If poetry exists independent of versification, it will naturally be asked, how then is it to be distinguished? Undoubtedly by its own peculiar expression; it has a language of its own."[49] More polemically, Thomas Gray (whom

Wordsworth identified as "the head of those who, by their reasonings, have attempted to widen the space of separation betwixt Prose and metrical composition, and was more than any other man curiously elaborate in the structure of his own poetic diction") wrote in a letter of 1742 to Richard West: "As a matter of stile, I have this to say: the language of the age is never the language of poetry. . . . Our poetry [in contrast to that of the French] has a language peculiar to itself; to which almost everyone that has written has added something by enriching it with foreign idioms and derivatives: nay sometimes words of their own composition or invention."[50] Samuel Johnson echoes Gray's notorious views as he explains Gray's tendency to drive a phrase "beyond apprehension": "Gray thought his language more poetical as it was more remote from common use."[51]

Commonplace

Gray's defense of poetic diction—of the "peculiarity" of poetic language —cannot be isolated from his use of what Heron calls "appropriated language and measures" in his own poetic practice. Gray preserved and enhanced the singularity of poetic language by following a "purely anthological principle" in his writing, by the compositional method of the commonplace book.[52] The poetic use of commonplace phrases—or commonplaces— corresponds to the verbal and social function of the cliché, the stereotype, and, at the level of form, to the effects of the poetic refrain. In the Renaissance study of classical rhetoric, commonplaces were common topoi associated with the art of memory: topics, themes, quotations (and ultimately clichés) essential to the mastery of a particular field.[53] One collected commonplaces (quotations of Greek and Latin authors) in a commonplace book, a practice that had evolved by the eighteenth century to include the incorporation of vernacular writing but also, eventually, of letters, dried flowers, and other types of "evidence"—in the manner of a scrapbook. As a pedagogical device, the commonplace book was at once an aid to reading or memorization and a compositional tool: a notebook or matrix of sources in which poems could take shape.

The production and use of commonplace books had always been oriented primarily to the genre of poetry, and, not surprisingly, Gray's personal commonplace book (which ran to a thousand pages) was the matrix of his own verse.[54] Yet the introduction of vernacular writing into school curricula in the mid-eighteenth century (during Gray's lifetime) brought about a shift in the types of poetry recorded in commonplace books. By the latter half of the eighteenth century, according to David Allan, "the familiar classics-heavy canon was not only being substantially supplemented. It was actually being supplanted, even among active commonplacers, by a growing preference for vernacular poetry in general and for comparatively recent British poetry in particular."[55] In addition to the dissemination of vernacular poetry, the rising popularity of new prose genres (fiction, essays, journalism) contributed significantly as well to the gradual demise of commonplace books as tools for writing poetry (and to their conversion into anthologies, scrapbooks, and diaries).

Concern about the lingering influence of commonplace books (and their rarefied poetic contents) is discernible in essays such as Edward Young's "Conjectures on Original Composition" (1759), which posed the question, "Why are *Originals* so few?"[56] Anxiety over the deleterious effects of commonplacing on poetic production evolved within a generation to William Hazlitt's outright scorn for the idolatrous cast of a classical education: "the ignorant, as well as the adept, were charmed only with what was obsolete and far-fetched, wrapped up in technical terms and in a learned tongue."[57] These shifts in the status of the commonplace, which reflect an unprecedented decline in the generic value of poetry, are recorded in transformations in the usage of the term: the "commonplace" went from being something to be revered, collected, and replicated to a synonym for the trivial, the insipid, the stereotypical—as reflected in our own contemporary usage of the term. What we mean by "commonplace" today is precisely the opposite of what it meant to Thomas Gray in 1750.

The incoherent history of the usage of the word "commonplace" extends as well to our assumptions about the class connotations of the types of poetry composed by commonplace methods during their decline. That is to say, we presume that the poets who remained wedded to the anthological method and classical materials of the commonplace book were anything but "commonplace." In fact, we tend to view belated classicists such as Gray, who insisted on the peculiarity and insularity of poetic diction, as elitists. Yet contemporaneous opinion indicates quite the opposite. Wordsworth, for example, who accused Gray of seeking "to widen the space of separation" between poetry and prose, also identified his "curiously elaborate" diction as the basis of "the popular Poetry of the day"—in contrast to his own "experiments" with ordinary language.[58] In the preface, Wordsworth warned that "in order entirely to enjoy the Poetry which I am recommending, it would be necessary to give up much of what is ordinarily enjoyed"—that is, the "inane phraseology" of Gray's poetic diction.[59] Hence, it was Gray, not Wordsworth, who was writing "popular" poetry.

The class connotations of this polemic become evident in the conflict between commonplace poetry and the emerging "literary"—ostensibly colloquial—poetry of Wordsworth's new program. Gray, we must recall, came from relatively humble origins (his mother was a milliner). In addition, his close friendship with Horace Walpole, the son of a prime minister, whom Gray met as a boy at Eton (the same Walpole who authored the first Gothic novel, *The Castle of Otranto*), was estranged for a time because of Gray's displeasure with Walpole's social priorities.[60] (On a lengthy Grand Tour of Europe—at Walpole's expense—the two parted in Italy over Walpole's habit of attending fashionable parties, which ran counter to Gray's inclination to visit antiquities.) Beyond these biographical indicators, one must also attend to evidence of class affiliations—the specter of working-class Gothic—embedded in Gray's most famous poem, "Elegy Written in a Country Church Yard," which calls attention to the graves of the "rude Forefathers" of the plowman and the swain: "Let not ambition mock their useful toil,/ Their homely joys, and destiny obscure."[61] Furthermore, as Joshua Scodel notes, "By imagining his own burial and monument in the churchyard, Gray links himself in death to the poor whose worth he defends against the 'proud.'"[62]

These symptoms of class affiliation become inverted—though the antagonism remains—in Donald Davie's comparison of Wordsworth's "sobriety" with the "glare and glitter" of Gray and other "poets of the uprooted."[63] By this cryptic phrase, Davie means to contrast "the uprooted, nomadic, and classless type of the governess and the paid companion" (a "classless" type encompassing Gray's poetic values) with the "urbanity" of poets such as Wordsworth and Shelley.[64] The vulgarity of Gray's diction (its "glare and glitter") stands in contrast, then, to the "purity of diction" cultivated by Wordsworth, which is at once "a sign of good breeding" (according to Davie) and a symptom of the emergent, bourgeois ideology of literature.[65] Hence the glare and glitter of Gray's alienated classicism resists, through its commonplace method of poetic composition, the aspirational goals and the patronizing colloquialism of "literary" poetry. By resisting the advancing bourgeois hegemony of literature (aligned with prose fiction and polite letters), by removing itself from "the language of the age," the substance of poetic diction exposes unlikely affinities between commonplace methods of composition and the nascent regime of the mass ornament, between high kitsch and low culture.

The correlation between the methodology of the commonplace book and Gray's own poetry (in the "Elegy Written in a Country Church Yard," if not the odes) is close enough for one critic to declare that "Gray's *Elegy* is composed in much the same manner as a commonplace book."[66] John Guillory indeed refers to "the cento of quotable quotations that *is* the poem," describing it as "an anthology of literary clichés" and noting that "its phrases sound familiar even in the absence of identified pretexts, as though it were the anonymous distillation of literary sententiae."[67] Judgments about Gray's anthological poems can be traced to controversies about the "nervous" diction echoing the poetry of Milton—whom Hazlitt condemned as "a writer of centos."[68] Following Milton's "delirious" example, Gray's "Elegy"—the most celebrated elegy in the English tradition—is said to function like a "rhapsody" (a term synonymous with "anthology"), an assemblage of poetic formulae stitched together by the poet. Mobilized against the reproductive bias of Gray's poetics (and the Gothic themes slumbering in his verse), Gray's critics twisted "a polemic on the nature and function of poetic language into a romance of compulsive mimesis—addiction and repetition."[69]

It is indeed curious that the profound intertextuality of Gray's "Elegy" has spawned such divergent notions of its reception. On the one hand, we find Hazlitt recalling that "Mr. Wordsworth had undertaken to shew that the language of the Elegy is unintelligible."[70] Views of this kind echo Gray's insistence on the peculiarity of poetic language and its estrangement from common speech. Yet the majority of readers have followed Samuel Johnson's judgment of the work: "The *Church-yard* abounds with images which find a mirror in every mind, and with sentiments to which every bosom returned an echo. The four stanzas beginning 'Yet e'en these bones' are to me original: I have never seen the notions in any other place; yet he that reads them here persuades himself that he has always felt them."[71] From Johnson's account, one might conclude that Gray was laying the groundwork for Baudelaire's poetic program of "inventing clichés"—essential to the enchantment exercised by kitsch—of writing poems as if they had been "uttered by the *Zeitgeist*" (in Guillory's phrase)—despite the peculiarity of their language. The language of Gray's "Elegy," as Gordon Teskey observes about the intertextuality of Milton's poetry, "gives the feeling of having been twice made."[72] Leslie Stephen describes how Gray's poem, a repository of poetic clichés, acts in turn like a commonplace book upon the memory of its readership: "The *Elegy* has so worked itself into the popular imagination that it includes more familiar phrases than any poem of equal length in the language."[73]

Johnson's recognition of the popularity of Gray's poem must be reconciled, however, with his acknowledgment that Gray's poetic diction is "remote from common use." The poem appears to be at once native and contrived, popular and arcane. This dichotomy reflects two prevailing yet divergent assessments: Gray's poetic diction is said to be unnatural, remote, and unintelligible, yet also popular, stereotypical, and familiar. Indeed, the seemingly contradictory features of Gray's poetic language would appear to fulfill Jeffrey's dialectical model of poetic popularity: "the most refined style to which he [the poet] can attain will be, at the last, the most extensively and permanently popular."[74] The key to this improbable achievement is the mechanism of repetition, the reproducibility of poetic language. Even the most obscure passage or phrase becomes, if it is repeated often enough, familiar and susceptible to mass consumption.

The dialectic of the popular and the arcane aligns itself, we should recall, with the antithetical usage of the word "commonplace." The practice of commonplacing, which is the methodological key to the aesthetic of kitsch, thus succeeds in *arresting poetry* in two ostensibly divergent ways: by removing poetic language from history and actual usage, so that it becomes increasingly insular and arcane—that is, by *secreting* the language of poetry within the domain of literature—but also by endlessly repeating poetic clichés, thereby cultivating an artificial, common language, a counterfeit vocabulary available to a mass audience. Ezra Pound, as I noted earlier, would later condemn this phenomenon in especially graphic terms as the "corpse language" of poetic diction.[75]

Lyric Fatality

The commonplace method does not imply that Gray's "Elegy" is a pastiche, nor are its "appropriated phrases and measures" used in an ironic fashion. The poem is not trifling or skeptical of its commonplace method and refrains from mocking its own "phraseology": it is not camp. The fatalism of Gray's rhapsodic (i.e., anthological) method may be contrasted to the wickedly satirical mode of Alexander Pope's poem, "Lines of a Person of Quality," a poem composed entirely of borrowed phrases, figures, and sentiments. Pope, unlike Gray, deliberately pushes his commonplace lines towards bathos and doggerel:

Thus the Cyprian Goddess weeping,
Mourned Adonis, darling Youth:
Him the boar in silence creeping,
Gor'd with unrelenting Tooth.[76]

Some of the same effects—though inadvertent—can be detected in Gray's
synthetic verse: the earnest cultivation of poetic clichés and tableaux, bar-
ing the wellspring of kitsch in poetry. Pope, by contrast, signals that the
bathos of his lines is deliberate; he ironizes the clichés by depicting and
exposing to ridicule the rhapsodic mode of composition:

Cynthia, tune harmonious Numbers
Fair Discretion, string the Lyre;
Sooth my everwaking Slumbers:
Bright Apollo, lend they Choir.

Yet the song culled from the borrowed "Choir" here is less an integral poem
(as Pope's title indicates) than a collection of disparate "lines," a spectacle
of poetic "stooping":

Thus when Philomela drooping,
Softly seeks her silent Mate,
See the Bird of Juno stooping;
Melody resigns to Fate.

The final line of Pope's satire suggests that poetry resigns itself to a pathetic
"Fate" by re-signing (signing again and again) the verbal clichés of the poetic
tradition.

Pope's own nonsatirical poetry is, of course, implicated in the stereotypical tradition he mocks, just as the "drooping" fate to which poetry resigns
itself evokes the graveyard setting—the commonplace—of melancholy:

Mournful Cypress, verdant Willow,
Gilding my Aurelia's Brows,
Morpheus hov'ring o'er my Pillow,
Hear me pay my dying Vows.

Gray, by contrast, views the "Fate" of commonplace poetry not as a satirical
subject but as equivalent to the "dying Vows" of the swain in the church-
yard. More precisely, the "dying Vows" of the melancholy figure in Pope's
poem signify quite literally, from Gray's perspective, the dissolution of the

traditional language of poetry. In essence, this caesura—the stilling of poetic diction—confronts poetry with its mortality, its own possible death, yet we have already seen that this verbal seizure is only one possible death among several advancing in the mid-eighteenth century on the genre of poetry: the waning of originality, Wordsworth's erasure of distinctions between the languages of poetry and prose, the correlation of poetry and feeling—apart from language (that is, the withdrawal of poetry's verbal character into the sensibility of the poet). Each of these possible developments pushes poetry towards dissolution, towards an impasse.

Much of Gray's poetry (he wrote fewer than a thousand lines) is pre-occupied with death, melancholy, and sensuous anomie in ways that are consistent with the narratives of poetic decline espoused by many poets and critics of the period (including Wordsworth and Jeffrey), which in turn derive from Giambattista Vico's genealogy of evolving abstraction (and en-ervation) in "the progress of poesy" (to borrow the ironic title of one of Gray's odes).[77] More specifically, the "Elegy" and "The Bard" (one of Gray's odes) feature melodramatic and perhaps influential suicides. Goethe's Werther, for example, encounters—before he takes his own life—a figure he calls "the wandering gray bard who reaches for the footsteps of his fathers on the vast heath and finds alas! only their tombstones."[78] Gray's "Elegy" is, of course, set in a graveyard, where the speaker imagines his own death and funeral, and composes the epitaph for his own tombstone. In addition, at least one Gray scholar has noted a premonitory aspect of Gray's serial suicides (in verse), prefiguring the notorious fate of the youth-ful forger, Thomas Chatterton, a spectacular suicide in 1770 (some twenty years after the publication of Gray's "Elegy").[79] One might even consider the suicidal drive of Frankenstein's monster—a poet of sorts—to be a leg-acy of Gray's doomed poets. Whatever may be the legacy of Gray's suicidal bards, there can be little doubt, as Jean-Pierre Mileur notes, that "death is especially privileged in this vision as the intersection of the poet's personal fate and the fate of poetry in the imminent future."[80] Furthermore, Mileur remarks, "for Gray, the inevitability of death extends to poetry, which is moving inexorably throughout the poem towards its ultimate reduction to epitaph."[81]

Before the speaker of the "Elegy Written in a Country Church Yard" be-comes witness to his own disappearance in the course of the poem, he re-counts a description—by "some hoary-headed Swain"—of his solitary and disturbed behavior (before his disappearance):

'Mutt'ring his wayward fancies he wou'd rove,
'Now drooping, woeful wan, like one forelorn,
'Or craz'd with care or cros'd in hopeless love.[82]

The possibility that the sudden disappearance of the speaker's alter ego
(noted by the Swain and his friends) may be a suicide is reinforced by lines
that formed the poem's conclusion in the original Eton manuscript:

Hark how the sacred Calm, that broods around
Bids ev'ry fierce tumultuous Passion cease
In still small Accent whisp'ring from the Ground
A grateful Earnest of eternal Peace

No more with Reason & thyself at Strife;
Give anxious Cares & endless Wishes room
But thro' the cool sequester'd Vale of Life
Pursue the silent Tenour of thy Doom.[83]

With his disappearance, the speaker becomes by the end of the poem a
spectator at his own funeral, overhearing a "kindred Spirit" read aloud (for
the illiterate swains) the lengthy epitaph the speaker has prepared for his
own gravestone, comprising the final twelve lines of the "Elegy." The poem's
closure with the epitaph of the speaker anticipates the restriction of Gray's
own poetic production to a few epitaphs composed for friends after he formally stopped writing poetry in 1753 (several years after he completed the
"Elegy") at the age of thirty-six. In 1757, he was offered the appointment of
Poet Laureate, which he refused.

The implied suicide of the speaker of the "Elegy" becomes explicit in
the fate reserved for the narrator of "The Bard," whose death is announced
precipitously in the final lines of the poem:

He spoke, and headlong from the mountain's height
Deep in the roaring tide he plung'd to endless night.[84]

The bard's suicide is emblematic, as Mileur notes, of the fate of poetry,
enunciated elsewhere in the poem:

'A Voice, as of the Cherub-Choir,
'Gales from blooming Eden bear;
'And distant warblings lessen on my ear,
'That lost in long futurity expire.[85]

Poetry suffers a similar fate in "The Progress of Poesy": "But ah! 'tis heard no more—/Oh! Lyre divine, what daring Spirit/Wakes thee now?"[86]

Ultimately, Gray's most significant poems reveal that the poetics of the commonplace—curating and distilling poetic language—enacts continuously the dying vows of poetry but also the verbal suicide of the poet: a speech act whose "felicity" is ensured only by its duration, its continuity, and indeed its endlessness. More precisely, and more in keeping with its Gothic implications, the "death" of poetry must be understood as a *live burial*, a secreting of poetic language within the liberal diction of literature. For if kitsch, the direct descendant of the commonplace method, can be understood as the self-inflicted and self-sustaining death of poetry (as so many modernists would argue), then poetry's ending, its self-consumption, is interminable, an enduring form of resistance to the middling, bourgeois ideology of literature.

Lest one presume that the confrontation between Gray and Wordsworth over the "gross and violent stimulants" of poetic diction did not establish the terms of a polemic that continues to haunt the fate of poetry, or that the lyric fatalities of Gray's poetic production were terminal events, one need only recall the notorious abandonment of poetry by one of modernism's most gifted poets, Laura Riding. After announcing her repudiation of poetry in 1938, Riding returned repeatedly to the grounds of her disavowal, explicating her poetic beliefs: "The difference of the poetic use of words was precious: the difference must be served with a devout separate-keeping of the poetic and the non-poetic verbal practice."[87] Further, she explains, "The price of poetic freedom of word was poetry's having the identity of a mode of verbal expression outside the norms of expression that language, as the common human possession, seemed to ordain to be natural, 'ordinary' practice."[88] Her commitment to poetic diction reached a crisis, however, with the "degeneration of the 'language' of poetry into a compound of super-ordinary 'ordinary language.'"[89] Assessing and reacting to the public "naturalization" of poetic language, she concludes, "I found poetic utterance *arrested* [emphasis added] even in its being poetic utterance: it adumbrated a potentiality that was not developable *within* it, its limits of achievement *was* the adumbration of potentiality. I ended, in my movement in the poetic path, at no-end."[90] As these statements demonstrate, the *arresting* of poetry over the "potentiality"—and dissolution—of poetic language continues to evolve, and to resonate, as a poetic event within the normative compound of literature.

Thieves' Latin

What survived poetry's inscription of its own epitaph in Gray's poetry was a disfigured model of the commonplace, which had succeeded in arresting the language of poetry even as it transformed itself into a prototype of the mechanism of repetition that would sustain mass culture and the genre of kitsch. The method of the lyric automaton prevailed even as the gingerbread details of poetic diction—archaism, elision, syntactic inversion—were revised and supplanted by a new repertoire of *special effects* derived from hidden deposits of the vernacular. In fact, Gray was among the early connoisseurs and fabricators (including Lady Wardlaw, James Macpherson, Thomas Percy, and others) of the ballads whose diction contributed to the "glare and glitter" of Gothic verse condemned by literary poets.[91] In the preface, Wordsworth targets not only the "vicious" substance of poetic diction, whether classical or pseudo-vernacular, but the instrument responsible for its popularity: the "mechanical device of style."[92] The method of the commonplace book—what Guillory calls Gray's "systematic linguistic normalization of quotation"—could be applied to Greek and Latin sources but also—in a more popular vein—to forged scraps of native "poesy."[93]

Jeffrey notes a continuation of commonplace methods, with a changing array of sources: "the new poets are just as great borrowers as the old; only that, instead of borrowing from the more popular passages of their illustrious predecessors, they have preferred furnishing themselves from vulgar ballads and plebian nurseries."[94] Poetic diction shifts, according to Jeffrey, from the "motley masquerade" of Gray's classicism to the vulgar repertoire of distressed native genres—both equally "popular" and equally removed from common speech: "instead of ingenious essays, elegant pieces of gallantry, and witty satires all stuck over with classical allusions, we have, in our popular poetry, the dreams of convicts, and the agonies of Gypsy women."[95] In fact, the poetic diction of Gothic verse—one of the first fully realized models of poetic kitsch—swings wildly between slang and "literary pomp," synthesizing a language of "calculated impurity," according to Davie.[96]

Poetic kitsch thus first appeared as a genre in the transitional space between "residual" and "emergent" cultures (to borrow Raymond Williams's terminology), between the antique confection of belated classicism and the new barbarism of counterfeit balladry. What is surprising about this transition—and essential to the popularity of kitsch—is that the "quaintnesses, hieroglyphics, and enigmas" of poetic diction are normalized, engraved in the popular imagination, by an accelerated and technologized mode of the commonplace book, by a kind of poetic automation.

Rejecting the mundane purity of diction intrinsic to the hegemony of literature, and contesting the premise that a basic model of the vernacular (Standard English) should be grounded in the "language of conversation" and polite letters, defenders of poetic diction sought to anchor the vernacular in deposits of archaic usage (whether native ballads, classical formulae, or rustic speech) possessing the atavistic trait of the commonplace. Gray was thus concerned to develop, according to John Guillory, "a poetic diction which replicated *within the vernacular* a distinction like the distinction between classical and vernacular literacy. This distinction could be articulated as an essential difference between poetry and prose."[97] More compellingly, Gray responded to the privileging of prose "by reworking the vernacular precisely in order to *estrange it from itself*, to invent a kind of vernacular Latin."[98]

Defenders of poetic diction weathered the demise of classical literacy by sourcing the vernacular to native, atavistic sources and by grounding the language of poetry in a vernacular estranged from itself. The persistence of verbal archaism in the neoclassical revival of the ballad may therefore be understood as an extension of the antiquarian cast of late classicism but also as a way of appropriating, and refashioning, the substance of the vernacular. Understandably—from the perspective of those defending a purity of diction based on polite conversation—Samuel Johnson condemned poets who "conceive it necessary to degrade the language of pastoral, by obsolete terms and rustic words, which they very learnedly call Dorick, without reflecting, that they thus become authors of a mingled dialect, which no human being ever could have spoken . . . joining elegance of thought with coarseness of diction."[99] Yet "Dorick" diction (an allusion to the earliest presumed order of Greek style) resembles in its "mingled aspect" the classical paradigm of a poetic vernacular: a synthetic language combining the "drab" with the enigmatic, the plain style with the jeweled.

In this polemical context, one can see quite clearly, as Guillory notes, that "poetic diction is not simply archaic: it represents a *reaction* against polite letters as the emergent discourse of the bourgeois public sphere."[100] While verbal archaism, as a device intrinsic to the replicative methods of the commonplace book, may certainly be regarded as a means of arresting poetry (and thereby popularizing it), it is also implicated in a more complex strategy of inversion, resistance, and *return*. For, as Owen Barfield notes, "True archaism does imply, not a standing still, but a *return* to something older, and if we examine it more closely, we shall find that it generally means a movement towards language at an earlier stage of its own development."[101] In this sense, poetic archaism—understood as a return to language in its youth, as youthful language—is, Barfield asserts, "the very opposite of conservatism."[102] Archaic (or invented) deposits of vernacular language, sequestered from the history of usage and mediation, thus offer a means of preserving and, at the same time, radicalizing poetic language, a fusing of archaic diction with the substance of the vernacular. Mingled in the new pop genre of Gothic verse, impressed upon the public by commonplace methods of inculcation, and challenging the ascendance of polite letters, these elements of poetic diction laid the foundation for the miscreant genre of kitsch.

4 The Spurious Progeny of Bare Nature

Balladry and the Burden of Popular Culture

Commonly referred to as the ballad revival, the complex appeal of tradi-tional balladry (to elite audiences) in the eighteenth century coincided, one must acknowledge, with the *decay* of indigenous oral composition and of the once ubiquitous broadside ballad in print culture. According to Albert B. Friedman, "ballad-making continued to become increasingly weaker on its native grounds during and after the revival. . . . Neither the traditional ballad nor the broadside was revived. Indeed, the eighteenth century witnessed a sharp decline in the quality of both."[1] Noting that the gradual disappear-ance of early printed ballads in particular gave rise to a robust market for poetic "relics," he declares, "It was actually the decay of the broadside ballad industry which gave the signal to antiquaries that the black-letter broadside was ripe for collecting."[2] Contrary to established historical narratives, one must therefore conclude that the so-called ballad revival coincided with, or was motivated by, the *eclipse* of traditional ballad making. In fact, most bal-lads composed by poets associated with elite culture—ballad imitations—diverge sharply from the unembellished narratives and diction of the tradi-tional ballad.

Any attempt, moreover, to explain the sense of "revival" by alleging a revival of *interest* in traditional balladry yields a similar negative account. For, with the exception of Philip Sidney's embarrassed allusion to the bal-lad of Chevy Chase in his "Defence of Poetry" of 1581 (the first critical ac-knowledgment of balladry by a canonical poet), references to ballads by elite poets are uniformly condescending (until the appearance of Joseph Addison's ballad papers in the *Spectator* in 1711).[3] Ben Jonson's expression of enmity is typical: "a poet should detest a ballad-maker."[4] Ballads had never been popular among educated poets.

How then should one begin to explain the so-called revival of ballad poetry in the eighteenth century? At the most basic verbal level, in terms of poetic form and diction, elite poets displayed a keen interest in the ballad's archaic language, but also its ingenious devices of repetition, especially the burden, the chorus, the refrain. In broader terms, however, the enterprise of humanistic literature—increased education, literacy, print culture— contributed to the demise of traditional balladry (even as the new supergenre of literature sought to assimilate and moderate the archaic diction of the traditional ballad).[5] Thus, it is essential to acknowledge that the unprecedented literary infatuation with balladry in the eighteenth century was a belated development, a sign of the intrinsic *decadence* of the ballad as a poetic model. Friedman is unequivocal on this point: "from the time the traditional ballad appeared upon the historical scene in the sixteenth century, it was in a state of decay."[6] The traditional ballad thus emerged into literary history through a process of attenuated mimeticism—as the last in a series—which in turn provided the impetus for a proliferation of "antique" genres in modern poetry. The iterability of the newly fashionable poetic refrain helped to re-kindle the generic reproducibility of the ballad itself.

The attenuation of the traditional ballad was inescapably intertwined with the allure of the archaic, with a desire for extinct social relations— for a lost totality—embodied, it seems, in the curious diction of the ballad. Ultimately, in a series of poetic events engulfed by scandal, obtaining the archaic substance of the ballad could be achieved only through counterfeiting—by faking ancient poetry. In addition, forged artifacts inevitably came under attack for emphasizing style over substance—the triumph of artifice—a charge often leveled against art that is perceived to be decadent. In this context, however, "decadent" is a term that should be used very cautiously, since decadence as a property of kitsch is entangled with the substance of the vernacular, with language in its youth. Hence the decadence of kitsch aligns itself with notions of backwardness, childhood, minority, and even innocence—with what Walter Benjamin calls "the worlds of childhood." Primitivism thus cannot be isolated from decadence in the ballad revival, a complex array of forces that contributed in turn to the emergence of popular culture in its modern aspect—a development first manifest through the regression, or "vulgarization," of poetry.

The eclipse and appropriation of balladry by the emerging institution of literature (a formation of bourgeois humanism) cannot be isolated from a paradoxical resistance to the eccentric diction of the ballad (and its spurious offspring) by the guardians of polite letters. If "literature" became the measure of standard usage, then the diction of poetry spawned by the ballad revival became, by contrast, a standard of *abuse*. Accordingly, the idea of popular culture as a distinctive topos depends on *resistance* to popular culture, as Michel de Certeau suggests when he asks, "Does popular culture exist without the gesture to suppress it?"[7] Popular culture in its modern aspect (and the controversies surrounding it) may be said to have arisen in the context of the ballad scandals, yet by the same token the dissolution of resistance to popular culture in our own age suggests that we may be witnessing the end of popular culture as a subaltern category. The eclipse of verbal and social textures associated with balladry by the emergent paradigm of literature in the eighteenth century may be slowly reversing itself today, as popular culture becomes ubiquitous—and dissolves in its own ubiquity.

At the same time, the middling, democratic thrust of literature, which maintains itself by contesting and dispersing the static domains of elite or demotic cultures, depends on the presumed defects of popular (or elite) cultures—and on literature's pretense of accommodation. Hence, if the rationale for the suppression of popular culture disappears, one faces not simply the dissolution of popular culture as a subaltern category but the decay of literature as a generic standard of the verbal arts—and as a vehicle of humanistic and bourgeois emulation. What might follow from such a crisis can be extrapolated from a retrospective analysis of the polarization of literature and popular culture—via the ballad scandals—and in poetry's historical alienation from literature (masking its affinities with popular culture). Poetry may at some point in the future recover its position as a generic standard of the verbal arts, in a reciprocative and newly equalized relation to an emerging—and perhaps unrecognizable—conception of popular culture.

Whatever the fate of the concept of popular culture in our own age, there can be little doubt that its generic features—along with the endless controversies about its aesthetic value—first arose in reference to the strange poems—a "chimera of verse, dance, and song"—brought to light by the ballad revival.[8] In Friedman's jarring epithet, the traditional ballad can be described as "illiterature" and, indubitably, as "a species of popular poetry."[9] In fact, the ballad (and its illegitimate offspring) is not simply "a species" of popular culture but its inaugural artifact—viewed from the perspective of elite culture—spawning the perpetual antinomies of debate about popular culture.[10]

Despite the poetological origins of our basic assumptions about popular culture, the developmental relation between elite poetry and popular culture (in opposition to literature) was aborted, as I explained earlier, by the modernist campaign against kitsch and displaced (under the guise of a defense of the avant-garde) into debates about visual or material culture. To expose the veiled affinities between "serious" poetry and popular culture (and to advance current reflections about the fate of popular culture in general), one must therefore revisit the ballad scandals of the eighteenth century. This historical perspective will make it easier to assess whether the incommensurable project of *arresting* poetry (aligned initially—and improbably—with the mechanism of popular culture) may also coincide eventually with the dissolution of popular culture (as a domain sustained by elite culture's negative judgments).

Exploded Beings and After-Poets

In his essay on the Oxford don and early ballad imitator, Thomas Tickell (1685-1740), Samuel Johnson notes derisively the "Gothick Fairies" populating Tickell's verse—legendary figures Johnson calls the "exploded beings" of folklore.[11] The mythological debris floating through Tickell's ballad imitations may also, however, be understood in material terms as the debris of poetic diction. Surveying the condition of modern poetry in the wake of the ballad revival, Francis Jeffrey contends, "Modern poetry is substantially derivative and, as geologists say of our present earth, of secondary formation—made up of the *debris* of a former world."[12] Elsewhere, Jeffrey coins the term "after-poets" to designate those compelled to fashion their verses from the "debris" of the poetic tradition yet who also go in "dread of imitation."[13] The principal legacy of the after-poet and his dreadful imitations is, of course, the "mingled" modernity of poetic kitsch.

The after-poet's restoration, or outright fabrication, of archaic sources—activities preparing the ground of poetic kitsch—attained a miscreant and rabid maturity during the ballad revival of the eighteenth century, in the context of what Adorno calls "the phantasmagoria of the folksong" (anticipating the "false glitter" of kitsch).[14] The activities of literary imposture, culminating in the practice of forgery, are the focal point (as I mentioned earlier) of Susan Stewart's study of "crimes of writing": "such practices are in fact inversions or negations of cultural rules and so have acquired a more 'properly' transgressive space for those aesthetic writings stretching from Romanticism to the avant-garde."[15] And Stewart sees kitsch as a permanent formation and legacy of the "crimes of writing" practiced in the eighteenth century.

Setting aside for the moment the potentially "transgressive space" initiated by poetic forgery, along with the precise implications of "inversion" (a term for sexual deviance)—which I will revisit later—let me emphasize, once more, the consistently pejorative tone of commentary (inherited at different stages by Jeffrey, Adorno, and Stewart) on poetic practices associated with the ballad revival. Contrasted implicitly to a domain of artistic originality, propriety, and authenticity, the poetic project of incorporating the archaic substance of the traditional ballad is by turn criminalized, dismissed as a phantasmagorical, and soiled by the "debris" of its poetic materials. The antithetical relation between folk culture and fine art, ballad imitation and lyric (or literary) poetry, transmitted by these rhetorical models becomes the basis for the antinomies of popular and elite cultures, of kitsch and avant-garde. In addition, the terms adopted (for dialectical purposes) by these critics (Jeffrey, Stewart, Adorno) transmit the earliest and most consistent judgments against ballad culture (judgments rendered from the perspective of canonical lyric poetry). Thus, as early as 1520, broadside ballads are condemned as "dongehyll matter" and discussed routinely as "slimy rhymes," "vicious triplets," or the "louzy ballad."[16] Even poets later associated with the ballad revival were complicit with this kind of rhetoric: Walter Scott shunned "legendary tales" (ballads set in pre-conquest England) as "lackadaisical trash," and Thomas Percy characterized his own momentous anthology of balladry as "a strange collection of trash."[17] (The term "trash" in this context can refer to anything of little value, but especially verbal "rubbish" or nonsense.)

It is surprising then to note that Percy's collection of ballads, which he labels as "trash," is called *Reliques of Ancient English Poetry*—a title evoking the practice of antiquarianism but also, more obliquely, the veneration of religious relics. The possibility that traditional ballads can be labeled at once as "trash" and as precious "reliques" (by the same editor) reveals that what Friedman calls "the antithesis of balladry to poetry" (the presumed dichotomy of popular and elite cultures) replicates itself *within* the domain of ballad culture.[18] This dichotomy appeared only as a back-formation during the ballad revival in the eighteenth century, when the existence of a true (oral) folk ballad (said to be marked by a distinctive "simplicity") was celebrated in contrast to the "modern" orientation of the printed broadside ballad. Although both terms of the ballad antithesis (folk and broadside) acquired greater specificity and renown with the historical decline of these activities, ballad scholarship in general was always built on a rolling dichotomy of orality and print, agrarian and urban, traditional and modern, pure and corrupt.

Even the inferior category of the broadside ballad breaks down, it turns out, into similar dichotomies of value, with the earlier, black-letter broadsides (printed in a "Gothick" font that went out of use by about 1700) prized by antiquaries for indicating the authenticity—and possible traditional origins —of a particular ballad. Thus, the debased term of the ballad dichotomy— the broadside ballad—could at times serve as a crucial indicator of its more highly valued contrary, the folk ballad.

In a polemic anticipating the modernist antithesis of art and kitsch, yet another variation of the ballad dichotomy emerged, contrasting the traditional ballad to its Romantic or Victorian progeny: the ballad-romance, the Gothic ballad, and the parlor ballad of "simplicity." Despite these replications of the contrast between high and low, real and fake, within the ballad tradition, Friedman reminds us that the properties shared by various forms of balladry represent to the elite tradition a unified object: "in their mutual opposition to sophisticated poetry the traditional and broadside ballad come very near to uniting."[19] Within this dialectical opposition, however, one also discovers an unsettling *equation* of balladry and the most conservative, anthological forms of lyric poetry.

The variants of this dichotomy between "sophisticated" poetry and balladry, or within ballad culture itself, reveal that the modern antinomy of elite and popular cultures, of art and kitsch, is rooted in controversies stemming from the poetic tradition. Thus, what we now call kitsch in material culture first assumed its aesthetic and social predicament, along with its basic physiognomy, as the inferior term in a dichotomy contrasting vulgar and refined forms of poetry. More specifically, the paradigm of kitsch evolved from controversies surrounding literary imitation of the traditional ballad. Not surprisingly, at the modern terminus of a long-standing historical antagonism, a series of immanent dichotomies develops within modernist definitions of kitsch as well. For example, both Siegfried Kracauer and Clement Greenberg seek to fortify their definitions of kitsch by drawing distinctions between the folk ornament and the mass ornament, between folk culture and kitsch (in addition to contrasting kitsch and high art). Greenberg contrasts kitsch (a product, in his view, of industrial capitalism) to folk art, declaring,

"Most of what we consider good in folk culture is the static survival of dead, formal, aristocratic cultures."[20] And his primary example of folk art is the traditional ballad: "our old English ballads, for instance, were not created by the 'folk,' but by the poet-feudal squirearchy of the English countryside, to survive in the mouths of the folk long after those for whom ballads were composed had gone on to other forms of literature."[21] For Greenberg, the antithesis of avant-garde and kitsch replicates earlier transactions between "aristocratic" ballad compositions and degraded "folk" ballads—except that the parasitic relation of kitsch to high culture, as Greenberg sees it, has become much more destructive.

Kracauer, as well, makes a distinction between "folk" and "mass" ornaments, without however disparaging what he regards as the emptiness and superficiality of the mass ornament. Concerning the peasantry and its folk "ornaments," Kracauer contends, "A current of organic life surges from these communal groups—which share a common destiny—to their ornaments, endowing these ornaments with a magic force and burdening them with meaning."[22] Mass ornaments, by contrast, are "brought about by emptying all the substantial constructs of their contents," which have "no meaning beyond themselves."[23] Displacing the organic meaningfulness and communality of the folk ornament, the emptiness of the mass ornament gives expression, by contrast, to the condition of anonymity: "the human figure enlisted in the mass ornament has begun the *exodus* from lush organic splendor and the constitution of individuality toward the realm of anonymity to which it relinquishes itself."[24] The mass ornament—defined by Kracauer as "the spurious progeny of bare nature"—lends moreover its productive "ambivalence" to the social being of anonymity (which begins to resemble, by analogy with the "spurious" lineage of the mass ornament, a forgery of the principle of identity).[25]

Kracauer clearly wishes to emphasize the superficiality of the mass ornament (the prerequisite of its monadological expressiveness) and its cultivation of anonymity, yet his characterization of the mass ornament closely resembles what many scholars say about the traditional ballad (as a paradigm of folk culture) and about the broadside ballad as well (which Friedman calls a "mass-produced and mechanical substitute").[26] Thus, in contrast to a theory of bardism or minstrelsy (which holds that a particular ballad bears the imprint of an individual author or singer), Friedman (like many scholars of balladry) refers to "impersonality as a hallmark of ballad style."[27] The distinctive anonymity of the ballad is held moreover to be a product of "the necessary submission of the ballad to mass sensibilities," an orientation that also explains the conventionality and invariable flatness of the ballad style: "ballads are uncompromisingly superficial; they indulge neither in psychological research nor close physical description . . . violence and sentiment are expressed in a flat, perfunctory fashion."[28] Far from being the antithesis of the mass ornament (Kracauer's conception of kitsch), the folk ornament—exemplified by the traditional ballad—appears to anticipate and to model many of the controversial features of modern kitsch, including its formulaic nature, its sentimentality, and its potential significance for a progressive model of social totality.

Live Burial

One trope, in particular, mapping the dichotomies we have been addressing requires closer scrutiny. I am referring in fact to a *chain* of tropes linking the topographies of kitsch and balladry. Hermann Broch offers, as I indicated in earlier chapters, a startling image of the vexed relation between art and kitsch: "kitsch . . . forms its own closed system, which is lodged like a foreign body in the overall system of art."[29] In a variant of this analogy, Adorno pushes kitsch into the realm of fairy-tale horror, animating the "foreign body" of kitsch and describing it as an inscrutable "imp": "kitsch . . . lies dormant in art itself, waiting for a chance to leap forward at any moment."[30] Here, we encounter the image of kitsch as an alien thing—a folk creature—buried alive within the precinct of art. Similar analogies—varying the imprint of Gothic iconography—arise tellingly in scholarly descriptions (by Friedman, in this case) of the polarized relation between literary poetry and balladry:

> Beneath sophisticated poetry lies another poetic system, which under earlier conditions, preserved a primitive mode of composition radically different from that of sophisticated poetry. As a species of popular poetry, therefore, the traditional ballad cannot be localized in any century. It is not the peer of literary genres, because it is not their type.[31]

Here, the strangeness of the "primitive" artifact—the ballad—entombed "beneath" the literary tradition is enhanced by the fact that its alternate "poetic system" lacks historical coordinates; it cannot be "localized" in time. Just as, for Adorno, "kitsch defies definition," so the traditional ballad appears in these analogies to exist as a foreign body outside of history: the slumbering "imp" of popular culture.[32]

What links all of these analogies is the notion of an alien artifact *buried alive* in the dominant "system" of art or literature. Broch confirms the implications of this rhetoric when he refers to the Romantic "necrophilia" spawning the "libertinage" of kitsch; as does Greenberg, when he contrasts the "decay" associated with kitsch to the "living culture" of the avant-garde.[33] (Ezra Pound, as I noted in earlier chapters, once referred to such "decay" as the "corpse language" of poetic diction.)[34] Yet the image and trope of *live burial* must be traced more precisely to the Gothic imagination, a primary site for re-animating the traditional ballad and a crucial branch of the genealogy of poetic kitsch. In her book on the conventions of the Gothic novel, Eve Sedgwick devotes a chapter to what she calls "Gothic topography" and, more precisely, to the structure of "live burial": "a darkness within a darkness, a tempest within a tempest . . . in each case the distinctness of the inner event, the way it resists assimilation to the outer, is the focus of attention."[35] At the same time, the topography of live burial replicates "the Gothic structure of submerged correspondences" between interior and exterior.[36] She focuses her attention principally on what J. Hillis Miller calls "the Piranesi effect": "a topography of depth and interiority" emphasizing "the spaciousness and vacuity of the imprisoning environment."[37]

Sedgwick insists, moreover, on a correlation between Gothic conventions (such as live burial) and the topic of language itself; hence, because the trope of live burial operates according to a series of unstable divisions, "the material details of live burial are thus a kind of emblem for the divorce of the sign from its meaning."[38] By analogy, the modernist repression of kitsch corresponds to "the rather grim interpretation of meaning as a kind of live burial."[39] With these tantalizing assertions about the live burial of meaning within language—about the correlation between live burial and a crisis of meaning at the level of the sign—one expects to find in Sedgwick's analysis a poetological approach to Gothic conventions, a close examination of the material and poetic features of language, comprising a live burial of meaning. Yet her argument rarely descends to the level of the signifier; she is concerned less with the live burial of language itself at the level of diction or form—despite her claims—than she is with live burial as a metaphor for Gothic conceptions of linguistic consciousness.

In contrast to Sedgwick's largely thematic and rhetorical analysis, the modernist adaptations of the trope of live burial to the abject domains of kitsch and balladry offer a perfect opportunity to carry out Sedgwick's unrealized anatomy: to dissect the "material details" of live burial at the level

of diction—in the operations of poetic language. One could at least momentarily put rhetorical analysis on hold in this case by noting that neoclassical
and Romantic forgeries (a crucial bridge between traditional balladry and
poetic kitsch) claim to be exhuming an ancient text, even as they conceal,
or bury, the text's false origin in its deceptive appearance: a way of aligning
poetic forgery—performatively—with the operation of live burial. In this
sense, live burial becomes the primal scene of imposture, of aesthetic judgment, and of the epistemology of secrecy: Is it alive or dead, but also is it
real or fake, art or kitsch?

One of the effects, or conditions, of live burial—of "the Gothic salience
of *within*"—is what Sedgwick calls "the correspondence of the internal and
the external" or, more radically, "the sameness of separated spaces."[40] The
living cannot be distinguished from the dead; the occupant of the crypt is
alive. In this sense, Broch's Gothic trope of live burial (of kitsch "lodged like
a foreign body in the overall system of art") implies the equivalence of art
and kitsch. Broch, in fact, draws precisely the same conclusion about the
"enemy within"—about kitsch—when he asserts that "the system and the
anti-system appear to be identical."[41] Seeking to define the dialectical nature of kitsch in the strongest possible terms, Broch reaches for an image
conveying the apocalyptic tone of warnings about kitsch: "the Anti-Christ
looks like Christ, acts and speaks like Christ, but is all the same Lucifer."[42]
The imp, or angel, of kitsch thus finds itself submerged in a Luciferian drama
of *inversion*—to use Susan Stewart's term for poetic imposture and deviance
(for "crimes of writing"). The demon of kitsch is an invert: man becomes
woman, living art becomes dead kitsch, good becomes evil, true becomes
false. And no one can tell the difference.

Addressing kitsch and the operation of live burial at the level of the verbal sign—where signified deviates from signifier, and meaning itself is buried alive—returns one to the question of poetic diction, archaism, and the
influence of the ballad revival. Specifically, it recalls the importance of repetition in the language and structure of the ballad—resembling the methods
of the commonplace book—along with the ballad's most salient and stirring
device of iteration: the burden, the chorus, the refrain. As a mechanism
that both arrests and compels a poem's development through repetition,
the refrain is commonly seen as incrementally revealing and enhancing the
full meaning of a particular phrase. Yet, in the course of its repetition, the
poetic refrain also progressively strips itself of meaning (as does verbal repetition in general) and induces in the poem recurrent episodes of empty

phrasing, sometimes verging on nonsense (as in any babbling refrain: *tra-la, tra-la, tra-la*). From this perspective, the priority of lulling over meaning, of sensibility over sense, exemplifies not only the archaism of the ballad but its childish decadence. It is precisely this aspect of the live burial of meaning —the technique of lulling—that links the operation of the poetic refrain to mass culture, consumption, and to episodes of fleeting collectivity: to a progressive remodeling of the concept of social totality.

At the level of diction, poetic phraseology (an oblivious and compulsory jargon of borrowed phrases) depends on practices of commonplacing and forgery as it accumulates a surfeit of *special effects* associated with "Gothicke mynstrellesie." The commonplace, or stereotypical, diction of the traditional ballad, continually succeeding itself in rhapsodic disorder, evokes a variation of live burial that Sedgwick associates with "the extended image of the palimpsest."[43] She writes, "This vision of the tissue of language, as a kind of orderly accident, is a way of subliming and abstracting the relationship of meaning."[44] The repeated and ostensibly accidental eruption of the poetic refrain, combined with the recklessly formulaic diction of the street, stall, or broadside ballad remakes poetry (or a militantly conservative variant of it) in the image of popular culture and mass consumption.

Illiterature

Refrain

Poetic kitsch descends from the illegitimate offspring of the ballad revival of the eighteenth century. This debt can be reckoned in terms of the verbal qualities of the poem, by emphasizing its commonplace and spurious diction, as well as its dependence on various devices of repetition—especially the poetic refrain. At the same time, just as analysis of the pop artifact itself is frequently overshadowed by a preoccupation with mediation and consumption, so too are discussions of the traditional ballad often diverted from questions of diction or form (alternating three- and four-beat lines arranged in quatrains or octaves) toward the ballad's more evocative (and inaccessible) conditions of performance. Thus, Albert Friedman maintains, "We define the ballad by the way it was produced and marketed: anything printed in the broadside format—not necessarily the many-column folio sheet—and intended for singing has a right to the name."[1] Tracing the genealogy of kitsch to a poetic artifact defined by the ways it was "produced and marketed" does indeed offer a useful framework for assessing poetry's relevance to the conditions of popular culture.

The relevance of the genealogy of ballad culture to kitsch reveals itself in the remarkable correspondences between the popularity of kitsch and the peculiar social ontology of the ballad. For the "spurious progeny" (in Kracauer's phrase) of the modern mass ornament replicates the mysterious expressive powers—a social monadology—of the stereotypical ballad. We have already seen how the relentless "superficiality" and "impersonality" of the traditional ballad anticipate the "pure externality" of the mass ornament. The "exodus toward the realm of anonymity" (as Kracauer calls it) documented by the mass ornament retraces the undetectable paths and the irresistible circulation of the broadside ballad: "an organ," in Friedman's view, "through which the general will had come to assert itself."[2] More precisely, Friedman claims, "the broadsides occasionally provided anonymities with the means of having their say."[3] The ballad thus functioned as a medium, a pivotal artifact, between the archaic signature of *Anon*, Romantic ideas about folk psychology, and modern formulations of anonymity (especially in relation to mass culture).

The idea that the ballad expresses the "general will," or impersonal sentiments, or anonymous intuitions, stems from Johann Gottfried von Herder's influential conception of the *Volkslieder*, generated by his enthusiastic readings of the Ossian forgeries and Percy's *Reliques of Ancient English Poetry*. According to the *das Volk dichtet* doctrine, "the folksong was the untrammeled expression of the *Volk*; in it the bona fide character of the race was embodied."[4] This doctrine of impersonal expression establishes a way of understanding the ballad—as a mode of choral lyric—which also accounts for the stereotypical allure of kitsch, for its representational incapacities: "Popular song is notoriously vague and inaccurate. Where balladry is of genuine value is in revealing the public reaction to political events, and in helping to reconstruct political and social atmosphere."[5] The "atmosphere" captured by the ballad and its spurious progeny is analogous to the social "substance" encrypted in the "pure externality" of the mass ornament. Based on the presumption that the ballad (like kitsch) provides "an invaluable index to popular feeling," the doctrine of anonymous expression flips around to become a model of verbal and ideological contagion, a matrix for transient social totalities, disclosing "the use of balladry for propaganda."[6]

The ballad's scope of expression and accessibility—the paradigm of a poetic mass ornament—is ensured by repetition and "jingles" of commonplace diction. For the antithetical usage of the term "commonplace"—meaning at once ordinary and extraordinary, trite and erudite, worthless and precious—became manifest in the earliest stages of the elite reception of the traditional ballad. In Henry Bold's *Latine Songs* (1685), for example, the "Ballad of Chevy Chase" appears in both dialect and Latin versions, a bizarre juxtaposition of unfamiliar tongues (one of them a variant of English) repeated in John Dryden's *Miscellany* (1702).[7] Similar hybrid rhapsodies of "Dorick" (i.e., rustic) songs and classical poetry, in which "the vernacular tags jar with the Latin context," appear in half a dozen volumes prior to Joseph Addison's ballad papers in the *Spectator* in 1711.[8] What accounts for these monstrosities is a perceived correlation between two types of obscurity: the difficulty of Latin and the rude vigor of poetry composed in dialect or archaic diction. Hence the idea of the vernacular, as it becomes manifest in the frozen diction of the ballad, is thrust away from "polite conversation" toward the domain of obscurity and archaism, fulfilling the dialectic of the commonplace. Furthermore, the pop arcana of the traditional ballad excited and advanced the evolving methods of *philology*, sometimes in circles far from traditional scholarship. Friedman reports that "the *Grub Street Journal* at this time was receiving into its columns serious emendations of 'Chevy Chase'"—a spontaneously erudite approach to balladry conducted in popular magazines.[9] One of the most influential anthologies of the period, *A Collection of Old Ballads* (1723-1725), is studded with annotations and lengthy headnotes. Friedman explains, "These trappings, of course, announce the arrival upon the scene of the curator with his labels, pins, and fixing fluids: the collector of *Old Ballads* may be said to have definitely inaugurated the 'museum life' of the ballad."[10] Though Freidman implies that these practices mark the onset of a period of decadence in the life of the ballad, they are in fact already in place at the earliest stages of the ballad revival.

Two factors conditioning the antinomian celebrity of the ballad must be emphasized here: first, the perplexing *curatorial* approach to the demotic registers of the poetic vernacular (an approach foreshadowing broader and more sophisticated methods of commodification). Secondly, the coincidence of obscurity and conventionality (the dialectical signature of the commonplace) is neither incoherent nor detrimental to a mode of poetry unconcerned with accuracy and specificity of representation. Under the sway of the curatorial imagination, the mass medium of the poetic vernacular gives expression—in ways that are fundamentally obscure—not to individuals but to collective identities, to social classes whose coherence and solidarity are undermined by shifting models of employment and consumption. As a prototype of kitsch, ballads offer a means of synthesizing genuine experience.

The choral—that is to say, impersonal—sentiments of the populace become manifest with particular force in the ballad and its spurious progeny through the lyric device of the burden or refrain. Exemplifying the mechanism of reproducibility that is essential to all popular culture, the poetic refrain gives expression to the sentiments and commentary of its anonymous listeners or readers: a collectivity mirrored by the *collectability* of the archaic ballad. In the oldest ballads, where the burden often recurs without variation, the refrain literally arrests the language of the poem—demonstrating the more general effects of stereotypical diction in the ballad—even as it serves as a pivot, an interlude, redirecting and invigorating the formulaic narrative of the poem. The refrain produces a disorienting echo, subjecting the poem to regular lapses of meaning or sense (especially when the refrain is itself nonsensical), thereby realizing the expressive conjunction of the formulaic and the obscure: the dialectic of the commonplace. The iteration of the poetic refrain, even when it is fully intelligible, may thus be said to effect a gradual separation of sound and sense, signifier and signified: a dislocation inducing a *live burial of meaning* within the poem.

Through repetition and episodic displacement, the poetic refrain makes a spectacle of lyric poetry's common dissolution of sense, robbing even the most transparent statement or sentiment—step by step—of fixed meaning. Assigning to the refrain the function of not making sense, rather than making sense, evokes aesthetic and sociological issues that are central to Deleuze and Guattari's conceptualization of the "refrain" (*la ritornelle*) and its relation to "territoriality." In their view—only partially consistent with the premise I have outlined here—the expressive disposition of the refrain, seeking to establish a "point of order" and a "circle of control," is "essentially territorial, territorializing, or reterritorializing."[11] The territorial function of the refrain—its ability to establish the coherence and solidarity of its audience—accounts for its mass appeal. Equally important to the symbolic economy of popular culture, the relationship of the refrain to territoriality is, according to Deleuze and Guattari, a function of *expression*, just as the efficacy of poetic kitsch is a matter of expression rather than representation.[12]

At the same time, a more concrete and precise analysis of the poetic burden reveals, in contrast to the views of Deleuze and Guattari, that its relation to territoriality inevitably involves operations of *deterritorialization*—of *not* making sense, of disorder and illegitimate control. The closer one looks at the territorializing function of the refrain, the more it appears to depend on its antithesis. For example, Deleuze and Guattari trace the origins of the refrain (and its territorial function) to birdsong, yet the oldest French word for birdsong, *jargon*, also refers to the slang of the criminal underworld, to the secret language of the demimonde. Hence the function of the poetic refrain aligns itself, in this case, with the *deterritorializing* powers of infidel speech: dialect, slang, archaism, obscurity, involution. My thesis regarding the live burial of meaning in the poetic refrain—a ruse of unraveling sense—thus contradicts in significant ways Deleuze and Guattari's equation of the refrain and territorialization.

The jargonal aspect of the refrain is borne out by the historical associa-tion between balladry and the demimonde, a genealogy of lyric deterrito-rialization comprehending the migration of the refrain from popular song to canonical verse, from vernacular to literary poetries. If "the refrain has been taken as the identifying feature of a given ballad," as Friedman claims, it usually takes the form of one or two lines recurring episodically through-out the song without variation (though the refrain may also be distributed irregularly).[13] In one of the most famous—and gruesome—of traditional bal-lads ("Edward, Edward"), the entire poem consists of a sequence of double refrains, alternating between a mother's questions and her son's answers (ultimately revealing a patricide):

> Quhy dois your brand sae drip wi' bluid,
>> Edward, Edward?
> Quhy dois your brand sae drip wi' bluid?
>> And quhy sae sad gang yee, O?
>
> O, I hae killed my hauke sae guid,
>> Mither, mither;
> O, I hae killed my hauke sae guid:
>> And I had nae mair bot hee, O.[14]

The same question and answer pattern is repeated by Dante Gabriel Rossetti in his celebrated ballad imitation, "Sweet Helen"—with the innovation of a "parenthetical refrain," a so-called ballad-burden trick that became a target of several Victorian parodies.[15]

The constant refrain is especially effective as a foil to the violence or sexual infamy depicted in ballads such as "Edward, Edward" (where the murderous son is revealed to be a pawn in an incestuous relation with his mother). An-other "homeopathic" refrain appears in the ballad, "Edom O'Gordon," where the helpless chatelaine rebuffs the predatory Gordon, shortly before he burns her alive and butchers her children as they drop from the castle walls:

> I winnae cum down, ye fals Gordon,
>> I winnaie cum down to thee. . . .
>
> I winnae give owre, ye false Gordon,
>> To nae sik traitor as yee.[16]

The gruesome scenes of the ballad are discharged by periodic "atmospheric refrains," a contrapuntal technique well suited to the aesthetics of shock,

horror, and scandal. The influence of these provocative devices runs through
Gothic verse, through a great deal of poetry of the nineteenth century (the
dark side of the pre-Raphaelite *phantastikon*), extending even to certain rebarbative poets in the twentieth century. One is struck, for example, by
the dark balladry in the super-sophisticated tableaux of the contemporary
American poet Frederick Seidel:

> All the way down to the wharf
> All the way down to the wharf
> All the way down to the wharf
> He-wolf and she-wolf went walking.
>
> Shut up, darling! I'll do the talking.
> All the way down to the wharf
> All the way down to the wharf
> The Stalker was stalking.[17]

Here, as in so many of his poems, Seidel constrains a sensationalistic narrative with the disaffected recitals of ballad composition—verging on a kind
of doggerel—combined with deliberately flat and colloquial diction. Seidel's
fussy and sadistic verses can best be understood as *high kitsch*, bringing up
to date a poetic tradition of mannered barbarism—and popular horror—
reaching back to the ballad revival.

   Within the ballad tradition itself, not to mention the pseudo-ballads of
generations of imitators, the unvaried refrain undergoes many permutations heightening the effects of, shall we say, deterritorialization. The so-
called "organic," or constant, refrain may be contrasted to its anomalous
kin: the "inorganic" refrain, the "incongruous" refrain, the "unconnected"
refrain, the "discordant" refrain. Such refrains, according to Friedman, are
"decorative and lyrical and never advance the story, to which indeed, they
are irrelevant and sometimes incongruous."[18] A traditional example can be
found in the ballad "The Cruel Brother":

> But it would have made your heart right sair,
> *With a hey ho and a lillie gay*
> To see the bridegroom rive his haire,
> *As the primrose spreads so sweetly.*[19]

The inorganic burden became the trademark of the pre-Raphaelite ballad,
including the irrelevant flower-refrain of William Morris's ballad "Two Red

Roses across the Moon" (from *The Defence of Guenevere*), in which the refrain (rehearsing the title of the ballad) dapples insensibly a song divided
between a lady and her knight.[20]

The discordant refrain becomes a meaningless refrain (like the irrelevant
flower-refrain) when a phrase or word is repeated continually and without
variation. A favorite burden of the sixteenth and seventeenth centuries, according to Thomas Percy, can be found in the song of "willow, willow." As
an example, Percy offers a "black-letter copy" from Samuel Pepys's collection of ballads—a variant, he notes, of the traditional ballad appropriated by
Shakespeare for Desdemona's willow song. The ballad is entitled "A Lover's
Complaint, being forsaken of his love. To a pleasant tune":

> A poore soule sat sighing under a sycamore tree;
> O willow, willow, willow!
> With his hand on his bosom, his head on his knee:
> O willow, willow, willow!
> O willow, willow, willow!
> Sing, O the greene willow shall be my garland.[21]

The devouring repetition of the willow refrain in a ballad of some 120 lines—
comprising nearly two-thirds of the total number of lines in the poem—
gradually empties the word "willow" of meaning, encrypting the signified in
the signifier, and turning the familiar word into a senseless "acoustic mirror"
(to use Kaja Silverman's term) of the melancholy singer.[22] The burden of a
song consisting mostly of refrains thus produces a hypnotic deterritorialization of sense, a live burial of meaning. Is "willow" a word in this context
or isn't it? Remarking on the typical contraction of the "burden," Friedman notes that the babbling refrain is conventionally "printed with the first
stanza and forgotten thereafter, or dwindles to a series of ampersands."[23]
Such is the case with Percy's example of the willow song, where the first
stanza is followed by a dozen abbreviated refrains:

> My love she is turned; untrue she doth prove:
> O willow, &c.
> She renders me nothing but hate for my love.
> O willow, &c.
> Sing, O the greene willow &c.[24]

And so on for 120 lines. The refrain continually interrupts and submerges
the poem, even as it is reduced to a typographical cipher marking an irresist-

ible lapse, iteration, stutter: a cipher of reproducibility forecasting the rise of mass culture. In essence, the sequence of the refrain, at once arresting and dissolute, concentrates the repetitional praxis of the commonplace diction of the ballad and, later, of kitsch in poetry.

In a final inversion of the territorializing effects of the refrain (essential to the mass appeal of kitsch), the babbling burden becomes simply unintelligible: "Hey, derry derry down," "Fa la la diddle," "Lillumwham! Lillumwham!" and so on.[25] Lewis Carroll's "Jabberwocky" offers a famous—and belated—example of the nonsensical burden, which appears at the beginning and the end of Carroll's poem:

> 'Twas brillig, and the slithy toves
> Did gyre and gimble in the wabe:
> All mimsy were the borogoves,
> And the mome raths outgrabe.[26]

Although "Jabberwocky" is typically understood as a parody of sense-making, the poem is actually a ballad imitation—like many of Carroll's poems—adhering strictly to ballad form. By implication the poem's nonsensical refrain should be viewed not as a parody but as an example of a common type of ballad refrain.

The inane chorus of Carroll's "King Fisher Song"—perhaps the culmination of the "inane phraseology" of poetic diction—brings to mind the form and function of the lullaby:

> Sing Beans, sing Bones, sing Butterflies! . . .
> Sing Prunes, sing Prawns, sing Primrose-Hill![27]

For the lullaby and its incantational charm exemplify, of course, the device of the nonsensical refrain: "So lulla lulla lulla lullaby bye." Some of the earliest examples of so-called children's poetry (often written in ballad form) were called, as I noted in an earlier chapter, "sonnets for the cradle."[28] In a rare essay on the genre of the lullaby, "Las nanas infantiles," Federico Garcia Lorca finds a connection between dreams and *la canción añeja* (the antique song) of the lullaby—a correspondence recalling Walter Benjamin's amalgam of dreams, kitsch, and "the worlds of childhood."[29] In her study of the verbal techniques of lulling, Marina Warner states, "lullabies resemble charms and magical wishes: spelling out what might happen in order to bind it is witchcraft. And this performative speech, the act of spell-binding, can either determine the future (make it come true) by chanting it into being or prevent through articulating it."[30]

Translated into the means of symbolic economy, lulling—"spelling out what might happen in order to bind it"—becomes a verbal technique essential to the dispersion of mass culture. The poetic refrain (epitomized by the repetitive burden of the lullaby) can thus be understood as an indispensable instrument of consumption and popular culture, capturing and territorializing its audience by repetition. Soothing the fractious child, the lullaby mesmerizes all who come within earshot—a siren song—establishing the modality of the helpless and enchanted listener, a prototype of the modern consumer.

Lullaby Logic

If we judge the ballad revival of the eighteenth century and the "folk phantasmagoria" (to use Adorno's phrase) of poetry following in its wake to be the hidden matrix of kitsch, then the standard Romantic genealogy of the origins of kitsch must be substantially revised. Friedman takes this view when he asserts, "The ballad revival in the first half of the eighteenth century was actually sponsored by neoclassicism."[31] Thus, we should not forget that the convergence of primitivism (or baby culture) and decadence in the antiquarian passion for vernacular poetry—which disclosed new sources of stereotypical poetic diction feeding the wellspring of kitsch—first occurred in the context of Augustan, or neoclassical, poetics. A poetological orientation towards kitsch pushes back the standard thesis about the Romantic origins of kitsch (first proposed by Broch, Greenberg, and others) by nearly a century.

Susan Sontag is exactly right—and nearly alone—in her determination of the historical genesis of camp (which shares some of its objects, though not its disposition, with kitsch): "the soundest starting point seems to be the late seventeenth and early eighteenth century, because of that period's extraordinary feel for artifice."[32] Furthermore, she identifies a sensibility that was "distributed throughout all of high culture," yet which satisfied its taste for artifice in part by fetishizing vernacular poems whose authenticity was almost continually in doubt.[33] Sontag's chronology can, of course, be sharpened considerably: although anthologies of Scottish folk poetry—known as "border ballads"—began to appear at the start of the eighteenth century, the inaugural and emblematic event of the ballad revival occurs, arguably, with the publication of a ballad called "Hardyknute," by a Scottish aristocrat, Lady Elizabeth Wardlaw, in 1719. This event embodies the characteristic features of the ballad revival in part because the authenticity of the poem, which was said to be a traditional ballad by an anonymous source, came almost immediately under suspicion and was ultimately shown to be a forgery.[34]

Lady Wardlaw's role in bringing "Hardyknute" to light—or producing it—reveals a crucial (but still largely ignored) network of female antiquarians responsible for cultivating the elementary materials of popular poetry in the eighteenth century.[35] Thomas Percy, in his prefatory (and caustic) remarks about "Hardyknute" in *Reliques*, reported that Lady Wardlaw "pretended she had found this poem written on shreds of paper employed for what is called the bottoms of clues" (the starting spools for balls of yarn).[36] Taking into account the domestic setting of this curious anecdote, which functions as the cryptic germ of countless "ballad scandals," Susan Stewart contends, "In Scotland, the production of ballad literature by aristocratic women, often done pseudonymously or anonymously, was part of the political and aesthetic production of the home and not part of a literary circle's attempts to validate a national literary tradition."[37] Here Stewart substitutes (tendentiously perhaps but with ample reason) domestic intrigue for Scottish nationalism as the essential matrix of the ballad revival. Elaborating, moreover, the implication of "the bottoms of clues" into an effective historical metaphor, she suggests, "It might be wise to reconsider all ballad imitators as a variety of fancy paper-cutters and embroiderers working from their vernacular allegiances."[38] In fact, as we shall discover, it is not simply the role of female antiquarians, but the origins of kitsch and a model of queer identity replicating the ambiguity of the forged artifact, that lie encrypted in "the bottoms of clues."

Lady Wardlaw's role in drawing attention to vernacular poetry—producing ballad imitations that left an indelible mark on literary history before being exposed as forgeries—indicates the importance of women in shaping the evolution of new poetic (but anti-literary) experiments leading ultimately to the formation of kitsch. She was not alone: a diverse and influential network of Scotswomen helped to establish—often without being fully acknowledged—a paradigm for poetic antiquarianism in the eighteenth century, anticipating in certain respects the "bluestocking" group of women writers and intellectuals gathered around Lady Elizabeth Montagu in Britain.[39] The Scottish circle was, however, considerably more diverse socially and economically than its later British counterpart, which experienced certain public tensions between its aristocratic and working-class members.[40] Some of the Scotswomen were primarily collectors and antiquarians, but many were poets, composers, and singers of ballads as well. The most notable collector was Mrs. Brown of Falkland, née Anna Gordon (1747-1810), the daughter of an Aberdeen professor, a number of whose ballads (collected from northeastern Scotland) went into Walter Scott's *Minstrelsy of the Scottish Border* and other influential anthologies.[41] Several of these collectors and poets were drawn from the Jacobite aristocracy: Wardlaw, but also Lady Jean Hume (1710-1770); the song composer Lady Carolina Nairne (1766-1845); Lady Alison Cockburn, née Rutherford (1714-1794), friend of David Hume and lyricist of the popular song "The Flowers of the Forest."[42] Lady Jean Elliot (1727-1805) as well penned a set of lyrics to this song in 1756. In addition to these well-born writers, the circle of Scottish Bluestockings included the folk poets Isobel Pagan and Jean Glover, along with Janet Little (1759-1813), who was a servant in the household of Mrs. Dunlop, the patroness of Robert Burns.[43] Like Joanna Baillee, Little wrote in Augustan English idioms and forms (as well as Scots vernacular), but her first book was presented as the work of "the Scotch Milkmaid."[44]

In the wake of controversies generated by Wardlaw's "Hardyknute," the ballad revival crossed over decisively into popular culture with the first—and wildly successful—staging of John Gay's *The Beggar's Opera* in London in 1728. Incorporating more than forty broadside ballads into a drama set in the criminal underworld, *The Beggar's Opera* made fashionable the familiar correspondences between ballad culture and the canting tradition of songs composed in the jargon of the demimonde.[45] The infidel slant of ballad culture can be detected as well in the work of Joseph Ritson, a prolific editor of ballad anthologies and early champion (against Percy) of a collectivist theory of the origins of balladry, who contributed antiquarian materials to Thomas Spence's ultraradical journal, *Pigs' Meat* (associated with the London Corresponding Society). Explaining why ballads are sometimes referred to as "fugitive poetry," Friedman observes, "The balladists had the reputation of being a drunken and beggarly lot; the disreputable ballad-vendors, both in fact and on the stage, were sometimes thieves or accomplices of thieves; the regular ballad public was drawn from the least refined strata of society."[46] At the same time—and more importantly for our purposes—*The*

Beggar's Opera (with its emphasis on a shorter and more lyrical variety of ballad) helped to launch a protean and popular tradition of ballad imitations, or pseudo-balladry, which constitutes the true matrix of poetic kitsch.

A survey of the permutations of the pseudo-ballad must take into account Gothic verse, the parlor ballad of "simplicity," poetic melodrama, peasant poetry, bardic fragments, and multiple shades of forgery. Additionally, the most popular form of the pseudo-ballad—the nursery rhyme—posits a peculiar, and distinctly modern, type of reader. To be more precise, the fractured and profane ballads gathered under the rubric of Mother Goose target the new and incoherent type of the *child-reader*, a figure resembling in ways the gullible connoisseur of native ballads, a consumer of potentially spurious artifacts. The child-reader posited by the nursery rhyme becomes, through an intricate web of verbal repetition, the subject of nonsense and enchantment but also of various punitive scenes of instruction.

The very first edition of Mother Goose rhymes was printed by John Newbery in London in 1765, the same year that Thomas Percy published *Reliques of Ancient English Poetry* (the most influential collection of ballads ever published) and that James Macpherson brought to light *The Works of Ossian*, assembling what were later shown to be mostly forgeries of poetic fragments by a fictive Gaelic bard. (A wider genealogy of kitsch would also note that a young Jean-Jacques Rousseau, after working as a tutor to the children of the Dupin household at Chenonceau, composed the first *melodrâme*, "Pygmalion," in 1762.)[47] Newbery's anonymously composed collection of nursery rhymes is entitled *Mother Goose's Melody, or Sonnets for the Cradle* and, in keeping with its obvious debt to the poetics of the ballad, it adopts certain graphic features associated with printed street ballads, including blackletter font (also known as "Gothic" type), used specifically for broadside ballads and for primers (works associated with childhood literacy) long after black-letter had ceased to be used for common texts.

Each of the fifty-one "sonnets" in *Mother Goose's Melody* was accompanied by a tiny woodcut illustration, a popular practice familiar from broadside ballads sold in the street. Moreover, the woodcuts of a second edition of Newbery's Mother Goose (1780) were done by the young Thomas Bewick, who later (with William Blake) produced illustrations for Joseph Ritson's "ballad garlands."[48] Bewick later became famous as an illustrator of natural history (something like an American Audubon): one might recall that the young Jane Eyre's favorite book (and a source of her Gothic paintings) was Bewick's *History of British Birds*—a fact reminding us of the correspondences between Mother Goose and the Gothic sensibility (both rooted in the ballad revival).[49]

Evidence of the vulgar intimacy between ballads and nursery rhymes—which are essentially a strain of ballad imitations—surfaces as well in the objections of literary poets to the popularity of these "fugitive" songs (such as Oliver Goldsmith's "Goody Two-Shoes"). Leigh Hunt, for example, complains to Wordsworth and Coleridge:

> Must a ballad doled out by a spectacled nurse
> About Two-shoes or Thumb, be your model of verse?[50]

It is hard to distinguish between the tenor of such complaints and the apologetic stance of early anthologists and antiquarians, who describe the "ancient" and popular verses they sought to preserve as frivolous, rude, artless—as poetic "trash." These partisans of vulgarity sought to offset their embarrassment and bad taste, as I indicated earlier, by a supercilious emphasis on philology—with bizarre allusions to Horace or Virgil. In his preface to the *Reliques* anthology, Percy disparages his own editorial efforts as "petty and frivolous research," as "minute and trifling," as "the amusement of now and then a vacant hour."[51] He refers repeatedly to his three-volume anthology as "this little work."[52]

A preoccupation with the minute and the trifling marks as well the first edition of Mother Goose, whose anonymous editor (thought to be Goldsmith) describes himself as "a very GREAT WRITER of very LITTLE BOOKS."[53] This ambivalent concern with trivial poems and "LITTLE BOOKS" manifests itself concretely in the diminutive size of the first edition of Mother Goose, which measures only 2.25 by 3.75 inches. The physical reduction of the book, expressing the minor stature of the poems contained within it, functions as one of the most powerful symptoms of the changes in our "handling" of poetry inaugurated by the elevation of the trivial, by the poetics of kitsch. The pragmatics of the miniaturization of the book turns, of course, on the idea that the book must be scaled down to suit the needs of its diminutive user, the child, making the book awkward to handle, or read, for adults: a toy-book modeling the eventual conversion of the physical book into a cult object of childish pleasures.

The physical diminution of the book mirrors the propagation of the child-reader: a sequestering of the entire collection within the emerging topos of infancy. The Mother Goose book—if indeed it may be called a book and not a toy—consists of two parts: first, a rhapsody of anonymous nursery rhymes; and second, a haphazard and frequently garbled collection of songs from Shakespeare's plays. The title page of the first section promises a selection of "Lullabies of the old British Nurses, calculated to amuse Children and to excite them to Sleep"; likewise, the title page of the second part advertises a book "containing the LULLABIES of Shakespeare."[54] Yet each section of the book contains only a single lullaby, properly speaking (verses sung to put a child to sleep). Evidently, the term "lullaby" here must refer to *all* of the poems contained in the tiny tome. This usage falls within the *Oxford English Dictionary*'s definition of the word "lullaby," which can mean "any soothing refrain"—in addition to songs associated specifically with nighttime rituals for children. If a lullaby is defined by its use of refrains to soothe but also to excite the listener (a strange alloy of sensations), then the songs of various kinds in *Mother Goose's Melody* may indeed be accurately described as lullabies.

Many of these lulling songs achieve their polarizing effects through devices of repetition—especially the use of many types of refrain: curses, counting songs, vendor's cries, cadences for walking, playground chants, and displays of "logic." The predominance of the refrain emphasizes, moreover, the degree to which all ballads (and their spurious progeny) may be described as lullabies. As such, the "lullaby logic" of spurious ballads—the matrix of kitsch—anticipates the methods of enchantment and indoctrination essential to modern consumerism.

By scaling the book to the stature of a small child and by assimilating all of its poems to the genre of the lullaby, the makers of *Mother Goose's Melody* appear to have created a book specifically for young children or, more radically, to have contributed to the invention of something called the *infant-reader*: a reader who is not yet able to read. Yet even a cursory glance at *Mother Goose's Melody* reveals that its child-reader is a most unlikely figure: the first book of children's verse is clearly a book made for adults. The title page announces that these "Sonnets for the Cradle" are "illustrated with NOTES and MAXIMS, Historical, Philosophical, and Critical."[55] In fact, the textual apparatus accompanying the rude "sonnets" of Mother Goose quickly reveals itself to be a work of pseudo-scholarship, with a mock introduction, facetious notes, nonsensical maxims, and learned, but fictive, sources. Cleverly fitted with incongruous accessories and a verbal "patina," the first edition of Mother Goose rhymes is at once a product of the ballad revival, steeped in archaic materials, and a satire of antiquarianism, with its pedantic dressing up of vernacular poetry: a new kind of commodity. In this framework, the first book of children's verse can be considered a toy, a toy-book (by virtue of its physical scale and its self-conscious elaboration of the trivial), only in the sense that its child-reader is also an adult: a consumer of childish and poetic trifles exquisite enough to be "bound and gilt" (the title page notes) for the carriage trade.

The modern, chimerical figure of the adult child-reader, cousin to the gullible connoisseur of "Gothicke" artifacts—the one who is "excited to sleep" by lullabies—subscribes to a peculiar "logic" illustrated by several lullabies in *Mother Goose's Melody*. The first is called "Aristotle's Story":

> There were two birds sat on a Stone,
> Fa, la, la, la, lal, de;
> One flew away, and then there was one
> Fa, la, la, la, lal, de. . . .[56]

At the end of the lullaby is an explanatory note attributed to *Sawwills Reports*: "This may serve as a chapter of consequence in the next new book of logic." It is unclear from this comment whether the term "logic" refers to the branch of philosophy—a model of rational thinking—or to the lulling technique of the nonsense refrain, a device capable of territorializing—and deterritorializing—the adult child-reader with its own brand of "logic."

A second attempt to interrogate—and demonstrate—the powers of "logic" occurs in a lullaby entitled "A Logical SONG; or the CONJUROR'S Reason for not getting Money":

> I Would if I cou'd,
> If I cou'dn't, how cou'd I?
> I cou'dn't, without I could, cou'd I?
> Cou'd you, without you cou'd, cou'd ye?
> Cou'd ye, Cou'd ye?
> Cou'd you, without you cou'd, cou'd ye?[57]

A "conjuror" is, of course, a wizard of sorts, someone clever with words, a sophist, but also a charlatan, a mountebank. Iona and Peter Opie identify this lullaby as a refrain extracted from a longer ballad; as a result, it is not clear, as in the case of the earlier lullaby, what sort of (failed) "logic" the conjuror is putting into practice, or being subjected to.[58] Certainly, the sense of logical deduction illustrated in this song for the adult child-reader is effective in part because it occurs as a refrain, as a lullaby. A note at the end of the "logical song" seeks perhaps to account for the origins of this double logic:

"Note. This is a new way of handling an old argument, said to be invented by a famous senator; but it has something in it of *Gothic* construction."[59] In the historical context, the meaning of the word "Gothic" here is highly unstable. In a letter of 1764, for example, a year prior to the publication of *Mother Goose's Melody*, Thomas Percy uses the term "gothic" to identify the properties of "minstrelsy" he is seeking to preserve in his soon-to-be published anthology of "ancient" ballads.[60] We might therefore feel confident that the phrase "Gothic construction" in the Mother Goose rhyme refers to the conjuring form of the ballad and, more precisely, to the "logical"—and barbarous—device of the refrain. The double logic of the lullaby also appears, however, to be conjuring a new Gothic sensibility, its first manifestation being (ostensibly) the publication of Walpole's gothic novel, *The Castle of Otranto*, in 1764. Yet the Gothic sensibility began as well to take shape contemporaneously in the proliferating subgenres of the pseudo-ballad: nursery rhymes, counterfeit epics, Gothic melodramas, lullabies for adults. The primary sources of the poetics of kitsch thus appeared in conjunction with one another for the first time in the years 1764 and 1765.

The Cult of Simplicity

The lullaby's cultivation of all things trifling, inferior, miniscule, immature, descends from the neoclassical infatuation with the idea of "simplicity." In 1724 (following in the footsteps of Wardlaw's "Hardyknute"), the poet Aaron Hill wrapped a "prettified copy" of the traditional ballad, "William and Margaret," in the following panegyric:

> There was a charming majestic Nakedness in the nervous Simplicity and plain Soundness of pathetick Nature, which went to the Hearts of our Forefathers, without stopping at their Fancy, or winding itself into their Understanding, through a maze of mystical Prettinesses.[61]

The contrast here between "nervous Simplicity" and "mystical Prettinesses" (the twin fonts of poetic kitsch) derives from terms established by Joseph Addison in the "Chevy-Chase papers" published in the *Spectator* in 1711. In these brief essays, Addison (most critics agree) not only inaugurates the so-called ballad revival of the eighteenth century but gives voice to an emerging doctrine of "simplicity"—a wide-ranging cultural discourse anchored specifically, as the preoccupation with balladry indicates, by the concept of *poetic* simplicity.

Addison's correlation of balladry and "simplicity" became, as Albert

Friedman notes, a curious replica of Augustan poetic values: "simplicity was the article in the neoclassic creed with which serious ballad criticism was most concerned—simplicity of thought, simplicity of style."[62] At the same time, the archaic ballad (with its "nervous Simplicity" and charming "Naked-ness") is lodged, to recall Broch's description of kitsch, like a "foreign body" in the system of neoclassical poetics: a "pathetick" double indistinguishable from its glorious host. Founding his theory of the ballad on a dichotomy that will turn out to be highly unstable, Addison praises "the Simplicity of the Stile" of "Chevy Chase" and places the "inherent Perfection of Simplic-ity of Thought above that which I call the Gothick Manner of Writing."[63] By "Gothick"—the ostensible contrary to "Simplicity"—Addison means the "epigrammatic turns and points of wit" associated with Cleveland, Cowley, and the Metaphysical poets.[64] By the mid-eighteenth century, however, as we have seen in the first edition of Mother Goose and in Percy's comment on the poetic "reliques" he collects, the term "Gothick" will be used to de-scribe the ballads and lullabies from which Addison's doctrine of simplicity is derived (before the term captures, more promiscuously, what we now call the Gothic sensibility).

Addison's neoclassical fashioning of the humble ballad launched an en-during and mutable cult of simplicity, converting "fugitive" songs into relics and poetic commodities prized by elite society. In his satirical poem "Taste: An Epistle to a Young Critic" (1753), John Armstrong complains,

> But thanks to Heav'n and Addison's good grace
> Now ev'ry fop is charm'd with Chevy Chase.[65]

Anticipating the contrived vulgarity of Goldsmith's Mother Goose and the "special effects" of Gothic verse, Addison reconciles the rude charm of the ballad and the delicate sensibility of the connoisseur—the fop—in what he called (borrowing a phrase of Dryden's) "the Fairy Way of Writing." A year after he published the influential "ballad papers," he drafted a set of rules and guidelines (in *Spectator* no. 419) for "a kind of Writing, wherein the Poet quite loses Sight of Nature."[66] He notes, for example, that "Spirits must not be confined to speak Sense, but it is certain their Sense ought to be a little discoloured." The poet who seeks to render the "discoloured" language of fairies should, Addison advises, "be very well versed in the Traditions of Nurses and old Women"—that is, in the lore and language of nursery rhymes. "Otherwise," he explains, the poet "will be apt to make his Fairies talk like People of his own Species, and not like other Setts of Beings, who converse with different Objects, and think in a different Manner from that of Mankind." Steeped in the "discoloured" language of ballads and lullabies, the poet of simplicity will be equipped to invent the diction of "Emblematical Persons," of the stereotypical figures found in works of what Addison calls "natural Prejudice": the ur-text of modern kitsch.

For examples of the unnatural diction—conforming however to "natural Prejudice"—essential to "the Fairy Way of Writing," we must return to a poet who was a master of writing for the "little folk" (whether fairies, children, or peasants): Oliver Goldsmith. Among the "Emblematical Persons" of the English countryside fabricated by Goldsmith is the figure (and language) of "The Hermit" (a pretty version of the traditional ballad "Edwin and Angelina"):

Turn, gentle Hermit of the dale
   And guide my lonely way
To where yon taper cheers the vale
   With Hospitable ray . . .

"Forbear, my son," the Hermit cries,
   "To tempt the dangerous gloom;
For yonder faithless phantom flies
   To lure thee to thy doom."[67]

The ornamental speech of the Hermit offers a generic example of a *synthetic vernacular*, a language never spoken by any class of persons, a "discoloured" and unreal diction essential to the "parlor ballad" of simplicity—and to the poetics of kitsch.

The same year that Goldsmith published "The Hermit" (1765), he also produced (anonymously, as I noted earlier) the first edition of Mother Goose rhymes, as well as the children's classic, *The History of Goody Two-Shoes*. The "ancient lullabies" collected (or fabricated) by Goldsmith offer a variant of the nonsensical, or "discoloured," sources feeding (in Addison's prescription) "the Fairy Way of Writing." Here is an alphabet song , for example, from *Mother Goose's Melody*:

GREAT A, little a,
Bouncing B;
The cat's in the cupboard,

And she can't see.[68]

And here is a ditty called "Caesar's Song":

> Bow, wow, wow,
> Whose dog art thou
> Little Tom Tinker's dog,
> Bow, wow, wow.[69]

In the curious, formal idiom of these "discoloured" songs, a dog barks a hybrid tongue of animals and humans, while the letters of the alphabet come to life, puzzling or mocking an oblivious cat. The "simple" show of absurdity prevails. Delighted and dislocated by the jargon of fairies, the reader becomes, by reveling in these dainty books, a prototype of the modern consumer: a grown-up transformed into the chimerical figure of the infant-reader. The tiny volume of Mother Goose depicts fanciful creatures, but it also produced a kind of monster.

The discolored speech of marginal "spirits"—of the inhuman—is haunted by specters of diminutive "folk" in the real world. One devotee of Goldsmith's books of children's verse suggests, for example,

> While they all evince a real genius for writing in a stile suited to the capacities of the little folk, there is a nameless something about them, which, far more than is the case with thousands of other books for the young, is calculated to enforce the attention and excite the interest of "children of a larger growth."[70]

The critic is alluding here to the miscreant figure of the adult child-reader, who resembles the feral and harshly managed "children" of *Mother Goose's Melody*. Hence, with a taste for the "nameless something" that will one day become the toxic substance of poetic kitsch, the fop is continually seeking the curious diction of his own *minority* in "very tiny books." By cultivating the pleasures of "minority," the man of good taste inadvertently cultivates the seeds of bad taste: an appetite for kitsch.

Even more alarming, the infatuation of the child-like man of taste with "little folk" and "discoloured" speech realized itself in a grotesque fashion of patronage in the mid-eighteenth century, transporting various "peasant poets" and their "rough verses" to high society. Aside from John Clare, perhaps the most famous figure in the cultural narrative of "discovery" (touching both patron and poet), was Ann Yearsley, "the Milkwoman of Bristol" (1753–1806), "discovered" by Hannah More and Elizabeth Montagu (as mentioned in my earlier discussion of female antiquarianism). But there were many others as well: Robert Tatersal, "the Bricklayer-Poet," author of

The Bricklayer's Miscellany (1734); John Frederick Bryant, "the tobacco-pipe maker of Bristol" (1753-1791); and John Jones (1774-1836), "an old servant" whose poetry served as the occasion for Robert Southey's belated *Lives and Works of the Uneducated Poets* (1831).[71] Southey cites a ballad by Jones, "The Red-Breast," addressed to a bird prized for its "simplicity":

> The Woodman seated on a log
>> His meal divides atween the three,
> And now himself, and now his dog,
>> And now he casts a crumb to thee . . .
>
> The Youth who strays, with dark design,
>> To make each well-stored nest a prey,
> If dusky hues denote them thine,
>> Will draw his pilfering hand away.[72]

Reviewing the diction of Jones and other poets in his anthology, Southey remarks, "The distinction between the language of high and low life could not be broadly marked"—a comment alerting the reader to a peculiar instability in the spectrum of poetic diction.[73]

Perhaps the most celebrated "discovery" of the early eighteenth century was Stephen Duck, "the Thresher-Poet" (1705-1756), subsidized by Queen Caroline, who in 1735 appointed him keeper of her library and the "subterranean building in the Royal Gardens at Richmond which was called Merlin's Cave" (according to the *Gentleman's Magazine* of 1735).[74] So great was the stir caused by Duck's "discovery" that he was rumored to be—only two months after his introduction to the queen—a candidate for Poet Laureate. On November 19, 1730, Jonathan Swift wrote to John Gay, "But the vogue of our honest folks here is, that Duck is absolutely to succeed Eusden in the laurel."[75] The prospect of Duck's elevation anticipated the uncanny ritual of the man of taste, the gullible connoisseur, placing his abject twin (one of the "little folk": a peasant, a fairy, a child) in the symbolic office of the laureate. Although this event, sadly, never came to pass, one should not underestimate its significance in the secret history of kitsch. For this ensemble of "minor" figures evokes the controversial type of the poetaster, or minor poet, of which the suffix, *-aster*, denotes a figure of small or inferior stature: a position occupied ambiguously by the peasant poet.[76]

In addition to threshers, bricklayers, and milkmaids, the vocation of the "honest" poet included an especially large contingent of shoemakers—a vocation at the very bottom of the hierarchy of trades, which would become an important trope in the infidel culture of Britain following the French Revolution.[77] Among the shoemaker-poets of the eighteenth century were John Bennet, "discovered" by Thomas Warton, professor of poetry at Oxford, in 1774; John Lucas, John Walker, and Charles Crocker; as well as Joseph Blacket (1786-1810), "discovered" by Samuel Jackson Pratt; and, most famously, Robert Bloomfield (1766-1823), whose book, *The Farmer's Boy* (1800), was illustrated with cuts by Thomas Bewick.[78]

Also in the company of shoemaker-poets was James Woodhouse (1735-1820), who was "discovered" by William Shenstone (1714-1763), the pale dean of simplicity, under emblematic circumstances. Shenstone had spent many years improving and "rusticating" the gardens of his estate at the Leasowes in Worcestershire, which became a destination for sympathetic cognoscenti. Southey explains, "Shenstone had at that time found it necessary to forbid that general access to his grounds which he used to allow, so much mischief had wantonly been done there."[79] In 1759, however, the shoemaker-poet Woodhouse addressed

> some verses to him [Shenstone], entreating that he might be exempted from this prohibition, and permitted still to recreate himself and indulge his imagination in that sweet scenery; and Shenstone, who was always benevolent and generous, when he had inquired into the character of the petitioner, admitted him not only to his grounds, but to the use of his library also.[80]

In this bizarre tale of discovery and "recreation," Woodhouse, an "honest" poet of the "laboring-class" is granted permission to enter a cultivated space of simplicity, a garden landscape (one of the earliest expressions of Gothic sensibility) in which he reads himself into an identity he already possesses (but without "polish"). In this narrative of transverse sublimation—the rites of kitsch—Woodhouse resembles Ann Yearsley's conversion into "Lactilla the Poetess," of whom Horace Walpole remarked, "Instead of real cows she tended Arcadian sheep."[81]

Seeking to polish and improve the rude verse of poetic adoptees and to appropriate altogether the domain of the traditional ballad, "the cult of simplicity, specifically its sentimentalizing faction," Friedman explains, "sponsored a numerous, insipid and now unreadable body of poetry, the ballad of simplicity."[82] Among the most popular early masters of poetic simplicity were Thomas Tickell, professor of poetry at Oxford, and David Mallet (1705-1765); but William Shenstone was the darling of what the *London Magazine*

called in 1782 "the gaunt and famish'd school of simplicity."[83] In contrast to
more "rustick" expression, Shenstone set about "prettifying the diction with
aureate phrases, borrowing bits of tinsel," in Friedman's assessment, as in
his ballad imitation of 1745, "Jemmy Dawson":[84]

Amid those unrelenting flames
She bore this constant heart to see;
But when 'twas mouldered into dust,
"Yet, yet," she cried, "I follow thee" . . .

The dismal scene was o'er and past,
The lover's mournful hearse retired;
The maid drew back her languid head,
And, sighing forth his name, expired.[85]

A similar plaintive tone and hapless simplicity can be found in Shenstone's
"Pastoral Ballad" of 1743 (belatedly published in 1755). At the same time, one
also detects the influence of Shenstone's study of Spenser (which helped
to establish Spenser's diction as a wellspring of kitsch) and the soon to be
fashionable theater of the horticultural imagination:

When forc'd the fair nymph to forego,
What anguish I felt at my heart!
Yet I thought—but it might not be so—
'Twas with pain that she saw me depart . . .

My banks they are furnish'd with bees,
Whose murmur invites me to sleep;
My grottoes are shaded with trees,
And my hills are white-over with sheep.
I seldom have met with a loss,
Such health do my fountains bestow;
My fountains all border'd with moss,
Where the harebells and violets grow.[86]

The correlation of simplicity and rusticity in these lines would eventually
develop into a "tradition of pathetic scenes of village life" (sometimes with
intimations of infidel resistance, as in Goldsmith's popular nostalgic poem,
"The Deserted Village," about the demise of rural life).[87] Shenstone's pallid
Spenserian diction could still be found, as Friedman notes, in "the late versions of the ballad of simplicity which glut the verse columns of the *Monthly*

Magazine, Gentleman's Magazine, Lady's Magazine, Monthly Register, Town and Country Magazine, and other polite journals of the 1780s and 1790s."[88]

Having adopted and sublimated quite literally an array of "little folk" in the form of living peasant-poets, the man of taste trained his delicate but insatiable appetite on similar objects in verse, so that the "pastoral ballad" came "to imply ingenuousness, an atmosphere of dulcet sentimentality, a preoccupation with the 'little,' the 'humble,' the 'pathetic.' "[89] Shenstone had considered calling his pastoral ballad an elegy, and so it was that the fetishistic regard for little things (and "little folk") found its most popular expression in elegies and, more succinctly, in poetic epitaphs. The most famous of such elegies is, as I discussed in previous chapters, Gray's "Elegy Written in a Country Church Yard," which concludes with the speaker's own epitaph (to be read by "some hoary-headed swain")—the sentiments of a poet who longs to be laid to rest among "the unhonor'd dead."[90]

In poems commemorating the socially humble, Friedman claims, "readers were invited to indulge their benevolent impulses vicariously by sympathizing with the plight of aged beggars, distressed vagrants, convicts, bereaved parents, women driven mad by the death or defection of their lovers, village idiots, and abused orphans."[91] Needless to say, such ballads and elegies were composed with a stock repertoire of phrases and epithets. The figures commemorated in these poems included some of the peasant-poets "discovered" (and then mourned) by the elite, as in Lord Byron's "Epitaph for Joseph Blacket, Late Poet and Shoemaker" (1811):

> STRANGER! Behold, interred together,
> The souls of learning and of leather.
> Poor Joe is gone, but left his all;
> You'll find his relics in a stall.
> His works were neat, and often found
> Well stitched, and with Morocco bound.
> Tread lightly—where the bard is laid—
> He cannot mend the shoes he made;
> Yet he is happy in his hole,
> With verse immortal as his sole . . .[92]

By comparing the "relics" of the shoemaker's trade to the poetic *reliques* produced by the shoemaker-poet ("stitched and with Morocco bound")—not to mention the title of Percy's anthology—Byron inadvertently conjures a materialist and working-class stratum of the poetics of kitsch.

Pets, Trifles, Toys

The poetic commemoration of the low, the humble, the inferior, took a final turn—directly related to kitsch—in epitaphs composed for domestic animals and pets. "In the mid and late eighteenth century," Joshua Scodel explains, "epitaphic commemoration of lowly creatures widened to include domestic animals."[93] It is thus not surprising, perhaps, to find that Byron composed an epitaph not only for a peasant-poet but for his pet dog, Boatswain, as well—verses that are inscribed on a monument at Newstead Priory (Byron's estate): "Tribute to the Memory of Boatswain, a Dog." In doing so, Byron may have been echoing an epitaph by the shoemaker-poet Robert Bloomfield, dedicated to his dog, "poor faithful TROUNCER," a lament already echoing "elegies to hares, goldfish, and robins by Cowper, Gray, and Rogers."[94] Byron's epitaph begins with "a comparison between pompous monuments raised to high-born but unworthy men and the unhonored, faithful dog."[95] In a final correlation of the poet with the humble creature he commemorates, Byron specified in his will that his own remains be buried with his dog in "a vault below Boatswain's monument."[96]

Evoking Pope's satire, "Bounce to Fop, an Heroick Epistle from a Dog at Twickenham to a Dog at Court" (published in 1736), the most famous eighteenth-century pet epitaph is Gray's "On the Death of a Favourite Cat, Drowned in a Tub of Gold Fishes" (1748).[97] The poem was occasioned by the death of Selima, a cat belonging to Gray's close friend Horace Walpole, who compared his grief to Queen Dido's mood at her lover's betrayal and departure: "I beg for empty time, for peace and reprieve from my frenzy."[98] Gray's elegy for Walpole's pet attracted (in a second edition of 1753) illustrations by Richard Bentley and, eventually, watercolors by William Blake in 1797. Gray wrote the pet elegy (inevitably recalling, tongue-in-cheek, his other, more somber "Elegy," also circulating privately in the late 1740s) in *tailed rhyme*, where the rhyme words occur in lines three and six of a six-line stanza:

> 'Twas on a lofty vase's side,
> Where China's gayest art had dy'd
>   The azure flowers that blow;
> The passive Selima reclin'd,
> Demurest of the tabby kind
>   Gaz'd on the lake below...

> Still had she gaz'd; but 'midst the tide
> Two beauteous forms were seen to glide,
>   The Genii of the stream:
> Their scaly armour's Tyrian hue
> Through richest purple to the view
>   Betray'd a golden gleam.[99]

Gray's elegy transforms "Selima" into one of the luxurious trifles (the "lofty" Chinese vase serving as a goldfish bowl, along with fashionable "Genii") surrounding her in the poem (and in reality at Walpole's estate at Strawberry Hill). For "goldfish were a relatively recent craze, more recent than the craze for blue-and-white Chinese porcelain."[100] In fact, the poem itself is often praised—or dismissed, in Samuel Johnson's case—as a trifle: "the poem on the *Cat* was doubtless by its author considered as a trifle, but it is not a happy trifle."[101]

The publisher of Gray and Shenstone (and other fashionable poets of the period), Robert Dodsley (1704-1764), was indeed the true bard (and dramatist) of "trifles." Dodsley, a poet and popular playwright, published (and staged) in 1735 *The Toy-Shop*, a "Dramatick Satire" in which the proprietor of a "toy-shop" receives customers seeking "Trifles and Gewgaws."[102] The emphasis here on toys and trifles is maintained in a later volume entitled *Trifles*, a selection of Dodsley's poems and writings for the theater published in 1745. The emblem on the title page of this volume promises "the least, the lowest of the tunefull Train."[103] Correspondingly, in the mercantile setting of *The Toy-Shop*, the proprietor offers to his customers (and verbally anatomizes) items such as gold rings and watches, snuff boxes, "ivory pocketbooks," horn-rim spectacles, "a mighty pretty Looking-Glass," a thimble, a cockle-shell, and, unforgettably, figurines of "Little Dogs!"[104] To one of his clients, the proprietor notes with special interest,

> But the most ancient Curiosity I have got is a small Brass Plate, on which is engrav'd the Speech which Adam made to his Wife, on their first Meeting, together with her Answer. The characters, thro' Age, are grown unintelligible; but for that 'tis more to be valued.[105]

This curious text mocks, of course, the antiquarian tastes sustaining the ballad revival, but it also evokes the inscriptional aspect of the pet epitaphs we have been reviewing.

Asserting that "the World is a great Toy-Shop and all its Inhabitants run mad for rattles," the proprietor offers an expansive commentary on his trade:

> I believe, from these childish Toys and gilded Baubles, I shall pick a comfortable
> Maintenance. For, really, as it is a trifling Age, so Nothing but Trifles are valued
> in it. Men read none but trifling Authors, pursue none but trifling Amusements,
> and contend for none but trifling Opinions. A trifling Fellow is preferr'd, a trifling
> Woman admired. Nay, as if there were not Trifles enow, they now make Trifles of
> the most serious and valuable Things.[106]

Enduring the proprietor's commentary on the toys he sells, one customer finds it "very odd that such serious Ware should be the Commodity of a Toy-Shop."[107] Even more acutely, another client remarks, "Your Shop is your Scripture, and every Piece of Goods a different Text," calling each toy an "allegory"—a treatise on consumption evoking the "discoloured" speech of fairies who "converse with different Objects."[108]

Gothic Verse and Melodrama

The Gothic sensibility is typically associated with drama and fiction, of which the first example, *The Castle of Otranto*, was published in 1764 by Horace Walpole, the close friend of Thomas Gray.[109] At the same time, the elemental (and sometimes apocalyptic) role of poetry in Gothic fiction suggests that the distinction between poetry and prose is never stable in the Gothic imagination. In terms of historical chronology, the dates and genre of the texts we have been considering (by Gray, Shenstone, Dodsley, and others) indicate that Gothic writing first became manifest in a genre of poetry that both elaborates and perverts the cult of simplicity. Experiments in poetic diction and sensibility (by Dodsley's stable of poets) offer the earliest evidence of what Broch calls "Gothick kitsch."[110] More specifically, with the unlikely fusion of simplicity and "nervous" diction in the Gothic ballad, poetic kitsch became associated with a synthetic and sometimes reckless *impurity* of diction, a falsification of speech without remedy: the eruption of *impolite* letters. Emphasizing the poetic origins of the Gothic sensibility exposes as well a crucial but neglected feature of Gothic writing: its extreme conventionality, which accounts for its generic reproducibility. The formulaic character of Gothic writing thus fortifies its preoccupation with the trivial, the pathetic, the captional, but also its fascination with imposture and illegitimacy.

On the face of it, it is difficult to reconcile the cultivation of minority (the trifling and formulaic orientation of these texts) with the more familiar

properties of Gothic: morbid scenery, inscrutable spirits, heightened feeling, illicit activities, extravagant diction. The gulf between what Susan Stewart calls the "ballads-in-drag" of Gothic verse and what Coleridge deems the
"homeliness of the diction" of simplicity would appear to be unbridgeable.[111]
Yet the poets who produced the earliest experiments in Gothic verse in the
1740s and 1750s found little difficulty in synthesizing what appear to us to
be anomalous elements.

Edward Young, for example, who, with Thomas Gray and Robert Blair,
attained a certain notoriety in the 1740s as one of the "graveyard poets"
(the first recognizably Gothic writers), was also the influential theorist of
"imitative genius" in his essay *Conjectures on Original Composition* (1759): "a
genius which stands in need of learning to make it shine . . . an infantine genius; a genius, which, like other infants, must be nursed, educated, or it will
come to naught."[112] Young's figure of "infantine genius" in need of instruction (which recalls the infant-reader of Mother Goose) is evidently a figure-
head of the poetics of minority, a genius determined by imitation—by the
methods of the commonplace book—who thereby produces the formulaic
and hyperlyrical diction of poets such as Gray and Shenstone. Additionally,
Young's essay on unoriginal writing—and on "a genius fond of *ornament*"—
begins, like his famous poem, "Night Thoughts" (1742-1745), in a graveyard:

> A serious thought standing single among many of a lighter nature, will sometimes
> strike the careless wanderer after amusement only, with useful awe: as monu-
> mental marbles scattered in a wide pleasure-garden (and such there are) will call
> to recollection those who would never have sought it in a churchyard walk of
> mournful yews.[113]

From Young's melancholy perspective, "amusement" and "serious thought"
evoke one another, like the "pleasure-garden" and the mournful "church-
yard" (a scene evoking Gray's humble but theatrical "church yard").

Even more germane are the affinities of what Young calls "the bespan-
gled": in his view, the "glittering pins" of a child's "oylet-hole suit" are com-
mensurable with "Achilles in his *Gothic* array."[114] To Young, the "spangles"
ornamenting both the child and the Gothic warrior are "very much on a
level."[115] In a related passage, he refers to "the temptation of that *Gothic*
daemon, which modern poetry tasting, became mortal," suggesting that
he associates the Gothic daemon with the *humanization* of language, with a
modern diminution of poetry, in particular—and hence with a poetry of the
minor sublime (the curious product of "imitative genius").[116]

Similar correspondences, confounding generic expectations, complicate Young's prototypical Gothic poem, "Night Thoughts" (which was first published by Dodsley). Throughout the poem, Young makes extensive use of apostrophe—directly addressing a listener or reader—a poetic device encompassing not only the lullaby but the diminutive, epitaphic compositions of the cult of simplicity. At the same time, as Jonathan Culler points out, apostrophes "serve as intensifiers, as images of invested passion"—an affective mode consonant with Young's Gothic temperament:[117]

> LORENZO! Such the glories of the world!
> What is the world itself? Thy world—a grave . . .
> The Roman? Greek? They stalk, an empty name!
> Yet few regard them in this useful light;
> Though half our learning is their epitaph.
> When down thy vale, unlock'd by midnight thought,
> That loves to wander in thy sunless realms,
> O Death! I stretch my view; what visions rise.[118]

Shifting address from "Lorenzo" to "Death" itself, the speaker enacts the apostrophic mode of the funerary epitaph, which is both an "empty name" and a legacy of "learning," only to discover a poetic language "unlock'd by midnight thought." Indeed, as Culler sees it, one must not dismiss the readerly temptation to embrace the "purely fictional time" of apostrophe: "one might be justified in taking apostrophe as the figure of all that is most radical, embarrassing, pretentious, and mystificatory in the lyric."[119]

Concentrated by its proximity to the "grave" and calculated to stir strong feelings by its naked address, the Gothic intensification of poetic diction is directly related to the musical innovation of the *melodrama* (the first one composed, as I indicated in previous chapters, by Jean-Jacques Rousseau in 1762). The poetic melodrama is an antiphonal form in which language alternates with music (instead of coinciding with it, as in opera) so that the two serialized media fortify—to the point of excess—the emotional impact of the work. The basic function of melodrama can be found, however, *within* the reverberating language of "simplicity," anticipating the impurity and sensationalism of Gothic diction. In the ballad of simplicity, Friedman notes, "these feeble, usually tragic or pathetic narratives of simple life are sometimes labeled 'old' and incrusted with a patina spuriously induced by consonants doubled at random and superfluous *e*'s."[120] Displaying a luxurious but spurious verbal "patina," some of the earliest productions of poetic simplicity, such as Shenstone's "The School-Mistress, a Poem in Imitation of Spenser" (published by Dodsley in 1742), marshal an array of poetic special effects designed to stir the sentiments of the reader and to evoke common—but strangely ornate—scenes of repose:

> See to their seats they hye with merry glee,
> And in beseemly order Sitten there;
> All but the wight of bum y-galled, he
> Abhorreth bench and stool, and fourm, and chair.[121]

The stretching and chopping of words here (recalling Aristotle's advice about supplementing poetic diction with "stretched words") must certainly be regarded as a kind of melodrama occurring at the level of the signifier (amplifying the expressive image), yet these special effects mark such verses as poetic (and expensive) *trifles* that might have appeared amidst the "commodities" for sale in Dodsley's *Toy-Shop*. Surely, these cosmetic and melodramatic effects—which could be applied to any type of poem—were designed with the "man of taste" in mind. Indeed, Shenstone only heightened the fetishistic allure of these details by affixing to Dodsley's first edition of the poem a "Ludicrous Index" annotating every one of the poem's thirty-two stanzas—a device suppressed following the poem's publication (but restored to the poem by Isaac D'Israeli in the early nineteenth century).

The lenticular, or mediumistic, function of melodrama (and its dyadic structure) helps to explain as well a fashionable variant of the epitaphic poems we have been considering: a form of apostrophe without appellation in English, but which we may call (with the help of Geoffrey Hartmann) a "nature-inscription."[122] In the mid-1750s, Mark Akenside and William Shenstone appear to have entered into a friendly contest of composing brief poems in imitation of "milestone" inscriptions from antiquity: an apostrophe whose locus classicus, *Siste Viator!* (Stop, traveler!), evokes a phrase inscribed on a piece of wood or stone, hailing a passing stranger in some secluded spot. Dodsley published several of Shenstone's "Rural Inscriptions" in 1755 and then a grouping of six of Akenside's "Inscriptions" in 1758. A revival of this epigrammatic mode occurred as well with the publication of eight of Robert Southey's inscriptions (which closely resemble Akenside's) in his *Poems* of 1797 and, more importantly, in inscriptional poems by Wordsworth (such as "Lines Left upon a Seat in a Yew-Tree")—evidence of his investment in poetic simplicity (which had become for him a stalking horse of "literary" values).

Like the epitaphic verses of Gray, Shenstone, or Young, the inscrip-
tion-poem may be regarded as a relic of simplicity, but it also serves as
a melodramatic, or captional, device in the *facture* of Gothic diction. The
Gothic dimension of Akenside's inscriptions remains implicit, perhaps, in its
choice of scenery and interlocutor, as in the following examples (each in its
entirety):

> For a Grotto
>
> . . . Enter in,
>
> O Stranger! Undismay'd . . .

Or:

> For a Column at Runnymede
>
> . . . O Stranger! Stay thee, and the scene
> Around contemplate well . . .

Or:

> The Woodnymph
>
> Approach in silence; it is no vulgar tale
> Which I, the Dryad of this hoary oak
> Pronounce to mortal ears . . . [123]

In each of these inscriptions, the lifeless stone marker addresses randomly a
passing stranger (recalling perhaps the plaintive—and promiscuous—query
of the beggar's chant, a forgotten infidel genre). Equally, in each case, as
Culler surmises, a "sinister reciprocity" takes place, in which the living are
"struck dumb" as the inanimate stone gives voice to the *genius loci*.[124]

The Gothic, or melodramatic, relation between the inscription and the
genius loci of the landscape becomes fully activated, however, only in Shenstone's inscription-poems, which were actually situated on the grounds of
his *ferme ornée* (as one of his admirers called his estate) at the Leasowes (a
pastoral theater anticipating Marie Antoinette's infamous toy farm). Dodsley published in 1755 the entirety of Shenstone's inscriptions in his own
text, "A Description of The Leasowes." In this fascinating text of some thirty
pages—an important document in the development of Gothic poetics—
Dodsley leads the reader on a descriptive walking tour of the extensive
grounds at Shenstone's country estate (where Shenstone carried out an

array of horticultural "experiments" for decades, bankrupting himself in the process—an enterprise that would mark him as an important figure in the history of landscape design).[125]

Dodsley devotes much of his locodescription of the landscape, which he calls "this perfectly Arcadian farm," to transcribing (and sometimes translating from Latin) Shenstone's inscriptions (about two dozen of them, some quite lengthy).[126] Many were carved, Dodsley notes, into benches offering views of various spots: "The Temple of Pan," "Virgil's Grove," and so on. Some of the inscriptions allude to, or cite, various poets (a form of commonplacing): Virgil several times, and a line from Pope's "Eloisha": "Divine oblivion of low-thoughted Care" (reminding us that Shenstone was the author of an "Ode to Indolence"—a topic and title later appropriated by Keats).[127] Other inscriptions are dedicated to friends, including one "To Mr DODSLEY," carved in a "bower" of oaks:

Come then, my friend! Thy sylvan taste display:
Come hear thy Faunus tune his rustic lay:
Ah? Rather come, and in these dells disown
The care of other strains, and tune thine own.[128]

The sincerity of Shenstone's apostrophes—and of Dodsley's infatuated reception of them—suggests that Dodsley's satirical approach to various "Trifles and Gewgaws" in The Toy-Shop masks more earnest passions, which could be indulged, as the inscription suggests, only in the secluded precincts of Shenstone's Arcadia. For surely Shenstone's inscriptions may be regarded as verbal toys, as Dodsley himself suggests in a poem supplementing his "Description of The Leasowes," where he describes the inscriptions as "pow'rful incantation, magic verse,/Inscrib'd on ev'ry tree, alcove, or urn."[129] At the same time, the historical development of melodrama—in keeping with the effects of "incantation"—reveals its importance as a means of inculcation and indoctrination at the Leasowes.

Dodsley associates the epitaphs and "magic verse" written across the landscape with what Addison called, as we discovered earlier, "the Fairy Way of Writing." Commenting on some verses carved on a "tablet" at the entrance to the gardens of the Leasowes, Dodsley declares, "These sentiments correspond as well as possible with the ideas we form of the abode of Fairies."[130] In this sense, the fairy way of writing—embodied by Shenstone's inscriptions—induces in the reader and spectator a sentimental vision of the landscape as "the abode of Fairies." The inscriptions serve as melodramatic captions, heightening and altering the perception of ornamental nature. In this sense, the juxtaposition of inscribed verse and horticultural scene models the antiphonal form of the melodrama, which seeks, as I indicated earlier, to heighten the spectator's emotional involvement in the scene. These poetic inscriptions, which expand the fairy way of writing into an environmental or ambient experience, thus function as a mediumistic device producing an array of special effects. Shenstone's "farm" could thus be described, in our present vocabulary, as an *installation* activated and sustained in part by poetry.

In the course of Dodsley's citational tour, it becomes clear that the Arcadian aspect of the Leasowes is converted, by inscription, into a setting for the cultivation of a Gothic sensibility. Dodsley frequently introduces a chiseled phrase by commenting on the atmosphere surrounding it: the idler comes upon "a beautiful gloomy scene called Virgil's Grove"; he notes the setting of a tablet dedicated to the poet James Thomson: "the whole scene is opaque and gloomy."[131] At other moments, the term "Gothic" serves as a placeholder, a key to the melodramatic spirit of the place: "we arrive unexpectedly at a lofty Gothic seat"; he finds himself in "a kind of Gothic alcove"; he returns to "the Gothic alcove on a hill well covered with wood."[132] Like the inscriptions themselves, Dodsley's use of the still-amorphous term "Gothic"—remember, this is ten years before the publication of the first Gothic novel—serves as a caption, a filter, through which the ornamental landscape begins to reverberate with antique imagery and modern sentiments.

Taking into account the melodramatic scenes and toy landscape cultivated by poetic inscription, one might reasonably conclude that the Gothic aesthetic is, at its origin, a mode of performance, a melodrama fueled by poetic "trifles" and "reliques"—most of them either borrowed or forged. Gothic fiction, by this account, could then be read as a replication of these clandestine and exclusive events, of poetic topoi: imagined yet real *commonplaces* that have all but disappeared from cultural memory.

Ultimately, in scenes rarely noted by critics, the neoclassical inscription becomes, finally, an emblem of Gothic obsession and paranoia in Mary Shelley's *Frankenstein*. For the monster is not simply a reader of Gothic texts (Volnay's *Ruins of Empires*, for example) but a writer of nature inscriptions resembling, but also perverting, the examples of Akenside, Shenstone, and Southey. In the final scenes of the novel, Victor Frankenstein pursues his "daemon" across the steppes toward the polar region. Along the way, on various objects in the landscape, he discovers unsigned inscriptions in the monster's hand, intended for his eyes:

> Sometimes, indeed, he left marks in writing on the barks of trees, or cut in stone, that guided me, and instigated my fury. "My reign is not yet over" (these words were legible in one of these inscriptions): "you live, and my power is complete. Follow me; I seek the everlasting ices of the north, where you will feel the misery of cold and frost, to which I am impassive. . . . You will find near this place, if you follow not too tardily, a dead hare; eat, and be refreshed."[133]

The monster's notes (the title of a poetry collection by the American writer, Laurie Scheck, predicated on the discovery of a box of the creature's writings) follow in part the classical prescription of *Siste Viator* ("eat and be refreshed"), thereby identifying the monster as a new kind of *genius loci* of the English countryside.[134] Yet the inscriptions can also turn malevolent, as the epigraph above indicates in unsettling ways—and as Frankenstein himself notices: "One inscription that he left was in these words:—'Prepare! Your toils only begin; wrap yourself in furs, and provide food, for we shall soon enter upon a journey where your sufferings will satisfy my everlasting hatred.'"[135] This epigraph combines solicitation and sadism in a way that raises interesting questions about the residual functions of apostrophe as a speech act.

The disconcerting ambivalence of these messages—at once solicitous and menacing—renders the specifically Gothic character of these inscriptions (and their deviation from the neoclassical type). More precisely, the narrative here involves the eccentric genre of the nature-inscription in a broader reading of Gothic conventions first articulated by Eve Sedgwick, who isolates and scrutinizes

> the tableau of two men chasing one another across a landscape. It is an importantly undecidable tableau, as in many other Gothic novels, whether the two men represent two consciousnesses or only one; and it is importantly undecidable whether their bond . . . is murderous or amorous.[136]

If the monster may be regarded as an icon of the prehistory of kitsch (a forgery, a creature made from borrowed or neglected parts), then the mixture of affection and paranoia radiating from the monster's notes must be consistent—in ways we are only beginning to understand—with the affective signature of kitsch: a compound of the abject—a queer negativity. The monster's dainty and malevolent inscriptions may be one of the lost genres of poetic kitsch.

Silver Proxy

It would take another sixty years before the laboratory of special effects curated by Mr. Shenstone and company at the Leasowes (parallel to
experiments undertaken by a circle centered on Thomas Gray and Horace
Walpole at Strawberry Hill) could be contained entirely within the medium
of poetic language, a development requiring the resolution of the dyadic
structure of melodrama into a single element. In the poems of John Keats,
who may be considered not only a prodigy of Gothic verse but a child-like
progenitor (a "pocket Apollo," some called him) of poetic kitsch, one discovers a dazzling inventory of special effects, a veritable "toy-shop" of poetic
commodities.[137] At the core of this poetic *phantastikon*, Keats becomes pre-
occupied with a trope that suggests how poetic kitsch acquired some of its
basic features from Romantic materialism and its articulation of aesthetic
ideology: the color *silver* as an emblem of pop metaphysics.

Keats (and he was not alone among his Romantic peers in dabbling in
Gothic colors) developed in his poems (especially "Lamia") the iconography
of an "airy texture" hovering between radiance and mass, agency and objecthood, medium and thing.[138] The most salient property of this protean, lyric
substance is its *silveriness*, associated principally by Keats with moonlight,
but also starlight and sometimes with lamplight: a color implicated in the
phenomenologies of reflection and dissolution, but also in a rhetoric of obscurity, since these sources of light can be experienced only at night. Keats
calls these "ambiguous atoms"—a wavering emblem of the special effects
associated with kitsch—a "silver proxy" and, emphasizing its solipsistic and
holistic aspects, "my silver planet."[139] This "fretted splendor," as Keats calls
it, is at once a place "where reason fades, in the calm twilight of Platonic
shades" and a program of derealization, a conversion of things into fleeting
specters: "We put our eyes into a pillowy cleft, / And see the spangly gloom
froth up and boil."[140] Irresistibly, it seems, the poet records, or manufactures,
scenes of dissolution: "The Spirit mourn'd 'Adieu!'—dissolv'd, and left / The
atom darkness in a slow turmoil."[141] Or again:

> She was a gordian shape of dazzling hue . . .
> And full of silver moons, that, as she breathed,
> dissolv'd or brighter shone, or interwreathed
> Their lustres with the gloomier tapestries.[142]

We should take Keats at his word when he describes his prismatic conjuring
of material substance as "a doubtful tale from faery land, / Hard for the non-

elect to understand," a statement encouraging us to see his poetry as a late example of Addison's "Fairy Way of Writing."[143] Yet Keats's poetic manufacture of special effects (and his discourse upon these effects) can also be seen as a powerful emblem of what Paul de Man condemns as the idealization of aesthetics initiated by Schiller—that is, an emblem of aesthetic ideology.[144] In this sense, the poetics of kitsch conforms precisely to de Man's notion of aesthetic ideology as a doctrine of synthetic artifacts, synthetic worlds, synthetic language.

Since Keats's poetry does in fact become a prime target of the modernist campaign against kitsch, one should not overlook the correspondences between a positivist critique of aesthetic ideology (exemplified by the later writings of Paul de Man) and modernist paranoia about kitsch. From the standpoint of de Man's eccentric positivism, the sham materialism attributed to kitsch by its modernist detractors undergoes a process of "internalization," turning away from perception (and reinforcing the "ideology of the symbol").[145] Kitsch, in this account, thus reveals itself to be the ultimate (and unavowed) object of idealist aesthetics but also, dialectically speaking, a matrix of "queer phenomenality"—a rejection of the world as it is "given" or perceived.[146] The aesthetic artifact becomes nothing more than a bundle of special effects: a mutation consistent with aesthetic ideology and therefore complicit, ultimately—in de Man's view—with the aestheticization of politics. One must bear in mind, however—when assessing the modernist (and ostensibly materialist) critique of kitsch—that the historical iconography of philosophical materialism itself cannot be isolated from captivating images of radiant objects and meteoric bodies.[147]

6 Queer Idylls
Imposture, Inversion, Unknowing

Topologies of Privacy

The experimental genre of the Gothic melodrama developed within the confines of a private estate, a secluded place transformed into a kind of delirium—a "silver planet"—by modes of poetic inscription associated with the antiquarian spirit of the age. An elaboration of what Addison called "the Fairy Way of Writing" thus converted a natural scene, in Dodsley's phrase, into a "fairy abode." At the same time, not surprisingly, these topical measures possessed the power to transform visitors to such places into "faeries," as we discover from verses inscribed on a tablet at the entrance of Shenstone's park:

> Here in cool grot and mossy cell
> We rural Fays and Faeries dwell;
> Tho' rarely seen by mortal eye,
> When the pale moon ascending high,
> Darts thro' yon' limmes her quiv'ring beams,
> We frisk it near these crystal streams.
>
> Her beams, reflected from the wave,
> Afford the light our revels crave.[1]

On a bench elsewhere in the park, Dodsley notes these verses in Latin (which he translates):

> May the cool grove,
> And gay assembled nymphs with sylvans mix'd,
> Conceal me from the world![2]

The various nymphs, fauns, sylvans, and fairies assembled in this secluded and cultivated spot (Shenstone's estate, that is) were usually all men. The visitors to the Leasowes thus formed a coterie of male friends: Shenstone and Dodsley, of course, but also Joseph Spence, Richard Jago, Richard Graves, and Thomas Percy. The names of most of these men were recorded on plaques distributed throughout the gardens, thereby inscribing them quite literally into the apparatus of the poetic melodrama, each becoming a "silver proxy" in the moonlit delirium of the landscape.

Shenstone's rural estate was not the only place where one could find—in Britain, in the middle of the eighteenth century—a coterie of male friends improvising the apparatus of Gothic melodrama, manufacturing various anachronistic topographies and texts, forging new kinds of poetry and sexual personae—not to mention joining the moonlit "revels" alluded to by Dodsley. More visible than the Shenstone Set was the Strawberry Hill Set, a world of "bachelors" gathered around Horace Walpole at his "Gothick" estate near Twickenham.[3] This "mimic republic" (as Walpole called it) included Thomas Gray, George Montagu, John Chute, and Richard Bentley (the illustrator of Gray's "Elegy on a Favourite Cat").[4] Walpole, Chute, and Bentley dubbed themselves "the Committee of Taste" (the name of a café open to visitors at Strawberry Hill today)—arbiters of elegance and promiscuity in the massive Gothic confection of Strawberry Hill. Numerous commentators—following Walpole's own views—have noted the correspondence between the setting of Walpole's Gothic novel, *The Castle of Otranto*, and Strawberry Hill, with the implication that one cannot be sure which topos (text or house) is the original or which one is more "real."[5] The deliberate confusion of textual and topographical (or architectural) strata produces what Walpole calls an "animated prospect"—a delirium anchored in the dyadic structure of melodrama.[6]

Shenstone as well cultivated a fluid and poetic correspondence between the physical setting of the Leasowes and the phantasm of a "Castle of Indolence" (the title of a lengthy poem by James Thomson, published in 1748). The epigraph of Thomson's "allegorical poem" reads:

> The Castle hight of Indolence
> And its false Luxury,
> Where for a little time, alas!
> We liv'd right jollily.[7]

In 1750, Shenstone published his own "Ode to Indolence" (a companion piece to the "syrenic" inscriptions of the Leasowes), though without any trace of Thomson's ambivalent censure of "indolence."

The persona of the shape-shifting "fairy" turns up frequently in the antiquarian (and melodramatic) productions of Strawberry Hill (as it does at the Leasowes). In Gray's poem "The Bard" (first published by Walpole's Strawberry Hill Press in 1757), the figure of "the Poet" betrays at once the aesthetic and the sexual ethos of Strawberry Hill when he applauds the spectacle of "truth severe, by fairy fiction drest."[8] Such masquerade is hardly distinguishable from the "forger's shadow" cast by the inventors of these secluded fairylands.[9]

Walpole himself had composed a mildly pornographic "fairy" text (called "Patapan, or the Little White Dog") in verse and prose (after a tale of La Fontaine), in which a female fairy ("of fairy race, Grifona is my name") declares, "A small queer cap'ring dog I will become."[10] She then transforms herself into "the smallest dog that nature ever produced," which could conjure "pearls and rubies and diamonds" from its silky, white ear—not to mention castles from the air.[11] Additionally, the creature in the story, Patapan, is named after Walpole's own dog (revealing the work's kinship to Gray's elegy on Walpole's cat), yet this trifling theme is surely not the reason the text did not see publication for some two hundred years (though it did circulate among Walpole's circle). Rather, the poem transforms Walpole's lover, Henry Fiennes Clinton, into "a tall, lean, dry, swarthy giant of an Ethiopian" guarding a castle: "he was tall, well-made and his complexion of a manly brown. He had every limb that promised strength and vigour; and his words promised a good deal more . . ."[12] And what this smutty fairy tale (or pet story) promised, it delivered—the reason, no doubt, for its restricted circulation—including a passage in which the Ethiope (with his "swarthy instrument") and the "Speaker" are caught *in flagrante delicto*.[13] The erotic dimension of this fairy tale leaves little doubt as to the sexual persuasion of the actors and readers within the special precinct—the erotic and architectural folly—of Strawberry Hill.[14]

One biographer of Walpole emphasizes the dialectic of privacy and publicity structuring the topos (a place that is at once real and imaginary) in which the earliest experiments of poetic melodrama (with their attendant sexual personae) came into being: "the enchanted castle of Strawberry Hill should be conceived of not only as an exercise in public relations, but as a large Gothic 'closet' to which Horace Walpole could sometimes retire when he wished to express his true persona with intimate friends."[15] The same may be said about the Shenstone Circle and the activities or poetic experi-

ments carried out at the Leasowes, in the 1750s and early 1760s.[16] These
private and ephemeral societies developed important models of social and
sexual inversion, revealing productive correspondences between the queer
sexual personae and the types of poetic artifacts—especially forgeries—
cultivated in these places.

From a theoretical perspective, what links such artifacts and personae is
their common investment in public structures of secrecy and dissimulation
—in what one may call a spectacle of obscurity. To describe either Strawberry Hill or the Leasowes as a "Gothic closet" inevitably brings to mind
the "topologies of privacy" articulated by Eve Sedgwick.[17] Taking into account the overall trajectory of her work, one can discern that her analysis of "the epistemology of the closet" originated with her interest in the
"Gothic topography" of Piranesi and de Quincey—a paradigm of what she
calls "live burial."[18] At the same time, her anatomy of the closet offers no
indication that a *topology* of privacy (as an ideological or psychoanalytic
model of queer taxonomy) might actually be grounded in historical—and
social—formations of Gothic *topography* (such as Strawberry Hill or the
Leasowes). Furthermore, Sedgwick's inattention to social history (or gre-
garious formations of privacy) reinforces her book's tendency to structure
the homosexual closet as a space (whether taxonomic or subjective) occupied by an individual, as an isolation cell.

To consider, by contrast, the possibility that places such as Strawberry
Hill or the Leasowes may be primary models for the epistemology of the
closet immediately introduces the thesis that the homosexual closet is, potentially, a social and indeed collective space. On this basis Rei Terada describes "the closet as a figure for the islanded mind with a good reason to
select its own society,"[19] a conception alluding to the transactional, or reciprocative, nature of relations within the reclusive "society" of the closet.

With these parameters—at once social and aesthetic—in place, the society of the Gothic closet at Strawberry Hill and the Leasowes begins to
look like a queer prototype of the modern avant-garde: a coterie of social,
sexual, aesthetic experimentation. At the same time, Timothy Mowl draws
attention to the *amateur*, and indeed amatory, nature of early Gothic sensibility (still under the sway of poetry): "at its best, the Gothick had always
an informal Rococo spirit clinging about its shoulders; its essential form, as
Horace [Walpole] would first practice it, was amateur and romantic."[20] In
the spirit of improvisation, for example, if funds were short for new proj-

ects at Strawberry Hill, a design for Gothic vaulted beams could simply be painted directly onto the ceiling: trompe l'oeil. Antique battlements could be made from cardboard.[21]

If the sociality of the closet eludes consideration in Sedgwick's account, her conception of its epistemology remains indispensable to the spectacle of social (and textual) obscurity animating the topographies of Strawberry Hill and the Leasowes. Possessing what Sedgwick calls "the projective potency of an open secret," the presumed opacity (to the outsider) of the homosexual closet should be regarded "not as a vacuum or as the blank it pretends to be but as a weighty and occupied and consequential epistemological space."[22] According to this model, the social obscurity of the Gothic closet thus continually frustrates (and refreshes) the question, "Is it true or not?" thereby sustaining (for those outside the coterie) an alluring halo of gossip and uncertainty. As we have already noted in reference to the inscriptions at the Leasowes, the members of these secret societies—visibly secret—emphasize the liberating effects of being "concealed from the world" in such places.

A premonition of the sheltered scene at Strawberry Hill can be glimpsed in an early poem by Gray (a curious satire conceived as a dialogue with the dead), describing his days at Eton with Walpole and other boys who would eventually form part of the Walpole Set. (In this setting, the friends called one another by pastoral pseudonyms: Walpole was Celadon; Gray was Orazmades; Richard West was Zephiron; Thomas Ashton Almanzor.) In Gray's poem, his soul—which he calls "that little, naked, melancholy thing"—finds itself in a park in heaven and spies the following scene: "Here Spirit-Beaux flutter along the Mall, / And Shadows in disguise scate o'er the Iced Canal."[23] The queer phenomenality of "Spirit-Beaux" and "Shadows in disguise"—a veil of special effects associated with poetic melodrama—receives its most delicate treatment in one of Shenstone's inscriptions at the Leasowes, dedicated to "Venus half-retired," carved on "a bason of gold-fish":

> While half withdrawn she seems to hide,
> And half reveals, her charms. . . .
>
> Let sweet Concealment's magic art
> Your mazy bounds invest,
> And while the sight unveils a part,
> Let Fancy paint the rest . . .[24]

The sexual ethos of "Venus half-retired" extends even to the landscape and its antique *emblemata*:

> Flow, flow, my Stream! this devious way . . .
> Nor let the pensive sage repine,
> whose latent course resembles thine.[25]

In this "fairy abode" furnished with "latent" figurines, nature itself becomes a cryptic place.

If Sedgwick's epistemology of the closet is founded on "sweet Concealment's magic art" (inheriting its modern complexion from the "mazy bounds" of Gothic inversion), then one would expect to discover, as its legacy, a spectacle of "unknowing." Gray's notorious reticence and Walpole's inscrutability (rooted in what one biographer calls "a successful front of normal sexuality he had put up to hide his true nature") typify the "topology of privacy" integral to these Gothic laboratories (and to the scene of "live burial").[26] Shenstone comes to be known as "the pallid bard of Leasowes," and Walpole resembles (in what has been called "the most important summary of him ever written") a specter: "you appear sometimes as I wish you were, sometimes as I fear you may not be, and perhaps never as you really are."[27] What remains implicit in the structure of secrecy—in the cryptology of Strawberry Hill—are the dreadful risks animating the fraudulent personae of its initiates: Walpole "may have been an outsider because of his sexual inclination, but he was only ever an embittered and belligerent outsider when that sexuality was threatened by a marriage which excluded him or by a public 'outing.' "[28] Only if the identity of its occupant remains unknown or uncertain can the Gothic closet be a space of productive and pleasurable invention.

The risk of exposure pertained, of course, to one's personal life, but it also threatened the queer orientation of the larger social and aesthetic experiment. For the inscrutability of life at Strawberry Hill or the Leasowes inevitably constituted, according to the premises of the epistemology of the closet, a *spectacle* of obscurity. Both Shenstone and Walpole opened their estates for public viewing. (Shenstone even furnished his "Arcadian farm" with peasant-poets, such as James Woodhouse, who served at once as protagonists and as spectators.) At Strawberry Hill, "Horace's life was a case of privacy turned inside out. His taste as expressed at Strawberry Hill was one of a deliberate rebel counterculture. He was proud of it and turned his retreat into a public showplace."[29] The epistemology of "privacy turned inside out" is sustained in part by what Walpole calls the "animated prospect," by the stratified experience of melodrama.

In 1774, the press at Strawberry Hill published Walpole's *Description of Mr. Walpole's Villa at Strawberry Hill*, which catalogs his collections (referred to by Walpole as "an assemblage of curious trifles") and, through a set of instructions for visitors, "organizes Strawberry Hill into a complicated but deliberate narrative experience, a series of framed and organized 'spots' seen in a certain order."[30] The imposition of Walpole's *Description* thus produces what Anna Chalcraft calls a work of "Gothic indoctrination."[31] Like Shenstone's inscriptions at the Leasowes (produced two decades prior to Walpole's *Description*), Walpole's text converts the estate by "animated prospect" into a melodramatic structure of special effects: "what in song or ditty/Is turn'd to fairy-ground" (according to the poem, "Strawberry Hill, A Ballad," appended to Walpole's *Description*).[32]

Although Walpole describes the melodramatic topos of Strawberry Hill (his "little Gothic castle") as a "plaything" and a "toy," it was also, according to the description I cited a moment ago, a monument to "a deliberate rebel counterculture." This assessment of Strawberry Hill as encompassing a kind of avant-garde—a place of resistance—cannot be isolated from the fact that homosexuality in eighteenth-century Britain was a crime punishable by death. Walpole's biographer sees a direct link between his sexual persona and his aesthetic agenda: "he was a sexual outsider and because of this he was also an aesthetic outsider, and a potent rebel in the heart of a nation's establishment."[33] As an "aesthetic outsider," Walpole cultivated the poetics of Gray's "methodical borrowing phrenzy": the replicative mania of Strawberry Hill mirroring the formulaic designs of Gothic fiction.[34] The militant mimeticism—at once sexual and aesthetic—of the Walpole Set was arrayed against the emergent, bourgeois category of "literature" (rooted in the "purified" idiom—as Wordsworth would have it—of conversation). The deliberate poeticism of Walpole's infidel stance thus defied the democratizing, aspirational tendency of polite letters.

The correlation among sexual, aesthetic, and political inversions—among kindred forms of deviance—can be detected in the curious evolution of the poetic melodrama, a mode intrinsic to the "delirious" compounds of Strawberry Hill and the Leasowes. A form that began in 1762 as a closet drama about the figure of Pygmalion (in Rousseau's inaugural *melodrâme*) for an aristocratic audience later developed in the English-speaking world into an instrument of political radicalism and infidel culture. For example, one of the first melodramas in English, *A Tale of Mystery*, was composed in 1802 by Thomas Holcroft, a Jacobin sympathizer (and member of Thomas Spence's radical London Corresponding Society), who had been tried for sedition and imprisoned briefly in 1794.[35] The separate but mutually reinforcing elements of melodrama (music and verse), which aim to heighten emotional and aesthetic response, thus migrated from a program of artistic special effects in a private setting to a public platform of propaganda and pedagogy. This surprising trajectory retained however—and radicalized—the original themes of Rousseau's "Pygmalion": imposture and sublimation of the social base. Holcroft's infidel compositions thus provided an explicit political agenda for the melodramatic experiments conducted by the societies of the Gothic closet.

Reliques

Sedgwick develops her theory of the epistemology of the closet in reference to subject-figures, or individuals, and to works of literature or philosophy elaborating such figures. Her anatomy of the closet remains oblivious, however, to the fact that poetry itself becomes, at certain historical moments, an irresistible object of "Concealment's magic art" (the eighteenth-century template of the epistemology of the closet). In fact, the eighteenth century's preoccupation with pastiche, replication, parody, "improvement," plagiarism, and forgery represents a decisive moment in the falsification and "secretion" of the poetic artifact.[36] At once disorienting, inexhaustibly controversial, and subtly influential, the ethos of falsification and disguise first established its basic theater of operation through editorial practices associated with the ballad revival—restoration, improvement, fabrication—culminating in acts of outright forgery (in Chatterton's Rowley manuscripts and Macpherson's Ossian fragments, most significantly). Certain kinds of fabricated texts became objects of poetic *inversion*—not simply a turning inward upon itself, concealing its origin, but a reversal of values, a form of deviance, a crime of writing. As a result of these practices and controversies, Susan Stewart contends, "imitation arises as a scandal," encompassing dubious "translations" of archaic languages (Ossian being the most famous), anonymous anthologies, "found" works (a narrative device adopted by Gothic fiction as well), and mysterious source-texts that never saw the light of day.[37] The use of italics and quotation marks in poetic texts during this period became pervasive and at times eccentric: much of Thomas Gray's ode "The Bard," for example, is placed in quotation—a practice betraying a more pervasive concern with authenticity.

All of these types of texts (old ballads, found manuscripts, forgeries, anonymous anthologies, lullabies rescued from oblivion) were enveloped—sometimes as soon as they appeared and some to this very day—in a cloud of uncertainty and controversy regarding their provenance. As long as their authenticity remained in doubt, texts of this kind could not be isolated from certain questions: Is it genuine or fraudulent, original or copy, real or fake, true or false? The persistent identification of many of these poems as "border ballads" (referring to their geographical origin between England and Scotland) betrays, according to Susan Stewart, a "recurrence of 'the border' as place of origin."[38] More pointedly, one could assert that many of these works are *borderline* texts—that is, of indeterminate origin and identity. Stewart hints as well at a submerged dimension of the border: "we see as well in the ballad's external history an eroticization of boundary."[39] This comment alludes to what has been quite obvious all along: the epistemology of the closet—"Concealment's magic art"—pertains not only to the borderline *personae* of the Gothic closet, but to borderline "authors" and texts as well.

The eighteenth-century space of the borderline—a nexus of social, sexual, and textual experimentation—can be understood as a prototype of what Nicolas Bourriaud calls "relational aesthetics": in relational art or poetry, its audience comes into being as a community; artworks and poetic texts become objects modeling, or producing, sociability.[40] "Artistic praxis," Bourriaud explains, is "a rich loam for social experiments, like a space partly protected from the uniformity of behavioral patterns."[41]

At the junction of social and aesthetic practice, the term "imposture" can mean at once impersonation and forgery. Questions about the authenticity of forged texts resemble queries about sexual orientation: in eighteenth-century Britain, the veiled identity of the forger (and controversy surrounding such artifacts) mirrored the epistemology of the sexual persona of the closeted homosexual. In the *OED*, the world "queer," as an adjective, can denote something "of questionable character; suspicious; dubious"; with a cognate verb meaning "to impose on, swindle, cheat" (note the verbal root of "imposture" here). At the same time, from a textual perspective, the traditional ballad becomes the object of spurious imitation, complicating the appeal of the modern persona-poem—a poetic mask—thereby casting in generic form the epistemology of the queer persona.

The correlation between sexual and textual personae (or forgeries), along with the controversies surrounding them, does not depend solely on associative or hermeneutic affinities. Rather, this correlation can be established on historical grounds as well: the members of the inner circles at Strawberry Hill and the Leasowes were instrumental in advancing the revival of ballad poetry, in addition to being among the earliest admirers of Macpherson's and Chatterton's forgeries. Robert Dodsley, the publisher of poets Gray, Young, and Shenstone (and a frequent visitor to the Leasowes), helped to sustain interest in Lady Wardlaw's notorious "Hardyknute" by printing a second edition of it in 1740. Dodsley (and eventually his younger brother, James) also printed the first edition of Percy's *Reliques of Ancient English Poetry* in 1765. Shenstone worked closely with Percy—often at the Leasowes—selecting and controversially "improving" many of the ballads eventually selected for the anthology. In addition, James Dodsley published books by Walpole (including a controversial essay seeking to rehabilitate Richard III), and was among the few publishers whom the forger Thomas Chatterton approached in 1770 to publish his Rowley manuscripts. Needless to say, the Dodsleys played a crucial role in assembling and promoting a nexus of poets essential to the prehistory of poetic kitsch.

More directly, Walpole and Gray had access (through Sir David Dalrymple) to Macpherson's Ossian fragments prior to their earliest publication in 1760 and helped to shape the burgeoning public controversy about their authenticity. In a letter of June 1760 to Horace Walpole, Gray records his first impression of the Ossian forgeries: "I am gone mad about them. . . . I was so struck, so *extasié* with their infinite beauty, that I writ into Scotland to make a thousand enquiries."[42] Gray's enthusiasm as a poet for the eccentric diction of Macpherson's text was tempered, however, by his perplexity over the manuscript's authenticity: "the whole external evidence would make one believe these fragments (for so he calls them, tho' nothing can be more entire) counterfeit: but the internal is so strong on the other side, that I am resolved to believe them genuine."[43] In Gray's conflicted response to Macpherson's forgery (and to the spectral figure of Ossian), one glimpses the nucleus of a controversy that would flourish for decades (concerning Macpherson's text), but also an allegory of the spectacle of "unknowing" generated by the topology of social and sexual inversion at Strawberry Hill.

Poetaster

The correspondence between textual and sexual forms of inversion, malfeasance, or forgery—between queer words and queer personae—is not without precedent in the poetic tradition (or counter-tradition). The most explicit model of such a correspondence can be found in the vocabulary of poems written in the jargon of the criminal underworld—in the canting tradition: here one finds verbal evidence of a direct correlation between "quyre whiddes" (queer words: the language of the demimonde) and the "quier cove" or "quier cuffin" (the cultural infidel, an initiate of the closed society of the canting crew).[44] A more canonical, if no less esoteric, model of the correlation between sexual and textual deviance occurs in Ben Jonson's elaboration of the figure of the *poetaster* (a word first introduced into English by Jonson): a poet of inferior stature who strives through imitation and plagiary to achieve artistic renown.

In Jonson's play *Poetaster, or His Arraignment* (1601), the poetaster (a character named Crispinus) is condemned as "a meer spunge" and "a Hydra of discourse."[45] Frequently compared to a dissembling courtier, Crispinus and his cronies are described as "errant rogues" (III.iii). Jonson's play participated in the notorious "Poetomachia" (1599-1601) a war of words among rival Elizabethan playwrights: Jonson, John Marston, and Thomas Dekker. In Jonson's play, the spurious language of the poetaster—who writes nothing but "worded trash" (III.i)—oscillates between two types of jargon: the learned diction of Marston and the infidel speech of Dekker (the Elizabethan playwright most obviously indebted to the canting tradition).

The dynamic of sexual imposture (replicating the crimes of writing committed by the poetaster) adheres to the play through the circumstances of its initial staging in 1601. The title page of an early folio edition notes the play as being "Acted in the yeere 1601 By the then Children of Queene Elizabeths Chappel." This statement reveals that Jonson's *Poetaster* was first performed by a "children's company" of prepubescent "boy players," a controversial performance practice in which young boys played all of the roles in the play—not merely the female ones—a practice revived by Jonson for this play and outlawed several years after its staging at the private Blackfriars Theater.

In contrast to Shakespeare's populist productions, Jonson's erudite plays were viewed as a form of coterie drama for gentleman "wits." The controversy about companies of "boy players" arose in part because of the sexual implications of the performance practice but also because of the rumored response of its "private" audiences. In 1583, Philip Stubbes, for example, complained that plays performed by boy players were corrupted by "such wanton gestures, such bawdy speeches . . . such kissing and bussing" that the playgoers would leave the theater together "very friendly . . . and play

the sodomites, or worse."[46] On the eve of Jonson's production, John Rainolds condemned the "filthy sparkes of lust that vice, the putting of women's
attire on men, may kindle in unclean affections."[47] More precisely, in the
case of Jonson's play, the imposture of the poetaster finds itself replicated
not only in the sexual inversion of the boy players but, perhaps even more
scandalously, in the imitative poetics of Jonson's own robust classicism.

The correlation between poetic inversion, or forgery, and the miscreant
personae forged in the laboratory of the Gothic closet (at Strawberry Hill
and the Leasowes) looks forward as well to modern configurations of kitsch.
It anticipates—in ways that require careful analysis—Hermann Broch's assertion of the correlation between the artifact of kitsch and what he calls
"kitsch-man." In Broch's view, "kitsch could not, in fact either emerge or
prosper without the existence of kitsch-man, the lover of kitsch; as a producer of art he produces kitsch and as a consumer of art he is prepared to
acquire it."[48] Remarkably, kitsch-man thus produces, consumes, and even
"loves" kitsch, believing it to be art, yet never refers to the coveted artifacts
as "kitsch." Even more germane to the eighteenth-century nexus of inversion and fabrication, Broch contends, "if kitsch represents falsehood (it is
often so defined, and rightly so), this falsehood falls back on the person in
need of it, on the person who uses this highly considerate mirror so as to be
able to recognize himself in the counterfeit image it throws back of him and
to confess his own lies."[49] From this description, one can discern that the
delusional kitsch-man (who mistakes kitsch for art) becomes (like his mirror image, the false artifact) an object of derision and contempt. Although it
will be necessary to re-assess the values of "falsehood" and "counterfeit"—
not to mention the "lies" and abject "confessions" of kitsch-man—one can
see quite readily that the configuration of falsehood attributed by Broch to
kitsch evokes indirectly the social topologies of inversion and fabrication.

Kitsch, Camp, and Homo-fascism

The most questionable feature of the social and aesthetic analogy I have
identified here lies in the choice of artifact—kitsch—expressing the subject
formation of queer identity. Traditionally, the aesthetic of *camp* has been
viewed as historically and specifically queer, in contrast to kitsch, which,
when it functions as a category of material culture, has been viewed more
broadly (by Broch, Greenberg, and others) as an expression of middle-class,
or bourgeois, tastes.[50] Comments by Susan Sontag and by Walpole biographer, Timothy Mowl, about the camp milieu of Strawberry Hill subscribe

to the presumed equivalence of camp and queer.[51] To move beyond this paradigm, the tensions between queer and kitsch must be given their full measure. In the first place, because kitsch has been targeted historically as embodying middle-class tastes—and, in the most extreme case, as an emblem of fascist aesthetics—the prospect of aligning queer and kitsch risks not only the generalization of queer identity but the equation of deviance and normativity, or homosexuality and fascism: a dubious and even dangerous operation.[52] Second, in contrast to the logic of identification fastening queer identity to camp aesthetics, kitsch attribution is rooted in contempt and paranoia, yielding powerful inhibitions against identification with its despised object. Kitsch, as it is usually conceived, appears (unlike camp) to be a category of objects without affiliation: no one claims to make or enjoy "kitsch" per se—since those who do so never use the word. Kitsch thus retains a persistent negativity, a trace of the abject that cannot be dispelled.

The importance of melodrama to the aesthetic experiments conducted within the homosocial enclaves of Strawberry Hill and the Leasowes would appear to support the equivalence of camp and queer in these environments. Yet my analysis of the role of poetic inscription at the Leasowes (or Walpole's *Description* of Strawberry Hill) indicates that melodrama in these contexts is less a matter of sentimentality and performance than of indoctrination, indolence, fabrication, triviality, and imposture. Poetry—a highly formulaic version of it—*imposes* on the viewer in these settings, captioning and falsifying the landscape for the viewer's consumption. Melodrama in this context also evokes the antiquarian fever of the age, the cultish appeal of the spurious artifact, and a residual poetics of hiding. The strongest arguments for linking queer and kitsch can therefore be found in the particular arrangements of these historical circumstances, in the actual investment of these queer communities in a "contagion of imitation," in forms of replication and inversion that mark the boundaries of kitsch. More precisely, it is only the revelation of kitsch as a distinctly poetic phenomenon (as a category originating in certain specific controversies in the history of poetry) that yields a substantial and productive model of the correlation of kitsch and queer. It is furthermore only the *poetics* of kitsch that reveals the importance of mimeticism and seriality as structures linking queer identity not only to forgery and imposture—in a progressive sense—but to the emergent mechanisms of popular culture.

Ultimately, it is precisely those qualities of kitsch threatening queer identity—its generality and its anathematic properties, its abject nature—that motivate the alignment of queer and kitsch. Most importantly, the indelible negativity of kitsch—its falseness, its contemptible lack of substance, its fraudulent nature—resonates with the original pejorative connotations of the word "queer." Eve Sedgwick is one of the few theorists to consider the correspondences between queer and kitsch (instead of queer and camp). She does so because the epistemology of the closet is a paranoid structure marking its occupant as an object of fury, contempt, and uncertainty; thus camp, because it becomes an object of identification and affectionate incorporation, can play no role in the drama of abjection structuring the cryptic space of the closet. The discourse of kitsch, Sedgwick acknowledges, reproduces the epistemology of the closet: "so it is necessarily true that the structure of contagion whereby *it takes one to know one*, and whereby *any* object about which the question 'Is it kitsch?' can be asked immediately *becomes* kitsch, remains, under the system of kitsch-attribution, a major scandal."[53] What Sedgwick fails to consider is the possibility of the uncloseted queer deliberately incorporating, or introjecting, kitsch *as* negation, producing a discourse of what Lee Edelman calls "queer negativity."[54]

The prospect of incorporating the negativity of kitsch—and associating it with queer subjectivity—arises, according to Andrew Hewitt, with the triangulation of fascism, kitsch, and homosexuality. Stable correspondences between fascism and kitsch, or homosexuality and camp, can be scrambled in the contemporary imagination by reading kitsch as if it were camp (a category rooted in identification):

> If kitsch and camp can become identical at the level of the object, there is always the danger that they will become identical in the subject. Rather than posing two forms of subject-formation—identificatory camp and alienating kitsch—we need instead to examine their virtual convergence as epistemological rather than straight-forwardly aesthetic phenomena: the surrender of the discourse of the Self to the dictates of the "Other."[55]

With the possibility of this "convergence" migrating from object to subject (mistaking kitsch for camp and fascist for queer), Hewitt contends, "the kitsch of fascism potentially becomes a homosexual camp."[56] Further, he explains, "If the homosexual can turn kitsch into camp—'mistake' kitsch for camp, in the example of fascist art—then he potentially subverts the kitsch logic of attribution (what we might otherwise call the logic of alienation) with the logic of identification."[57] In contemporary equations of fascism and queerness—via the faulty nexus of kitsch—the imaginary fascist (like the

susceptible queer) performs a similar inversion of camp and kitsch, exposing the queer lining of fascism.

As a result of this dangerous—but potentially dialectical—transaction,

> the homosexual . . . acknowledges the "fascist within" . . . (recognizes, in fact,
> that the "within" is a mere function of the definitive "without"). . . . It is not so
> much a question of the homosexual "being" fascist, as it is of the homosexual
> acknowledging the supplemental inference of the Other in the self.[58]

Though Hewitt contends that a homosexual identification with kitsch—a
catastrophic likening of queer and kitsch—produces in the contemporary
imagination a compound he calls "homo-fascism," he does not allow for
the possibility (nor is it to be expected in the context of his argument) of a
deliberate queering of fascism through the garbled relay of kitsch. He does
not review the possibility, or the value, of "queer negativity" as a calculated
stratagem.

The possible alignment of kitsch and queer, which is enabled in part by
the transitivity, or fluidity, of anathematic elements, thus re-establishes the
powers of horror and negation associated with the word "queer" (which
have in fact receded with the recent transvaluation of the term). The
miscreant substance of kitsch makes available to aesthetic and political discourse an inconceivable figure: the persona of the *nazi-queer*—a position,
an imposition, revealed only by the anti-system (as Broch calls it) of kitsch.
The extremity of this term seems to defy, even as it requires, examination
of what it would mean to adopt the imposition of the nazi-queer, an identity synthesizing the abject properties of kitsch. In abetting the political
and cultural agency of the nazi-queer, the fraudulent verbal resources of
kitsch would necessarily reassert their queer affinities—without limit or
constraint—their atavistic relation to infidel culture.

At the same time, the alignment of queer and kitsch has the potential
to abstract or generalize—as one feared it would—the historical specificity
of queer identity, exposing its appeal as a cultural and political model in a
wider context. Society at large (at least its vast bourgeois domain) begins
unknowingly to turn queer—as both the perpetrator and the fascinated witness of imposture—through its identification with the kitsch. When, for example, large numbers of people begin to fear digital exposure, or "mining,"
of personal archives, when one sees evidence of mass fantasies of inscrutability (stemming from fantasies of the violation of privacy), one must acknowledge the queer *sociality* of the closet in the broadest possible terms.

Even stranger is the possibility that the epistemology of the closet may ultimately become a theory of crowd psychology, of mass culture unfolding in
the dark. The prospect of a *queer totality* escapes from the confines of the
closet: a spectacle of obscurity fueled by mass paranoia.

1800 Words

The eccentric spelling of the word "reliques" in the title of Thomas
Percy's famous anthology of ballads is itself what we would now call "distressed": in its original context, it meant to convey the allure of the archaic
and has since become an amusing gesture of failed seriousness. The spelling
is kitschy, but it is also *queer*. The basis of these connotations can be fully recovered only by examining more closely the queer affiliations, and the controversies over poetic diction, determining the reception (and sometimes
the production) of these sorts of poetic texts. At the same time, one must
bear in mind that the polarized structure of identification and alienation determining the value of kitsch replicates the inexhaustible controversies surrounding the poetic practices of polite "improvement," fabrication, and outright forgery in the eighteenth century. Opinions on these matters among
members of the Walpole Set or the Shenstone Set (who helped to promote
or condemn, and sometimes fashion, such texts) were by no means uniform. Indeed, because the stakes in defending or attacking the authenticity
of the latest "found" manuscript (or phantom author) replicated the drama
of concealment and exposure—the epistemology of the closet—enveloping
homosexual identity, the positions on these texts adopted publicly by members of these circles reverberated with unpredictable and sometimes devas-
tating effects.

Approaching this historical nexus of poetic forgery, one must note at
the outset that the problems of corruption and authentication were built
into the presentation of the earliest editions of these influential texts. Already, for example, in the second edition of the notorious "Hardyknute"
(published by Robert Dodsley in 1740), a section of "General Remarks and
Notes" addresses the authenticity of Wardlaw's "Fragment" (which appears
to the editor to be "less encumber'd with the Rust of Antiquity") and its elusive author ("I shall not trouble you with any whimsical Conjectures about
him").[59] The dance of authentication we find in these comments—which
deliberately garbles the gender of the impostor—figures even more prominently in the inaugural appearance of Macpherson's Ossian texts, *Fragments
of Ancient Poetry* (1760), where the first sentence of Macpherson's preface

declares, "The public may depend on the following fragments as genuine remains of ancient Scottish poetry" (as if the reader would have any reason to
think otherwise).[60] Ten years later, Thomas Chatterton's fabrication of texts
by a fictitious fifteenth-century monk, Thomas Rowley, encompassed an
elaborate web of authentication, including the invention by Chatterton of
a secondary scribe, "William Canynge," who supplements the bogus Rowleyan poems with equally fake documents on the law, heraldry, genealogy,
and medieval "peyncteynge" (to which Chatterton attached ten pages of explanatory notes when he sent the forgeries to Walpole at the age of sixteen).

In the minds of the initiates at Strawberry Hill or the Leasowes, these
infamous texts (and spectral poets) appear to have existed in a kind of submerged constellation of dubious but palpable intrigue. In a letter of April
1760 to Walpole, for example, Gray suggests that the "charm" of the Ossian
fragments is due in part to their uncertain origin: "I am so charmed with
the two specimens of Erse poetry that I cannot help giving you the trouble
to enquire a little farther about them, and should wish to see a few lines of
the original."[61] Gray's curiosity about the Ossian "specimens" (a designation
marking their unstable position between philology and poetics) summons
his thoughts about Lady Wardlaw's production: "I have often been told that
the poem called Hardicanute (which I always admired, and still admire) was
the work of somebody that lived a few years ago. This I do not at all believe,
though it has evidently been retouched in places by some modern hand."[62]
Walpole's opinion of the Ossianic corpus is, by contrast, less credulous and
enthusiastic: "I will trust you with a secret, but you must not disclose it, I
should be ruined with my Scotch friends—in short, I cannot believe it genuine."[63] Tellingly, Walpole feels compelled to wrap a secret within a secret—
evidence of the general economy of secrecy and speculation governing
these circumstances.

This constellation of poetic forgeries (yielding a monadological pattern
of uncertain persuasion) can be recomposed, more reliably, as a genealogy
of imposture. Macpherson boldly advanced the poetics of the "retouched"
text (inaugurated by "Hardyknute"), while the Ossianic "remains" provided,
in turn, reckless inspiration for the poetic experiments of Gray, Shenstone,
Percy, and Chatterton. In the process of selecting and "improving" old
ballads for Percy's anthology (a collaboration conducted at the Leasowes),
Shenstone recommended to Percy the example of Macpherson's liberties:
"Let the Liberties taken by the translator of the Erse-Fragments be a Precedent for you. Many old Pieces without some alteration will do nothing,

& with your amendments will be striking."[64] More specifically, concerning Percy's "amendments" to the ballads "Edom o' Gordon" and "Gentle Herdsman," Shenstone confirms his enthusiasm for what Dante Rossetti later calls the "modern antique": "I believe I shall never make any objection to such Improvements as you bestow upon them, unless you were plainly to contradict Antiquity, which I am pretty sure will never be the case."[65]

Percy adopted the recommendations of the "elegant Mr. Shenstone" frequently enough to become associated in the minds of critics with the controversial methods enveloping the Ossianic fragments—since Shenstone's doctrine of "Improvements" could be seen as a potential path to forgery. "Macpherson's and Percy's methods were very often similar," one critic maintains.[66] As a consequence, Percy felt compelled to defend such liberties in the preface to his anthology. Referring to himself in the third person, he acknowledges that the editor "must plead guilty to the charge of concealing his own share in the amendments. . . . Yet it has been his design to give sufficient intimation where any considerable liberties were taken with the old copies."[67] (In fact, Percy gave no "intimation" of the amendments he made to numerous ballads in the anthology.) The motive for taking such liberties becomes clear, he explains, "when, by a few slight corrections or additions, a most beautiful or interesting sense hath started forth."[68] Echoing Shenstone's defense of poetic effects (of amendments that are "striking"), Percy urges the production of a sense that "starts forth" from the doctored text. One should also note, however, that Percy never misses a chance in his prefatory notes to individual poems to knock Lady Wardlaw—with misgivings—for her shadowy involvement in the production of certain ballads included in the anthology.[69]

Sympathetic responses to various shades of poetic forgery (often involving attempts to mask such practices) from eminent figures such as Gray, Shenstone, and Percy (or from those motivated by Scottish nationalism and Jacobite sympathies) inevitably produced spirited and sometimes harsh resistance.[70] Samuel Johnson, for example, devoted considerable time to investigating and denouncing the forgeries of Macpherson and Chatterton. The most vehement (and influential) of such critics was Joseph Ritson, who mounted a ferocious campaign against literati who were, he claimed, "addicted to literary imposition."[71] Foremost among his targets was Percy, whose aims, Ritson argued, were "secretly to suppress the original text, and insert his own fabrications for the sake of provideing more refine'd entertainment for readers of taste."[72] In Ritson's view, as a result of the "fabrication" endemic to Percy's anthology, "the purchasers and perusers of such a collection are deceived and impos'd upon; the pleasure they receive is derive'd from the idea of antiquity, which, in fact, is perfect illusion."[73] One must emphasize here Ritson's antagonism towards "entertainment" and "illusion" in the production of Percy's ballads—terms anticipating the popular aesthetic of kitsch—a stance opposing Shenstone's and Percy's "addiction" to spurious poetic effects.

As Ritson's defense of the "original text" (along with his scornful reference to "readers of taste") indicates, the controversy about the motives and verbal effects of forgery was often framed as a conflict between the inclinations of the "antiquarian" and those of the "reader of taste," that is, between philology and poetics. Hence, in contrast to Ritson's antiquarian bias, Shenstone (admired by some as an *arbiter elegantiarum*) feared that Percy's "fondness for antiquity should tempt him to admit pieces that have no other sort of merit."[74] Ritson, of course claimed quite the contrary about Percy's methods. Subject to attack from both ends of the critical spectrum, Percy sought to negotiate this polemic by situating himself between the two positions. Referring to himself in the third person in the preface to his anthology, Percy remarks, "His object was to please both the judicious antiquary, and the reader of taste; and he hath endeavored to gratify both without offending either."[75] As the stakes in the controversy over forgery intensified, however, Percy sought increasingly to distance himself from the motives and milieu of the reader of taste—that is, from Shenstone, the "pallid bard of Leasowes."[76]

The fierce debates over the poetic appeal and verbal authenticity of the ballad-poem should be seen as a rivalry between complementary figures of the cultural infidel. For Joseph Ritson, absolute commitment to the "meagre stuff" of ballad texts, to remnants of what he believed to be pure, vernacular poetry, signified cultural and political radicalism. At the same time, the verbal impositions of the reader of taste—of the elegant Mr. Shenstone—could certainly be regarded as "reliques" of poetic experimentalism in a different vein: as enigmatic toys of the sexual infidel. From this perspective, just as one can trace correspondences between poetic and sexual inversions in Shenstone's example, so Ritson's militant antiquarianism evolved in concert with his radical Jacobite, and later Jacobin, sympathies. Both figures, despite their antagonism over fidelity to the letter—that is, to the diction—of the text, may be regarded as poetic and cultural infidels.

Affinities between textual and cultural militancy found expression in

Ritson's compulsively annotated anthology of Robin Hood ballads (with woodcuts by Thomas Bewick, the illustrator of an early edition of *Mother Goose*), a project in which he sought to link the raw material of the ballad-poem—via the figure of the outlaw—to the ultraradical politics of post-revolutionary London. Ritson's eccentricities (including vegetarianism and the development of a peculiar system of orthography) culminated in his maniacal death in 1803, when he barricaded himself in his rooms at Gray's Inn (as he worked to complete a pamphlet "proving Jesus Christ to be an imposter") and set fire to masses of rare manuscripts.[77] (Ritson's stringent editorial bias, it should be noted, eventually became the de facto standard of modern textual conservatorship.)

The struggle between the zealous antiquary (the philologist) and the elegant man of taste (the poet) over the verbal "relique" of the ballad occurs principally as an effort to stabilize and regulate the poetic vernacular, but also as a conflict between competing registers of poetic diction (a dispute instrumental, as I have frequently noted, to the foundation of poetic kitsch). John Pinkerton (an anthologist of Scottish ballads), whose manuscripts Ritson denounced as "palpable and bungling forgery," took an equally forceful stance (in the person of the "editor") against the textual fetishism of the antiquary: "the editor has in no instance sacrificed the character of a man of taste to that of an antiquary; as of all characters he least chuses that of an hoarder of ancient dirt."[78] Shenstone as well warned Percy against ballads that were "subobscure in point of Language; And this, at the beginning of your work, might perhaps be liable to give disgust."[79] Percy, accordingly, adopted a stance in his editorial practice against retaining "antique words and phrases" that he deemed "extremely incorrect."[80]

In contrast to the "ancient dirt" prized by the verbal antiquary, Shenstone advocated the manufacture of "improved Copies," urging Percy, "I would wish you to consult for Simplicity as much as possible."[81] Shenstone acknowledged that certain doctored texts might have to "be rejected for their modernism," using a term—one of the earliest uses of the word "modernism"—associated with frivolous poetic effects (as in Swift's reference to the "quaint modernisms" of scribblers and hacks).[82] Shenstone nevertheless recommends to Percy that he approach the raw material of his controversial "found" manuscript of ballads—adopting the analogy of numismatic forgery—as if it were an opportunity to literally *coin* new poetic language: "Suppose then you consider your MS. as an hoard of gold, somewhat defac'd by Time, from which however you may be able to draw supplies upon occasion, and with which you may enrich the world hereafter, with more current Impressions."[83]

Among the spurious poetic coin to be found in what some critics have called Percy's "counterfeit anthology" are words such as "meed," "dight," "eke," "thrall," "forfend," "gear," and "paramour"—precisely the kind of diction Wordsworth condemned as "the vague, the glossy, and unfeeling language of the day."[84] Later critics inadvertently pinpoint the origins of poetic kitsch when they dismiss Shenstone's manner of "prettifying the diction with aureate phrases, borrowing bits of tinsel," or condemn the "tawdry feebleness" of Percy's interpolations, which produce an "objectionable *més-alliance* of true and false."[85]

Within the historical nexus of eighteenth-century poetic forgery, which functions as a polemical site for experiments with poetic diction, a kind of rupture (or rapture) occurred with the physical manufacture and private circulation of Thomas Chatterton's Rowley manuscripts. Chatterton's fraudulent project, unprecedented in scope and variegation, collapsed the antithesis of antiquarian fidelity and forged "simplicity," a development essential to the poetics of kitsch. He was not, ostensibly, in the business of manufacturing "quaint modernisms"—as befitted the man of taste—yet "Chatterton had gone on to an altogether different plane of deception, moving beyond plagiarism and literary reconstruction into the realm of the fake, once he started to supply corroborative detail, contextual padding, and all the props of bogus authentication."[86] The palpability of Chatterton's forgery (he actually fabricated an array of manuscripts) heightened the prospect of catastrophic exposure—a climactic scene already suggested, but also deferred, by Macpherson's and Percy's withholding from public inspection the archaic manuscripts said to be the source, respectively, of their "translations" and anthologies.

At the core of Chatterton's fraudulent project is the language he invented—a peculiar and incomparable diction—for an imaginary medieval poet, Thomas Rowley. Chatterton scholars have determined that the Rowleyan jargon "consists of about 1800 words, virtually all of which can be traced to probable sources."[87] At the same time, apparently, only about 7 percent of the archaisms adopted by Chatterton are entirely authentic or correctly used.[88] The Rowleyan tongue can thus be regarded as a fantastic realization of the thesis (advocated by Gray, Goldsmith, and others) that poetry possesses its own "peculiar" language—exhibiting properties at once of the non sequitur and the cliché—a self-contained idiom preserved through replication. Chatterton's made-up language offers proof of poetry's verbal eccentricity, even as it echoes the timeless vernacular of its origin.

The Rowley poems are composed in a truly *miscreant* idiom, grounded in canonical sources (Chaucer, Shakespeare, and Spenser, primarily, in addition to certain dictionaries), yet mostly inauthentic in its deployment. Chatterton's fidelity to legitimate sources (even if it is a form of plagiarism) is perverted by his eccentric system of orthography (a principal device of his experimentation with poetic diction). Virtually every word in much of the Rowley corpus is extravagantly misspelled:

> Whann Autumpne blake and sunn-brente doe appere,
> With hys goude honde guylteynge the falleynge lefe,
> Bryngeynge oppe Wynterr to folylle the yere
> Beerynge uponne hys backe the riped shefe.[89]

Chatterton's production of what one critic calls "stretch-limo spellings" yields a stunning illustration of one of the oldest recipes for poetic diction: the use of what Aristotle calls "expanded words," which leads, in excess, to "barbarism."[90] Chatterton's orthography follows a few crude principles: make as many words end in "e" as possible; duplicate or otherwise add consonants freely. A closer historical analogy for this method, perhaps to be associated with the mania of antiquarian fidelity, would be Joseph Ritson's curious system of orthography, which also features a surfeit of e's. One would also want to invoke at the same time the renegade orthographic and pedagogical systems of the ultraradical organizer, Thomas Spence.[91] The corresponding orthographies of Chatterton, Ritson, and Spence together yield a palpable matrix of political and poetic infidelity. The verbal poetics of kitsch can thus be conjoined with a mode of infidel scholarship.

The orthographic barbarism of Chatterton's forgeries inhibits the reader's experience of both the musical and the semantic dimensions of the poems, since the spelling interferes with efforts either to scan the poem or to read it for meaning. In the Rowleyan poems, one is confronted initially by the sovereignty of poetic diction—the trademark of kitsch—at the expense of meaning and prosody. One can therefore appreciate—even if one is baffled by the choice of terms—why Keats called Chatterton "the purest writer in the English language" and later dedicated "Endymion" to him.[92]

For Keats's extravagant diction—a wellspring of kitsch—finds its illegitimate standard in Chatterton's experiments in poetic tone:

> Fayntelie the mone her palyde lyght makes gleme;
> The upryste sprytes the sylente letten fylle,
> Wythe ouphant faeryes joynyng yune the dreme;
> The forreste sheenethe wythe the sylver leme.[93]

The impenetrable surface of Chatterton's forgery produces a fairyland of indirection, a melodrama of pure connotation. Here Keats discovers not only the alchemy of the "silver proxy"—a dazzling and fraudulent diction—but also the queer phenomenality of a place he calls "my silver planet": a queer totality.

Poison

Chatterton's audacious imposture scrambled the ranks of polemical response, even among the closeted society of forgers. Oliver Goldsmith, for example, the anonymous compiler (and fabricator) of Mother Goose rhymes, became "an adherent of the Rowley cause," which set him at odds with Percy, who privately condemned Chatterton's manuscripts as "undoubtedly modern and spurious."[94] Publicly, however, Percy maintained a notable silence on the Chatterton controversy. "The most likely explanation," one critic contends,

> is that Percy wished to distance himself from his earlier mode of *litérrateur* and gentleman-author. . . . It may also be that Percy observed the possible links people would make between the *Reliques* sensation of the 1760s, and Chatterton, sensation of the 1770s. . . . The thought may have struck Percy that he was in some buried sense one of the progenitors of Chatterton's poetic mode.[95]

Even without attempting to postulate the motives for Percy's silence, however, it is quite evident that the open secret of the forger's closet became more volatile, more dangerous, following the scandal of Chatterton's exposure.

Prior to the publication of any of the Rowley poems, Chatterton poisoned himself by taking arsenic (on August 24, 1770) at the age of seventeen. Chatterton's suicide—an event without redress, explanation, or resolution—exposed and heightened the isolation of the forger's closet, alluding to a "buried sense" of cancelled affiliations, to a host of silent "progenitors." Speculation about the motive for Chatterton's suicide, which cannot be isolated from the private circulation and reception of his texts prior to his death, continued for nearly half a century, culminating in a constellation of poems about Chatterton by Wordsworth, Coleridge, Shelley, and Keats. The treacherous matrix of speculation about Chatterton's suicide (and its effects on opinion about his spurious texts) entangled several prominent figures (as I noted in Percy's case) long before he became a Romantic martyr. With the denouement of the Chatterton affair, forgery and imposture—perhaps all acts of imposture—could not be isolated from the ethical and figurative matrix of suicide. A vivid icon of this correlation can be found in Henry Wallis's pre-Raphaelite painting *The Death of Chatterton* (1856), which depicts the tattered leaves of the notorious manuscripts beside Chatterton's body at the moment of his death.

The most cogent explanation for the perceived association of forgery and suicide would be the obligatory erasure of the self—and the true author of a text—as a basic condition of imposture. The correlation may also explain why the numismatic analogy of forgery, employed frivolously by Shenstone, was used more often to suggest the criminality of poetic imposture. Joseph Ritson, for example, declared, "A man who will forge a poem, a line or even a word will not hesitate, when the temptation is greater & the impunity equal, to forge a note."[96] And one could add to Ritson's warning: a forger of words would not hesitate, by the same logic, to forge a persona, an identity. In addition, forging a banknote or veiling the true source of a counterfeit text calls to mind the breach of faith—the criminality—of suicide.

The impulse to criminalize Chatterton's poetic imposture (thereby aligning it with the transgressive act of suicide) found one of its agents in a source who was intimately invested in the production and concealment of textual (and sexual) personae. In a public letter of 1779 to the editor of a newly published selection of Chatterton's writings, Horace Walpole wrote, "All of the house of forgery are relations," and "[Chatterton's] ingenuity in counterfeiting styles and, I believe, hands, might easily have led him to those more facile imitations of prose, promissory notes."[97] Here Walpole, like Ritson, draws a correlation between poetic imposture and counterfeiting banknotes. Walpole had become ensnared in the Chatterton controversy as a result of a brief correspondence he had with the young poet a year and a half prior to his death—and widespread speculation about a connection between Walpole's conduct and Chatterton's suicide. Documenting Walpole's ambivalence toward Chatterton—he called him "the young villain" but also "that marvelous creature" (anticipating Wordsworth's reference to Chatter-

ton as "the marvelous Boy")—Walpole amassed four volumes of Chatterto-
niana in his personal library at Strawberry Hill.[98]

The affair had begun in 1769 when Chatterton, age sixteen, sent Walpole
the transcript of a "curious manuscript" entitled "The Ryse of Peynceteynge,
yn Englande, wroten bie T. Rowlie, 1469" (a fabrication carefully baited to
interest Walpole, who had just published *Anecdotes of Painting*). Although
initially conveying "a thousand thanks"—and an offer to print some of the
Rowley poems—Walpole grew suspicious when Chatterton claimed to have
found the Rowley manuscript in "an Iron Chest in Redclift Church" in Bristol.[99] Given the fact that Walpole's own novel *The Castle of Otranto* (published anonymously in 1764), begins with the conceit of a manuscript found
in a trunk (from which the narrative of the novel is said to be recovered), it
is no surprise that Walpole's faith in Chatterton's enterprise quickly evapo-
rated. With Chatterton's claims, he had been confronted, in fact, with a
new and especially potent variant of the fashionable tale of a found manuscript of ancient texts (echoing the backstories of Wardlaw, Percy, and
Macpherson): the unmistakable signature of imposture. He declined further
correspondence with Chatterton—never having met him—and returned his
transcripts.

In response to Walpole's rejection, Chatterton wrote angry letters and a
poem (never sent), accusing him of coldheartedness and class prejudice:

> *Walpole*, I thought not I should ever see
> So mean a heart as thine has prov'd to be.
> Thou who, in luxury nurst, beholds with scorn
> The boy, who friendless, penniless, forlorn,
> Asks they favour—thou mayest call me cheat.
> Say, did thou never practice such deceit?
> Who wrote *Otranto*?[100]

Reminding Walpole that his own novel was an imposture of sorts, Chatterton sketches here a portrait of authorial hypocrisy that, once it received
wide circulation, haunted Walpole's career for the remainder of his life,
establishing an indelible account of Walpole's guilty accusations. In a letter of 1779, Walpole wrote, "Someone has published the poems of Chatterton the Bristol boy, and in the preface intimates that I was the cause of
his despair and poisoning himself, and a little more openly is of the opinion
that I ought to be stoned."[101] (Walpole refers here to the editor whom he
upbraided in the public letter cited earlier, intemperately placing Chatter-

ton in the "house of forgery.") Walpole was not exaggerating the effects of the scandal, since even his neighbors at Strawberry Hill observed that he "began to go down in public favour from the time he resisted the imposition of Chatterton."[102]

The idea of Walpole *resisting* "the imposition of Chatterton" is significant since it portrays Chatterton's imposture as a personal "imposition," an act of cheating that observers surmised Walpole might have some reason to entertain—and forgive. The mistake of resisting Chatterton's imposition implies the possible allure imposture was imagined to hold for Walpole and how he might be expected to respond to the spectacle of a fraudulent text or persona. It seems possible, then, that the event of Chatterton's suicide became coherent in the literary and public imagination only once it had been assimilated to a certain crime of writing (which calls for the disguise, or extinction, of the author) but also to a sexual persona that is contingent on "Concealment's magic art." Ultimately, one could conclude that the legal, poetological, and sexual codes of the public imagination required Walpole to be punished for condemning acts of imposture that he himself had exploited both as the author of *Otranto* and as a closeted homosexual.

In this web of correspondences, we become witness to the transactional, or complementary, constructions of the closeted homosexual, the "suicidal person," and the poetics of the fraudulent text—all of which become objects of interminable speculation. The persistent toxicologies, at once poetic and psychosexual, of the Chatterton affair are reminiscent of Adorno's intermittently hysterical, yet rhetorically apt, report on the noxious chemistry of kitsch: "Kitsch is like a poisonous substance that is mixed in with art. Discharging that poison is one of the most difficult tasks art faces at the present time."[103]

7 Kitsching the *Cantos*

Totality, Fascism, and *les Paradis Artificiels*

> The whole is a riddle, an enigma, an inexplicable mystery. Doubt, uncertainty, suspense of judgment, appear the only result of our most accurate certainty, concerning this subject. But such is the frailty of human reason, and such is the irresistible contagion of opinion, that even this deliberate doubt could scarcely be upheld.
>
> David Hume

Vortex and Cream Puff

Kitsch in poetry became more and more widespread—principally through the cottage industry of parlor ballads and the cult of simplicity— during the nineteenth century, yet the basic verbal platform of kitsch established in the eighteenth century remained largely intact: imposture, archaism, sentimentality, stereotypical diction, melodrama—all diffused through an evolving "Fairy Way of Writing." It was only with the emergence of modernist antagonism to kitsch in the twentieth century that the attenuated doctrine of poetic "simplicity" began to develop new and unprecedented strategies of survival and elaboration. The most significant reverberations of poetic kitsch in the early part of the twentieth century are to be found not in the countless examples of ballads filtered through the matrices of decadence, medievalism, and orientalism but, surprisingly, within the emergent paradigm of modernism. Despite its vehement opposition to kitsch, poetic modernism failed ultimately to rid itself of its nemesis. In this sense, an evolutionary aspect of poetic kitsch in the era of high modernism surfaced within polarized structures encompassing both the hyperlyrical substance of kitsch and its antithesis, the reptilian diction of modernism. These experimental forms—the great legacy of poetic modernism—enlist the verbal substance of kitsch in the construction of highly synthetic (and unstable) forms of poetic and cultural totality. From this perspective, the modernist commitment to epic poetry activated inadvertently the repressed constellation of kitsch, poetic diction, and totality.

The most ambitious and influential example of such a work is Ezra Pound's experimental epic, the *Cantos*. Of course, to describe the *Cantos* as advancing the poetics of kitsch is nothing short of blasphemy; I do not take this step lightly. No epithet more contrary or perverse could be applied to Pound's innovative and learned poem, or indeed to any canonical work of high modernism. The cultic substance of the *Cantos* has lost none of its potency, which explains why the poem remains, when viewed from the perspective of kitsch, apotropaic—inscrutable to eyes blinded by the dogmatic principles of modernism. The element of kitsch in the *Cantos* promises to disclose the apocalyptic dimension of an aesthetic category associated historically with complacent pleasures and artistic degradation.

The fate of poetic kitsch under the regime of modernism reveals the extent and the usefulness of the paradigm of kitsch: it becomes necessary to apply it not simply to poetry whose sugary diction and alienated posture conforms quite obviously to the historical legacy of poetic kitsch, but also to concede, to diagnose, the properties of kitsch in poetry whose commitments to it are submerged or inconsistent. Even more provocatively, the veiled significance of kitsch to the ultimate achievement of the *Cantos* urges us to test the outer limits of kitsch by seeking its verbal substance in poetry that is ostensibly and vigorously opposed to it.

Any exploration of the relation of the *Cantos*, a modern epic, to poetic kitsch must start with a consideration of the poems written by Pound well before he began to compose the *Cantos*. Like many of the writers involved with the early formulation of Anglo-American modernism, Pound's pre-modernist poetry was steeped in the legacy of nineteenth-century poetic kitsch (from the pre-Raphaelites to orientalism to writers associated with Aestheticism and the Decadent movement). A quick glance at any of Pound's first six collections of poetry (published prior to the emergence of Imagism in 1913) will confirm, moreover, that this early stage of his career was more deeply influenced by the legacy of nineteenth-century kitsch than that of any of his modernist peers. In addition, his extensive commitments as a translator and comparatist only intensified his engagement with the competing dictions of the poetic tradition. As a result of this active immersion in the legacy of kitsch (condensed from the residues of the poetic tra-

dition), Pound's struggle to rid himself of that influence, once he embraced
(and helped to invent) the tenets of poetic modernism, was more difficult,
more ambivalent, and more protracted, than that of any of his peers. This
struggle within Pound's poetry between his modernist principles and the
legacy of kitsch did not, moreover, simply disappear once he committed
himself to the composition of the *Cantos*. On the contrary, this struggle
became a permanent part of the poetic, ideological, and ultimately political
development of the *Cantos*.

The question of how the values of Pound's early poetry are related to
the modernist achievement of the *Cantos* must focus initially on the pivotal moment of Imagism and, more specifically, on certain latent features of
Pound's conception of the poetic image. Although writing ballad imitations
is not customarily associated with the precepts of Imagism, a surprising
piece of advice appears in the earliest statement on the principles of Imagism (published in *Poetry* magazine in April 1913): Pound advises the would-
be Imagist poet to sample the pleasures of "Saxon charms" and "Hebridean
Folk Songs," in order to "fill his mind with finest cadences he can discover."[1]
Pound's interest here, as is evident from his own attempts at ballad-making,
encompasses not only the "cadences" but the synthetic diction of the vernacular genres (charms and folksongs) associated with the ballad revival.
His "Ballad of the Goodly Fere" (displaying what T. S. Eliot claims is Pound's
"great knowledge of the ballad form") offers a prickly example of the archaism and pseudo-dialect ("Ha' we lost the goodliest fere o' all") that Pound's
early poetry frequently adopts.[2] Astonishingly, given the poem's boldly "distressed" diction—which reveals the odd correspondences between archaism, kitsch, and poetic populism—Pound extolls the poem for its accessibility: "For the first time in my life I had written something that 'everyone
could understand' and I wanted it to go to the people."[3] Some two hundred
years after the earliest symptoms of the ballad revival had emerged in Addison's "Chevy Chase" papers and Lady Wardlaw's "Hardyknute," ballad writing had become part of the formation of the modernist poet. Pound, we see,
felt compelled to learn how to use an existing palette of antiquated diction
(comprising the matrix of poetic kitsch) in order, paradoxically, to make his
poetry, he thought, more popular and accessible.

In Pound's case, as students of modernism well know, this regimen of
imitation encompassed not only native sources (Anglo-Saxon, Scots dialect,
etc.) but also various "oriental" and Romance (especially medieval) traditions. Pound's absorption (or invention) of this palette of diction is closely

bound up with his influential practice and theorizing as a translator during the development of Imagism. At times, the functions of translator and poet overlap in significant ways in Pound's practice. When he is "translating," for example, from a language he doesn't know (or know well), the practice of "importing" exotic diction (still under the sway of the cult of simplicity) becomes indistinguishable from the invention of poetic personae. The motivation for this kind of "translation"—so important to the emergence of poetic modernism—has less to do with the invention of new poetic forms than it does with elaborating—and rebranding—registers of poetic language associated with the ballad revival.

One simple way to illustrate the convergence of kitsch and modernism is to take a fresh look at the inaugural icon of Anglo-American poetic modernism: Pound's two-line (or three, counting the title) poem, "In a Station of the Metro":

> The apparition of these faces in the crowd:
> Petals on a wet, black bough.[4]

Most critics and readers see this poem as an archetype of poetic modernism, as exemplifying the basic principles of Imagism: direct treatment of the thing, "austere" diction (exhibiting "hardness and gauntness," as Pound asserts), and a commitment to use as few words as possible.[5] While the "Metro" poem fulfills the latter requirement, the words it does employ (except for the title) are hardly gaunt, austere, or even direct (unless one sees the poem as simply a description of a crowd next to a blossoming tree). But clearly the diction of the poem suggests more: it conjures a dappled vision of the underworld.

The vocabulary of the poem is unmistakably poetic in a prescriptive sense but also quite fashionable and up to date: anyone familiar with early twentieth-century tastes in poetry will recognize the "Metro" poem as an orientalist tableau, whittled down—for the sake of "brevity"—to haiku-like form, and inserted in a modern, urban setting.[6] A less "austere" example of Pound's chinoiserie from the same period (a bit later, actually) can be found in the poems he "translated" for *Cathay* (1915), including a passage from "The Jewel Stairs' Grievance":

> The jeweled steps are already quite white with dew,
> It is so late that the dew soaks my gauze stockings.
> And I let down the crystal curtain
> And watch the moon through the clear autumn.[7]

A close reader of Pound's pre-Imagist poetry will recognize the "Metro" poem as a variant of what Pound calls "the vision of the blossom," which appears in his poetry as early as 1909:

> . . . the perfect faces which I see at times
> When my eyes are closed—
> Faces fragile, pale, yet flushed a little,
>   like petals of a rose.[8]

Yet another variant of what he calls elsewhere "peach-trees in magical blossom" appears in an early draft of the first few cantos (five years after the "Metro" poem): "the thousand-year peach trees shed their flakes/into the stream, out of a former time."[9]

Taking into account the persistent aestheticism of the "vision of the blossom" in Pound's poetry, describing the "Metro" poem as a fine example of orientalist kitsch is no less appropriate than describing it as an icon of modernist poetics. It would not therefore be inaccurate to assert that much of Pound's Imagist verse shares certain disreputable properties with, for example, the saturated lyrics of Djuna Barnes's Decadent modernism (written during the same period as the span of the Imagist campaign, 1913-1916). This correspondence suggests that the parameters of the tiny canon of Imagist verse should perhaps be re-defined, not to mention the basic presumptions that we hold about Pound's writing of poetic Imagism.

Taking a somewhat broader perspective, acknowledging the phantasmic aspect of the "Metro" poem (a vision of apparitional figures in the underworld), it becomes impossible to isolate it from a massive formation of necrophilic imagery and diction distributed throughout Pound's early poetry prior to the formal proclamations of Imagism in 1913. Well over a third of the poems in Pound's first six books of poetry (76 of 214 poems in the *Collected Early Poems*) treat the subject of death in a manner echoing the poetry of the pre-Raphaelites and of the Decadent poets Ernest Dowson, Arthur Symons, and Lionel Johnson. Pound later referred to the sum of his early poems as "a collection of stale cream puffs" (*CEP* 314). The poems abound with eroticized references to tombs, ghosts, cadavers, murder, suicide—all staged with a marvelous array of furnishings from various defunct cultures (ancient Egypt or China, medieval France and Italy).

More importantly, the diction of these tender and frequently luxurious tableaux echoes the depleted charm of poetic kitsch, as in the following passage from "Dance Figure," a poem set in an Egyptian tomb:

Gilt turquoise and silver are in thy place of rest
O Nathat-Ikanaie . . .
Thine arms are as a young sapling under the bark;
Thy face as a river of lights. (*P* 91)

In another poem, the reader finds a portrait of the melancholy "singer" haunting the crypt:

Poor wearied singer at the gates of death
Taking thy slender sweetness from the breath
Of the singers of old time.[10]

A sketch of the poet—not uncommon in Pound's crypt poetry—frequently offers a glimpse of Pound's insular and retrospective poetic program:

They tell me to 'Mirror my age'
God pity the age if I do it,
Perhaps I myself would prefer
To sing of the dead and the buried . . .
I sing of risorgimenti
Of old things found that were hidden.[11]

It is not simply that Pound sings of "the dead and the buried" but that he sings, as the previous citation indicates, with "the breath / Of the singers of old time"— that is, with their words, with the diction, the phrases, of the poetic tradition.

In this sense, the exquisite melodrama of Pound's crypt poetry offers a repertoire of stock figures and phrases, but it is also a veiled example of commonplace methods, of the immobilization of poetic language that lies at the heart of kitsch. At moments in Pound's cryptology, a correlation emerges between the poet's idolatrous stance towards poetic phraseology and the namelessness, or anonymity, of that language:

I die in the tears of the morning,
I kiss the wail of the dead . . .
Exquisite, alone, untrammeled
I kiss the nameless sign
And the laws of my inmost being
Chant to the nameless shrine.[12]

Evoking the varieties of funerary and epigraphic poetry fashionable in the eighteenth century, Pound appears to draw a connection between the impersonal "laws" of the poet's "inmost being" and the stultifying, memorial phrases of the epitaph, the gravestone. From this perspective, Pound's crypt poetry, which supplies at once the protocols of imposture and the epitaphic charm of the "Metro" poem, sustains and renews a conservative program of poetry haunted by the past, a program that will survive, despite Pound's best efforts to kill it off, into the composition of the *Cantos*.

The "Metro" poem is contaminated, without question, by the tastes Pound acquired during his long apprenticeship in the gloomy, exquisite—but often rather silly—conservatory of the dead. At the same time, the "Metro" poem emerges, in more familiar fashion, as a new kind of icon directed against the cult of the dead: a slender blade to be driven through the heart of the "corpse language" (as Pound calls it) of his own youthful poetry.[13] Humphrey Carpenter, for example, describes Pound's book, *Canzoni* (1911)—published shortly before the emergence of Imagism—as "the last twitch of a poetic corpse."[14] But corpse language—which survives in the replicant idiom of Imagism itself—is hard to kill off. In fact, the Imagist movement—a rather hasty campaign—was only the first in a series of failed attempts by Pound to arrest the infection of corpse language in his own poetry.

Not long after the first public explanations of Imagism, Pound backed away from the belletristic emblem of the Image as a Chinese ideogram, acknowledging implicitly the ambiguity and "softness" of the original stance (embodied in the "Metro" poem). A more forceful approach was required. Within a year of the Imagist manifesto, he converted Imagism into Vorticism and seized on the more dynamic emblem of the "vortex" as a means of heralding his campaign against the "mushiness" and "putrefaction" of corpse language. Yet the poetry and translations that Pound published during the period of his association with Vorticism (especially the seminal translations of Chinese and Japanese poetry in *Cathay* and *Lustra*) continued to display the resonant and elegiac diction of his early poetry. Alluding to a series of failed interventions, Pound described *Lustra* (1916), his first book of poems after launching the Imagist movement, as "absolutely the *last* obsequies of the Victorian period" (*L* 23). It was not, however, to be his last attempt to put the past behind him.

A significant new axis emerged in Pound's Vorticist polemic against "corpse language"—an orientation that would come to dominate his final attempts to rid his poetry of "putrefaction" and dissolution. In the first issue of the Vorticist magazine, *BLAST*, in 1914, Pound gave a new emphasis to his attack on what he calls "rhetoric" in the arts: "Hedonism," he declares, "is

the vacant place of the vortex."[15] Indulgent pleasure thus occupies the vacant crypt of the modernist Image (conceived as a vortex). At the same time,
the vortex consumes the regime of vacuous pleasures, whose object—we
must bear in mind—is the corpse language of poetry conceived and consumed in perpetual twilight. Equating corpse language with "hedonism"—
with complacent pleasure—not only acknowledges the libidinal and trifling
nature of Pound's poetic cryptology, it confirms the correlation of corpse
language and kitsch. Even more significantly, insofar as hedonism occupies
the dead center of the vortex—of modernist poetics—Pound's cryptology
of the modernist Image (targeting the insidious corpse language of late Victorian poetry) bears a striking resemblance to Hermann Broch's Gothic topology of kitsch as "a foreign body lodged in the system of art."

Pound's polemic against hedonism—exemplified by the effete pleasures of
"beauty" corrupted by the marketplace—receives its fullest treatment in the
long poem "Hugh Selwyn Mauberley," published in 1920: a work described by
one critic as an "elaborate autopsy" of the Imagist period (which we must now
see as spanning the years 1908-1920).[16] The poem chronicles the etiolated existence (and apparent suicide) of Mauberley, a poet whose passivity and languid
sensibility stand in contrast to the virility and pragmatism of another writer in
the poem, "E.P." Six years, then, after condemning poetic hedonism in *BLAST*,
Pound is still trying to bury the figure of the hyperaesthetic, pleasure-loving
poet. More than any other document in Pound's long, futile campaign against
corpse language and hedonism, "Hugh Selwyn Mauberley" draws explicit comparisons between poetic and cultural manifestations of kitsch.

Mauberley is said to practice "an art in profile": his "fundamental
passion"—a passion without passion—dwindles in his poetry to

> This urge to convey the relation
> Of eye-lid to cheekbone
> By verbal manifestation;
> To present the series
> Of curious heads in Medallion (*P* 198, 200).

Mauberley's poetic sensibility is consistent, Pound infers, with "the age" he
inhabits and its taste for kitsch: "a tawdry cheapness / Shall outlive our days
. . . / We see *to kalon* / Decreed in the marketplace" (*P* 186-187). In these lines,
a perfume marketed in Pound's day under the name of the ancient Greek
word for "beauty" (*to kalon*) becomes a symbol for the antithesis of modernist values in poetry, a symbol condemned ultimately by the obituarian

aspect of the poem—and exemplified by the art of the pseudo-Imagist Mauberley: "The 'age demanded' chiefly a mould in plaster" (*P* 186). Ultimately, in "Hugh Selwyn Mauberley," death captures the poet who is captive to pleasure (especially the "tawdry" pleasure of kitsch). Mauberley's epitaph, evoking the Vorticist polemic Pound had initiated six years earlier, reads, "I was / And I no more exist; / Here drifted / An hedonist" (*P* 203).

Although "Hugh Selwyn Mauberley" condemns Mauberley's hyperaesthetic sensibility, the language of the poem frequently succumbs to the forbidden allure of poetic kitsch:

> Thick foliage
> Placid beneath warm suns
> Tawn fore-shores
> Washed in cobalt oblivions (*P* 201).

In another passage,

> The coral isle, the lion-coloured sand
> Burst in upon the porcelain revery:
> Impetuous troubling
> Of his imagery (*P* 199).

The fact that Mauberley is both an image-maker and a self-destructive addict of beauty suggests that Pound's early crypt poetry, which we must now, by analogy with Mauberley's art, regard as kitsch, is one of the hidden wellsprings of Imagism. Furthermore, it is Mauberley's death—some would say suicide—in the poem from an excess of pleasure that establishes the terms for a phantasmic revival of kitsch in the *Cantos*.

Contraband

By the time Pound published "Hugh Selwyn Mauberley" in 1920, he had already composed and published drafts (in 1918) of several cantos. The contradictory stance toward kitsch evident in "Mauberley"—alternately condemning it and yielding to its vacuous pleasure—became the model for the episodic incorporation of kitsch into the *Cantos*. Pound quietly renounced the possibility—betraying his own modernist principles—of an absolute embargo on kitsch in the *Cantos*. Ultimately, kitsch finds a permanent place in the *Cantos*: it functions as a poetic substance—a form of contraband—that can be admitted in part through the practice, or romance, of translation—that is, by summoning various archaic personae. In effect,

the open structure of the *Cantos*—produced by what Pound called the ideogrammic method of composition—became a kind of smuggler's paradise.

The many passages in the *Cantos* that betray the rhapsodic sensibility
of kitsch frequently occur at the three principal sites of Pound's historical
imagination (which he calls the "*phantastikon*"): medieval Italy or France,
ancient China, and Greek (or Roman) antiquity. Often, the scenes mix details and references to several places or cultures at once, as in this Chinese
tableau (from Canto 20) alluding to the Roman god of sleep:

> Plain, as the plain of Somnus,
> > the heavy cars, as a triumph,
> Gilded, heavy on wheel,
> > and the panthers chained to the cars,
> Over the suave turf, the form wrapped,
> Rose, crimson, deep crimson,
> And, in the blue dusk, a colour as of rust in the sunlight.[17]

The Hellenic version of this scene usually involves some nudity, lots of
water, and perhaps a peep at a pagan god:

> Bathing the body of nymphs, and Diana,
> Nymphs, white-gathered about her, and the air, air,
> Shaking, air alight with the goddess,
> Fanning their hair in the dark. (Canto 4, *C* 14)

Other variations of these bucolic and naughty tableaux (with the Tech-
nicolor palette of a Fairfield Porter poster) may combine a bit of chinoiserie, a vision of a dead Italian queen in a Mongol court, or a Troubadour poet
floating in a pagan landscape:

> Ivory rigid in sunlight
> And the pale clear of the heaven
> Phoibos of narrow thighs,
> The cut cool of the air,
> Blossom cut on the wind, by Helios
> Lord of the Light's edge, and April
> Blown round the feet of the God. (Canto 29, *C* 145)

As these passages indicate, the language of epic kitsch is highly eclectic and
ambiguous in its provenance: an artificial language to render an artificial
paradise.

The eruptions of kitsch into the text of the *Cantos* are frequent and unmistakable; the diction of these passages, usually no more than half a dozen lines, betrays immediately an air of languid and fugitive pleasure. The early cantos in particular are thickly strewn with rhapsodic fragments of pseudo-medieval, Attic, or pan-orientalist embroidery, yet the distinctive tonality of kitsch surfaces at moments throughout the *Cantos*. The spare lines of the final canto (Canto 120) betray the essentially passive, libidinal, and paradisiacal inclination of kitsch:

I have tried to write Paradise

Do not move
    Let the wind speak
        that is paradise (Canto 120, *C* 803).

This confession is Pound's final statement on a subject of considerable controversy within the *Cantos*. In the Pisan cantos (written while Pound was incarcerated immediately following World War II in a temporary prison compound in Italy), Pound repeats the French phrase "Le Paradis n'est pas artificiel" six times—first in Canto 74 and for the last time in Canto 83 (*C* 438, 528).

The lines I have cited from Canto 120 appear to complicate and perhaps even contradict Pound's mantra in the Pisan cantos. This is not surprising, since Pound's repeated disavowal of Baudelaire's project of writing *Les paradis artificiels* should be understood, contrary to the opinion of most critics, not as a reiteration of the presumed ethos of the *Cantos* (epic *realism*) but as a stammering confession of his own failure to write an artificial "Paradise" (with a capital "P")—a stern self-rebuke, precipitated only by his incarceration as a POW. Pound here identifies—and renounces—the unifying aim of his experimental epic. The *Cantos* had always been, he admits in these dire circumstances, a grandiose and catastrophic attempt "to write Paradise": a Baudelairean project—but without irony or deliberate perversion.

As evidence of his attempt to "write Paradise," the intermittent spells of kitsch in the *Cantos* function, along with the didactic sampling of discursive texts (starting in the middle cantos), as indispensable ingredients in what would eventually become a Fascist, totalitarian epic. Manifestations of kitsch in the vast middle section of the poem (where Pound overtly aligns his poem with Italian Fascism) tend to coalesce in individual cantos devoted entirely to voluptuous fantasy, which serve as counterpoint to the ranting of the didactic cantos (unlike the hybrid texture of individual cantos in the first third of the epic). Ultimately, the allure of kitsch remains irresistible to Pound throughout the poem. The steady recrudescence of kitsch in the *Cantos*—from beginning to end—provides evidence of a sustained ensemble of aesthetic and ideological principles advancing (or devolving) throughout Pound's work: from crypt poetry to Imagism to paradisiacal epic, from Decadent modernism to Fascist utopia.

Remarkably, in what one may call a "spectroscopic" analysis of the *Cantos*, matching the profile of Keats's "silver planet" (as well as Warhol's "silver factory"), one detects a silver substance or hue—marking the fugitive presence of kitsch—cast inscrutably over the whole of the *Cantos*. The synthetic (and synthesizing) properties of this atmospheric substance can be traced to Pound's early poetry, where one discovers it (in a poem titled "The Alchemist," for example) in the "pallor of silver" and the "pale lustre" of the charlatan's elusive profile (*CEP* 226). Even as it symbolizes the fetishized materials of Pound's borrowed diction, the color silver subtly infuses the ornamental nature of Pound's monotonous "planet": the floating world of kitsch is laced with references to "silver shafts," "silver harness," and "silver hounds"; to the "silver of the leaf," to "a silver reed," and "the silver rustling of the wheat" (*P* 20, 138, 70, 71, 58).

In the *Cantos*, where the alchemy of kitsch continues to operate in unexpected ways, a panoply of the elemental silver emerges: the color of epiphany and even of epic poetry. The first thirty cantos in particular betray a fascination with silver as a promiscuous medium consisting of air, water, and light—with mercurial substances and reflections:

> The silver mirrors catch the bright stones and flare,
> Dawn, to our waking, drifts in the cool green light;
> Dew-haze blurs, in the grass, pale ankles moving (Canto 4, *C* 13).

Veiled by the color silver, the body—even the landscape—disappears and returns under a spell:

> And in the water, the almond-white swimmers,
> The silvery water glazes the upturned nipple (Canto 3, *C* 11).

Or, more abstractly:

> Lifting, lifting and waffing:
> Ivory dipping in silver
> Shadow'd, o'ershadow'd
> Ivory dipping in silver (Canto 4, *C* 14).

The archaic elisions employed here are part of the same verbal fabric in which the word "silver" appears and reappears as the index of a lost world, as a talismanic substance, a reflective yet crepuscular medium, unifying the disparate worlds of Pound's epic:

Where memory liveth
  it takes its state
Formed like a diafan from light on shade
Which shadow cometh of Mars (Canto 36, *C* 177).

The silvery, diaphanous "state" of memory summoned here by Pound (in a translation of Cavalcanti) is at once the languid totality of a poetic "silver planet" and a violent utopia ("Which shadow cometh of Mars"). Even as late as Canto 41, which begins with Pound handing over a copy of his poem to Mussolini (a moment of Fascist idolatry), things appear "frosted with silver" (Canto 41, *C* 204). Yet in the final cantos, where one finds Pound pitting "Disney against the metaphysicals" (kitsch vs. labored conceit), Pound sides with Disney: the slippery substance of "silver" veers between "the crystal body of air" (the poem's body) and "a little light, like a rushlight/to lead back to splendor."[18] The "poor, wearied singer" returns to the Magic Castle.

The Kitsch of Apocalypse

Clearly, the gulf between the loftiness of the epic genre (as an emblem of high modernism) and the triviality of kitsch (a contrast dependent on the ideology of formalism, which favors novelty, privation, and complex patterning without ornamentation) presents a significant obstacle to any thesis asserting the importance of kitsch in the fabric of the *Cantos*. One way of addressing this disjunction is to identify a counterargument *within* the discourse of modernism—and within the *Cantos*—for an esoteric form of kitsch consistent with the principles of high modernism. From this counterperspective, for example, Christmas tree ornaments painted with Hitler's portrait belong in the same aesthetic domain as the runic insignia of the SS uniform; likewise, the aggressively modernist installations of the 1932 Fascist exhibition in Rome provide the context for processions of Italian youth dressed in togas. The sources of these two ostensibly divergent modalities of kitsch are identical: the cryptology of myth, nostalgia, and death.

In the context of Pound's work, the spirit of modernist, totalitarian kitsch emerges from Mauberley's grave: the cult of beauty revives as a formal paradigm of "possession," modeled after the tropes of ethnographic collecting and symbolized by the principle of *paideuma*—a discourse that Pound appropriated from the German ethnographer Leo Frobenius (as I will explain in greater detail below). According to this paradigm, the Fascist poet is possessed not simply by objects of beauty (though that experience, too, persists in the *Cantos*) but by "dead" objects charged with mythological significance, which the poet has rescued from a distracted modernity and arranged in a collection according to the esoteric and didactic impulses of Pound's aesthetic ideology. This collection is itself a monadic "image" (in the sense that a museum collection is an image) of a Fascist utopia. The anachronistic and totalitarian features of kitsch become evident in the *Cantos* not merely through the sentimental or rhapsodic effect of some of its images but, by implication, through the praxis of collecting that governs the *Cantos*. This collection provides in turn a simulacrum of the mythological community to which the nostalgic images refer. Pound's poetic praxis in the *Cantos* thus fuses kitsch and high modernism most obviously in its atavistic seizures of pre-Raphaelite beauty (which occur like blackouts in the experimental ethos of the text), yet also in its sometimes hysterical impulse to display its verbal booty, its contraband, its sentimental treasure. In addition, directly imitating the kitsch sensibility of certain kinds of Fascist propaganda, sections of the later cantos use melodrama and simplistic myths to mobilize support for the Italian Fascist regime.

A cryptological account of kitsch first emerged in the analysis of Hermann Broch, who associates kitsch with "that atmosphere of quite indecent necrophilia which so largely dominates Romantic literature."[19] More recently, the historian Saul Friedländer has examined the necrophilic dimension of kitsch, as well as its nostalgic character, in relation to Fascist culture. In an essay on kitsch and the apocalyptic imagination, he refers to "the use of kitsch and death motives in representations meant to exercise the past by re-invoking its specific kind of fascination."[20] In his seminal work, *Reflections of Nazism: An Essay on Kitsch and Death*, Friedländer develops a conception of what he calls "kitsch of the apocalypse," and observes, "The paradox of kitsch and modernity is that kitsch is often an antimodern face of modernity."[21] Further, he claims, "kitsch death is a means to digest the past" (40), signaling "a cult of primitive and archaic values" (33). Thus he associates kitsch with "exorcism" and the "work of mourning" (85)—an *aberrant* mourning that calls to mind the permutations of Pound's fascination with death in his early poetry. Friedländer's necrological and apocalyptic reading of kitsch focuses on the phenomenon of myth, which he defines as "a footprint, an echo of lost worlds, haunting an imagination invaded by excessive rationality and thus becoming the crystallization point for thrusts of the archaic and the irrational" (49). "Kitsch," he argues, "is a debased form of myth, but nevertheless draws from the mythic substance" (49).

Quite clearly, Friedländer's understanding of kitsch, as it appears in the context of Fascist culture, calls to mind many of the features of Pound's archaism, as well as the more specific features of his mythological revision of the poetic ideogram (which occurs under the spell of Fascism, in concert with the ethnographic doctrine of paideuma)—a revision I will examine more fully below. Although Friedländer echoes the formalist condemnation of kitsch as contingent on unreflective, immediate emotional response, he also lays the groundwork, through his conception of myth, for a theory of high kitsch, of esoteric kitsch, which would help to account for Pound's Fascist modernism. He refers, for example, to "the pseudo-spirituality that envelops such kitsch, finding there constant exploitations of esotericism and mystery as well as the no less frequent evocation of the universe of legends and myths" (46). He also notes that "the kitsch of death, of destruction, of apocalypse, is a special kitsch, a representation of reality that does not integrate into the vision of ordinary kitsch" (26)—not at first glance, one must add. Friedländer is referring here to the ostensible gulf between the triviality of kitsch and its apocalyptic aspects—a division that is breached in Pound's elaboration of poetic kitsch. A variant of Friedländer's historiographic model, which presents kitsch as a phenomenon that is *alternately* immediate or esoteric, Pound views myth—the modernist matrix of high kitsch—as being implicated simultaneously in the mundane details of totality and in a secretive doctrine. For Pound, myth (like kitsch) is at once brutally obvious and mysterious in its function: a veritable black box of aesthetic production.

The mythological dimension of kitsch becomes fully operative in the *Cantos* when its two modalities—low and high, vulgar and refined, immediate and esoteric—coincide. While works of reactionary modernism such as the *Cantos* may invoke the hierarchies implicit in the concept of kitsch (vulgar and refined, muddled and clear), they also call into question such distinctions; hence, the esoteric mode of kitsch, which submits the "possessive" logic of the collection to the principles of high modernism, aspires to complete transparency and immediacy (just as the obscurity of the poetic ideogram is actually an effect of a positivist doctrine of unmediated presentation). Cantos 72 and 73, originally published in 1945 but withheld from the standard edition of the *Cantos* until 1987, offer an illustration of the synthesis of these two aspects of kitsch. Written by Pound in Italian and published in an official newspaper of the Fascist Salò Republic near the end of the war, these cantos represent some of the most blatant and simplistic material Pound wrote in support of the Fascist regime.[22] They fulfill to a remarkable degree Friedländer's thesis that "kitsch related to death scenes and ceremonies of sacrifice seems to be at the very core of a certain type of extreme political motivation."[23] That is, these cantos display the basic features of "ordinary" kitsch (stereotype and sentiment) placed in the service of a totalitarian regime (a function of kitsch emphasized as well by Broch) and permeated by an atmosphere of death.

The fact that these cantos were written and published in Italian indicates Pound's desire to present these emblematic narratives to what he imagined to be his immediate audience (the Italian populace) as directly as possible (in a manner recalling his eccentric notions about the transparency of archaism in the ballad) and thereby demonstrating his steadfast commitment to Italian Fascism in its final, desperate hours. Canto 72 presents the poet absorbed in a visitation from the underworld by three ghosts, including the recently deceased Fascist and leader of the Futurist movement, F. T. Marinetti. Pound's former nemesis, whose Fascist views have apparently softened Pound's antagonistic stance towards Futurism, asks Pound to lend him his body so that he may continue fighting for the Fascist cause—a bizarre episode of body snatching which serves well as a curious emblem of late modernism.

Canto 73 presents a related scenario, with considerably less ambiguity concerning its political aims: Pound receives a dream-like visitation from Cavalcanti's ghost, who tells Pound (and the reader) what is supposed to be an uplifting tale of heroism from the battlefront of World War II. The story involves an Italian peasant girl, "un po' tozza ma bella" (a little stocky, but pretty), who meets a group of Canadian soldiers in the Italian countryside with several German prisoners in tow, scouting for stray enemy combatants in the final months of the Allied cleanup in northern Italy. The girl, a Fascist partisan, leads the Canadian outfit into a minefield, where she and the Canadians are killed, while the German prisoners escape to fight once more. The poet celebrates the girl's heroism, claiming, "The brave young girl's spirit/was singing, singing with joy/. . . Glory of the Fatherland!/Glory! Glory/To die for the Fatherland/in Romagna!/The dead are not dead" (*C* 440-441).

This melodramatic narrative exemplifies, without qualification, the features of what Friedländer calls the "kitsch of apocalypse," seeking to elicit
from its audience, through mythical scenes of death and sacrifice, an emotional, unreflective response. (More specifically, Canto 73, in particular, clearly
aims to mobilize support for the German-backed Salò government.) At the
same time, however, the dramatic setting of these cantos—a conversation with
the dead—cannot help but recall the interview with the dead in Canto 1
that inaugurates the *Cantos*, thereby suggesting that these cantos, inspired
by Fascism, subscribe in an obvious way to the impulse guiding the *Cantos*
as a whole. There is also a formal continuity: these cantos are composed
according to the high modernist principles of the ideogrammic method.
Canto 72, in particular, like the cantos that precede it, is fragmentary, al-
lusive, and didactic. Restored to its place within the *Cantos*, Canto 72 follows the last of the Adams cantos, which are composed almost entirely of
citations from other texts and therefore provide a good example of Pound's
textual foraging—under the guise of the ideogram—at its most extreme.
Canto 72 thus sustains the logic of preservation, accumulation, and display
that informs the collection of curiosities stored in the *Cantos*: in addition to
Fascist ghost stories, Canto 72 serves up familiar and scurrilous references
to Churchill and usury, to medieval history and the "mysterious bed of divine Isotta," to Confucius and Gemisto (musty figures from the repertoire of
Pound's allegorical imagination).

   In this context, Friedländer theorizes that "cumulation is a characteristic
of kitsch," that the language of kitsch is "one of accumulation, repetition
and redundancy: a massive use of synonyms, an excess of similar epithets,
a play of images sent back, in turn, from one to the other in echoes without end."[24] The phenomena of accumulation and "possession" are central
not only to the ideogrammic logic of the collection but to the rhapsodic
and repetitive matrix of poetic kitsch. Despite the ostensible opposition
between avant-garde and kitsch, the esotericism, allusiveness, and formal
complexity of high modernism are not necessarily antithetical to kitsch. Indeed, as Clement Greenberg contends, these avant-garde strategies are easily appropriated by the "system" of kitsch—a condition suggesting that the
Cantos should be regarded as an unstable amalgam of avant-garde and kitsch
combined in a single poetic monument.[25] In Pound's case, the totalitarian
scope of kitsch coincides with the cryptic dimension of Imagism in poetry
(its kitschy preoccupation with death) just as the transparency of kitsch in
the *Cantos* may be viewed as the "afterlife" of literary positivism—an after-

life shrouded in secrecy, violence, and "racial" memory. Indeed, the dialectical relation between modernist and collector helps to explain the surprising
lack of tension or incongruity as the poem moves from the ideogrammic
construction of Canto 72 to the Fascist parable of Canto 73. On one level,
this parable of death is simply one more "curiosity" in the excessive and
nostalgic collection of the *Cantos*, yet it is also, in its susceptibility to complex ideological diversions, a parable not only of Pound's strange modernist
"museum" but of the forms of "possession" on which it is founded and to
which it is a monument.

Epic, Rhapsody, Seizure

Friedländer's modeling of what he calls "kitsch-death," or "kitsch of the
apocalypse," offers a rationale for asserting the continuity of the aesthetic
ideology of the *Cantos*. First, it demonstrates beyond a shadow of a doubt
that poetic kitsch is an elemental feature of Fascist epic and, further, that
the polarized surface of the *Cantos* in its early stages, accommodating kitsch
within the experimental structure of montage, must be read as consistent
with its later development into a Fascist, totalitarian epic. Second, Friedländer's cryptological model of kitsch, grounded in myth, nostalgia, and
millenarianism, provides a conceptual framework for identifying kitsch as
a submerged paradigm linking Pound's early "necrophiliast" poetry and his
visions of Fascist apocalypse. Taking Friedländer's model a step beyond the
boundaries it observes, the example of the *Cantos* confounds the formalist
opposition of avant-garde and kitsch, of lofty epic and cultish trivia.

The ambiguous meaning of the word *epos* in the Greek lexicon lends surprising support to the hypothetical substance of epic kitsch. Although, in its
most rudimentary sense, *epos* means simply "word," it is not at all clear what
sort of word it denotes. The kind of totality associated with *epos* as a poetic
phenomenon must (if we take into account the Greek translation of the bib-
lical Genesis) be quite unlike that intrinsic to *logos*. "In the beginning," one
does not find the *epos*. Logos is the more abstract term, meaning "concept"
or "thought," as well as "word." *Epos*, by contrast, is more concrete, more
deliberately concerned with the powers of language in particular. Beyond
the root meaning of "word," *epos* in Greek can mean "a pledged word" (I give
you my word), personal "counsel" (a word to the wise), a proverbial saying,
an oracle, poetry in its entirety, or the particular genre of epic poetry.[26]
Some of these definitions possess a pragmatic (as in speech-act theory) or
persuasive—even charismatic—dimension. As for the idea that epic verse

may be charismatic—oracle and proverb—it is useful to bear in mind that Pound, in addition to describing the *Cantos* as "the tale of the tribe" and epic as "a poem containing history," also referred to Dante's *Divine Comedy* (his primary model for epic) as "a cycle of mystery plays."[27]

The idea that an epic poem is, for Pound, "a cycle of mystery plays" is helpful in explaining the modus operandi of the *Cantos*, an epic addicted to the mesmerizing effect of kitsch and, as the poem develops, to utilizing kitsch (and other textual accessories) to sweeten the mythical dimension of Fascist utopia. At the same time, the poetic strategies generating this matrix of irrationalism and populism can be defined more precisely by examining the compositional principles shared by epic poetry and kitsch. It is common knowledge, for example, that the Homeric epics are founded on a matrix of poetic formulae, epithets, and commonplace phrases. The Homeric singer, or rhapsode (from a Greek verb meaning "to stitch together"), arranges and re-arranges this repertoire of formulae in a manner of composition that finds little need for poetic originality.[28] This anti-subjective mode of composition, combined with epic poetry's fidelity to collective rather than individual experience, forms the basis of epic's enduring profile as a genre of poetry distinguished by the communal nature of its verbal materials, as well as its modes of production and reception. The ultimate goal of epic poetry—to produce a vision of the totality of a particular culture—cannot be achieved without *arresting poetry* and its drive towards particularity and originality, without immobilizing the renovation of poetic materials (from epithet and metaphor to historical narrative). In order to see the whole picture, to reveal the unseen horizon of a "nation" (however limited), poetry must come to a standstill. Epic verse—in terms drawn from its own technicity—organizes the structure and teleology of its verbal materials according to the function of two of poetry's most basic techniques: caesura and refrain (forms of poetic suspense that function at once as interruption and repetition).

The basic criteria of epic poetry exhibit a basic affinity with a model of kitsch grounded in the replication of poetic clichés and commonplace phrases—with a mode of poetry that spurns originality, particularity, and subjectivity. Poetic kitsch and epic both function according to the logic of the refrain—a poetic seizure—by ceaselessly replicating their verbal materials and therefore arresting the development of poetic diction. Epic poetry, insofar as its formulaic composition may be regarded as a kind of prehistory of the invention of modern poetic clichés, could not exist without a verbal matrix of something resembling poetic kitsch. Conversely, modern kitsch is "epic" in its lack of originality, its impersonality, and its rendering of social totality as a closed language. Both genres—kitsch and epic—are poetic categories anchored in the practice and sociology of replication. From this perspective, the shared principles of kitsch and epic poetry are essential— as Brecht's concept of "epic theater" suggests—to the fate of mass culture and political solidarity.[29]

The role of nationalism in shaping epic poetry into a vision of social and cultural totality is of course axiomatic, starting with *The Iliad* and extending to William Carlos Williams's *Paterson*. Yet nationalism is equally important as a principal site for the utilization of kitsch in the service of cultural and political solidarity. This convergence manifests itself in the political knick-knacks and ephemera produced to support all nation-states (including fascist regimes). Correspondingly, in a poetic vein, the sentimental tableaux, the emblematics, and the phraseology of the *Cantos* demonstrate its commitment to the Italian Fascist state.

Closer to home, the congruence of kitsch and nationalism is frequently on display in the national hymns sung (after a coin toss) as prelude or coda to public sporting events:

> O say can you see by the dawn's early light,
> What so proudly we hailed at the twilight's last gleaming
> Whose broad stripes and bright stars through the perilous fight,
> O'er the ramparts we watched were so gallantly streaming!

Sampling the kitsch of "The Star-Spangled Banner" and its references to "bombs bursting in air," it is only appropriate to mention that Ossian's *Fragments of Ancient Poetry*—the most influential poetic forgery in history and a crucial text in the development of kitsch—is an epic closely linked to the rise of Scottish nationalism. James Macpherson claimed that the poetry of Ossian was an ancient epic poem recounting the exploits of the Gaelic hero Fingal (a name said to mean—how Gothic!—"white stranger"):

> Ghost of Fingal! do thou, from thy cloud
> direct Comala's bow. Let him fail
> like the hart of the desert. It is Fingal
> in the crowd of ghosts.
> Raise ye bards, the song;
> raise the wars of the streamy Carun![30]

154 My Silver Planet

It is also the case that one of the longest texts in Thomas Chatterton's pseudo-medieval forgeries is an epic of some 1300 lines, *The Battle of Hastings*. Kitsch, forgery, and nationalism are familiar friends (or false friends).

Surveying the verbal patterns produced by the ideogrammic composition of the *Cantos*—a text assembled according to the principle of montage—Pound's repetition of foreign phrases, fixed epithets, and stock situations in the *Cantos* (a deliberate and insistent *phraseology*) subscribes at once to the methodologies of epic and kitsch. Repetitive procedures of this kind sustain the didactic and propagandistic aims of epic (which are essential to the *Cantos*), even as they induce the lulling effects of kitsch—the rhapsodic and rumorous operation of Pound's translational personae. Indeed, only within the framework of epic kitsch can the disparate meanings of the term "rhapsody" be integrated: the *Cantos* is, on one hand, a rhapsody in the archaic sense that it is a poem "stitched together" from various epithets, catchphrases, and poetic clichés—a model identifying rhapsodic composition as the earliest form of montage. Yet the *Cantos* is also, at least in part, a rhapsody in the modern sense of the term: a poem animated—and unified—at moments by gusty feelings and formulaic language. Even more remarkably, the rhapsodic compound of epic kitsch in the *Cantos* appears to resolve the dialectical tension between montage and synthesis—a basic criterion of the presumed antithesis of avant-garde and kitsch.

Pound's early assessment of the rationale for writing a modern epic poem was accompanied (in 1922) by his reflections on the virtues of poetry (in contrast to prose) as the appropriate medium for epic: "Most good prose arises, perhaps, from an instinct of negation; is the detailed, convincing analysis of something detestable; of something which one wants to eliminate. Poetry is the assertion of a positive, i.e. of desire" (*LE* 324). With these views, Pound was participating in a larger public debate about the disparate values of poetry and prose that flourished as he was developing his own model for the *Cantos*. Georg Lukács's theory of modern epic (outlined in *The Theory of the Novel* in 1920) proceeds, by contrast, under the assumption that prose is the true medium of modern epic: "the novel is the epic of an age in which the extensive totality of life is no longer directly given, in which the immanence of the meaning of life has become the problem, yet which still thinks in terms of totality."[31] Both Pound and Lukács are thinking about epic as a means of engaging the problem of totality, but Pound considers prose to be essentially critical and reflective—limited in its capacity to motivate the reader to act historically or to envision new forms of totality. Poetry, Pound believes, is fundamentally libidinal, imaginative, motivational. Poetry, like prose, can yield images of an existing but submerged totality, but it can also produce holistic images of *paradise*: it can induce the reader—because poetry itself is designed to be pleasurable in subversive ways—not only to *desire* and envision paradise in earthly, social, or political forms but to strive to achieve it. From this perspective, Pound aims to exploit the pleasures associated with poetry to political ends, positioning it as rival to the pleasures of commodification (in its ability to conjure new worlds and incite the reader to work towards their realization).

Bad Infinity

In the *Cantos*, Pound synthesized the modalities of epic, kitsch, and avant-garde as a way of producing a utopian vision of cultural and political totality. By the mid-1930s, Pound had embraced Italian Fascism as a partial realization of this utopian vision, aligning the *Cantos* with Mussolini's regime and using his poem as an eccentric tool of Fascist propaganda. With alarming fluency, Pound assimilated his most fundamental poetic beliefs, innovations, and tastes (the theory of poetic personae, Imagism, Vorticism, the ideogrammic method, paideuma) to his newfound Fascist ideology. Even after the war, when Pound expressed some regret for his delusional views—when the last quarter of the *Cantos* were written—he found it nearly impossible to systematically isolate the core of his poetic values from the demonologies of Fascism and anti-Semitism. The autonomous modalities of kitsch and epic had become in Pound's poetry inalienable properties of Fascist ideology. The prospect of a modern, redemptive totality had reverted to archaic totalitarianism. On its own terms, as a poetic vision of utopia, the *Cantos* is a failure: it is not, as Pound claimed, "a poem containing history" but a poem containing, and consumed by, *myth*: by delusional, bourgeois myths—which Pound converts into neo-pagan "mysteries"—of class and racial hatred.

At the same time, the provisional motives and horizons of Pound's failed project should not be dismissed altogether. In order to isolate the mistakes he made as a poet struggling to forge a holistic vision—and to avoid repeating them—but also to salvage some tutelary value from the wreckage of the *Cantos* and to gauge the reparative powers of epic and kitsch, one must establish a context for the figurative strategies and auxiliary concepts Pound used to wed his poetic values to Fascist ideology. To do so effectively, one must acknowledge and try to understand how Pound's investment in the principles of collectivism and totality (via kitsch and epic) echo indirectly, and sometimes anticipate, certain features of the contemporaneous Marxist discourse of totality.

Pound, as I indicated earlier, began to explore the idea of epic (and totality) in his poetic program about the same time that Lukács sparked debate about these categories for Western Marxism in *The Theory of the Novel* (1920) and *History and Class Consciousness* (1923). For purely political reasons, of course, Lukács is an unlikely figure to use as an index for measuring the historical resonance of Pound's conceptions of totality, yet the convergence of some of their views on this topic is potentially revealing in a variety of ways. Pound's public migration towards totality and epic began somewhat earlier than Lukács's—shortly after the eruption of Vorticism in 1914—and can be understood more precisely, at least initially, in relation to the influence of the British anarchist poet-philosopher, T. E. Hulme. One discovers in Hulme's ideas (developed during a brief period before his death in World War I) the nucleus not only of Pound's efforts to modernize his own poetry (via the principles of Imagism) but also of a radicalized political profile that would only become fully evident in Pound's career when he began to gravitate towards Fascism. Hulme's influence on the poetics of Imagism is indisputable—and substantial—though not widely acknowledged: the concept of a modern, poetic "image"—and the first "imagist" poems—appeared in Hulme's work (prior to Pound's inauguration of the Imagist movement) between 1908 and 1910. Pound even published a small selection of Hulme's poems in his own volume of poetry, *Ripostes*, in 1912 and makes cryptic reference in an introductory note to a "'School of Images' which may or not have existed" (acknowledging obliquely Hulme's formulation of the image-concept at the Poets' Club in 1908).[32] Drafting what would become the archetypal terms of Anglo-American poetic modernism, Hulme called for a new aesthetic of discipline, restraint, and "dry hardness": Pound turned this renegade platform—with mixed results—into Imagism.[33]

Hulme was provocative as well and innovative—in Britain, at least—in the radicalism of his philosophical and political theories (in ways that seem completely unmoored from his equally revolutionary poetics).[34] Most importantly—and this is where Pound and Hulme may again converge—Hulme published in installments in A. R. Orage's socialist journal, *The New Age*, in 1915 (where Pound had been writing weekly columns since 1911) a translation of the incendiary anarcho-syndicalist text *Reflections on Violence*, by the French activist and thinker Georges Sorel.[35] Coinciding with Pound's commitment to the artistic militancy of Vorticism (exemplified by *BLAST*, the short-lived journal edited by Wyndham Lewis—who was also a Hulme disciple), Hulme's presentation of Sorel could not have gone unnoticed by Pound.

There are important reasons to contrast Pound and Sorel, who was anti-elitist and anti-Jacobinist to the core, as well as anti-statist. Pound, once he showed his Fascist colors, was none of these things. Yet the irrationalism of Sorel's socialist platform, with its discordant appeals to syndicalism, charismatic leadership, and secular religiosity, would have resonated with Pound's unstable amalgam of aesthetics and politics. Sorel's assertion of the holistic nature of socialist revolution served as an impetus for further development of the Marxist concept of totality, which found its most important theoretician in Lukács in the early 1920s.[36] Furthermore, Sorel's dynamic model of totality is crystallized in his concept of collective "social myths": historical yet necessarily irrational narratives or "pictures" that have the power to motivate masses of people (in accordance with a "general strike") to undertake spontaneous revolutionary actions.[37] Although Pound's conception of the transformational power of myth remained, unlike Sorel's, steadfastly rooted in religious feeling—with a reverence for the state as its primary historical dimension—the synthesis of myth, militancy, and poetic totality in the *Cantos* bears a notable resemblance to the Sorelian model introduced by Hulme into the turbulent context of the Vorticist movement. At the same time, Pound—unlike Hulme—lived long enough to find ways to integrate (via his commitment to Fascism in the 1930s) the analytic and synthetic registers cultivated by Hulme, to forge the atomized particulars of poetic Imagism into a charismatic and politicized vision of totality: a combinatory operation, an epic sleight of hand, yielding an unholy alliance of positivism and kitsch, realized on a gargantuan scale in the *Cantos*. Experiments in poetic diction involving—contrary to modernist orthodoxy—the verbal substance of kitsch became a permanent feature of Pound's modernist epic, thereby disclosing the latent correspondences between saturated diction, kitsch, and totality. He ended up producing something like what Hegel calls—in attempting to describe a boundless aggregation of disparate elements—a "bad infinity."[38]

Although Pound certainly intended the epic totality of the *Cantos* to be regarded (beginning in the 1930s) as a poetic analogue of Fascist culture, it is difficult, if not misleading, to separate categorically Pound's model of totality from its counterpart in Western Marxism. Historically, the political contamination of the idea of totality, which coincides with the repudiation of kitsch (and suspicion about the lulling effects of poetic diction), followed from the formation of deliberately totalitarian cultures in the 1930s. Yet the basic poetic and political features of the *Cantos* came into focus during the late 1910s and early 1920s—the same period that Marxist thinkers entered into fierce discussion about the nature of totality as a progressive idea and tested its validity as a theoretical and pragmatic framework. Even if Pound was not directly familiar with specifically Marxist theorizations of totality, his own thinking about epic and totality could not have escaped—via Hulme and Sorel—the spirit of an age that produced a burgeoning Marxist polemic on the subject. The era of high modernism was an era infatuated with the idea of totality in many forms.

By drawing attention to these correspondences, I do not wish to claim that the *Cantos* can somehow be redeemed as a crypto-Marxist text: Pound perverted his poem by making it serve the ends of Fascism, thereby sacrificing a potentially progressive experiment directing poetry towards overt political engagement. As a utopian vision of cultural unity, a progressive epic, the *Cantos* is a failure. But it is not an absolute failure—in the motives for some of its basic political aspirations. To condemn the *Cantos* as completely misguided in its use of poetic strategies toward political ends would be to reject categorically in a poetic context any possible creative or progressive application of the idea of totality. Furthermore, because recognition of kitsch as a mode of progressive political expression depends in part on its reciprocal relation with the concept of totality and the form of epic, the fate of poetic kitsch cannot be separated, in certain respects, from the vicissitudes of modern epic. One may condemn the susceptibility of epic to totalitarian values (and its suppression of difference or individuality) for the same reason that one ridicules the complete lack of originality and particularity in kitsch: generality and falsehood appear to be two sides of the same coin. Yet the revolutionary potential of epic and kitsch reside precisely in the enigma of the formulaic, the typical, the cliché—on the limitation, or suspension, of differences.

The medusal appeal of the "riddle" of totality (as David Hume refers to it) can be traced in the Marxist lineage of the concept. Most Western Marxists tend to agree that Marx was a holistic thinker, an orientation easily discernible from the frequent appearance of the word "totality" and other synonyms for the concept of the whole in his writings. For Marx, according to Martin Jay, "history was to be understood descriptively as a totality and normatively as promising a new totalization in the future."[39] More narrowly, the development of the kind of Marxist thinking that has proved historically germane to the humanities is inconceivable without the concept of totality. Lukács, who is largely responsible for making the concept philosophically respectable in European intellectual life, approached the question of totality initially through a reconsideration of epic and the modern novel's assimilation of that ancient genre. It is in his study *The Theory of the Novel* that Lukács first identifies totality as a concept pertinent specifically to the domain of culture, an orientation that would increasingly emphasize the cultural, rather than political or economic, matrix of totality. In *Theory of the Novel*, Lukács declares, "A totality of men and events is possible only on the basis of culture."[40]

In *History and Class Consciousness* (1923), Lukács develops the concept of totality at greater length in relation to political struggle, laying the groundwork for an astonishing proliferation of ideas on the topic by many of the most celebrated Marxist thinkers of the twentieth century. Renewing his insistence on the cultural framework of totality, yet shifting its significance to the core of Western Marxist methodology, Lukács declares,

> It is not the primacy of economic motives in historical explanation that constitutes the decisive difference between Marxism and bourgeois thought, but the point of totality. The category, the all-pervasive supremacy of the whole over the parts, is the essence of the method which Marx took over from Hegel and brilliantly transformed into the foundations of a wholly new science. *The primacy of the category of totality is the bearer of the principle of revolution.*[41]

Without a vigorous conception of *cultural* totality, Lukács contends, the imperative of economic and political revolution cannot advance.

The generalizing and synthetic properties of totality adumbrated by Lukács arise quite specifically in opposition to positivism, to Cartesian rationalism and, generally, to modes of analytic reasoning that lead to the atomization of experience or knowledge. Totality is thus essentially speculative or synthetic in nature; it presumes the operation of dialectical reasoning (as the subtitle of Lukács's book indicates), of mediation and reflection, to produce a plausible image of the whole. Indeed, through the lens of Lukács's dialectical approach, it is only the whole—not the particular details constituting the whole—that is true. By implication, knowledge of the whole comes at the expense of the minutiae of isolated facts. In reaction, moreover, to the radically anti-metaphysical orientation of nineteenth-century positivism (Ernst Mach, Avenarius, Henri Poincaré), not to mention the orthodoxies of vulgar Marxism, dialecticians such as Lukács adopted a dismissive attitude toward what Jay calls "the fetishism of facts."[42]

The tension between the vulgar materialist (or positivist) emphasis on physical evidence and the more dialectical reasoning of Marxists such as Lukács produced a similar dichotomy in T. E. Hulme's work, for example, between the "hard" facts of the poetic image and the totalizing, intuitionist appeal of Sorel. To reconcile the tension between the part and the whole, between concreteness and synthesis—and to address the complaints of vulgar Marxism—dialectical thinkers, beginning with Marx himself, developed models of what Marx calls "concrete totality."[43] Renewing Marx's dialectical (and paradoxical) equation of concreteness and totality, Lukács contends that only through "knowledge of the concrete totality . . . can knowledge of the facts hope to become knowledge of reality."[44] In other words, facts become real only in the context of the totality—which is itself (in Hegelian terms) the only true, concrete entity. The magical reconciliation motivating this paradigm, which synthesizes a constellation of particulars into a "concrete totality," is precisely what appealed to Pound about the Chinese ideogram as a model for the poetic image and, ultimately, for the paratactic method of composition governing the totality of the *Cantos*. In these corresponding political and poetic models of totality, Marxist theorists and modernist poets seek to reconcile the contradictory modalities of analysis and synthesis, montage and mediation, imagist fragment and epic.

In order to comply with its materialist foundations, Western Marxism continually seeks to materialize and historicize the metaphysicality of the whole. To account for the concreteness of totality, to identify the actual *substance* of relations between particular elements forming a whole, a variety of hypotheses have emerged within the Marxist discourse of totality. One of the oldest and most variegated models for explaining the substance of relations unifying the whole pertains to the role of language. Verbal media can be construed as historicizing and materializing social totality. Giambattista Vico, who is the most important pre-Marxian philosopher of history and social totality, placed a significant emphasis on the role of language—and specifically poetic language—as the actual substance of myths governing the unity of archaic cultures.[45] Later, Antonio Gramsci echoed Vico's theory of the intersubjective construction of a "sensus communis" through language: "Great importance," Gramsci asserts, "is assumed by the general question of language, that is, the question of collectively attaining a single cultural 'climate.' "[46]

Seeking a more rigorous approach to this verbal model, contemporary Marxist theorists of totality, such as Jürgen Habermas, have turned to the philosophy of ordinary language to posit a matrix of linguistic intersubjectivity as the historical medium of totality.[47] Combining Vico's mythologizing of poetry with Habermas's theory of linguistic consensus as a way of explaining the concreteness of social totality yields a conception resembling the historical web of verbal commonplaces sustaining the poetic tradition. From this perspective, the rhapsodic network of epic poetry, for example, can be seen as a way of materializing collectivity. In a contemporary context, the formulaic and repetitive language of kitsch could be viewed as a matrix of poetic but ultimately ephemeral totalities—a volatile medium akin to the language of advertising jingles.

Ethnofascist Souvenirs

Other Marxist formulations of totality, in addition to the linguistic model, betray an affinity with the *Cantos*: notions of open or partial totalities, for example, or expressive totalities (a paradigm that views the part as expressing the whole). Yet the variants of Marxist totality most germane to Pound's conception of a modern epic poem, which grounds its vision of the future in a garbled, retrospective collection of verbal fragments, are those treating the correlation of totality and *memory*. Illustrated by Hegel's parable of Minerva's owl flying only at dusk (when history draws to a close), the idea of memory as a synthetic, totalizing power is implicit in Vico's thesis that one knows truly only that which one has made (*poesis*) and that all true knowledge is therefore retrospective. In a specifically Marxist context, Lukács emphasizes the dialectical effects of memory in his theory of epic: "Only in the novel and in certain epic forms resembling the novel does memory occur as a creative force affecting the object and transforming it. The genuinely epic quality of such memory is the affirmative experience of the life process."[48] In Lukács's conception, the "affirmative experience of the life process" is precisely the revolutionary objective, the progressive outcome, of a totalizing approach to history.

Although Lukács placed less emphasis on the retrospective nature of totality in *History and Class Consciousness* than he did in his study of epic, the redemptive power of memory has figured prominently in the thinking of other Marxist theorists (Walter Benjamin most notably but also Siegfried Kracauer). Perhaps the most insistent and comprehensive theory of social recollection occurs, however, in the Freudian-inflected model of "anamnestic totalization" developed by Herbert Marcuse (who joined the Frankfurt school in the 1930s, near the end of its active period). Seeking to overcome the oblivion of reification, Marcuse's theory of emancipatory recollection focuses, according to Fredric Jameson (a student of Marcuse's), on the "memory of a prehistoric paradise . . . which the individual can regain only through its externalization, through its re-establishment for society as a whole."[49] To enter a remembered "paradise" requires that the individual (all individuals) reconstruct paradise in society in the present. In a variant of this logic discernible in the epic ambitions of *Cantos*, "to write Paradise"—or recollect it—coincides with actualization in the present.

Seeking, at the same time, to avoid the equation of remembrance and nostalgia, Marcuse reconfigures social memory as a symbolic operation, so that it becomes "not regression to a previous stage of civilization, but return to an imaginary *temps perdu* in the real life of mankind."[50] Totality, then, becomes equivalent to a cultural landscape resembling Sorel's "social mythology": a sense of the whole based on *imagined* episodes in "the real life of mankind"—a dialectical sleight of hand disclosing the potential appeal of anamnestic totalization to fascism (and hence to a writer like Pound). To avoid the dangers of Marcuse's platonic valorization of memory, Ernst Bloch (yet another Marxist absorbed by the concept of utopian recollection) proposed the operation of what he calls "anagnorisis," in which the details of the past are read as *figural* traces of a utopian future.[51]

The correlation of memory and totality, which plays such an obvious and dominant role in the nostalgic and ultimately Fascist orientation of the *Cantos*, actually informs some of Pound's earliest conceptions of the poetic image. Specifically, his famous definitions of the image as a "radiant node or cluster" (*GB* 92), a "complex" (*LE* 4), and a Chinese ideogram are tropes that depict the poetic image as a constellation of archaic elements recuperated by cultural memory and synthesized into a whole by irresistible forces.[52] These models could all be described as instruments of *projective* memory, deployed increasingly by Pound to map an idealized past onto the present or future. In addition, quite obviously, this ensemble of tropes seeks to resolve the tension between the destructive operation of analysis and the intuitive magic of synthesis, between montage and "totalitarian" harmony.

The Imagist trope of the constellated ideogram—a static structure—does not, however, supply a proposition indicating how the isolated "radicals" of the poetic ideogram are to become fused into a whole. As a tentative solution to this problem, Pound defined the image as a "radiant node or cluster," a metaphor that yields a dynamic model of integration related to the fluidity of the image as "vortex." The idea of the "radiant node" suggests that poetic synthesis occurs by analogy with some kind of electromagnetic energy (a metaphor borrowed from physics). A similar principle is at work in Pound's definition of the image as a "complex," a model whose discursive context offers, it turns out, a more articulate explanation of the problem of poetic synthesis—and one that anticipates as well Pound's explanation of the totality of Fascist culture.

The idea of the "complex" is one of Pound's earliest formulations of the poetic image (articulated when he was still indulging in the pleasures of crypt poetry): "An 'image' is that which presents an intellectual and emotional complex in an instance of time. I use the term 'complex' rather in the technical sense employed by the new psychologists, such as Hart" (*LE* 4). Bernard Hart was one of the few Freudian psychologists practicing in England prior to World War I. Pound's knowledge of Hart may have come through A. R. Orage, the editor of *The New Age*, who was an early supporter of Freudian psychoanalysis (as well as a socialist). In 1912, Hart published two books (*Subconscious Phenomena* and *The Psychology of Insanity*) in which he discusses Freud's recently developed notion of an unconscious complex. In *Psychology of Insanity*, Hart calls the complex "a system of connected ideas, with a strong emotional tone" and further states, "The mode of thought produced by the activity of a complex is quite different from that occurring in genuine logical thinking."[53] The complex, according to Hart, is a "system" of ideas infused with unconscious feeling.

Pound's famous definition of the poetic image as a "complex," a term usually understood only in its formal connotations, is therefore grounded in psychology: it suggests a constellation of elements charged with subconscious "energy"—a system opposed to "logical thinking." Hart explains the significance of this dynamic: "complexes . . . are causes which determine behavior of the conscious stream, and the action which they exert upon consciousness may be regarded as the psychological analogue of the conception of 'force' in physics."[54] As a complex the poetic image represents a moment when conscious thought and actions fall under the sway of unconscious "forces" (analogous to the image conceived as a "radiant node or cluster"). Captive to the influence of hidden powers, disparate ideas and objects form a magical (and irresistible) totality. In its essence, the idea of the complex offers an account of the experience of *possession*.

Calling to mind Hart's comparison of subconscious energy and electromagnetic force, one of Pound's most famous analogies for the image-complex is what he calls "the rose in the steel dust": a form imposed on iron filings by the proximity of magnetic energy. In an essay on Vorticism published in 1915, Pound compares "magnetised iron filings" to "automatic painting"—a mediumistic art in which the image is produced under the sway of "unconscious or sub-human energies."[55] The idea of a form organized by "subhuman energies" is analogous, moreover, to the ethnographic concept of *paideuma*, which Pound borrowed from the German ethnographer Leo Frobenius (who developed it at the same time that Freud was formulating his theory of unconscious complexes).[56] Frobenius's eccentric study of African societies, especially the holistic concept of paideuma, would become in the 1920s a central feature of Pound's theorization of Fascist culture.[57]

Pound's knowledge of Frobenius was often mediated (for linguistic reasons) by Douglas Fox, an American assistant of Frobenius in Germany, with whom Pound corresponded extensively in the 1930s. Of particular importance in this respect is an essay by Fox entitled "Frobenius' Paideuma as Philosophy of Culture." Pound arranged for the essay to be published in six parts in 1936 in the *New English Weekly* (where Pound's work appeared frequently—thanks to his longstanding friendship with the editor, A. R. Orage).[58] This document, providing a summary of the paideuma concept (drawn directly from the works of Frobenius), clearly played a crucial role in Pound's views: references in Pound's writing to specific features of Frobenian ethnography can often be traced directly to the content of Fox's article.

Fox begins his article by distinguishing between the concept of paideuma and a related term used by Oswald Spengler, *Kulturseele* (culture-soul): "to avoid the word *Kulturseele* to which Oswald Spengler gave a definite meaning and which, since then, has often been misused, Frobenius introduces the word Paideuma."[59] What Fox does not make clear is that Spengler borrowed the concept of the *Kulturseele* from Frobenius, whose book on the paideuma concept was originally entitled *Paideuma: Umrisse einer Kultur- und Seelenlehre* (literally, *Paideuma: An outline for a doctrine of culture and a doctrine of the soul*).[60] The word *Seelenlehre* is an archaic term in German for "psychology." (Pound's use of the term "psychology"—in contrast to psychoanalysis—in the title of his early essay "Psychology and Troubadours" has similar connotations.) Frobenius thus originally conceived of his "science of culture" (paideuma) as a counterpart to *psychology*.

Spengler's debt to Frobenius is not limited, however, to the idea of the

Kulturseele, which entered the ideological repertory of National Socialism (hence Fox's protest against the term's "misuse"). Paideuma, according to Frobenius, is "bipolar," governed by temporal and spatial modalities. The spatial dimension manifests itself through *Gestalt* (form) or *Gestaltende* (molding, shaping). Spengler, in turn, makes a similar division in his concept of *Kulturseele*, which he describes, according to Fox, as a *Weltbild* (world-picture). Spengler's theory superimposes the idea of a "world-picture" on the paideuma concept, while retaining the emphasis on *Gestalt*. Furthermore, the concept of *Gestalt* was developed as a visual analogue of totalitarian power by the German proto-Fascist, Ernst Jünger, in the early 1930s.[61] It is also worth mentioning in this context that the Heideggerian concept of the *Weltbild*, or modern world-picture, though far removed from the ethnographic framework of paideuma, is indebted as a basic concept to Spengler's notion of a world-picture.[62] Taking this intricate nexus of influence into account, along with its submerged relation to Freudian psychology, Pound's understanding of paideuma derives from a constellation of related concepts that refer, variously, to a form, soul, or "image" of culture as a whole (to models of totality). Each of these concepts is entangled, moreover, with the historical crisis of fascism.

As an illustration of how the paideuma, or "soul-membrane," functions in the world of objects, Fox offers an anecdote that is supposedly drawn from Frobenius's personal life (a corollary perhaps of Freudian fort/da game). Frobenius ("the scholar") gives his four-year-old daughter three spent matchsticks to play with, suggesting that she pretend they are Hansel and Gretel and the witch. (The fact that this story involves a child may not be incidental —the term "paideuma" derives from the Greek word for child, *pais*.) After playing for some time while her father is working, the girl leaps up in fright and begs her father to take back "the witch." Fox explains, "Here we have the sudden transfer of an idea from the surface of the unconscious (or what Frobenius calls *Gemüt*) to the conscious. The child does not formulate the idea 'witch' but is seized (*ergriffen*) by it."[63] Further, he writes, "in the match, she *experiences* the real witchness of the witch and identifies the match not with the witch but *as* the witch." In this extraordinary moment, an "inactive thing suddenly seizes the soul and is formulated by the mind. In such seizures man is one with reality."

The relation between the soul-membrane of the paideuma and the world of objects is thus articulated in a "moment of *Ergriffenheit* or seizure," which eliminates any kind of mediation or separation between the soul/paideuma and material reality. The soul (of culture, of the individual) and the object are both "bewitched": the paideuma (the soul-membrane of totality) and the individual object are united, indistinguishable. The crucial divide between the human realm of desire and the external realm of physical nature dissolves in the moment of *Ergriffenheit* (possession). What is more, Fox emphasizes not only the "spontaneity" of possession but its tyrannical power over the mind: "the seizure is spontaneous and completely dominates the child."

As a philosophy of culture, paideuma thus describes a world of enchantment in which disparate objects fall under a spell and are thereby unified in the structure of the "world-soul" or world-picture. Furthermore, as Adorno explains in his account of the Spenglerian *Kulturseele*, "real history is ideologically transfigured into a history of the soul in order to bring what is antithetical and rebellious in man, consciousness, all the more completely under the sway of blind necessity."[64] In this moment of possession, *all* the constituent features of a given culture (artifacts, ideas, actions) bear a "family resemblance" to one another, which identifies them as "symptoms" of the paideuma or *Weltbild*.[65] Composed according to the inscrutable logic of the *Weltbild*, bewitched by the fetish-membrane of world-soul, the haphazard details of existence are synthesized into a coherent and irresistible *Gestalt*: a totality.

Forrest Read suggests that the mythological features of paideuma and the ideogrammic method in Pound's writing are related to the supernatural elements of his earliest poetry (which coincide with its necrophilic aspect and its kitschy obsession with beauty): "In going back to the unconscious in the individual Pound was, like Frobenius, going back to the collective racial myths of prehistory and to its magical view of the world. Pound's early poetry abounds in 'states of mind' attributed to the inspiration which precedes poetry, an individual analogue to the mythic perceptions which precede history."[66] More specifically, the new "methodology" associated with Frobenius became inextricably linked in Pound's mind to the rise of fascism—a correlation that he emphasizes in his 1937 article, "Totalitarian Scholarship and the New Paideuma": "To know today's Deutschland we need a worthy translation of Leo Frobenius."[67]

Pound's cultural symptomatology, with its fetishistic regard for individual facts, locates the "radiant" force necessary to synthesize these details in mythological (and racial) categories that typically help to sustain fascist ideology. In the same article, he writes, "I assert most positively the mutual need of the different racial vigours in our Paideuma," and further, "the first postulate of a realist world-order is that each race must contribute initially that which it has in higher degree than the other races." Thus the ostensible materialism (or "realism") of Pound's ideogrammic method is constructed on a mythic foundation of "racial vigours." All cultural "symptoms" or facts point beyond history—and beyond economics—to the magical dimension of blood and race. The symptom, fact, detail, is "bewitched" by the medium of race in a moment of *Ergriffenheit*, so that it becomes part of a constellation of elements, but also expresses by itself the hidden totality of race. Pound's eccentric understanding of the concept of the "totalitarian" thus accounts for the enchanted relation between the constellation of the poetic ideogram and its radical elements.

The cultural or mythological dimension of the unremembered "complex" is therefore implicit in Pound's earliest conceptions of the image. As a Vorticist, and later in his formulation of totalitarian culture, Pound employs the rhetoric of primitivism to illustrate the shock of "possession" characterizing the image-complex and paideuma. The same logic governs the ethnographic (and fascist) revision of the ideogram, which provides a way of illustrating, in Pound's view, the reversion of society to its mythological foundations. The "objectivity" and magical integrity of a textual ideogram are thus guaranteed by its indexical relation to the unseen paideuma (just as the iron filings render the invisible force of magnetic energy). Charged with "subhuman energies," the ideogram expresses the "racial" paideuma of a culture. Possessed in this manner by the "world-soul," the cultural ideogram makes visible an unseen totality and is itself "totalitarian" (in Pound's use of the term). A similar relation obtains between a historical society and its paideuma: in the context of Italian Fascism, according to Pound, the disparate elements of society must be possessed by its mythological image. The result of this seizure is what Pound calls "totalitarian" culture.

The iconography of the poetic image (complex, ideogram, vortex, paideuma) is thus embedded from the start in the problem of totality, which explains in part its susceptibility to the cultural poetics of fascism and totalitarianism. Pound's rhetoric oscillates wildly between rigor and delirium, positivism and mysticism, between a defense of concrete fact and surrender to the fluidity of possession: between Imagism and the synthetic powers of kitsch. The term "rhapsody," denoting at once an epic poem stitched together from verbal formulae, and something inducing emotional overload, captures both sides of this dialectic.

Kitsch, with its combination of redundancy, triviality, and irrational authority, operates with unacknowledged agency in the *Cantos*. The unseen forces of synthetic magic unifying the elements of the complex, the ideogram, originate with the demonic energies of possession to which Pound surrenders in his crypt poetry (the wellspring of kitsch in his writing). The energies of synthesis and attraction radiate ultimately from the magnetic substance of poetic kitsch riddling Pound's poetry from beginning to end. Kitsch, then, takes possession of the language of the *Cantos* in discrete episodes, signifying the momentary appearance of a forbidden realm of beauty and archaic language. Yet kitsch is also the source of the mysterious energy that *dissolves* boundaries between the individual curiosities in the museum of kitsch, yoking together the epithets and formulae of epic. Ultimately, kitsch in the *Cantos* becomes the dark matter that constellates and unifies a horde of textual relics that are at once proverbial and esoteric—along with the garbled voices of a sinister paradise.

8 Junk

A Shopper's Guide to Poetic Language
(and the New York School)

Thermofax: Warhol, Malanga, and the Art of Suicide

For American poets, the traumatic legacy of Pound's fascism and anti-Semitism converted the *Cantos* into a vast, partially abandoned minefield, riddled with hidden dangers and unspeakable ambitions. Any attempt to defend the *Cantos* could assess the poem only in fragments, thereby ignoring its scope as an epic, its synthetic powers, its vision of cultural and political totality. The integrity of the poem's experiment could be salvaged only by isolating (and purifying) its formalist agenda, which meant that the appeal and function of kitsch in the *Cantos* could not even begin to be acknowledged, debated, or tested. The emergence of so-called late modernism—a mandarin, hyper-formalist variant of the original movement—suppressed any discussion of the possibility that the diction of the *Cantos* alternated, in fact, between the "silvery" substance of kitsch and the "hard" phrasing of modernism.

The medusal effects of Pound's perilous example could not last forever: the catalyst for re-assessing the forbidden constellation of synthesis, totality, and kitsch emerged with a new wave of experimental poets eager to test—in concert with pop art—the opposition between kitsch and avant-garde. A wayward signal of the possible rapprochement between modernism and pop culture can be detected, appropriately enough, in the epigraphic folly of a minor poet in the 1960s. In the dedication to a book in which his poems alternate with photographs of silkscreen works by Andy Warhol, Gerard Malanga draws a correlation that seems bizarre, if not absurd: he equates Andy Warhol with Ezra Pound. Malanga dedicates his book *Chic Death* to "Andy Warhol, *il miglior fabbro*" (Andy Warhol, the better crafts-man).[1] This inscription echoes T. S. Eliot's dedication of *The Waste Land*:

"For Ezra Pound, *il miglior fabbro*" (a phrase echoing in turn Dante's praise for the Provençal poet Arnaut Daniel). Malanga's correlation of Pound, the über-modernist, and Warhol, the queer purveyor of pop art, seems faintly ludicrous—even today—in part because the prevailing (modernist) doctrine contrasting kitsch and avant-garde has been so effective in suppressing any hypothesis that questions or defies this antinomy. All the same, should we take seriously the idea that Warhol was the new Pound?

Perhaps Malanga was also alluding to a lost genealogy of another kind— an atavistic affiliation engulfing and animating his generic poems. Perhaps Warhol's Death and Disaster series (from which Malanga appropriated the totemistic images for his book of poems) belongs, retrospectively, in a genealogy of forgers and suicides. What if the suicide/forgery axis of the Chatterton affair in the eighteenth century had established an abiding signal— relayed in part through the modernist necrophilia of the *Cantos*—triggering the appropriation of kitsch by vanguard poets in America following World War II? Yet, even if none of these connections could be traced, several Chatterton forgeries did in fact appear, like alien hieroglyphs, in a generative anthology of young New York School poets in 1961: John Ashbery, Kenneth Koch, James Schuyler, and Harry Matthews published a "Special Collaborations Issue" of a transatlantic journal called *Locus Solus* in Paris that summer. The poetic collaborations selected for the issue range from works between poets in the past (of various languages and traditions), between existing poets, and between existing poets and past poets. One finds traditional Japanese and Chinese forms, collaborative works by canonical British poets (Shakespeare and Fletcher, Cowley and Crashaw, Coleridge and Southey), along with a number of French Surrealist experiments. Among the works by existing poets are a cento by an unnamed poet, appropriations of nonpoetic texts (by various American poets), and "Six Collaborations" by Ashbery and Koch.

The issue also contains works that do not fit neatly into any of these categories: for example, immediately following a collaboration between Suckling and Waller, one finds two of Chatterton's Rowley poems and two forged poems by the fictitious poet Ern Malley. (The Ern Malley hoax, as I will explain more fully below, was perpetrated by two Australian poets in 1944.) Although the Ern Malley poems could be considered collaborations (since they were in fact produced by two poets working together), Koch explains—in an important Afterword to the issue—that Chatterton, like Ern Malley, is a poet in collaboration with "already existing languages."[2]

Although Koch's comment about Chatterton is mildly perplexing, there can be no doubt that Koch and his fellow editors must have considered Chatterton's poetic imposture (and the Ern Malley forgeries) to be notable ingredients in the mock tradition forged through collaboration—and appropriation—by the New York poets published in *Locus Solus*. Forgery, one would surmise from the inclusion of Chatterton and Ern Malley, must be a precursor to the vanguard activity of poetic collaboration.

In February of 1962, John Ashbery published his second book, *The Tennis Court Oath*, a collection strongly influenced by Dada procedures of appropriation, collage, and collaboration, with a number of poems resembling the work that had appeared the previous year in *Locus Solus* 2. A few months later, in July of 1962, Andy Warhol had his first solo show (with soup cans and Brillo boxes) at the Ferus Gallery in Los Angeles. Between 1962 and 1965, Ashbery showed a marked interest in Warhol's early photo-silkscreen images—especially his Marilyn Monroe images and the Death and Disaster series—reviewing five separate shows in which Warhol's paintings appeared, most notably a catalog essay for the first New York exhibition devoted to what was then called the "New Realism" (pop art) in November 1962. Ashbery also wrote reviews of Warhol's first two solo shows in Paris in 1964 and 1965, praising the "unambiguous ambiguity" of the work.[3] In addition, Ashbery included a poem called "The New Realism" in *The Tennis Court Oath*.

Warhol returned Ashbery's attention: he showed up for one of Ashbery's rare New York readings (Ashbery was living in Paris) at the Washington Square Art Gallery in August of 1964. (A photograph of the event shows Warhol seated between Taylor Mead and Barbara Guest.) Warhol also asked Ashbery to sit for one of his three-minute *Screen Tests*—the first poet to do so—in 1965. Later, when asked whether he had a favorite poet, Warhol replied, "John Ashbery, and Gerard Malanga. Do you know him?"—a curious intimation of the compound identities frequently adopted by Malanga in his poetic collaborations.[4]

In 1965, Ashbery wrote a review of Warhol's second solo show in Paris, *Death in America*, a title referring to the provocative paintings on display: appropriated images of suicides and car crashes. In this review, Ashbery compared Warhol to Oscar Wilde, thereby placing Warhol in a constellation of scandal and simulation that some critics see as encompassing Chatterton the forger.[5] Countering the received notion of Chatterton as a harbinger of Romantic poetics, Jerome McGann, for example, reconfigures the legacy of

Chatterton's imposture: "This is no 'tender night' of Romantic imagination, it is the brainy world of an artist whose delight lies in hoaxing and masking. The line to Oscar Wilde is direct."[6] The appearance of Chatterton in the collaborations issue of *Locus Solus* (edited primarily by Koch) may in fact have been part of a Chatterton "moment" in Paris in the sixties, a moment mixing pop art and high theory. In 1967—the same year Roland Barthes published his seminal essay, "The Death of the Author"—Serge Gainsbourg released a song called "Chatterton," which places the "marvelous boy" in a genealogy of famous suicides:

Chatterton killed himself
Isocrates killed himself
Cleopatra killed herself
Goya
Out of his mind
As for me, as for me,
Things aren't going too well.[7]

Akin perhaps to Gainsbourg's pop *chansonnerie*, though at the far end of the spectrum of French letters, is Michel Foucault's iconic essay, "What Is an Author?," published in 1969, which replicates the suicide/forgery axis when it asserts, "Writing has become linked to sacrifice, even to the sacrifice of life: it is now a voluntary effacement."[8] One year later, in 1970, Foucault takes note of Warhol's Death and Disaster series, finding "the equivalence of death in the cavity of an eviscerated car" and "the sudden illumination of multiplicity itself—with nothing at its center."[9]

On a parallel track, others have found links between Lacan's assault on ego-psychology in the 1960s and Warhol's seriality, along with his attempt to eliminate any trace of the artist's hand from the photo-silkscreen process (an execution allegorized in Warhol's appropriated images of suicide and electric chairs).[10] Ultimately, Chatterton presides explicitly over the binary figure of suicide and the vanishing "author function" in Foucault's brief essay on the "pleasure" of suicide, which he contributed to the inaugural issue of *Le Gai Pied* (an underground gay tabloid published in Paris in the 1970s). Beneath the title of Foucault's essay, "Un plaisir si simple," one discovers—without caption or explanation—a reproduction of Henry Wallis's pre-Raphaelite painting of Chatterton's suicide.[11]

The genealogy running from Chatterton to Wilde to Warhol (and Foucault) implies that Warhol's "suicidal mimicry" should be seen as replicating the suicide/forgery axis first articulated in the Chatterton affair.[12] The correlation of suicide and mimeticism in Warhol's art is borne out by the evolution of his early work. Warhol has stated that he first used the photo-silkscreen process and initiated the Death and Disaster series (based on appropriated newspaper photos of car crashes and executions) shortly after Marilyn Monroe's suicide on August 5, 1962.[13] Thus the earliest Marilyn paintings (especially the serial *Marilyn Diptych* of 1962) should be seen as triggering the Death and Disaster series, followed by the appropriated newspaper photos of suicide (usually falling, or fallen, bodies) in 1963.

Traces of Warhol's preoccupation with suicide can be found as late as March 1965, when he made the rarely seen film *Suicide* (originally conceived as number 3 in the Screen Test series). In addition, one should note that the Death and Disaster series—more than Warhol's other silkscreen paintings—consists of serial images *within* the picture frame. Taking into account the fact that Warhol's earliest serial images are generally viewed as allegories of commodification and consumption, the process of seriality—the structure of commodification—may be especially pertinent, in Warhol's view, to the subject of suicide and violent death.

Certainly, the Disaster images are sensationalistic and evocative of mass culture, as many critics argue, but the suicide paintings in particular are also, I am suggesting, emblematic of the emergence of seriality and the suppression of the "artist function" in Warhol's work. The same could be said about the appearance of the suicide/forger, Chatterton, in a collection of poetic collaborations (in *Locus Solus* 2). Just as Chatterton's "suicidal mimicry" supplies an icon of the effects of collaboration, appropriation, and forgery on the "authorial function," so too must the suicidal poetics of Thomas Gray be seen—in the context of eighteenth-century imposture—as an expression of his "methodical borrowing phrenzy." It is not poetry in its essence or entirety that perishes by its own hand but a certain mode of poetry. What survives—and indeed what governs—the procedures of collaboration, appropriation, and mimicry is the poetics of kitsch, both as a development of aesthetic ideology and as an evolving set of procedures contesting, but also rivaling, the allure of the commodity in the marketplace.

What one may call the poetics of suicide received a virtuosic treatment, or demonstration, in the volume containing Ashbery's alignment with the emerging strategies of pop art and the New Realism: according to Andrew Ross, "the deepest poetics of *The Tennis Court Oath* is to eradicate at all levels, formal and material (through decontextualization and collage), the experience of an original work created through autonomous authorial agency."[14] At the same time, Ross acknowledges, in contrast to the intentions of the historical avant-garde, "The instances of shock on the accidental surface of *The Tennis Court Oath* are more ambiguous: it is the commitment itself that seems random and, often, conspicuously absent."[15] What one may call Ashbery's infidel passivity, a new model of avant-garde practice stirred by indifference, set the standard for a whole generation of poets.

Ashbery's ambiguous demonstration of the poetics of suicide—a puzzling combination of provocative technique and indiscernible, or vacuous, intent—realized itself fully (as a new prototype of kitsch) in the collaborative project I alluded to earlier by Gerard Malanga (Warhol's production assistant starting in 1963). Malanga's book—the same one in which he equates Pound and Warhol—incorporates images from Warhol's serial disasters, as I indicated a moment ago, but it also borrows lines and phrases from John Ashbery's poetry. One could even say that Malanga's status as a minor and derivative figure—a downtown de Quincey—identifies him (and not Ashbery) as the generic agent in this largely forgotten episode of the early formation of pop art.

At the same time, Malanga's "minority" must not be taken as evidence that his own poetic practice had no influence over Warhol's evolving pop aesthetic, or that Warhol's dependence on Malanga for exposure to new poetry in the early sixties was insignificant. On the contrary, Warhol indicated that he regularly attended poetry readings in the late 1950s and became more responsive to Malanga's experimental poetic practice when Malanga started working for him in 1963.[16] Malanga then became his guide to the downtown poetry scene in the early 1960s.[17] Malanga, like other poets seeking to break with the academic tradition of poetry in the early 1960s, had quickly taken up the radical procedures of *The Tennis Court Oath* (which Ashbery had been experimenting with since the late 1950s).

It is precisely because the innovations of Ashbery and Warhol depend on appropriation and collaboration that one must reconsider the significance of a minor poet like Malanga, whose poetry illustrates in an absolute sense the properties distinguishing the work of poets who may be considered, perhaps incoherently, to be more original. If Ashbery's poetry is defiantly derivative, then Malanga is a genius of unoriginal writing. This orientation obliges one to regard the poet "without qualities," the minor poet, as the exemplary figure of the New Realism in poetry, the generic agent of changes associated with the echolalia of poetic kitsch. Malanga's collaboration with Warhol and

Ashbery may thus help us to gauge the aesthetic and social significance of minority within a shifting paradigm of poetic substance and exposure.

Malanga's project, appearing in several different manifestations—often recycling the phrase "chic death"—sought to involve poetry in the topology of Warhol's Disaster series: suicide, celebrity, fashion, and violent death. In December of 1964, Malanga gave a reading at the Leo Castelli Gallery, which was holding an exhibit of Warhol's work. The poster for the event referred to "Poem Visuals [sic] by Andy Warhol and Gerard Malanga," promising "The New Realism, Yeah, Yeah, Fashion, and Disaster Series read by Gerard Malanga."[18] To an interviewer at the event, Malanga explained that he was planning to publish a new magazine called *Chic Death*, which would "combine the death image with fashion, using fashion models posing in front of automobile wrecks."[19] Though the magazine was never produced, Malanga salvaged (so to speak) the phrase "chic death" for the title of a book of his poetry published in 1971, which includes the "serial disaster" poems he read at the Castelli Gallery, alongside cheap reproductions of silkscreen paintings from Warhol's Death and Disaster series.

Malanga's emphasis on fashion and celebrity in his collaboration remains faithful to and, one could even say, restores the occluded origin of Warhol's Death and Disaster series: the serialized image of a celebrity suicide (Marilyn). In addition, taking into account the connotations of the phrase "chic death," one could conclude that Malanga is simply rehearsing in his picture-book of poems a version of Warhol's serial disasters: grainy newsprint photos of electric chairs and car crashes, overlaid with delicate hues of lavender, gold, rose, mint green—as though death itself had been overtaken by questions of style and commodification. At the same time, the inadvertent kitschiness of Malanga's phrase "chic death" hints at an inversion embedded in the orthography of the word "chic": the possibility—uncovered by reversing (loosely) the spelling of the word "chic"—that kitsch is the inversion of the logic of chic and that Malanga, by calling his own work chic, secretes its true identity as kitsch, wedding its fate to inversion. Isn't "chic" just "kitsch" spelled backwards?

The *kitsch-death* exposed by Malanga's so-called collaboration with Warhol (and Ashbery) is fully legible in a series of works produced by Malanga in 1964 and 1965, combining his poetry and photographs resembling Warhol's "serial disasters." The works were produced on a Thermofax machine, an early photocopying device using a heat transfer process and coated paper. Thermofax copies are literally burned onto the paper (hence the origin of the phrase, "to burn a copy"), producing an overall sepia tone and unstable shading (which may have influenced Warhol's modulation of the photo-silkscreen process in his serialized images). Malanga produced Thermofax copies of newspaper photos of car crashes and shootings, leaving a blank area beneath the blurry image, where Malanga typed his poems (many of which he read as examples of the New Realism—a phrase he grabbed from Ashbery at the Castelli reading). With a blurry sepia image affixed to coated and curling paper, the Thermofax "poem" could not conceal its essence as a copy, displaying a kind of tackiness that Ashbery compared (in reference to Warhol) to "a rubbing of the surface of a kitchen table oilcloth."[20] When Malanga asks in one of the poems in *Chic Death*, "What false secrets did the thermo-fax hold?" one is tempted to answer: the "false secret" of kitsch.

In one of the Thermofax works, Malanga's poem, "The Young Mod" (dedicated to the model Jean Shrimpton), is coupled with a gruesome image of a body spilled from a car crash; the poem itself veers from borrowed advertising copy (feeding the poetics of kitsch) to a jarring reference at the end of the poem to the Thermofax image of the car crash:

> The naked wool bolero-back skimmer
> Is just the sort of almost-nothing weight
> She'll need for sun and sea. A man lies
> Dead along the wreckage of his auto
> Another is still pinned behind the steering wheel.[21]

Malanga appears to be positioning Shrimpton as his own "Marilyn" (or Liz) and combining—in a move that veers towards kitsch—references to celebrity and violence (which Warhol kept apart).

Malanga's Thermofax "combines" (text and image) are representative of the "New Realism" he heralds in the poster for the Castelli event (where he read some of the Thermofax poems). Pop art made its first significant appearance in the US under the rubric of "the New Realists," the title of a large group show in New York held at the Sidney Janis Gallery in November of 1962 (a phrase borrowed from the French critic Pierre Restang, who had applied it to French proto-pop in the early sixties). John Ashbery, living in Paris at the time, wrote a poem called "The New Realism" (first published in *Locus Solus* 3/4 in February of 1962 and later included in *The Tennis Court Oath*), thereby insinuating a poetic variant of pop art before it reached the public eye in New York. Ashbery also wrote a catalog essay ("The New Realists") for the Sidney Janis show. Gerard Malanga then picked up the phrase, which floats through his poetry of the period, including a poem entitled "The New Realism," which he published in *Chic Death*.

What sort of art (or poetry) did the New Realists produce? In his catalog essay, Ashbery contends, "As the name indicates, it is (like Surrealism) another kind of Realism."[22] At the same time, he notes, "New Realism is not new. Even before Duchamp produced the first readymade, Apollinaire had written that the true poetry of our age is to be found in the window of a barber shop."[23] Thus the earliest precedent Ashbery mentions for the New Realism (for pop art) is to be found in a kind of poetry that appropriates its language from popular sources, thereby initiating a shift in poetic diction towards the language of advertising and undermining art's autonomy (in relation to everyday existence). The New Realism is evidently, Ashbery contends, a form of realism, yet it also appears to place the nature of art in question: "what these artists are doing is calling attention with singular effectiveness to the ambiguity of the artistic experience; to the crucial confusion about the nature of art."[24] To put it another way, art or poetry associated with the New Realism inevitably incites controversy—like kitsch—about whether it is truly art, which in turn reveals a basic "ambiguity" and "confusion" about art itself.

Ashbery's poem "The New Realism" offers a bold demonstration of the methodology of the poetic "readymade," with lengthy chains of appropriated phrases punctuated by momentary reflections on the method: "Reading from the pages of the telephone directory . . . all I can smell here is newsprint . . . perched on some utterly crass sign / Not the hardest either, but adoption is no way."[25] Likewise, "for Malanga," Reva Wolf contends, " 'new realism' came to stand for a way of creating art—and of living—that paralleled Warhol's practices and raised compelling questions about copying (or 'stealing') words and images."[26] In Malanga's practice of poetic New Realism, it should be noted, neither Warhol nor Ashbery ever consented to, or participated in, the so-called collaborations of Malanga's *Chic Death*—though his book does adopt some of the strategies of collaboration showcased in *Locus Solus* 2.

The figurative equation of suicide and collaboration in Malanga's poetry becomes unmistakable in a poem called "Some Suicides" (published in *Chic Death*), which makes no reference to suicide per se, but samples a passage from Ashbery's "The Skaters" (via Ted Berrigan's appropriation of the same passage). Here is the passage from Ashbery's poem (which is itself a demonstration of collage method):

> We are nearing the Moorish coast, I think, in a bateau.
> I wonder if I will have any friends there
> Whether the future will be kinder to me than the pasts, for example[27]

Here is Berrigan's version in his book *The Sonnets* (1966):

> I wonder if Jan or Helen or Babe
> Ever think about me, I wonder if Dave Bearden still
> Dislikes me. I wonder if people talk about me
> secretly.[28]

And here is Malanga's allusion to Ashbery, through Berrigan:

> I wonder if Kenny Lane bought a new wristwatch today,
> Or whether Charles Henrie Ford is back at the Dakota,
> And if everyone is beginning to talk about me, seriously,
> For a change?[29]

The rolling sequence of allusions and samplings shared among the three poets demonstrates the fluidity of motives and practices encompassing Malanga's experiments.

Critics have condemned Malanga's poetry for being "parasitically fastened to the works of a poet as contemporary as Ashbery," yet it's quite clear that the poetics of kitsch-death in Malanga's poetry subscribes to the Dada principles Ashbery enunciates in a poem in his first collection, *Some Trees*:[30]

> All beauty, resonance, integrity,
> Exist by deprivation or logic
> Of strange position.[31]

In a poem of Malanga's dedicated to Ashbery in *Chic Death*, the art of leaving things out ("deprivation"), or rearranging things in odd ways ("the logic of strange position"), becomes what Malanga calls a "strange science":

> That men
> Wish to be part of the "quotation," and
> That not to "explain" would make "them" light
> In a fast world that's convincing and photogenic.[32]

Here, it seems, the poetics of suicide can be located at the convergence of the experience of ontological "quotation" (a practice evoked by the poem itself), photogenesis, and a refusal to explain. The "strange science" of kitsch appears to be a proxy for the New Realism.

Dada Kitsch

The profusion of "allegorical suicides" in the early pop productions of Warhol and Malanga can be traced to Dada, which had adopted "theoretic suicide" as a leitmotif in its assault on art.[33] For example, Jacques Rigaut, a French Dadaist, published an essay in 1920 entitled "Suicide Must Be a Vocation."[34] Although the work of the New Realists, poets and painters alike, could not be accused of trying "to kill art" (as Dadaism aimed to do), it certainly placed in question, as Ashbery emphasized, prevailing notions about the nature of art. More specifically, the references to artistic suicide I mention here are drawn from an anthology of Dada writings and manifestos, *The Dada Painters and Poets*, edited by Robert Motherwell and published in 1951, which was widely available to the poets and painters I have been examining here. In fact, the anthology—which Frank O'Hara described as "the Gospels for myself and many other poets"—was so influential that New Realism, or pop art, was referred to interchangeably as the "New Dada."[35] Warhol's early work, for example, was tagged as "neo-Dada."[36] And Warhol himself mused, "Dada must have something to do with Pop—it's so funny, the names are really synonyms. . . . Johns and Rauschenberg—Neo-Dada for all these years, and everyone calling them derivative and unable to transform the things they were—are now called progenitors of Pop."[37] One detects here the queer passivity of kitsch in Warhol's emphasis on a *lack* of originality in the art of Rauschenberg and Johns as the basic link between Dada and pop art.

Ashbery, too, in his catalog essay for the *New Realists* show in 1962, explains the significance of the legacy of Dada for pop artists (and poets): "The explosion of Dada cleared the air by bringing these new materials violently to the attention of the public. Today's New Realists are not neo-Dadaists in the sense that they copy the Dadaists; they are using a language which existed before Dada and has always existed. The way back to this language is what Dada has forcibly laid bare."[38] Here, Ashbery describes a new form of Dadaism bent not on the destruction of art but on exposing an *existing language*—and the desirability of that language as a found object or text. Likewise, attempting to explain the new fascination with appropriated

"signs" and advertising—the New Realists were also called "Sign Painters"—
Barbara Rose (in a review of a 1962 show at the Pasadena Museum) writes,
"The attitude of worship is as common to new Dada as the attitude of negation was to the Dada of the past."[39] What could not yet be reconciled in the
criticism of the period was the possibility of a polarized relation between
fascination and repulsion, between desire and critique, in the New Realism
—a compound essential to a dialectical poetics of kitsch.

In the correlation between the New Dada and the poetics of kitsch, I
have been stressing the revival of procedures such as replication, appropriation, and collaboration—what Wolf calls, for example, "Ashbery's use
of dada-like collage techniques, phrases copied from a wide range of texts,
disjunctive language."[40] Malanga, as well, borrowing a fashionable phrase of
Tristan Tzara's from the Motherwell anthology, identifies one of the collage-
poems in *Chic Death* ("All the Beautiful People") as a "cut-up."[41] Yet the copycat mentality of the New Dada (a.k.a. New Realism, pop art, etc.) can also
yield a somewhat different formulation—one that helps to explain why a
poet like O'Hara could describe Motherwell's Dada anthology as the "gospel" of poetic experimentation for him and other poets. Viewing the Dada
revival from a somewhat different vantage point, it is not simply a question of using certain procedures—regardless of content—but of varying the
kinds of content one appropriates. Hence Rose, enumerating the "new Dada
concepts" in her review of the 1962 Pasadena show, lays emphasis on "the
use of the ordinary and the commonplace, the familiar and the banal in
art."[42] In essence, the twin axes of the New Dada (appropriation and ordi-
nariness) revive the dialectic of the "commonplace": the New Realist borrows and divulges the commonplace.

If Rose's understanding of Dada's contributions to the New Realism (to
pop art) makes it easier to regard O'Hara's *Lunch Poems* as a work subscribing to the principles of Dadaism—of the historical avant-garde—it remains
unclear how one could also view O'Hara's poetry as the antithesis of the
avant-garde. Yet this is precisely how the conservative gatekeepers of the
modernist avant-garde (associated with abstract expressionism) during this
period viewed the painting and poetry of the New Realism. In fact, a chorus
of indignant voices equated the New Dada—accused of being a fraudulent
avant-garde—with *kitsch*. In a 1962 essay entitled "Kitsch into 'Art': The New
Realism," Gilbert Sorrentino attacks the New Realism for converting Dada
into mere "fashion" and condemns its fraudulent "art" as "one-of-a-kind

kitsch."[43] Hilton Kramer, too, dismisses pop art as "fraudulent," as a series of "clichés."[44]

In a related attack on the "new vulgarians" of "Neo-Dada," and its "central idea—kitsch," Max Kozloff declares, "Not merely do the images appear pre-created, but the artist expects us, rather than himself, to contribute the imaginative values. He poses as the agent, not the author of the work."[45] These attacks were acknowledged and echoed by the godfather of the campaign against kitsch, Clement Greenberg, who in 1962 condemned those "artists in this country who have now gone in for 'Neo-Dada,'" with its "ironic comments on the banalities of the industrial environment."[46] For work that displays little more than "a conventional and pretty cubism," Greenberg declares, "novelty, as distinct from originality, has no staying power."[47] By disparaging the prettiness and mere novelty of works associated with Neo-Dada, Greenberg is clearly sounding the old battle cry of vanguard opposition to kitsch—even if kitsch now stems from a revival of techniques associated with Dada—with the historical avant-garde.

Greenberg extended his renewed attack on kitsch to poetry, and even art criticism, associated with Neo-Dada—to O'Hara's writing in particular. In a 1962 essay entitled "How Art Writing Earned its Bad Name," Greenberg, seizing on a phrase from O'Hara's monograph on Jackson Pollock ("an abyss of glamor encroached upon by a flood of innocence"), declares, "The widening gap between art and discourse solicits, as such widenings will, perversions and abortions of discourse: pseudo-description, pseudo-narrative, pseudo-exposition, pseudo-history, pseudo-philosophy, pseudo-psychology, and—worst of all—pseudo-poetry."[48] Clearly, Greenberg intends O'Hara's "pseudo-poetry"—as a "perversion" of discourse—to be equated with the falsehood of kitsch. Indeed, the fraudulence of such poetry—fake poetry—is singled out by Greenberg precisely because art criticism was being "perverted" by a strain of "poetic appreciation," by a flood of pseudo-phenomena exemplified by O'Hara's poetry.[49]

Greenberg, certainly, would have been familiar—in the context of his own life—with O'Hara's perceived vulnerability as an amateur critic without credentials in art history, trying to make an impact in the art world. For Greenberg was himself, when he published his essay "Avant-Garde and Kitsch" in 1939, an aspiring poet with no academic training in art history. Indeed, a quick glance at Greenberg's unpublished poetry, which he continued to write through the 1940s, suggests that his own "pseudo-poetry" may have been the submerged and alienated model for the kitsch he attacked in his famous essay, as well as the prototype (in his mind) for the poetic kitsch he thought he discerned in O'Hara's poetry. Certainly, Greenberg's poetry is full of feeling and not afraid to be frank (or "Frank") about his personal life:

> If you ruin your life at 26, can you ever pick it up again
> Will you ever find someone to love you.
> Time isn't big enough. It takes years to find a loving heart
> For yourself. Love's Pilgrim. Oh weary road.[50]

Nor was he afraid of pastiche (of Eliot's "Prufrock," in this case):

> Among adolescent maids who've never prayed
> William P. Yerrington finds his earthly troubles.
> Physio-chemical engineers
> Who pressure to vent skeptical sneers.[51]

Without making too much of the correlation between Greenberg's own poetic kitsch and his condemnation of O'Hara's "pseudo-poetry," the imitative and derivative nature of Greenberg's juvenilia cannot easily be isolated from O'Hara's enthusiasm for the Dada "gospel" of appropriation and collaboration—a strange science, indeed!

Neo-modernist critics complained that kitsch was the new Dada: the revival of techniques associated with Dada (appropriation, collage, collaboration) had produced a deceptive variant of kitsch. The works of the New Realism in painting and poetry were little more than singular clichés, they claimed, examples of "one-of-a-kind kitsch." To a remarkable degree—though in ways the defenders of modernism could scarcely acknowledge or sanction—these charges are true.

At the level of practice, there can be no doubt that many painters and poets associated with the New Realism experimented—under the influence of Motherwell's transformative anthology—with Dada techniques and became more interested in using vernacular materials and documenting everyday experience. That much is beyond dispute. The fact that poets such as Ashbery, Koch, Malanga, Schuyler, and O'Hara were composing poetry based on Tzara's instructions for making a Dadaist poem—following a recipe—was evidence that a paradigm shift was under way. Public evidence of this shift—with regard to a distinct pop sensibility—first became manifest in poetry, with the publication of the *Locus Solus* collaborations issue in the summer of 1961. A year or so later, the first public exhibitions of pop art—the New Realism—were held in New York and Paris.

Dada, one must bear in mind, was a crucial component of the historical avant-garde: poetry or painting influenced by Dada cannot therefore be dubbed "kitsch" without calling into question the Greenbergian dichotomy of avant-garde and kitsch. How can kitsch be opposed to the avant-garde if it becomes an offspring of the avant-garde? The accusations of kitsch hurled by neo-modernist critics against the New Dada raise important questions about the nature of the avant-garde and, more specifically, about the relationship of kitsch to the avant-garde.

Dadaism, according to Peter Bürger, was "the most radical movement within the European avant-garde," exemplifying its campaign to destroy the autonomy of art in bourgeois society—that is, the solipsism and isolation of art from everyday life.[52] More precisely, Bürger explains, "the historical avant-garde movements negate those determinations that are essential in autonomous art: the disjunction of art and the praxis of life, individual production, and individual reception."[53] In other words, the "historical avant-garde" (which is distinct from, and conceivably at odds with, the strictly formalist orientation of modernism) seeks to integrate art into the practice of everyday life and to cultivate collective forms of production and reception. Techniques employed by Dada painters and poets (and adapted by American artists and poets of the New Realism) are the means by which the historical avant-garde seeks to achieve those ends. These objectives can only be fulfilled, according to Bürger, by progressing through three distinct (and increasingly difficult) stages: "self-criticism" and exposure of the autonomy of art; negation of the autonomy of art; and integration of a new paradigm of art into an evolving "praxis of life."[54]

The avant-garde objectives Bürger attributes to Dada practice provide the basis for a dialectical reading of the postwar modernists' scornful equation of Neo-Dada and kitsch. For his emphasis on the importance of collective production and reception, as a means of integrating art into "the praxis of life," necessarily implies the evolution of the avant-garde towards the condition of popular culture. From this perspective, it is entirely conceivable that kitsch may indeed be the future of Dada, of the avant-garde. At the same time, Bürger is fully aware of the danger, as he sees it, of popular culture's tendency to produce what he calls "a false sublation of autonomous art"—a fraudulent displacement of high art by mass culture.[55] In his view, "pulp fiction and commodity aesthetics prove that such a false sublation exists. . . . Here literature ceases to an instrument of emancipation and becomes one of subjection."[56] Despite his emphasis on collective production and reception as crucial features of the avant-gardist work, Bürger thus appears unable in these statements to acknowledge the prospect of a critical variant of "commodity aesthetics" (whether pulp fiction or poetic kitsch) as a vehicle of the avant-garde. Though he is referring here to commercial art on a mass scale (and not to works of the "neo-avant-garde" such as pop art), his statements are surprisingly reminiscent of the neo-modernists' unqualified rejection of kitsch.[57]

The furious critical debates that followed the emergence of the New Realism in poetry and art focused less on the *formal* influence of Dada on pop art—since that was beyond dispute—than on the intentionality and reception of the techniques used by the New Realists. That is to say, American critics took up the question of "the false sublation of autonomous art"—not as a condition of popular culture but as a feature of the neo-avant-garde (pop art). Were the techniques of the New Dada used in the critical and adversarial spirit of the original Dada, or had they become tools of an art that was essentially "affirmative" (to use Marcuse's term)—supportive of marketplace values and the aesthetic ideology of autonomous art (which Dada had sought to expose and destroy)? Asserting the latter possibility implies, of course, that the Dadaist project had indeed been corrupted—converted into kitsch (according to the Greenbergian model of the parasitic nature of kitsch), though it also denies the possibility of art (or poetry) that is fundamentally dialectical in relation to bourgeois values.

A survey of the polemical debate on these issues in 1962 reveals broad support for the Greenbergian position. In his review of what he calls the "new vulgarians," Max Kozloff contends, "The spectator's nose is practically rubbed into the whole pointless cajolery of our hardsell," an effect of "the injection of merchandising and 'direct mail' techniques into art" (a view equating advertising and art).[58] To Gilbert Sorrentino, the New Realism is little more than the objectification of "a specious reality"; it is, he claims, "a poor art, distinguished by sterile facility, cynicism, and middle-class opportunism."[59] Stanley Kunitz explains the problem by contrasting old and new Dada: "The profound difference is that Dada was essentially a revolutionary movement. . . . Now the New Dada instead *embraces*, in a sense, the bourgeois symbols."[60] Hilton Kramer, too, sees in pop art a betrayal of Dada: "its social effect is simply to reconcile us to a world of commodities, banalities and vulgarities—which is to say an effect indistinguishable from advertising art."[61] In all of these comments, one discovers a contrast between an avowedly political sublimation of kitsch by Dadaism and what is perceived to be a purely aesthetic sublimation of commercial culture—in the service of bourgeois consumerism—by pop art.

Among the polemical voices (Kramer, Kunitz, Dore Ashton, and others) at a "Symposium on Pop Art" held in 1962, only Leo Steinberg offered a tentative, but acute, model for assessing the enigma of the New Realism apart from the conventional militancy of the neo-modernists. In response to Peter Selz's question, "If this art is as closely related to advertising and the whole campaign of Madison Avenue as some people say it is, what is its relation to Dada?" Steinberg contends that the New Realist, unlike the abstract expressionist, occupies the position of *"the non-dissenter."*[62] He explains, "Sure, Dada was revolutionary. Every art movement we have known for a hundred years was revolutionary. And it may be that the extraordinary novelty and the shock and dismay and disdain that is felt over this movement is that it doesn't *seem revolutionary* like every other."[63] Steinberg is not saying that the New Realism is *not* revolutionary but rather that the revolutionary stance of the *non-dissenter* is inscrutable, inexplicit, equivocal, perhaps divided within itself, and therefore puzzling. Steiner's position suggests that the sublimation of kitsch ventured by pop art is something more than purely aesthetic or affirmative.

When Bürger addresses the problem of "the false sublation of autonomous art" in the works of the neo-avant-garde (that is, in the New Dada of pop art), he is of two minds. On the one hand, referring to the "snare pictures" of the French pop artist Daniel Spoerri, he finds the affirmations of pop art to be unequivocal: "the neo-avant-garde institutionalizes the *avant-garde as art* and thus negates genuinely avant-gardist intentions."[64] Addressing, on the other hand, one of Warhol's serialized images, he acknowledges, "The painting of 100 Campbell soup cans contains resistance to this commodity society only for the person who wants to see it there."[65] From this perspective, the critical and adversarial character of the Warhol painting is ambiguous: it may or may not be a genuine work of the avant-garde. In this sense, the work of the New Realist is truly a "snare picture" (had Bürger been able to appreciate the full significance of this term), confronting the viewer with a series of unresolvable questions: Is it avant-garde or not? Is it art or kitsch? Adorno as well, Bürger notes, takes a similar view of the possible sublation of autonomous art in the work of the neo-avant-garde: "one cannot say in general whether someone who does away with all expression is a mouthpiece of reified consciousness or the speechless, expressionless expression that denounces that consciousness."[66] Thus the intentionality and therefore the value of the "expressionless" Warholian artifact remains—like the attitude of the *non-dissenter*—inscrutable, duplicitous, unverifiable.

Bürger's and Adorno's characterization of the fundamental ambiguity of the neo-avant-garde work—Is it genuine or not?—replicates the enduring "mystery" of the kitsch artifact: Is it fake or not? Is it art or kitsch? Bürger, perhaps reflecting his bias against kitsch and popular culture, regards this ambiguity in the neo-avant-garde work as a deficit, a failure to achieve a more decisive and definitive position concerning its resistance to commodification. What Bürger fails to grasp is that the unverifiability of kitsch—insofar as it is truly a *snare picture*, appealing to the consumer as an artifact that is simultaneously desirable and alienating—offers a significant new paradigm for the work of the avant-garde.

After After-Poets: Collaboration and Collective Writing

In the domain of innovative poetry, the 1960s was an era of what Francis Jeffrey (in the early nineteenth century) called "after-poets," whose writing is "substantially derivative and, as geologists say of our own present earth, of secondary formation—made up of the debris of a former world."[67] The "debris" gathered by the after-poets of the mid-twentieth century derived, however, not only from the poetry of the past but from texts of all kinds and, frequently, from the writing of one another—an orientation departing from Walter Benjamin's conception of poetic kitsch, which in his view is always "the debris of a former world" (to use Jeffrey's phrase). From this perspective, the poets of the New Realism are "after-after-poets"—not historically or temporally, but in the sense that their poems always duplicate or serialize parts of other texts that have themselves been composed from the "debris" of other poets.

The immediate impetus for these experiments came, as I have indicated, from the revival and example of Dadaism, yet one must acknowledge that they also constitute a revival of the conservative methods of the commonplace book: citation, appropriation, replication, collaboration. Warhol's "serial disasters" and Malanga's parasitic rituals of verbal "suicide" thus expose, scandalize, and resituate these traditional techniques. From a purely technical standpoint, then, the methods of the neo-avant-garde during this period adopted the unmarked yet enduring compositional logic of middle-brow poetry, of magazine verse and poetic kitsch: a closed circuit of unoriginal writing. The postwar avant-garde was intent, it appears, on reviving and reorienting the poetics of kitsch.

Radicalizing the techniques of the commonplace book—the archaic *action* of the poetics of kitsch—begins with the concept of *collaboration*, since the first glimpse of poetry that would soon be intertwined with Warhol's radical aesthetic came in the *Locus Solus* issue devoted (as I indicated earlier) to that practice. The issue opens with an epigraph from Lautréamont's *Poésies: Preface à un livre futur*: "La poésie doit être faite par tous. Non par un." (Poetry should be made by all. Not by one.) Although Koch and his fellow editors captured the essence of Lautréamont's recipe for future poetry, they neglected to use a somewhat bolder statement of the same principle in Lautréamont's essay: "Plagiarism is necessary. Progress calls for it" (a slogan adopted by the Situationist Guy Debord in his 1970 manifesto, *The Society of the Spectacle*).[68]

The enunciation of this principle at the beginning of the *Locus Solus* issue helps to account for the inclusion of two of Chatterton's Rowley poems—indicating a correlation between forgery and collaboration—along with examples of the Australian Ern Malley forgeries of 1944 (which have been compared to Chatterton's poems).[69] It is certainly the case that the new Dadaist "collaborators" made use of devices common to eighteenth-century imposture: found texts, invented sources, assumed identities, multiple authors. Embracing the poetics of forgery also underscores the complications of the term "collaboration" pertaining to complicity, betrayal, and other treasonous activities.

It is worth examining the Ern Malley affair more closely—American interest in this hoax was occasioned by publication of a new edition of the texts in 1961—in order to understand why the editors of *Locus Solus* may have viewed these forgeries (and the context of the scandal) as pertinent to the practice of collaboration.[70] The reception of the Ern Malley poems has occasionally unfolded in unexpected ways, sometimes resulting in the migration of imposture into canonical settings, as with John Tranter's inclusion of all of the Ern Malley forgeries in the *Penguin Book of Modern Australian Poetry*.[71] In addition, the historian of New York School poetry Mark Ford reports that John Ashbery and Kenneth Koch included the Ern Malley poems in their teaching syllabi at Brooklyn College and Columbia University.[72] Ashbery, apparently, used the poems for an exercise in which students were asked to identify the forged text among unattributed poems, including examples of Geoffrey Hill's *Mercian Hymns*. The juxtaposition of the Ern Malley poems with the pseudo-Anglo-Saxon diction of the *Mercian Hymns* resonates with the historical conditions of imposture: the appeal of archaism and the question of authenticity (Is it real or not?) associated with poetic forgery during the eighteenth-century ballad revival. Ashbery's pedagogical exercise suggests that the anxieties associated with poetic imposture cannot be entirely eliminated from the Neo-Dada procedures of collaboration and appropriation. The "new collaboration" is not simply an exercise in constructivism: it aims, instead, to re-enchant the unreliability of the artifact as a way of producing a counterfeit commodity, a device that is simultaneously seductive and critically engaged.

The Ern Malley poems were produced by two Australian poets, James McAuley and Harold Stewart, who sought to discredit the poetic values of modernism by placing the forgeries in a small Australian avant-garde journal called *Angry Penguins*, edited by two young poets, Max Harris and John Reed. Sixteen Ern Malley poems were published under the title, *The Darkening Ecliptic*, in the summer issue of *Angry Penguins* in 1944. In his initial enthusiasm over the poems, Harris described the fictitious Malley as "one of the two giants of contemporary Australian poetry."[73] The hoax was soon exposed, however, by a journalist investigating the affair. Even so, eminent critics such as Herbert Read—who described Ern Malley as a "modern Ossian"—continued to find value in the poems.[74]

The rationale for the *Locus Solus* editors' inclusion of Ern Malley poems in their issue on Dada-inspired collaboration can be found in part in statements made by the forgers, McAuley and Stewart, about the procedures they used to produce the texts:

> We produced the whole of Ern Malley's tragic life-work in one afternoon, with the aid of a chance collection of books which happened to be on our desks: the *Concise Oxford Dictionary*, a collected Shakespeare, a dictionary of quotations, etc. . . . We opened books at random, choosing a word or phrase haphazardly. We made lists of these and wove them into nonsensical sentences.[75]

Viewed within the larger framework of correspondences between imposture and collaboration, the Ern Malley procedures function like a bridge between Chatterton's fabrication of the Rowleyan tongue (utilizing dictionaries and editions of Spenser and Shakespeare) and the instructions for writing Dada poetry which Ashbery, O'Hara, and other poets found in Motherwell's postwar anthology. Notice the affinities between the Ern Malley procedures and Tzara's recipe for avant-garde poetry:

> To make a Dadaist poem
> Take a newspaper.
> Take a pair of scissors.
> Choose an article as long as you are planning to make
> Your poem.
> Cut the article.
> Then cut out each of the words that make up this article
> And put them in a bag.
> Shake it gently.
> Then take out the scraps one after the other
> In the order in which they left the bag.
> Copy conscientiously.[76]

Remarkably, these instructions for writing *real* avant-garde poetry are not terribly different from the forgers' description of producing *fake* avant-garde poetry (except for the divergent sources). The "collaborators" in the *Locus Solus* issue might just as easily have produced their cut-ups utilizing the Ern Malley procedure as Tzara's Dada recipe.

Of these two compositional models, the fraudulent angle is certainly the more interesting, since it lends a disreputable air to the vital amateurism of the avant-garde procedure, even as it acquires a subversive—and mystifying—sense of purpose. The "tragic life-work" of one of Australia's greatest modern poets can be whipped up in a single afternoon; the "suicidal" Dadaist poem can be thrown together like a casserole in the kitchen. Just follow directions. These do-it-yourself artifacts are closely related to Warhol's "paint-by-numbers" pictures (exhibited alongside his "serial disasters") and to Ted Berrigan's "fill-in-the-blank operation" (a text circulated among multiple poets), which was inspired, Berrigan says, by Koch's "anthology of collaborations" in *Locus Solus* 2.[77]

The two Ern Malley poems in *Locus Solus* immediately follow a half-dozen Surrealist collaborations in the issue, including a *cadavre exquis* by Paul Eluard and others, thereby intimating a correlation between imposture and automatic writing. The Ern Malley forgeries are followed in turn by cut-up texts "by Gregory Corso and Dwight Eisenhower"; by "Daniel Krakauer, Aeschylus, the N.Y. Daily News & a Handbook on Birdlife"; and by Shakespeare and the Soviet cosmonaut "Uri Gagarin," combined with various news items from the press ("arranged" by Ruth Krauss). It is not surprising in the least, then, to find among these garbled texts a collage by Ern Malley, "Sybilline," pushing the Surrealism of Eliot's *Waste Land* towards absurdity and, with a grim determination, towards kitsch:

> Would it be strange now to meet
> The figure that strode hell swinging
> His head by the hair
> On Princess Street?[78]

Milton's Satan and Dante's Bertrand de Born appear to be fused here in the "sybilline" figure of a drag queen cruising the shadowy purlieus of Princess Street.

Following Lautréamont's epigraph about the necessity of collective writing, *Locus Solus* 2 opens with a text that is emblematic of the collaborative enterprise: an unattributed cento of some fifty-two lines called "To a Waterfowl" (the title of a poem by William Cullen Bryant). Although John Ashbery is identified in Koch's notes (at the end of the issue) as the composer of the text, the lack of attribution effectively signals the suppression of the author function in extreme forms of "collaboration." At the same time, although the composer of the cento is anonymous—having written none of its lines—one should not therefore presume that the particular selection of lines does not betray the intentions of the composer or that the texture of the sampling may not be of some significance. In the case of Ashbery's cento, the complexion and authorial "weave" of the selections appear to be at odds with the radicalism of the Dada techniques introduced by the procedure of the cento. This kind of polarization is entirely in keeping with the ancient, generic motivations of the cento, a type of poem first written in antiquity from bits of Old Testament scripture in the service of christological beliefs, as a way of rewriting, but also discrediting—and dialectically preserving—the phraseology of the older system.

What kind of poetry does Ashbery choose to fill the poetic form inaugurating this anthology of experimental writing? The most frequently cited authors in "To a Waterfowl" are Keats (with seven lines) and Tennyson (with six). These selections are in keeping with the canonical—and distinctly lyrical—tenor of all of the fifty-two lines chosen by Ashbery. In fact, echoing the preponderance of Keats and Tennyson, the diction of the appropriated materials never strays far from a tonality that is supersaturated with poetic effects—that is, from the echo chamber of poetic kitsch. Here is a sampling of lines (which are unattributed in the cento):

> The vapours weep their burthen to the ground
> [Tennyson, "Tithonius"]
> And many a nymph who wreathes her brow with sedge
> [Collins, "Ode to Evening"]
> Calm was the day, and through the trembling aire
> [Spenser, "Prothalamium"]
> Last noon beheld them full of lusty life
> [Byron, "Waterloo"]
> Steady thy laden head across a brook
> [Keats, "To Autumn"]
> She dwells with Beauty—Beauty that must die
> [Keats, "Ode to Melancholy"]

There is even a sequence of lines from Whitman, Campion, and Waller devoted to a repertoire of poetic blossoms: lilies, roses, and lilacs. In the end, it would not be inaccurate to describe the cento as a "garland"—a treasury—of poetic kitsch.

The relation of these appropriated materials to the ostensibly radical procedures associated with collaboration can be interpreted in several ways. At first glance, the anachronistic diction and the procedure of the cento—radicalized by its proximity to various Dada techniques—appear to be incongruous, incommensurable. Yet it may be that one of the functions of these sampling techniques is to import—one might even say to smuggle—unfashionable (and in this case lyrical) notions into the militant precinct of the avant-garde (in a manner resembling, as we have seen, the function of translational personae in the *Cantos*). Ashbery, for example, prefaces an early essay on the Surrealist Joseph Cornell with a quotation from Rimbaud's *Season in Hell*:

> I loved stupid paintings, decorated transoms, stage sets, carnival booths, signs, popular engravings, old-fashioned literature, church Latin, erotic books with nonexistent spelling, the novels of our grandmothers, fairy tales, childrens' books, old operas, silly refrains, naïve rhythms.[79]

Taking into account their unfashionable allure, the appropriated lines in Ashbery's cento may be compared to the forms of kitsch—a rhapsody of bad taste—celebrated in Rimbaud's manifesto—and to the wayward impulse to secretly embrace the disenchanted, the outmoded. From this perspective, Ashbery (and Rimbaud before him) is taking a cue from Baudelaire's poetic radicalization of bad taste (a topic about which I shall have more to say in the next chapter).

Yet perhaps this correspondence does not go far enough in explaining the puzzling relation between the avant-garde procedure of appropriation (or collaboration) and its "stupid" but glamorous materials. Perhaps, as I suggested earlier, the Dada technique of sampling corresponds in fundamental ways to the mechanism of replication that sustains the poetics of kitsch. This interpretation of Ashbery's perverse selection of markedly lyrical diction foregrounds the essential difference between the polarized substance of kitsch under high modernism and its more dialectical elaboration in the context of late modernism, pop art, and the New Realism.

In addition, one might then see that both versions of replication—Dada and the polarized sublimation of kitsch—model the capitalist logic of fashion. In this case, the vanguard techniques of Dada resonate with, or may even derive from, the replicative and delirious structure of kitsch. At the same time, there is a divergence between the explicitly political sublimation of clichés practiced by Dada poets and the implicitly aesthetic sublimation of clichés (or poetic commonplaces) by Ashbery and other poets of the New York school. Indeed, any of these practices will inevitably be situated along a spectrum ranging from militantly political to unabashedly aesthetic modes of appropriation—though none of them is entirely one or the other.

Ashbery did not republish "To a Waterfowl" in any of his books, but the poem resembles—in its uninflected concatenation of poetic baubles—other poems composed under the influence of Dada that Ashbery did publish in *The Tennis Court Oath* and the book that followed it, *Rivers and Mountains* (1966). The elements of these catalogue-poems can be construed in diverse ways. For example, the 111 brief telegraphic sections composing Ashbery's detective epic, "Europe," may be read as inscrutable clues to a submerged narrative or crime:

2.
A wave of nausea—
Numerals.

3.
A few berries

4.
The unseen claw
Babe asked today
The background ropes roped over
Into star jolted them

5.
Filthy or into backward drenched flung heaviness
Lemons asleep pattern crying.[80]

As the riddling crime (of writing?) unfolds, the poem drops fragments of
Auden, Hopkins, Coleridge, Marvell, and D. H. Lawrence—along with sections of a forgotten children's story, *Beryl of the Biplane*, about "a mysterious
aviatrix in World War I."[81]

The tantalizing elements of the catalogue-poem are serialized differently
in another poem written (in 1961) under the influence of Dada, "Into the
Dusk-Charged Air." The title evokes an old-fashioned adventure yarn, and
the poem itself delivers a breathless travelogue of 152 of the world's rivers,
each line containing at least one name of a river:

The landscape around the Mohawk stretches away:
The Rubicon is merely a brook.
In winter the Main
Surges; the Rhine sings its eternal song. . . .
And above the glistering Gila
A sunset as beautiful as the Athabasca
Stammered. The Zambezi chimed. The Oxus
Flowed somewhere. . . .[82]

Instead of clues, the elements of the catalogue-poem here become geographical "features," locations, and destinations—all alluring in their remote-
ness, all consumed verbally at a breakneck pace by the armchair traveler.

The rituals of conspicuous consumption, which remain implicit in Ashbery's centos and early catalogue-poems, become overt when, in a poem
such as "Daffy Duck in Hollywood," Ashbery turns his attention to commodity culture. Here the rivers and the clues and treasured citations of the
catalogue-poem turn into commodities:

La Celestina has only to warble the first few bars
Of "I Thought about You" or something mellow from

Amadigi di Guala for everything—a mint-condition can
Of Rumford's Baking Powder, a celluloid earring, Speedy
Gonzales, the latest from Helen Topping Miller's fertile
Escritoire, a sheaf of suggestive pix on greige, deckle-edged
Stock—to come clattering through the rainbow trellis
Where Pistachio Avenue rams the 300 block of Highland
Fling Terrace . . .[83]

Here, all it takes to cause a flood of gewgaws and trifles to come crashing through the "rainbow trellis" is a "few bars" of a song—a lyric: a chance event replicating the effects of appropriation in Ashbery's catalogue-poems. The correlation between scraps of poetic kitsch (in "To a Waterfowl") and commodities takes a final step in *The Vermont Notebook*, where in one poem Ashbery simply streams a list of corporations:

Gulf Oil, Union Carbide, Westinghouse, Xerox, Eastman Kodak,
ITT, Marriot, Sonesta, Crédit Mobilier, Sperry Rand, Curtis
Publishing, Colgate, Motorola, Chrysler, General Motors,
Anaconda, Crédit Lyonnais, Chase Manhattan, Continental Can,
Time-Life, McGraw Hill, CBS, ABC, NBC.[84]

In this passage, brand names (of corporations) have replaced names of far-away rivers, or emblems of poetic kitsch in a cento, inviting us to consider whether poetic kitsch may function like a brand name: saturated, ambient, impersonal (a dialectical form of advertising).

The Neo-Dada techniques of appropriation and montage play a crucial role in isolating the kitsch of Ashbery's catalogue-poems from the aesthetic of camp. In Ashbery's catalogues and centos, Andrew Ross contends, with their "Rousselian voyeurism" and their "obsessive attention to gratuitous notation and visual detail," there is "never any sense of order, aesthetic or otherwise, an order upon which camp stylism depends for its construction of an entirely mannered world."[85] Furthermore, in contrast, say, to O'Hara's campy "I do this I do that" style of delivery, "Ashbery seldom takes advantage of the consummate sense of tone, timing, and delivery that comes with the full-blown naïve (as opposed to deliberate) camp sensibility. . . . Ashbery refuses to *humanize* the tone of camp."[86] Techniques such as appropriation and montage therefore tend to isolate the borrowed line, the mundane object, the trifle, the commodity, from affect and value—certainly from any sort of identificatory embrace. The items in Ashbery's kitschy catalogue-poems remain at a distance—neutral, dehumanized, interchangeable—and therefore susceptible to accumulation (as his poems demonstrate) and to allegorical readings.

Ashbery's catalogue-poems have important things to tell us about the particular poetic effects produced by some of these experimental procedures. As an emblem of techniques of appropriation and montage, the cento reinforces the integrity of the poetic line as a basic unit of composition. Commenting, for example, on Ted Berrigan's "method arrangement," which relies heavily on the appropriation and shuffling of individual lines, Alice Notley refers to "Ted's conception of the line in *The Sonnets* as something that once established becomes rigid in its repetition no matter the syntax involved."[87] Because the line is also the integral unit of the poetic refrain—which amplifies, in turn, the expressivity of the line—and because the lines appropriated in a cento are often repetitions of lines written by other poets (or of parts of other texts), the effects of poetic experimentation in this context may be understood as redefining the use and form of the refrain—a device essential to the poetics of kitsch. The elaboration of a refrain becomes more prominent in collaborations where constraints require the repetition of certain words in every, or every other, line.[88] Another type of redistribution of the refrain occurs when particular lines are utilized by multiple poets, as in Malanga's and Berrigan's use of an Ashbery title (which is itself appropriated): "How Much Longer Will I Be Able to Inhabit the Divine Sepulcher . . ."[89]

Methods of collaboration tend therefore to isolate and reinforce the poetic line, or portions of it, as a repeating or alternating unit. This is especially true with collaborations between two writers, when the poetic "labor" is divided by alternating lines (as is the case in some of Koch's and Ashbery's collaborations in *Locus Solus*).[90] In addition, the alternation, or calculated distribution, of lines lends itself naturally to the collaborative composition of short dramas, a practice favored by Ashbery, Koch, O'Hara, and their coterie of friends. Even more broadly, decoding and redefining the iterability of the verbal refrain (as a tool of advertising and indoctrination) may be compared to the development of seriality in Warhol's photo-silkscreen paintings—a correspondence cultivated in particular by second-generation New York school poets (Berrigan, Ron Padgett, Joe Brainard, Diane di Prima, and others).

The poetic effects generated by techniques that collapse the distinction between kitsch and the avant-garde (appropriation, collage, collaboration), extend notably to the *diction* of a text —a decisive feature of poetic kitsch. In the context of twentieth-century poetic experiment, the mechanism of appropriation is often trained on the vernacular, on the language of everyday experience (which may, of course, take many forms), resulting in a marked relaxation of the diction of poetry.[91] Sublimating the vernacular has also, however, always been a significant operation of poetic kitsch, even if the poetic "vernacular" turns out to be a synthetic, and even disfigured, medium far removed from ordinary speech.

At the same time, as we see in the "garland" of high lyrical kitsch serialized in Ashbery's cento, "To a Waterfowl," the device of appropriation can, in a more conservative vein, shape contemporary diction by exposing it to archaic usage, specialized vocabularies, and formulaic poetic language: textures and tonalities that appear to be at odds with the "experimental" procedures driving the poem. Within the rarified and residualized domain of kitsch, the production of elevated special effects coexists with the transcription of idiomatic speech, precisely because the language of poetic kitsch consists entirely of verbal samples, produced through an endless process of appropriation, replication, and collaboration. The texture of kitsch in Ashbery's writing, whether high or low, is synthetic, residual, *plastic*:

> 56.
>> songs like
>> You came back to me
>> you were wrong about the gravestone
> that nettles hide quietly
> The son is not ours.

> 57.
> Precise mechanisms
> Love us.

> He came over the hill
> He held me in his arms—it was marvelous.

> But the map of Europe
> shrinks around naked couples[92]

Ashbery's synthesis of torch songs and Audenesque sonneteering may be contrasted with the way Malanga sequences the endless distractions framed by the New Realism of kitsch:

> I will visit the nation bearing the evidence of fresh
> Death and suspicion.
> Yet we come out of it in the photo
> Stat. Stings and complaint. The smirk.[93]

Malanga's lines sample the tonalities of rhetorical inflation, journalism, and certain specialized jargons, combined with the artless tone of a diary. Ted Berrigan's diction, by contrast, veers between the profane and the pre-Raphaelite:

> Summer so histrionic, marvelous dirty days
> Is not genuine it shines forth from the faces
> Littered with soup, cigarettes, the heavy
> is a correspondent the innocence of a childhood
> Sadness graying the faces of virgins aching
> and everything comes before their eyes. . . .
> they weep and get solemn etcetera.[94]

Not surprisingly, given Berrigan's poetic "stalking" of O'Hara's charismatic susceptibility, Berrigan learned a thing or two about tone from his master, whose poetry redefines the art of verbal promiscuity:

> Vagrants, crushed by such effulgence,
> wrap their wild twigs and bruises in straws
> and touch themselves lightly, like buttered bees . . .
> Oh, March! You have not decided whom you train.
> Or what traitors are waiting for you to be born,
> Oh, March! Or what it will mean in terms of diet.[95]

The dappled vocabulary of O'Hara's synthetic aria (enriched by "vagrants" and "buttered bees") easily accommodates as well the dead register of "what it will mean in terms of diet." According to Lytle Shaw, O'Hara's poetry facilitates "the collapsing of vocabulary registers . . . the rubbing of vernacular diction against opera and high art."[96]

The deliberate turn toward idiomatic language in all of these passages would appear to be a polemical gesture, recalling Wordsworth's militant commitment to "common language"—in contrast to markedly poetic diction. Yet the inclusion in these passages of precisely the sort of "phraseology" that Wordsworth abhorred suggests otherwise. This is borne out by the fact that few poetic manifestos of the late 1950s or early 1960s make exclusive commitments to the diction of everyday language.[97] Rather, judging by the use of idioms in the passages I have cited, the turn to the vernacular appears in this context to be more gestural, materialistic, acquisitive—and therefore not incompatible with the infusion of richer, or more generic, poetic stuff.

Compositional distraction leads to a consumerist or curatorial approach to poetic language: I *like* this I *like* that (a variation of O'Hara's "I do this I do that" model). In terms of the poetics of kitsch, these passages combine what are essentially idiomatic gestures—or jingles—with spells of heightened diction. What results from this synthesis—similar perhaps to the effect of Thomas Gray's "methodical borrowing phrenzy"—is a poetic tone that is simultaneously obscure and familiar, contrived and colloquial. The authenticity of these poetic dummies may be in question, but they do not cross over into camp and become a mask or a prop. They retain the vulgar refinement and the insularity of kitsch—its doll-like composure. Dada procedures of appropriation and collaboration therefore permit—without sanctioning—a curatorial model of poetic diction. Rooted in questions of taste, this approach veers inevitably towards a consumerist model of exchange, in which all verbal textures become, in principle, interchangeable and therefore subject to higher levels of abstraction. Commodification produces in turn an allegorical dimension of poetic diction, harboring the "secrets" of the symbolic economy to which poetry has succumbed.

This development reached a peak in the mid-1960s, with the so-called second generation of New York school poets—Berrigan, Padgett, di Prima, Malanga—a group that found in Warhol's practice and ideas a model for their own poetic agenda. At the same time, these poets were radicalizing the ancient methods of the commonplace book—what Berrigan called "the precious art of reading aggressively"—by combining the activities of reading and writing into a single event.[98] Describing an exercise in what he called his "method," Berrigan remarks, "Part of the time Ron [Padgett] read to me from different books while I wrote, so that I wouldn't run out of things to say."[99] And, about the same time Berrigan was developing the "method" that would produce his *Sonnets*, Warhol remembers seeing Gerard Malanga at the Factory in 1965 engaging in a similar practice of modified commonplacing: "Gerard was usually over in a corner doing poetry that he based on lines from other people's work, so he would have an open book in one hand and be writing with the other."[100]

The commonplace methods, or intertextuality, of this group's writing could involve the work of older poets whom they admired, as we have already seen in Malanga's appropriation of Ashbery's poetry, or in the writing of Ted Berrigan (whom Geoff Ward calls a "Pepsi-generation de Quincey" in his adoring but tenuous relation to O'Hara).[101] The circles of appropriation or collaboration could also extend to multiple poets, as Daniel Kane explains: "The consistent intertextual references by Second-Generation New York school poets to First-Generation poets are so preponderant that a single poem by Frank O'Hara found itself re-cycled in literally dozens of other texts."[102] John Ashbery's poetry as well was the object of appropriation by numerous poets, including Ron Padgett, Malanga (as I have already indicated), and Berrigan, who freely acknowledges the borrowed sources in much of his writing: "my entire poem 'Frank O'Hara's Question' from 'Writers and Issues' by John Ashbery' in my book *Many Happy Returns* is entirely by John, i.e., some quotes from Frank surrounded by prose by John, which I 'found' à la Andy Warhol."[103] In addition, the title of Berrigan's volume of selected poems, *So Going Around Cities*, was lifted from Ashbery's poem "Rivers and Mountains."[104]

A number of the most important books to emerge from the second generation of New York school poets came about through the active collaboration of multiple poets. Ted Berrigan's major work, *The Sonnets*, is essentially a labyrinth of "collaboration" in various forms. In addition, Berrigan and Padgett wrote the book *Bean Spasms* together and considered calling it "Lyrical Bullets" (after Wordsworth and Coleridge's collaborative volume).[105] More provocative appropriations occurred as well, as Berrigan indicates in describing his use of a poem by his friend Dick Gallup as source material: "I took it and I rearranged a few lines, moved the things around, changed a couple of things. I mean it was a sonnet I made from all lines by him. There was no attempt to hide that it was all by him."[106] In essence, as Reva Wolf observes of Berrigan, "What intrigued him was the idea of making a copy of a copy and the question this raised about the 'ownership' of words."[107]

Berrigan even went so far as to produce outright fabrications: in his notorious "Interview with John Cage," for example (in which Cage played no role) he simply invents statements or, more interestingly, attributes Warhol's words to Cage. In one passage, Berrigan has Cage utter a kind of maxim: "to speak is to lie. To lie is to collaborate."[108] These statements leave no doubt that, for Berrigan, collaboration veers towards imposture, a development familiar (as we saw in earlier chapters) from the "contagion of imitation" spawned by the ballad revival in the eighteenth century.[109] Taking into account the transgressive aspect of these "collaborations," one might conclude that the sampling procedures of the second generation of New York School poets appear to be motivated, at times, by more deliberately political intent (the goal of destabilizing authorial integrity) than the experiments carried out by the contributors, for example, to the *Locus Solus* issue of collaborations (first-generation New York School poets). Drawing distinctions on the basis of political intent alone, however, calls to mind the precarious, and perhaps untenable, contrast between the political sublimation of clichés associated with Dada and a more purely aesthetic sublimation characteristic of kitsch.

A variegated repertoire of sampling strategies emerged in this context, from Ashbery's cento, "To a Waterfowl," and Berrigan's palimpsest poems to his "fill-in-the-blank operations" involving multiple poets. In terms of *reception*, however, the most important question concerning these kinds of texts becomes: Does the reader recognize the source (or sources) of these poems? What is the reader consuming, or does she imagine herself to be consuming? Clearly, the paradigm of a single author producing original work is irrelevant and misleading; these are forms of collective writing, whose most engaging qualities become evident in relation to other poems. Depending on the nature of the collaboration, or the types of material appropriated, one could argue that the reader is, to some degree, consuming scraps of the poetic tradition or, in a narrower sense, the mock tradition—I will call it—of the coterie. At the same time, the reader may be overhearing a slew of commercial or demotic gleanings in a poem that also samples the finery of the lyric tradition. It is precisely at this point, if one understands poetic kitsch to be the product of innumerable incidents of replication, imitation, and collaboration, that the underlying structural principles of the echo chamber of kitsch coincide with the collectivist (and sometimes political) procedures of the avant-garde.

Now, I am not claiming that one's experience of an Ashbery cento, or catalogue-poem, is identical to reading a poem by a naive poet who unconsciously repeats the clichés of a thousand other lyric poets. Rather, by composing in this manner, Ashbery has insinuated his poem into a deliberate collective process that, were it to progress far enough, would replicate the echolalia of kitsch—even as it acknowledges explicitly (as traditional kitsch does not) its collectivist formation, thereby seeking to alter, or influence, the praxis of everyday life. However, even if Ashbery's cento were to be circulated and replicated at length over time—like an artifact of mass culture—it is not clear whether the alienating effects of montage in the cento could ever become thoroughly synthesized and naturalized. The defamiliarizing impact of montage—related to shock—comes into conflict with the familiarizing effect of repetition. In works of this kind, the formal innovations of modernism (such as montage) are juxtaposed with the basic mechanism of kitsch (replication). The ultimate effect of this juxtaposition—on the reader—remains uncertain and open to question. It is entirely possible, however, that a critical eye (unlike the ordinary consumer of lyric clichés) might experience poetic kitsch of the most conventional sort as a concatenation of formulaic phrases—an assessment that would suspend the conflict between montage and replication.

One could also take this model of reception a step further, as John Shoptaw has done in relation to Ashbery's poetry, by arguing that intertextuality sustains a poetics of "misrepresentation," with the result that one should regard the collaborative surface of writing as a "cryptonymy."[110] Shoptaw views the cryptonymy of Ashbery's poetry in particular (facilitated in part by Dada procedures) as equivalent to what he calls "homotextuality": a consistent practice of poetic "misrepresentation," obscuring (and obliquely disclosing) the experience of queer subjectivity in the 1950s and 1960s.[111] Yet one can also broaden the spectrum of the cryptonymous text produced by avant-garde procedures, in reference to its evocation of the poetic tradition. In other words, it matters what sort of poetry is sampled in a cento or collage-poem: one may discern in a given selection a covert politics of the example. More specifically, the technique of appropriation can be used to smuggle into the collage-poem materials that may be out of fashion, or even at odds, with the presumed ideology of the procedure itself (as we saw in the case of Ashbery's cento, "To a Waterfowl"). Appropriation can permit outlawed registers of poetic diction—that is, kitsch—to be encrypted in the modernist text, as we discovered in examining the diction of Pound's *Cantos*.

The cryptonymy of the appropriated text can also operate at the level of vernacular expression, or depersonalized forms of public language—such as advertising copy—whereby the common phrases or idioms sampled in a poem may disclose submerged conditions of social antagonism or distress. Of the poetry I've examined so far in this chapter, the most obvious example of using verbal clichés from the public domain as a matrix of the New Realism occurs with Malanga's cut-up texts in *Chic Death*:

> The passageway flunked you
> Against something suddenly to the fireworks tired of setting.
> I saw that because I'm going to see
> This. We back up into the only paradox.
> We have acquired the eternal grace of pure reason.[112]

Cognitively, the language Malanga employs here means virtually nothing; it functions solely as a means of *expressing* social conditions (the collision of radicalism and consumption, for example) that are accessible only as a residue of the various registers of diction Malanga employs. At this level, avant-garde practice and the poetics of kitsch share the contraption of allegorical expression, a mode of expression consistent with the inherent ambiguity of kitsch (Is it art or not?) and with the poetics of imposture.

Coterie and Melodrama

Ashbery, O'Hara, Koch, and Schuyler—it hardly needs to be stated—formed the nucleus of the first generation of New York School poets. A second generation of New York School poets—dubbed "the *soi-disant* Tulsa school" by Ashbery—clustered around Ted Berrigan and Ron Padgett—who had been friends in Oklahoma before they set up shop at the Poetry Project of St. Mark's in Manhattan. These two (sometimes overlapping) generations of poets are best described, according to leading scholars in the field, as poetic coteries. Geoff Ward sees in the density and vigor of New York School affiliations a modern counterpart to the coterie around Alexander Pope in the eighteenth century—though it would be more accurate, perhaps, to draw a comparison with the Shenstone Set or Walpole's Strawberry Hill Set. Shaw describes the New York coteries as "temporary queer families," and it is certainly the case that the majority of insiders were male and homosexual: Ashbery, O'Hara, Schuyler, Edwin Denby, John Wieners (a satellite figure), Joe Brainard, Kenward Elmslie—not to mention Allen Ginsberg and William S. Burroughs, but also John Cage, Jasper Johns, Robert Rauschenberg, Cy Twombly, and so on.[113]

The immediate connotations of the term "coterie" (insular, elitist, arcane, trifling) are not to be dismissed—Shaw calls the concept of coterie "community's evil twin"—but one cannot begin to appreciate the full significance of the concept without attending to the historical origin of the term: from the word "cots" (short for "cottages"), the *Oxford English Dictionary* has "coterie" meaning, at its source, "a certain number of peasants united together to hold land from a lord."[114] Though this definition may seem laughable when applied to the sophisticates of the New York school, it reveals that the concept of "coterie" is rooted in social and economic resistance. Even more surprisingly, "coterie" originally pertained, contrary to assumptions about its elitist orientation, to the experience of the underclasses. In addition, a social formation we now associate with exclusivity and privacy originated with incidents of public insurgency. A similar oscillation between private and public, and between divergent class associations, comprehends as well, we should recall, the historical vicissitudes of melodrama: a poetic (and musical) practice originating in private, aristocratic circles, which then became a vehicle of infidel propaganda and public subversion.

When Geoff Ward writes of the New York school, "The unashamed promotion of the coterie of poets as such probably reached its high-point with Berrigan," he is not referring solely to the social interaction of the coterie —if such a distinction were possible—but also to the collaborative poetic practices that governed and objectified the sociality of the coterie.[115] It is on this basis that Ward, invoking the example of the Jena Circle of German Romantic writers, proposes "to read the term 'coterie' textually"— that is, to read the poetry produced within the coterie as exemplifying its social praxis—and vice versa.[116] More to the point, the examples of the Shenstone Set and the Walpole Set serve as historical models of a "textual coterie," oriented around the axes of queer personification and textual imposture.

Accordingly, in Shaw's treatment of New York School poets, "coterie illuminates crucial assumptions about the ways that styles of referentiality are taken to encode models of audience."[117] Since, in the "relational aesthetics" of the textual coterie, the audience cannot be distinguished from the community, the violation of poetic convention coincides potentially with the infidel complexion of the audience/community. Thus, Shaw claims, "because the charge of coterie tends to involve a claim about an aesthetic and social breach, it becomes a moment when historically inflected assumptions about community (and its relation to reading) get articulated."[118] Furthermore, though Shaw does not directly invoke Bürger's model of the historical avant-garde, he contends, "Reading a coterie thus might be considered an exemplary problem in considering the seam between the textual and the empirical"—between art and life (in Bürger's terms).[119] Works of art in this context thus become, in Nicolas Bourriaud's view, "objects producing sociability" or "moments of sociability" in themselves.[120]

The interdependency of the queer coterie (as a model of social subversion) and poetic collaboration becomes evident in curious and sometimes cryptic ways. Two forgeries by Chatterton appear, as I indicated earlier, as premonitory models of poetic collaboration in *Locus Solus*. A closer look at the content of the poetic impostures selected by Ashbery and Koch reveals a coterie scene recalling Shenstone's realm of "indolence"—or a party on Long Island, where Ashbery, Koch, O'Hara, and Schuyler might have performed one of their collaborative dramas:

> The ealdermenne doe sytte arounde,
> Ande snoffelle oppe the cheorte steeme.
> Lyche asses wilde ynne desarte waste
> Swotelye the morneynge ayre doe taste,
>
> Syke keene theie ate; the minstrels plaie,
> The dyne of angelles doe theie keepe.[121]

> (The gentlemen do sit around
> And snuffle up the pleasant steam.
>
> Like asses wild in desert waste
> Sweetly the morning air do taste,
>
> Such delicacies they eat; the minstrels play;
> The din of angels do they keep.)

In the many closet dramas written by O'Hara as well—a deliberately socialized mode of imposture—one finds allusions to collaboration, to methods used to compose these dramatic texts. In "The Coronation Murder Mystery" (a masquerade of individuals associated with the New York school), "John Myers" (the director of the Tibor de Nagy Gallery) announces to "Larry Rivers" that "they want to do a feature story on you in *Angry Penguins*" (the defunct Australian magazine where the Ern Malley forgeries first appeared).[122] And in "Flight 115: a play, or Pas de Fumer sur la Piste" (a theater piece O'Hara wrote with Bill Berkson on a flight from Rome to New York in 1961), a portion of one of O'Hara's "collaborations with the French language"—a Surrealist farce he published originally in *Locus Solus* 2—fits easily into the antic milieu of the play.[123] Collaboration becomes a model for coterie as well—and vice versa—in *A Nest of Ninnies*, the novel written together by Ashbery and Schuyler, in which the method of composition enacts the relational values of the queer coterie evoked in the title.

Some of these collaborative theater texts, especially O'Hara's "Noh dramas" and "eclogues," emerge directly—in formal terms—from the discontinuous, lineated, alternating mode of the poetic collaborations by Ashbery, Koch, Berrigan, Padgett, and others. Bill Berkson, for example, recalled the influence of Ashbery's *Tennis Court Oath* on the theater piece "Flight 115" he wrote with O'Hara.[124] Much of the collaborative work in poetry I've examined here could in fact be converted into dramatic texts—into what O'Hara called "eclogues": dialogues—modeled on the ancient poetic genre of the eclogue and alluding to a kind of "queer idyll"—between two or more "shepherds" (usually players in the New York art scene).

One could say a great deal about the performative qualities—the camp humor—of some of O'Hara's plays, but the same material can be seen from a formal or sociological perspective as kitsch. For example, one of O'Hara's "eclogues" ("Love on the Hoof") was written (with Frank Lima) for Warhol —though never produced—in the mid-1960s. The two characters in the play, "Frank I" and Frank II," spend most of their time, like Warhol, on the telephone—indeed, the whole piece seems to want to assimilate the eclogue form (and its queer idyll) to the fashionable Warholian practice of seriality and its deadpan cultivation of kitsch: Virgil (poet of the *Eclogues*)— and his double, O'Hara—go to the Silver Factory.[125]

The poetics of collaboration thus finds its paradigmatic form in the coterie dramas written, performed, and experienced (as casual spectators) by Ashbery, Koch, O'Hara, and their friends (often, though not always, in a private setting). Insofar as these closet dramas meet some of Bürger's basic criteria for establishing genuine avant-garde work—especially the negation of individual production and reception—one can regard these collective and ephemeral texts as crystalizing momentarily some of the aspirations of the Neo-Dada revival of the 1960s. In addition, these works reach beyond the purely formal aspects of vanguard practice to the question of socialization. They anticipate the model of relational aesthetics, developed by Bourriaud, in which,

> form only assumes its texture (and only acquires a real existence) when it introduces human interactions. . . . Each particular artwork is a proposal to live in a shared world, and the work of every artist is a bundle of relations with the world, giving rise to other relations, and so on and so forth, ad infinitum.[126]

In this sense, the experimental dramas of the New York School poets combine formal techniques of Dadaism with an evolving project of integrating art into the praxis of everyday life.

In O'Hara's experimental coterie dramas, the collaborative conditions of production and reception recapitulate certain basic features of what one might call the situationist mode of Gothic melodrama in the eighteenth century. The substance of these correspondences reveals as well the relevance of kitsch (apart from camp) to O'Hara's little theater. Formally, we recall, melodrama depends on the mimeticism of its structure: one medium, or element, imposes on the other, echoing it and producing a new kind of ambient artifact, a "delirium" of the "twice-made." William Shenstone's poetic inscriptions and epitaphs on the grounds of his estate inscribed his coterie of friends (who adopted classical pseudonyms) into the "queer idyll" of the Leasowes, into a melodramatic space fusing art and life. O'Hara, to similar effect, helped to write and stage poetic melodramas (especially "Kenneth Koch: A Tragedy" and "The Coronation Murder Mystery") populated by characters from his coterie of friends in the New York art world. The cast in these melodramas—the "originals" of the characters in the play—sometimes played their namesakes, and sometimes not. (Ashbery, for example, played "Schuyler" in "The Coronation Murder Mystery.") In addition, O'Hara wrote a melodrama about the admirers of his poetry among the second generation of New York poets: Ted Berrigan, Joe Brainard, and Ron Padgett (with cameo appearances by Gregory Corso, Allen Ginsberg—and "Barry Goldwater"), all of whom appear as characters in the play. Evoking the real-life activities of these poets, the dialogue puts a flamboyant and playful spin, for example, on the founding of Ted Berrigan's influential poetry magazine, C, suggesting that the initial stands for "Carole Lombard," or "Communist," or "Courbet," or "Davy Crockett"—or "Caraway seeds."[127]

The Metaphysics of Kitsch

In the dialogue of "C Revisited," the diction and the profiles of the coterie figures are largely interchangeable: one character seems to be much like another. The generic quality of the diction is symptomatic of kitsch (even if the humor may be described as campy). One is reminded of Berrigan's fabricated interview with John Cage, in which statements made by Warhol in a 1963 interview are attributed to Cage:

> CAGE: . . . Somebody said that Brecht wanted everybody to think alike. I want everybody to think alike. . . . Everybody looks alike and acts alike, and we're getting more and more that way. I think everybody should be a machine. I think everybody should be alike.

INTERVIEWER: Isn't that like Pop Art?
CAGE: Yes, that's what Pop Art is, liking things.[128]

In these statements of Warhol's (which Berrigan transcribed almost verbatim), Cage becomes like Warhol, a condition grounded in "liking"—the *affect* characteristic of pop art—which makes one thing like another. Berrigan, too, likes Warhol, which explains the likeness of his fraudulent interview to the mimicry of Warhol's art. O'Hara—Joe LeSueur acknowledges—lived with the myth that "Frank liked everything": an affective regime, an ideology of affection, accounting in Warholian terms for the interchangeability of characters in O'Hara's melodramas.[129] The connection between liking and being alike also explains the potentially malicious nexus of "likeness" governing the social and textual relations of the coterie.

Warhol declares that "everybody should be alike," yet he also expands the mimeticism of the coterie—the denizens of the Silver Factory, in this case—to encompass a fugitive *totality*. Remarkably, and astutely, he finds common ground between pop art and Brecht's vanguard agenda—though he rejects Brecht's governmental "Communism," in favor of a pop regime of liking and being alike.[130] The shift from coterie to totality reminds us that coterie is a microcosm or, as Shaw contends, "as much an idea about the social possibilities of affinity as it is a concrete sociological fact."[131] That is to say, coterie may be at once a particular historical nexus and a speculative model of utopia, an artificial paradise (as Pound sought to inscribe in the *Cantos*).

Warhol's conception of fugitive totalities finds expression most commonly in his attraction to, his thoughts about, synthetic or reflective substances: plastic and silver. The infatuation with silver (the most traditional of phantasmatic substances) appears to emerge fortuitously with Ondine's (Billy Name's) coating of all the interior surfaces of the original Factory (Warhol's studio) with tinfoil—hence the name it acquired, the Silver Factory. Transformed by these reflective surfaces, the physical site of Warhol's coterie and art making became a sordid clubhouse and workplace of infinite, muddled reflections: a specious totality. Warhol's silver wig and the polyurethane balloons he called "silver pillows" or "silver clouds" were allegorical features of this silver totality, but silvering the Factory was definitely "an amphetamine thing" (on the part of Ondine and the other queer "A-men" who did the work).[132] When pop and Dada and kitsch converged in the early 1960s, Warhol remembers, "it was the perfect time to think sil-

ver. Silver was the future, it was spacy—the astronauts wore silver suits—
Shepard, Grissom, and Glenn had already been up in them, and their equipment was silver, too."[133] The future looked silver—when all the equipment
would be silver—because wearing "silver suits"—a second skin—makes everyone look alike. And not just the future: "Silver was also the past—the
Silver Screen—Hollywood actresses photographed in silver sets," Warhol
muses.[134] Everything is the color of mirrors: the past, the future, the astronauts, the stars, the sets, the equipment. And it is "all amphetamine busy-
work"—vacuous, compulsive, inexhaustible—a coterie of "mole people" pa-
pering a "silver tenement": a "silver planet," in Keats's phrase.[135]

If, in Warhol's pop laboratory, silver is the hectic, cloudy tint of kitsch,
then plastic is its true substance: a synthetic material converting the idea
of *surface* into a *Gesamtwerk* of feedback and liquid projections. Warhol
produced the early performances of the Velvet Underground as a multime-
dia show called the *EXPLODING PLASTIC INEVITABLE* (initially called the
ERUPTING plastic inevitable).[136] Here, "plastic" is the emblematic property of
a show that covers everything: a bogus and fluid totality.

In a meditation on plastic written in the late 1950s, shortly before Warhol would equate plastic with the substance of pop art, Roland Barthes observes that plastic, "despite having names of Greek shepherds (Polystyrene,
Polyvinyl, Polyethylene) . . . is in essence the stuff of alchemy."[137] Further, he
states, "In the hierarchy of major poetic substances, it figures as a disgraced
material, lost between the effusiveness of rubber and the flat hardness
of metal."[138] As a result of this retrograde "evolution in the myth of 'imitation' materials," he states, "plastic is, all told, a spectacle to be deciphered."[139]
In the modern dogma of this cryptic substance, "the age-old function of
nature is modified: . . . an artificial Matter, more bountiful than all natural deposits is about to replace her, and to determine the very invention
of forms."[140] Plastic, Barthes explains, is "the first magical substance which
consents to be prosaic."[141]

In Warhol's eccentric use of the word "plastic," its fraudulent, totalizing,
featureless essence becomes more pronounced in proximity to commercial
culture: "Vacant, vacuous Hollywood was everything I ever wanted to mold
my life into. Plastic: White-on-white. . . . It looked like it would be so easy
to just walk into a room and say those wonderful plastic lines."[142] In addition
to his fantasies about speaking "plastic lines"—faking language—his taste in
pop music (despite his cultivation of the Velvet Underground) betrayed a
similar liking for the indistinct, for "white-on-white": "the Beach Boys," he

once claimed, "were the most wonderful group in America because they ac-
cepted life in California for the mindless glory it is, without apologizing for
it or being embarrassed about it."[143] Yet perhaps in Warhol's mind, the Beach
Boys and the Velvet Underground are both "plastic," since the substance of
plastic captures—for Warhol—the neutralizing power of *abstraction* (which
would allow both bands to exist in the same totalizing dimension). Referring
to his friend the poet Ronnie Tavel, Warhol once remarked, "He understood
instantly when I'd say things like 'I want it simple and plastic and white.' Not
everyone can think in an abstract way."[144] Warhol is praising the ability to
"think in an abstract way" (one of the keys to his art), but also the ability to
think *plastic*—to think *silver*—as a mode of abstraction: generality, totality,
simplicity. A plastic world—with its "plastic lines" of poetry—is without
qualities, without parts, without volition. Ultimately, as Barthes contends,
"The hierarchy of substances is abolished: a single one replaces them all: the
whole world *can* be plasticized, and even life itself."[145]

9 Inventing Clichés
The Lost Legacy
of Baudelaire's Muddy Halo

> I long for the return of the dioramas whose enormous,
> crude magic subjects me to the spell of a useful illusion. I
> like going to the theater to look at the backdrop paintings
> on stage, where I find my favorite dreams treated with
> consummate skill and tragic concision. Those things, so
> completely false, are for that reason much closer to the
> truth, whereas the majority of our landscape painters are
> liars, precisely because they fail to lie.
>
> Baudelaire, *Salon of 1859*

Plastic Poetry

In the final stage of my attempt to outline a genealogy of poetry and
kitsch, I want to identify a somewhat anomalous source for the modern
synthesis of kitsch and vanguard poetry, a source inspiring the *paradis arti-*
ficiel of Pound's polarized epic poem but also prescribing the synthetic and
poetic "debris" of the New York school: Baudelaire's nakedly symptomatic
and contradictory prototype of the avant-garde. More narrowly, I want to
trace the impact of Baudelaire's poetic radicalization of bad taste through
the legacy of what he calls *"argot plastique"* (the poetic medium of *les paradis*
artificiels).[1] With its celebration of bad taste (via the trivial universe of aesthetic failure and distressed artifacts) and its "queer" relation to commodity
culture, Baudelaire's "plastic poetry" prefigures the *plastic inevitable* of Warhol's artificial paradise.

When Warhol equates the substance of plastic—an emblem of synthetic
and counterfeit realities—with his latest ideas about art, he is clearly drawing a correlation between art and commerce, between aesthetics and commodification. It is precisely, however, his willingness to conceive of the art-

work and the commodity as composed of the same synthetic substance that compels Peter Bürger to reject Warhol's serialized images as authentic expressions of the avant-garde—in contrast to the unambiguous negation of autonomous art (and commodification) offered by the works of Dadaism. Bürger elaborates his account of the essential negativity of the avant-garde by adopting a model of allegorical production and reception that he attributes—without any particular evidence—to the writings of Dada painters or poets. In fact, to be more precise, Bürger's model derives not from Dadaism but from Walter Benjamin's reading of Baudelaire's poetry: "Benjamin's allegory concept can function as a central category of a theory of the avant-gardiste work of art."[2]

Briefly, in Bürger's view, allegorical production (reflecting Benjamin's conception of Baroque allegory) corresponds to the Dadaist techniques of appropriation and montage: fragments of outdated artifacts are torn from their original context (an act robbing them of the illusion of intrinsic meaning), which the artist/allegorist then recombines into expressive constellations. Because appropriation and montage rob the displaced fragments of intrinsic meaning, allegorical reception exposes the inescapably subjective and historical determination of meaning, thereby revealing the deluded assumptions of the viewer in the present. Allegory is essentially a mode of expression revealing to the viewer the reality of the historical *present*—via alienated fragments of obsolete works from the past.

Benjamin's important revision of his concept of Baroque allegory in the 1930s did not, however, reflect the influence of Dadaism, as Bürger's hypothesis indicates. Benjamin regarded Dada (whose manifestations he witnessed directly during his most active years as a critic) as a premonitory or provisional movement whose techniques and intentions would be realized fully only in the mass medium of film.[3] Thus, instead of focusing on Dadaism, Benjamin—the most influential theorist of art's relation to commodity capitalism of the twentieth century—applied his conception of allegory to film but also, quite deliberately, to lyric poetry. He re-discovered allegory, it turns out, in the travails of the "lyric poet in the era of high capitalism"—in the poetry of Baudelaire. Benjamin's decision to focus his political and critical agenda (during the most mature phase of his work in the 1930s) on poetry lacking the radical posture and techniques of Dadaism remains essential to his final conception of allegory, which reflects his understanding of how lyric poetry in particular might pose a significant challenge to the delirium of commodity capitalism.

Taking into account the indispensable role of Baudelaire's poetry in Benjamin's Marxist revision of his theory of Baroque allegory in the 1930s, it appears that Bürger, by applying Benjamin's conception of allegory to Dada without qualification, misconstrues Benjamin's later formulation of allegory. (Bürger rarely mentions Baudelaire, for example, in his theorization of the avant-garde.) In particular, with regard to Benjamin's statement that "the structure of *Les Fleurs du mal* is monadological," Bürger fails to acknowledge the persistence of Leibniz's theory of *expression* in Benjamin's Marxist reformulation of allegory.[4] Bürger's embrace of the literal meaning of Dada practice—destroy autonomous art!—would appear to preclude altogether the need for a model of allegorical expression. Bürger's misappropriation may also account for his dismissal of Benjamin's view that the work of Dada must be regarded as a provisional phenomenon—the precondition, I have argued, of a full-blown elaboration of radicalized kitsch: a dialectical kitsch of apocalypse.

In his late criticism, Benjamin contrasts the violent tactics of Dadaism to Baudelaire's poetics of the "secret agent."[5] Concerning the random verbiage of Dadaist writing, Benjamin remarks, "Their poems are 'word salad' containing obscenities and every imaginable waste product of language."[6] The form and diction of Baudelaire's verse are, by contrast, Benjamin notes, embedded in a familiar but inscrutable matrix of poetic identity: "The incognito was the law of his poetry. His prosody is like the map of a big city in which one can move about inconspicuously."[7] Likewise, Benjamin acknowledges Baudelaire to be largely apolitical as a writer. In contrast to the direct and unequivocal political sympathies of a poet such as Pierre Dupont—a friend of Baudelaire's—Benjamin emphasizes "the profound duplicity which animates Baudelaire's own poetry. His verse supported the oppressed, though it espoused not only their cause but their illusions as well. It had an ear for the songs of the revolution and also for the 'higher voice' which spoke from the drumroll of the executions."[8] It is therefore not the unequivocal militancy of Dada writing that dominates Benjamin's thinking about revolutionary modernity—and poetry's task in revolution—but rather the "profound duplicity" of Baudelaire's lyric poetry. Baudelaire's poems are revolutionary precisely because they are disconcertingly *symptomatic* of the modern loss of historical experience ("a matter of tradition," according to Benjamin) and of the impersonal delirium of commodification.[9]

The political reserve and the formal conservatism (apart from the experiment of the late prose poems) of Baudelaire's verse compel Benjamin to read his poetry allegorically. Only by penetrating the rebarbative surface and the exaggerated gestures of the poem, by treating these qualities as a vehicle of allegorical expression, can one access its "profound duplicity," its apocalyptic tension between repulsion and attraction, *spleen et ideal*—its abject politics. More broadly, the allegorical equation of poetics and commodification in Baudelaire's verse reflects, in Benjamin's view, the poetic nature of the commodity (one of the sections of his unfinished study of Baudelaire is called "The Commodity as Poetic Object"). Baudelaire's poetry discloses a modern revival—and revision—of the conditions of allegory: "the commodity has taken the place of the allegorical mode of apprehension."[10] Baudelaire's poetry thus not only treats commodities as poetic objects, it deliberately invites the reader to consume and enjoy the poem allegorically as a commodity.

Baudelaire's insistence that the poem *rival* the allure of the commodity —in order to become an object of allegorical expression (a political artifact)—sets his poetic platform and its revolutionary potential apart from the unqualified negativity of Dadaism. Baudelaire's poems, according to Benjamin's analysis, can be described as "counterfeit capital" intended to disrupt the symbolic economy.[11] Directly at odds with Bürger's warning about the "false sublation" of autonomous art (and his valorization of pure negativity as a revolutionary stance), Baudelaire reaffirms the poem's fetishistic properties—its allure as a commodity—to enhance, rather than diminish, its efficacy as a tool of protest and subversion. Baudelaire's poetry must be read, according to Jennifer Bajorek, as "a 'new technology' of historical inscription and cultural transmission specifically adapted to capital."[12] She therefore understands Baudelaire's poetry to be, as the title of her book announces, a form of "counterfeit capital": a poetic forgery of the modern fetish, a dialectical falsification of the falsehood of commodities, a form of commodification without exchange. Baudelaire indeed produced his poems to subsist within a landscape of commodities or, as Benjamin contends, "to live in the heart of unreality (semblance)."[13] In contrast, then, to the deliberately and purely political sublimation of kitsch later practiced by Dadaism, Baudelaire outlined a program of poetic militancy and anarchism rooted in the aesthetic sublimation of kitsch—a program whose "profound duplicity" is its most significant contribution to the prehistory of the avant-garde: a legacy that has been largely ignored in favor of greater ideological purity.

A poetics of treachery and secrecy may indeed account, as Benjamin suggests, for the deceptive traditionalism of Baudelaire's prosody: his retention of rhyme, stanza, refrain, the alexandrine—all the trinkets, accessories, and baubles traditionally available to lyric poetry as a technology of desire. In a broader sense, the fetishizing and instrumentalizing of formal accessories may also help to explain the persistence—and the political valence—of the poetic "burden" in the gilded (and distressed) genre of poetry I have examined in this study. The refrain is the most obviously redundant—and potentially seductive—of poetic devices. These poetic trifles isolate, as Geoff Ward contends, "a gratuitousness which as Baudelaire foresaw would have to be made brazen rather than disguised."[14] This is precisely the view of pop art adopted—in opposition to the militancy of the neo-modernists—by Leo Steinberg who, citing the example of Baudelaire, suggests that "what the artist creates is essentially a new kind of spectator response. . . . The idea seemed to be to out-bourgeois the bourgeois."[15] At the same time, Steinberg explains, "the artist does not simply make a thing, an artifact, or in the case of Baudelaire, a poem. . . . What he creates is a provocation."[16] Baudelaire thus sought to provoke a new response in the reader by forcing his poems to contest the pleasures of the commodity—by equaling or excelling them.

The ravishing commodity is also, however, a stereotypical object. Echoing Baudelaire's ambition to "invent clichés" in his poems (an ambition that all future poets, Benjamin claims, would share), Benjamin declares, "The mass-produced article was Baudelaire's model. . . . He wanted to create a *poncif* [cliché]."[17] The verbal cliché thus served as a model for assimilating poetry to the condition of the commodity. From this perspective, Baudelaire placed his poems under the obligation of sustaining an aesthetic sublimation of clichés—combined with a desublimation of the lyric vocation (a strategy to be contrasted, as I have noted, with the starkly political sublimation of clichés by Dadaist poets). The lulling iterability of the cliché, which finds its aesthetic counterpart in the commonplace book, the advertising jingle, and the poetic refrain, corresponds in substantial ways to the reproducibility of the commodity.

The profound habituation induced by repetition creates conditions that help to explain the allegorical disposition of the cliché and the commodity as poetic objects. In his study of clichés, Anton Zijderveld points to the cliché's "capacity to bypass reflection"—that is, to its iceberg-like formation, in which the greater part of its meaning lies submerged.[18] In this respect, to paraphrase an observation made by Eric Partridge in his *Dictionary of Slang*, clichés are "things better left *unsaid*."[19] What is more, in keeping with its allegorical bent, the cliché's resistance to reflection—its superficiality and its scant meaning—result in what Zijderveld calls a heightened "social functionality."[20] Thus, it is precisely the blankness of the cliché that allows it to function, like the commodity, as an expressive medium, an allegorical screen.

The stuttering logic of the cliché, akin to the melodramatic space of the commodity, may be seen as arresting poetry—bringing the poem to a halt in a revolutionary gesture of neutralization. The poetics of the cliché thus helps Baudelaire to accomplish—not to suffer—the predicament of what Benjamin calls "petrified arrest": "to interrupt the course of the world—that was Baudelaire's deepest intention."[21] Dialectically speaking, this impulse—abetted by the poetics of the cliché—echoes and suspends the condition inducing the irritability of poetic *spleen*: "catastrophe in permanence."[22] For the modern poet, "that things are 'status quo' *is* the disaster. It is not an ever-present possibility but what in each case is given."[23] From this perspective, just as the poem rivals the allure of the commodity, so the process of inventing clichés and arresting poetry mimics, but also surmounts, the state of "catastrophe in permanence," of "petrified unrest." It is precisely with these goals in mind that Warhol—an artist sometimes compared to Baudelaire—serialized images of disaster and suicide, as a means of trivializing, but also surmounting, the ontology of "catastrophe in permanence."

The substance of the poetic cliché—of kitsch—is equivalent to what Benjamin calls "the enigmatic stuff of allegory."[24] The lifeless, bewitching matter of clichés and allegory is related, in turn, to the curious substance of the aura surrounding a work of art: "What, then, is aura? A strange tissue of space and time: the unique appearance of a distance, however near it may be."[25] The correlation between the "stuff of allegory" and the "strange tissue" of the aura may help to explain why Benjamin, remarkably, draws a comparison between the scandalous publication of Ossian's poetry and the impact of *Les fleurs du mal*.[26] The flickering aura of dubious originality enveloping the Ossian fragments cannot be isolated from the irresistible novelty of its antiquated diction—the stuff of poetic commodification. Judging from the spell it first cast over the public—the gist of Benjamin's comparison—Baudelaire's poetry appears to be made of the same "enigmatic stuff" as the Ossianic corpus. The decaying aura of Baudelaire's diction invites allegorical analysis.

Baudelaire, of course, has his own way of identifying the "strange tissue" of the spoiled, auratic poem. Seeing a basic correlation between his poetic practice and the fashionable genre of graphic *caricature* (often to be found in newspapers), Baudelaire identifies and embraces what he calls *"l'argot plastique"*: the medium of *les paradis artificiels* created by the poet, but also the medium of the artist's violent response to commodification and celebrity.[27]

The phrase means literally "plastic jargon," though both terms yield multiple inflections. "Plastic" implies mutability, pliability—the performative aspect of poetic language in its attempt to jinx the jinx of commodification—but the word also evokes, if not the alchemy of a "disgraced material," then a hint of charlatanism, fakery. Jinx, jingle, jargon. The word "jargon" (*argot*) refers to slang, the idiom of the criminal underworld, but also to any specialized vocabulary—including poetic diction (or advertising copy). In this sense, the caricatural diction of *l'argot plastique* is the medium of poetry's incorporation—and suspension—of the commodity fetish.

Ultimately, *l'argot plastique*—a poetic compound of cliché, aura, and allegory—finds expression in the figure of the halo in Baudelaire's poem "Perte d'aureole" ("Lost Halo"). The poem occurs as a dialogue between two figures:

> What! You here, old friend? You, in such a low quarter? You who sip the quintessence, who drink ambrosia? There's something surprising here.

> Friend, you know my terror of horses and carriages. A few minutes ago, hastily crossing the boulevard, jumping over the mud . . . my halo, jarred, slid off my head into the muck on the asphalt. I hadn't the courage to retrieve it . . . Now I can stroll about incognito, do mean things, launch into debauches, like ordinary mortals. So here I am, just like you, as you see.

> You should report your loss of halo, or go to the police lost-and-found.

> Heavens no! I like it this way. You are the only one to recognize me. Besides, dignity bores me. And I enjoy the thought of some bad poet picking it up and wearing it shamelessly.[28]

Benjamin quotes the entirety of this poem in his essay "On Some Motifs in Baudelaire" and, after noting Baudelaire's project of "inventing clichés," remarks, "To Baudelaire, the lyric poet with a halo is antiquated."[29] Thus the angel's muddy halo is analogous to the soiled aura of the lyric poet. The French word for halo, *aureole*, contains the word "aura" and although "the renunciation of the magic of distance is a decisive moment in Baudelaire's lyric poetry," it is also the case, as Benjamin insists, that "Baudelaire's enterprise was to make manifest the peculiar aura of commodities."[30] Hence the fate of the poet's derelict halo is bound up with the decay, but also the radiance, of the aura of commodities.

The magical substance of aura is at once reproduced and renounced, incorporated and negated, by the *argot plastique* of Baudelaire's poetry—

by the fetishized apparatus of the poem. It may be helpful in this context to recall Giorgio Agamben's conversion of the obliterating substance of the commodity into what he calls (borrowing from Baudeliare) a "profane halo"—into "the good that humanity must learn how to wrest from commodities."[31] To this end, the "profound duplicity" of Baudelaire's poetry reverberates with the allure of the commodity, even as it aims to surmount the "catastrophe in permanence" created by the ubiquity of commodities. No artifact of political or cultural subversion can be effective, according to Baudelaire, without rivaling or equaling the lure of the commodity.

Liar, Liar

In an effort to illustrate the Baudelairean legacy of producing poems as a form of "counterfeit capital," I want to examine five twentieth-century American poets whose work betrays the influence of Baudelaire's model of lyric modernity: three poets with direct or tangential relations to the New York school (John Wieners, Barbara Guest, and Jack Spicer), along with two other writers (Djuna Barnes and Frederick Seidel) whose poetry succumbs without scruple or shame to Baudelaire's corrosive example. The work of each of these poets illustrates, to varying degrees, the poetics of reverberation and fabrication characteristic of kitsch, displaying a curatorial approach to diction and employing eccentric or attenuated procedures of appropriation to produce a resonant but vaguely formulaic tonal complexion. On a scale demarcating the ideological spectrum of kitsch, these poets appear to adopt such procedures not to compel a political sublimation of commodified language—the program of original Dada—but to cultivate the aesthetic sublimation of clichés and poetic commonplaces (with political intentions that may be obscured by the cosmetic ethos of kitsch or accessible only to allegorical readings). In this sense, these poets are the true heirs of Baudelaire's consubstantiation of "disaster," which seeks to eradicate the substance of aura—the lyric halo—even as it "insists on the magic of distance."[32] The work of these poets therefore advances indirectly the aestheticization of Dada techniques evident in the "collaborations" of the first-generation poets of the New York school, though their poems are more inclined to mask the alienation effects of montage. The diction of these poets is sometimes redolent of lyric "phraseology," more highly synthesized, confronting the reader with the queer stance of "the non-dissenter" and the "profound duplicity" of the lyric poet in an era of late capitalism.

Of the five poets under consideration here (Wieners, Guest, Seidel,

Barnes, Spicer), Wieners is the most helpless disciple of Baudelaire's infidel doctrine of the "useful illusion," of art "so completely false" that it tells
the truth—a doctrine against artists who are "liars precisely because they
fail to lie."[33] This renegade brand of kitsch surfaces as well in John Ashbery's ambition to "create a counterfeit of reality more real than reality"
and in Berrigan's statement that "to speak is to lie. To lie is to collaborate."[34]
Living mostly in Boston (with stints in San Francisco and New York), John
Wieners was an evanescent figure in the postwar New York scene—John
Wilkinson calls him "a New York poet of exquisite shyness."[35] His career
was launched by Frank O'Hara's poem "To a Young Poet," written in 1957 to
the twenty-two-year-old Wieners, praising his "beautiful style."[36] (Wieners
later wrote an elegy for O'Hara entitled "After Reading *Second Avenue*.")[37]
Extending O'Hara's regard for Wieners's poetry, Ted Berrigan continued to
arrange readings for Wieners at the Poetry Project in New York City during
the 1960s. In addition, Malanga made a film, "April Diary," in 1970, involving
John Wieners, Anne Waldman, and Charles Olson (with whom Wieners had
studied at Black Mountain College).

   In his superb essays on Wieners's poetry—to which my insights are
largely indebted—John Wilkinson inquires of Wieners's writing, "Could
the poem as an enticing untruth, interrupt the poem of everyday life, the
poem of everyday life itself having interrupted the poetic diversions of refined sensibility?"[38] Modeling his question after the historical spiral of kitsch
traced in the alternation of postwar American poetry between "everyday"
and "refined" sensibilities—and in Wieners's own verse—Wilkinson answers
this question by turning to one of the infidel lyrics of Wieners's first book,
The Hotel Wentley Poems:

> We make it. And have made it
> For months now together after midnight.
> Soon I know the fuzz will
> interrupt, will arrest Jimmy and
> I shall be placed on probation. The poem
> does not lie to us. We lie under
> its law, alive in the glamour of this hour.[39]

Wilkinson proceeds to illuminate what he calls "a poem for liars," explaining, "The poem cannot lie *to* us . . . instead, the poem lies: and the relationship it demands is that 'We lie under / its law.' . . . But if we submit to the poem's lying, we too may become true liars."[40] Ultimately, in its fidelity to the

dispossessed, the poem relies on "infidelity to its own occasion, interrupting itself to secure to the reader the endless promise of poetic mendacity."[41]

Giving priority to Wieners's affinity with Robert Herrick and his debts to Edna St. Vincent Millay and to the ballad tradition—all significant features of the genealogy of kitsch—one can make a significant case for the role of Baudelairean "interruptions" in the echo chamber of Wieners's diction. Wilkinson finds "a macaronic first person composed of multiple voices and discourses but simultaneously their virtuoso . . . an individual voice which skitters across textual decoupages and is reshaped incessantly by the surfaces it crosses. The treatment of earlier, shapely verse as material for collage amongst fan-mags, newspaper stories and other stuff, is noteworthy."[42] Ultimately, Wilkinson suggests that Wieners's virtuosic program of interruptions (veering between canonical lyric and "fan mags") stands at the crossroads of schizophrenic language (characterized by automaticity) and the poetics of kitsch—that is, "the amateur and popular practice of poetry, where the formulaic determinants of what constitutes poetry tend to overcome the felt necessity for personal expression."[43] Wieners's poems thus record, yet also cultivate, the submersion of the individual voice in a faultlessly synthesized texture of alternately profane and sumptuous vocabularies.

Barbara Guest's poetry as well moved toward a mode of synthesized or saturated lyric, after absorbing the influence of the New Dada in the late 1950s and early 1960s. The poems in her first book, *The Location of Things* (1960), reveal that Guest was experimenting with Dada techniques (appropriation, montage, etc.) at least as early, if not earlier, than Ashbery in *Tennis Court Oath* (1962).[44] In "The Hero Leaves His Ship," Guest appears to be addressing issues (including the emergence of the New Realism) that would receive much wider attention with the first exhibition of pop art in 1962:

> I wonder if this new reality is going to destroy me. . . .
>
> I am about to use my voice
> Why am I afraid that salty wing
> Flying over a real hearth will stop me?
>
> Yesterday the yellow
> Tokening clouds. I said "no" to my burden.[45]

The alienation of the speaker's voice, the ordeal of the poetic "burden," find expression in the syntactic and tonal "interruptions" evident in many of these early poems:

The quality of the day
That has its size in the North
and in the South
a low sighing that of wings

Describe that nude, audacious line
Most lofty, practiced street
You are no longer thirsty
Turn or go straight.[46]

In addition to poems anticipating Ashbery's more famous Roussellian or Dadaist experiments, Guest did collaborative work with painters and writers, including several plays and two exuberant comic strips with Joe Brainard in 1964. One of these comics, "Joan and Ken," resembles one of O'Hara's "eclogues," in which two figures trade nonsensical lines. Ken: "You were there in the arcade reading winsome"; Joan: "I broke my arm stroking that cat."[47] Maggie Nelson locates the diction of these comics in "the dissonance between their Pop idiom and their mysterious non-sequitur speech"—an amalgam evident in the final panel of the comic, which garbles the advertising copy of the domestic scene: "The secret is violet soap and living in an old house and never making repairs. . . . I mean using consciences that repeat."[48]

As Nelson suggests, even Guest's most elliptical experiments early in her career are characterized by a dissonance between a pop idiom more characteristic of her peer-poets in the New York school and a "mysterious non-sequitur speech." (Guest once gave a talk entitled "Mysteriously Defining the Mysterious.") Already by the mid-1960s, Guest's poetry was beginning to reverberate with the "special effects" of poetic diction, as in this segment of "Fan Poems":

Classically perchance am I your robin
Or rossignol, not hirondelle, that dark
Word ending in dress? At the top of stairs
Stands the Marquis wearing a burnt
Ribbon, wearing an "air," so they say,
I wonder at its quaintness, I wonder also,
At my hoops, my stays are "pinching,"
Let us take the night air in an ice.[49]

Guest playfully adopts the fortified diction of canonical lyric —a bit too rich, and deliberately so. Yet she also garbles phrases and tropes, as if they were borrowed—or bought—as if she were feeling antsy (her undergarments—

her "stays"—are pinching), as if she were an intruder assembling the "air" by some cheap formula.

The lyric saturation becomes more grotesque, more charming, and more compulsively reflexive, in the long poem "Knight of the Swan," a poem retailing—and anatomizing—a trove of lyric commonplaces:

> Sensing the token and ridding it of dispiritedness a cold
> foam bath and icy smiles the lips permitted and the knight
> was refreshed then also the mountains had reviving airs
>
> nesting in the hollows from peak to golden peak and there were
> lairs for robbers which altered the loneliness.[50]

Calling "Knight of the Swan" a "masterpiece of textual facture," Marjorie Welish writes, "for Guest, medieval romance is already given as text, not history—which means in her poetics, surface and facture, not illusion, are the protagonists to the rescue."[51] Evoking the long history of medievalist kitsch and its cosmetic "facture"—anatomized under Guest's restless gaze—Welish explains, "More apt to yield verbal delirium than noise-music, Guest's lyrical pulse brings early modern materiality of language into vital relation with the free-ranging experiment that is lyric."[52] More provocatively, the experiment that is *kitsch* names the cold "delirium" that Guest summons by composing in the fraudulent hand of the ballad. Essentially, Guest produces a ravishing but alienated lyric "facture" (kitsch) by using the disruptive techniques of Dada—without programmatic intent—within the echoing chamber of the poetic commonplace. In the hands of poets such as Guest and Wieners, poetic kitsch becomes a radicalized form of lyric, an ironic commodity, a form of "counterfeit capital" betraying—and surfeiting—the symbolic economy of verse.

The poetry of the third writer to be considered in light of Baudelaire's *argot plastique* would not—at first glance—be confused with the trifling, experimental verse of the New York school. Frederick Seidel, to be sure, never succumbed to the influence of Dadaism. His models were Pound, Eliot, and Robert Lowell—though it is difficult to find any trace of the first two poets in Seidel's writing after his first book, *Final Solutions* (1963). His poetry is routinely compared, however, to that of Baudelaire and, in at least one poem, the poet finds the image of Baudelaire staring back at him when he looks in the mirror.[53] Seidel revives the figure of the urban dandy for modern poetry—an icon defined historically in part by Baudelaire's poetic persona. His poems are seen as sharing the savage sophistication, the abject (heterosexual) eroticism, and the perverse sentiments of Baudelaire's poetry. Comparisons of this sort are not necessarily misleading, but what sets Seidel's decadence apart—and aligns it with poetic kitsch—is its mincing and menacing tone, its bad taste, its cancerous diction. Here's a sample:

> The most expensive hotel in the world ignites
> As many orgasms as there are virgins in paradise.
> The epileptic foaming fits dehydrate one,
> But justify the cost of a honeymoon.
> The Caribbean is room temperature,
> Rippling over sand as rich as cream.
> The beach chair has the thighs of a convertible
> with the top down.[54]

And another:

> A string of women like a string of fish
> Kept dangling in the water to keep them alive.
> Washed down with Lynch-Bages to assuage the anguish
> Of eating red meat during a muff dive.[55]

In Seidel's deadpan recitation, the cold delirium of Guest's lyric "facture"—the poem's diction— becomes genuinely scary, delivering the alienated substance of kitsch in candied phrases. No other poet demonstrates so clearly the gulf between camp and kitsch—a difference that reveals itself through a phraseology so glossy, so flat, so resistant to "polite" analysis, that it can only be experienced as menacing, baleful.

In some of Seidel's earliest poems, the polarizing attraction of kitsch is unmistakable:

> Never to wake up in the blond
> Hush and gauze of that Hyannis sunrise.
> Bliss was it
> In that dawn to be alive.[56]

The soothing idioms are faintly skewed here, producing a dissonance that becomes characteristic of Seidel's lyric:

> Fall leaves inflame the woods.
> It is brilliant to live.

The sorrow that is not sorrow,
The mist of everything over everything.[57]

Seidel lulls the reader initially with aimless rounds of kitsch, often end-stopped, only to swerve into a more vulgar, insinuating tone:

The attitude of green to blue is love.
And so the day just floats itself away.
The stench of green, the drench of green, above
The ripples of sweet swimming a bay
Of just-mowed green, intoxicates the house.
The meadow goddess squeaking like a mouse
Is stoned, inhales the grass, adores the sky.[58]

In the nervous—even pathological—diction of these lines, Seidel combines, characteristically, the polarized aspects of kitsch: its complacent and affectionate phraseology—infused with contempt. The gaudy spells of kitsch become the insinuating vice of disdainful regard: a kind of melodrama with sadistic overtones. Also evident in these lines are the singsong rhythms and rigid linearity (enforced by crude rhymes and capital letters at the start of each line) that form the basis of what Ange Mlinko calls "the prosody of atrocity" in Seidel's verse.[59] Curiously—and this is crucial to its affinity with kitsch—Mlinko compares the minacious tone and rhythms of Seidel's poetry to the children's verse of Dr. Seuss. Here is a sample of Seidel's doggerel:

I call him Nancy.
He is so fancy.
It is alarming
He is so charming.
It is the thing he does and knows.
It is the fragrance of the rose.[60]

And here is a passage from Dr. Seuss (which begins to sound eerily decadent when placed next to Seidel's tumbled vernacular):

I spent the summer in Bologna.
Bologna is my town.
Bologna is so brown.
I ate shavings
Of tuna roe on buttered toast.

Despite the heat,
Brown waxy slices of fishy salt
As strong as ammonia, Bologna.
Bologna, it takes a prince to eat *bottarga*.[61]

Although Mlinko hears the rhythms of Dr. Seuss in Seidel's doggerel, a more resonant analogy would be the jingles of Mother Goose ("It was a little pig not very big. / When he was alive he lived in clover. / But now he's dead and that's all over."), an echo that reveals even more directly Seidel's place in the genealogy of kitsch.

The traditionalism of Seidel's prosody and the neutrality of his diction, like Baudelaire's, are deceptive. They produce a weird synthesis of triviality and horror evoking the "petrified unrest" of Baudelaire's mimicry of catastrophe. At the same time, oddly, the distracted libido and incessant name-dropping of Seidel's poetry evoke a sensibility resembling O'Hara's "I do this I do that" approach. Crucially, however—for the allegorical dimension of kitsch—Seidel's sadistic imposture functions as nemesis and supplement to the *Frank Likes Everything* school of poetry. The sociopathic undertow of his flowing accents, the Warholian disaffection of his *poshlost*, the stereotypical diction of his torture-ballads set in the beau monde, make it impossible to ignore the mix of longing and revulsion at the heart of kitsch—and the social antagonism to which it gives voice.

The fourth poet to be considered here, Djuna Barnes, shares Seidel's love of stale diction (along with his voluptuous and brittle contempt), yet her verse is closer historically to the lingering example of Baudelaire's anathematic tone and therefore helps to expose the insidious effects of fin-de-siècle kitsch on the origins of poetic modernism. Barnes is certainly the nearest thing we have in English to Baudelaire's fulgurating sensibility. In addition, her fondness for archaic, and specifically Jacobean, diction in her great novel, *Nightwood*, is well known, but one should recall that she developed this verbal palette as a poet at a time when Imagism and Vorticism—the earliest formulations of poetic modernism—were beginning to make an impact. Like Ezra Pound's proto-Imagist (and indeed Imagist) poetry, Barnes's verse sounds at once modern and still mesmerized by the vacuous and hyperlyrical diction of the 1890s. Neither Pound nor Barnes ever relinquished the cultic substance of stale diction in the writing for which they are best known—and celebrated.

Barnes's early poetry, much of it written between 1910 and 1920, draws

on many of the same idiosyncratic sources of poetic language feeding Seidel's polarized diction, including, her attraction to the circular and stilted
rhythms of ballad-making:

> A woman riding astride came
> Riding astride;
> A golden ring on her finger fore
> Came to the bride's door.
> To the bride's door came a bride
> Riding astride.[62]

Though the hovering accents of the ballad form do not fully resolve themselves here, the sexual conceit presses forward unmistakably, as it frequently does in the saturated tone of Barnes's Gothic modernism:

> The flame of your red hair does crawl and creep
> Upon your body that denies the gloom
> And feeds upon your flesh . . .
>
> The dark comes up, my little love, and dyes
> Your fallen lids the stain of ebony.[63]

The exoticism of the poem's title, "Six Songs of Khalidine" (from an Arabic
word meaning "immortal ones"), functions in part to authorize the ener-
vated and faintly conspiratorial diction of the poem. At the same time, the
allusion to immortality, while it may refer to the immobility and feigned
timelessness of Barnes's language—to the verbal regime of kitsch—it also
fails to mask the erotic fervor of the necrophile, the habitual posture of the
speaker seduced by horror in Barnes's poems.

The belated Gothicism of Barnes's poems surrenders at moments to the
ostensibly timeless cult of "simplicity":

> A little trellis stood beside my head,
> And all the tiny fruitage of its vine
> Fashioned a shadowy cover to my bed,
> And I was madly drunk on shadow wine!
>
> A lily bell hung sidewise, leaning down,
> And gowned me in a robe so light and long;
> And so I dreamed, and drank, and slept, and heard
> The lily's song.[64]

With its array of diminutives ("little," "tiny") and its miniature furnishings, the poem evokes—with a bohemian twist—the counter-modernist revival of fairy literature between 1910 and 1930 (Edmund Duke, Conan Doyle, Cicely Mary Barber) but also, more remotely, "the Fairy Way of Writing" that Addison associated with archaic ballads. The iconography of fairies coincides here with the embrace of a precious but generic poetic language, a movement towards generality, vagueness, and superficiality that becomes more insistent and even dogmatic in a poem like "A Last Toast":

> My tears are falling one by one
> Upon the silence of this bed;
> Like rain they crown his quiet head
> Like moons they slip within his hair;
> They came like wine and passed like prayer
> Into the goblets of the dead.[65]

Like the enigmatic "quiet dead" evoked here, the featurelessness of the poem's language—its lack of distinction—defies the reader's attention, as if the poem were somehow alien to the particularity of its own medium (to English, that is).

The vexing hyper-transparency of a language seemingly without qualities becomes fully operative as a medium of kitsch when Barnes's poems betray a destructive (and self-destructive) impulse common to Seidel and to Baudelaire. In a poem called "Suicide," Barnes subtly mocks the two cadavers on display in the poem:

> Corpse A
> They brought her in, a shattered small
> Cocoon,
> With a little bruised body like
> A startled moon;
> And all the symphonies of her
> A twilight rune.[66]

The nasty streak in Barnes's poems often surges unexpectedly, as in Seidel's poems, from veils of sugary indulgence:

> Ornate the autumn with the wane of her,
> The flutter of her satin-sandaled feet;
> And more demure and more than quite discreet
> The hem that dusts her ankles with its fur.

The light was pulsing with the quaint surprise
Of ribboned wings that aureoled her head
The bister and the blue beneath her eyes.[67]

Reverberations of Baudelaire's poetic and psychological "duplicity" alternate in Barnes's notorious *Book of Repulsive Women* (1915) between verbal lassitude and provocation:

Though her lips are vague as fancy
In her youth—
They bloom vivid and repulsive
As the truth.[68]

The word "repulsive" here (and in the phrase "Repulsive Women" of Barnes's title) refers antithetically, the reader discerns in the course of reading the pamphlet, to lesbian sexuality. Barnes may have appropriated this term (and its duplicity) from Baudelaire, who sneers at the "repulsive behavior" of lesbians, yet who also wrote banned poems about lesbian passion and regarded the figure of the lesbian, according to Benjamin, as "the heroine of *la modernité*."[69]

In the poetry of *The Book of Repulsive Women*, Barnes's tone, like Baudelaire's, combines sensuous indulgence and condescension:

You, the twilight powder of
A fire-wet dawn;
You, the massive mother
Of illicit spawn;
While the others shrink in virtue
You have borne.[70]

In these lines (and others I have cited here), the volatile and alienated compound of kitsch is at once excessive and jejune: a language "vague as fancy" veering unpredictably towards shock and the vice of self-annihilation. Returning to the eccentric framework established by Benjamin's allegorical reading of Baudelaire's poetry, it is precisely in the nakedly symptomatic flux of kitsch that one glimpses a cosmetic "anti-system" (to use Broch's term for kitsch) of mimicking—and resisting—the flux of modern commodification.

I want to turn finally to the work of Jack Spicer, a poet whose polarized disposition—combining perspectives that are at once strikingly innovative and deeply traditional—often frustrates efforts to situate his work within prevailing models of poetic affiliation. The poetics of kitsch offers, by contrast, a useful paradigm for reconciling some of the contradictions within Spicer's work. The book that first brought readers' attention to his work, *After Lorca* (published in 1957), presents, the introduction claims, a collection of "translations" of Lorca's work—though numerous poems in the book do not derive, it turns out, from Lorca's writing. Some of the poems in the book (most beginning with the phrase "Ballad of . . .") are based on Lorca's poems (whether closely translated or loosely rendered), but others with similar titles (starting with the word "ballad") are original poems of Spicer's. In fact, as the editors of Spicer's *Collected Poetry* confirm, *After Lorca* contains "nearly a dozen original Spicer poems masquerading as translations."[71] The volume begins, moreover, with a counterfeit introduction by Lorca, expressing his disdain for the execution of the translations. Quite obviously Spicer's first volume of poetry aims to revive the scandalous procedures of imposture for the poetic avant-garde, anticipating the more explicit masquerades and hoaxes of Ted Berrigan and his pals in the New York school. Spicer's book resembles (in its ballad imitations, mock introduction, and facetious notes) Oliver Goldsmith's notorious production of Mother Goose, published some two hundred years earlier.

Several years following the publication of *After Lorca*, Spicer developed a theory of what he called poetic "dictation" to explain the sources and methods of his writing, identifying *After Lorca* as his first "dictated" volume.[72] In his Vancouver lecture of 1965, where he explains his theory of "dictation," Spicer makes reference to the poet Helen Adams's "ballad metric" as exemplifying the effects of poetic "dictation."[73] Alluding to an affinity between balladry and "dictation" is certainly more instructive about Spicer's poetics than his facetious references to "martians" as the source of his writing, yet one must probe more carefully to understand the practical significance of poetic "dictation." For example—oddly enough, given his alignment with what Robin Blaser calls "the practice of the outside"—Spicer repeatedly valorizes a *lack* of originality in poetic diction. The letters addressed to Lorca in *After Lorca*, which are both part of the ballad series and reflections on that series, offer a lively commentary on "what tradition seems to have meant lately—an historical patchwork. . . . But tradition means much more than that. It means generations of different poets in different countries patiently telling the same story, writing the same poem. . . . Invention is merely the enemy of poetry."[74] For Spicer, the poetic tradition—and its principal mechanism, "dictation"—are characterized by a suppression of originality and by

imposture: a system (or anti-system) of values intrinsic to the "fake translations" of *After Lorca*.[75]

Spicer's hostility to poetic "invention" coincides with his frequent reflections on the subject of poetic diction. His emphasis on the process of replication (whether true or false) comprehends an affinity for restricted (and, by
definition, overused) deposits of language (exemplifying the territoriality of
diction in general). In one of the letters to Lorca, for example, Spicer twice
repeats the dictum "The perfect poem has an infinitely small vocabulary,"
alluding perhaps to the verbal formulae of the ballad tradition but also to
the "infinite" expressivity of a proverbial model of poetry.[76] The expressivity
of a small vocabulary is, of course, intrinsic to the poetics of kitsch.

In his collection *Admonitions* (unpublished in Spicer's lifetime but composed during the same period as *After Lorca*), Spicer includes portions of
letters he wrote to Joe Dunn and Robin Blaser, in which he offers further
thoughts on the correlation of the poetic tradition and intertextuality (suppressing originality): "Poems should echo and re-echo against each other.
They should create resonances. . . . A poem is never to be judged by itself
alone. A poem is never by itself alone."[77] In these formulations, we find
that Spicer's innovative model of the poetic series (as an echo chamber)
is directly related to his conception of the poetic tradition as a whole. In
the same collection (in a letter to Blaser), Spicer offers a memorable image
of the constellation of poems and the reflective relations holding them together: "Each of them is a mirror. . . . The frightening hall of mirrors in
a fun house is universal beyond each particular reflection."[78] In this analogy, we discover the "universal" chamber of poetic kitsch described—quite
appropriately—as a "fun house" but also a "frightening hall."

Spicer adapts Baudelaire's theory of symbolic "correspondences" (a forest of "living trees" returning our "familiar glances") to his model of poetic
"dictation," which encompasses at once the practice of "fake translations"
and the "fun house" of the poetic tradition.[79] His embrace of Baudelairean
"correspondences" extends as well to haunted structures of affective sym-
pathy, where the "frightening hall" of the poetic tradition becomes what
Spicer dubs "the poisonous candy factory."[80] Recalling, but also remapping,
the Baudelairean affinities of Guest, Barnes, Wiener, and Seidel, Spicer's poetry thus exemplifies an alternative vanguard of "duplicity" and symptomatic expression.

Spicer conceives of his model of poetic dictation in opposition to Dada (though he does not disavow the "destructive moment" or Dada's opposition to originality). In a poem written on the occasion of something called Dada Day in 1955, Spicer contrasts the exclusively critical agenda of Dada to the alienated aestheticism (which he calls "barbarism") underlying his conceptions of "dictation" and intertextuality: "Darling,/The difference between Dada and barbarism/Is the difference between an abortion and a wet dream."[81] He continues:

> An ugly vandal pissing on a statue is not Phidias
> Pissing on a statue. Barbarism
> Is something less than a gesture.
> Destroy your own gods if you want Dada:
> Give up your vices, burn your jukebox.[82]

Separating the "ugly vandal" of Dadaism from the classical "Phidias," even as he defends the "vice" of dictation and the "jukebox" of the poetic tradition, Spicer concludes,

> "Beauty is so rare a thing," Pound said,
> "So few drink at her fountain."
> You only have the right to piss in the fountain
> If you are beautiful.[83]

Citing Pound—in a passage whose diction is nakedly poetic, for the most part—Spicer condemns the mere vandalism of Dada, in favor of the childish affront to beauty perpetrated by the maker of beauty (Phidias). Spicer clearly has no intention of burning the "jukebox" of poetic kitsch (though, as a maker of beauty, he has earned the "right" to do so).

With this judgment, Spicer embraces and exemplifies the characteristically ambivalent (or duplicitous) gesture of the Baudelairean avant-garde: poetry's "barbaric" cancellation of its own lyrical beauty—a homeopathic, if not suicidal, remedy to poetry's collusion with the contemporary marketplace of commodities and pleasurable consumption. Spicer condemns the suicidal impulse of Dada, even as he retains the prerogative to sacrifice beauty by exaggerating it: a self-consuming gesture essential to the logic of kitsch.

Afterword

In the Poisonous Candy Factory

At the beginning of this book, I promised that learning more about the submerged relationship between kitsch and poetry would revise significantly our assumptions about the nature of kitsch as a category of material culture. I also claimed that revealing this secret history would alter our assumptions about the development of modern poetry—that is, our understanding of how the introduction of renegade sources of diction—the matrix of kitsch—into elite poetry transformed the writing and reception of English poetry beginning in the eighteenth century. Let me begin to assess whether those promises have been kept by attending first to the former topic, the body of received ideas about the nature of kitsch in material culture. In the most rudimentary sense, continuing to ignore poetry's genetic relation to kitsch would ultimately condemn to irrelevance the concept of kitsch as a framework for understanding popular culture. Disclosing fully the implications of poetry's role in the genealogy of kitsch provides the basic terms for initiating a vital revisionary account of relations between high and low culture, thereby ensuring the continued relevance of kitsch as an index of high culture's ever-increasing susceptibility to mass culture. Central to the importance of poetic kitsch in particular is the manner in which it reveals kitsch to be a medium, a bridge, between elite and vernacular cultures. A poetological model of kitsch may indeed hold the key to understanding elite culture as a polarized dimension of popular culture, to understanding art as a variety of kitsch.

Looking at kitsch through the medium of poetry introduces fundamental changes to our assumptions about its origins: Romantic Germany remains an important locus in the genealogy of kitsch (as modernist critics asserted), but the importance of the ballad revival (and all of its dubious progeny) in sparking controversy about the nature of vernacular culture points to the borderlands between England and Scotland in the early eighteenth century as the true geographical and historical locus of kitsch. Viewing kitsch as a "borderline" phenomenon exposes the importance of certain volatile issues—some obvious, some not—embedded in its formation: nationalism, feminism, domesticity, consumerism, queer sociality, anglophony, literacy, philology, antiquarianism, canon formation, and the emergence of the supergenre of literature. The prehistory of kitsch is entangled with all of these issues in various ways.

Revising the genealogy of kitsch along these lines accounts not only for the enduring affinity of poetry and kitsch but also—via the contagion of poetic imposture associated with the ballad revival—for the presumed illegitimacy of kitsch. Kitsch is consistently condemned as unoriginal, imitative, and even fraudulent, precisely because its inaugural artifacts—poetic forgeries—were quite literally counterfeit. As an aesthetic category associated with falsehood and fakery, kitsch stems from the production of real fakes and from the confused reception of these artifacts. The conditions of poetic imposture thus account for the enduring ambiguity of the kitsch artifact: Is it real or fake, true or false, art or kitsch?

These entrancing and sometimes scandalous texts found some of their earliest champions, imitators, and interpreters in communities of individuals whose sexual preferences produced corresponding social veils of inscrutability and speculation. The secret history of poetry and kitsch therefore discloses meaningful structural analogies between the uncertain reception of poetic imposture—Is it authentic or not?—and the historical foundations of the modern, homosexual coterie (what Eve Sedgwick calls the epistemology of the closet). Controversy over the authenticity of certain poetic artifacts thus appears to have become interfused, rather deliberately, with the uncertainty of public opinion about the sexual preference of the exclusive social circles that helped to neutralize the "toxins" in these dubious artifacts.

The influence of the eighteenth-century homosexual coterie (specifically, the Shenstone and Walpole circles) in shaping the prehistory of kitsch depended in turn on the innovative methods of collection, redaction, and dissemination practiced by female antiquarians who gathered (and "improved") some of the earliest "reliques" of the ballad revival. Especially germane to the mediumistic properties of kitsch (traversing high and low cultures) is the economic and class diversity of the Scottish circle of female antiquarians, anthologists, poets, and performers who helped launch the ballad revival from "the bottoms of clues" (as Thomas Percy said of Lady Wardlaw's "Hardyknute"). The mingling of vernacular and elite sensibilities in the circle of Scottish "bluestockings" communicates essential qualities about a poetological inflection of kitsch, which in turn forces significant revisions of our received ideas about kitsch in general. Reflected in the heterogeneous social matrix of female antiquarianism (and its domestic setting), kitsch can no longer be viewed as an isolated product of vernacular or industrial working-class culture, but must be seen as a hybrid of high and low cultures—a bridge between the two. This relation is reciprocal: Clement Greenberg is essentially correct in saying that kitsch (in its pop variant) has a parasitic relation to high culture, yet it is also increasingly true that high culture feeds off popular trends and artifacts (to the extent that the distinction between the two realms becomes ever more uncertain). The true significance of kitsch derives from its mediumistic function. This transactional model also helps to explain the rarely acknowledged variance between different *levels* of kitsch in contemporary material culture: mass market, midcult, high-brow. On this basis, the phenomenon of high kitsch can no longer be considered anomalous or contradictory: on the contrary, it illustrates perfectly the transactional nature of kitsch.

The mediumistic properties of poetic kitsch—its capacity, for example, to reveal affinities between rarefaction and the cult of simplicity—became manifest as well in the disparate tastes of various poetic circles functioning as laboratories to combine the curious diction of the ballad with the "inane phraseology" (to use Wordsworth's epithet) of elite verse. In this sense, composing poetic kitsch is, at its origin, an *experiment* (a disposition that would later reassert itself in the scandalous correspondences between Dadaism and kitsch). Thomas Gray and William Shenstone were both deeply traditional poets whose formulaic verse is a direct product of the compositional paradigm of the commonplace book. At the same time, however, these poets were also instrumental in producing the synthetic (and disfigured) vernacular that became the common medium of ballad imitation (made-up folksongs, bardic fragments, and other spurious "reliques"). The echoing, replicative methods of the commonplace tradition thus produced an impure and excessively poetic (though also modern) diction that is remote from conversational speech. As a result, Gray's and Shenstone's poetries could be condemned (by "literary" poets such as Wordsworth) as being at once arcane and formulaic, obscure and clichéd. Strangely—

from a modern perspective—it was not the Wordsworthian advocates of poetry's equivalence to polite conversation, a purified version of speech, but the defenders of the "peculiar language" of poetry (Gray, Goldsmith, Shenstone, even Coleridge), who saw an affinity between the "phraseology" of traditional poetic diction and the synthetic folk language recovered, or coined, through successive waves of ballad imitation. They discerned in the counterfeit vernacular of the ballad revival a verbal counterpart to the petrified diction produced by commonplace methods.

Grounded in the mechanism of replication, the synthesis of counterfeit vernaculars and elite poetic diction yields a hyperlyrical medium that effectively immobilizes poetic language—even as it promises to make available a domain of lost experience. As a consequence, a blueprint emerged for an unprecedented alliance between a militant, conservative poeticism and a promiscuous model of vernacular "poesy" sustained by archaism and "vicious" phrasing. From this strange alliance emerged the substance of kitsch as an amalgam of elite and popular cultures—a substance binding commonplace poetry to the mythological foundations of popular culture. This conjunction produced a conception of the pop artifact released from its allergy to obscurity, since its accessibility and familiarity depend not on simplicity of diction or design but on endless replication. Even the most obscure phrase or image becomes familiar if experienced repeatedly.

A poetological approach to kitsch reveals the profound traditionalism of all forms of kitsch, especially if (as T. S. Eliot claims) the poetic tradition is defined by the substance of *minority*. Embodied by the formulaic nature of kitsch, the echoing phenomenon of tradition evokes, yet also promises to overcome, a pervasive loss of historical experience induced by the assimilation of modern technology. Kitsch entices, Walter Benjamin argues, by promising a rehabilitation of historical experience: an orientation that helps to explain, for example, Timothy Morton's renegade application of kitsch to *ecology*—generating what he calls "ecological kitsch" as a way of posing in the starkest terms the progressive concept of an "ecology without nature." Kitsch thus exposes modernism's failure to revise the domain of historical, or collective, experience; it exposes the vestigial nature of modern experience without renouncing its viability, invoking indeed the recovery of nature as a social and aesthetic totality.

In its holistic orientation, the traditionalism of kitsch comprehends various fugitive genres that appear to defy the values of elite culture: ballad imitations, folk songs, amateur epics, bardic forgeries, melodramas, Gothic

verse, maxims, mottoes, and jingles (a key to Benjamin's interest in the language of advertising as a form of poetic kitsch). In addition, insofar as these
"distressed" genres may be regarded as symptoms of the "cult of simplicity," they must also be understood as expressions of *minority*: the verbal
manifestations of children, animals (*talking* animals), and the members of
repressed social, economic, and racial classes. A genealogy of poetry and
kitsch exposes a conception of minority grounded in triviality, imposture,
melodrama, and nonsense. At the same time, the traits of minority determine (according to Eliot) the scope of tradition, which is sustained by minor
poetry—by what he calls inferiority and mediocrity. A "minor literature"
can never be more than a travesty, a distortion, of the tradition from which
it derives, according to Gilles Deleuze, even as it preserves the essence of
that tradition. Conceived as an index of tradition and experience, kitsch
is distinguished above all by its *weakness* as an aesthetic category. Kitsch
functions as an emblem of *aesthetic failure*, precisely because it harbors the
cultic substance of lost experience and a fading, or frozen, tradition.

The inherent traditionalism of all forms of kitsch defeats the impulse
to equate kitsch solely with industrial culture—though this affinity is real
and substantial—even as it appears to strengthen the grounds for opposing kitsch to the avant-garde. Yet a poetological approach to kitsch reveals
(through the example of Baudelaire's militant bad taste and the neo-Dada
experiments of the New York school of poets) that this antithesis is far
from absolute or secure. Grounded in a novel reassessment of the aesthetic
potential of the cliché—a static form of everyday language—these poetic
developments advanced the possibility of a dialectical overcoming, or sus-
pending, of kitsch as a rationalized mythology of regressive and delusional
sentiments.

Counterfeit Capital

Returning to the question of how kitsch matters to our understanding
of modern poetry, I hope I have demonstrated in the preceding chapters
that the project of "kitsching" modern poetry produces some surprising
and significant results. To begin with the question of literary history in
the most basic sense, thinking about kitsch inevitably foregrounds the
importance of eighteenth-century poetry and poetics not only to certain
neglected, or censured, aspects of modern poetry but, more surprisingly,
to certain formations—yet to be fully realized—of the avant-garde. If satire and didacticism—two genres essential to canonical eighteenth century

verse—are not especially important to twentieth-century poetry, it is also true that the neoclassical taste for pastiche is directly related to the "vicious" subgenres of the "minor" eighteenth century that form the matrix of modern kitsch: nursery rhymes, bardic fragments, peasant poetry, Gothic verse, and melodrama. In fact, the eighteenth-century fascination with poetic imposture is an expression of that period's taste for pastiche—a sorcerer's apprentice—just as the forger Chatterton can be seen as a radical *pasticheur* (rather than a precursor of Romantic pathos and invention, as he is usually received). This genealogy, rooted in neoclassical poetics, extends to experiments in collaboration and "unoriginal writing" in the twentieth century. From this perspective, developing a genealogy of poetry and kitsch not only draws attention to influential episodes of poetic forgery but also suggests that taking imposture seriously may spur unexpected insights into the history of canonical and noncanonical poetries. Forgery matters, both as a historic event and as a poetic model.

A hypothesis about the enduring importance of poetic kitsch finds support in the fact that the legacy of the ballad revival in poetry has endured for nearly three hundred years: from Lady Wardlaw and Thomas Gray to Coleridge, Lewis Carroll, and Frederick Seidel, from Swinburne and the Rossettis to Ezra Pound and Djuna Barnes, poets writing in English continue to practice the art of simplicity—or a twisted version of it. Poets (and songwriters) of all kinds continue to rewrite the demotic fantasy of the ballad, producing increasingly eccentric imitations (of imitations) and innumerable shades of spurious diction. Like the poetic assimilation of classical languages, the deliberate incorporation of vernacular language—sometimes fabricated—into elite poetry permanently altered the spectrum of poetic diction in the English tradition. Even in the context of modernism, the monstrous example of Pound's *Cantos* (and the crypt poetry from which its episodes of kitsch derive) can be regarded as a pivotal work in the genealogy of poetic kitsch: consuming, replicating (and disfiguring) the legacy of nineteenth-century kitsch, the poem also fashions a polarized verbal matrix, combining hard and soft diction, an amalgam that anticipates the more effective synthesis of kitsch and avant-garde in the New York school of poets.

Turning to the question of poetics, thinking about kitsch inevitably generates renewed attention to the moribund concept of *diction*, which lies at the very core of the operations of poetic kitsch. It is no accident that the interrelated phenomena of diction and kitsch became—in tandem—objects of incomprehension or suspicion within the dominant paradigm of modernist and neo-modernist formalism. As a result, issues that properly belong to the question of diction (such as the importation of various kinds of language through techniques of sampling, appropriation, or translation) are often discussed tendentiously—and obtusely—in terms of formal innovation. It is not that questions of form and diction do not overlap—open or paratactic forms, for example, can facilitate experiments in diction—yet the two should not be confused. Diction, unlike form, inevitably engages issues directly relating to ethnic, sexual, regional, and class identities (to matters of anglophony) and to the historical stratification of language (archaism, standard usage, slang, pidgen).

The problem of diction also addresses—in ways that escape the question of form entirely—the *manipulation* of verbal identities: diction exercises control over the prospect of simulating or counterfeiting the verbal substance of ethnic, sexual, regional, and class identities. For this reason, along with the importance of replication in preserving a particular province of poetic diction, mass culture (and its genetic basis in reproducibility) finds its most reliable link to poetry through the operations of diction. The harmonic relation of the tonalities of poetic kitsch to mass culture is vividly staged as early as the contrivances of Mother Goose, in the basic functions of "lullaby logic": simulation, enchantment, indoctrination.

The unexpected comity of recondite poetry and emergent forms of popular culture in the eighteenth century points to one of the most startling consequences of thinking about poetry's relation to kitsch: the revelation of an enduring conflict between militant poeticism (grounded in the methods of the commonplace book) and the middling, bourgeois supergenre of literature. The schism between poetry and literature (and literary poetry) arises from a dispute about the nature of poetic diction and, more specifically, about the diction of the emerging category of vernacular poetry (and its upscale version, "literary" poetry). Kitsch thus develops when operations normally associated with rarefaction and decadence (redundancy, attenuation, immobility) come to define the substance of the vernacular, of language in its youth (so to speak). In kitsch, the seriality of decadence—its mechanical unwinding—becomes associated not with decrepitude but with what Benjamin calls "the worlds of childhood," with backwardness, minority, innocence, and childish language.

The antagonism between poetry and literature occurs, essentially, as a fight over who owns, or gets to define, vernacular language. On one hand, Wordsworth and his cohort of literary poets seek to ground poetry in a model of the vernacular based on a "purified," or sublimated, residue of speech: the standard of "polite" letters. By contrast, poets such as Gray, Shenstone, and Goldsmith emphasize a model of the vernacular rooted in the allegedly native diction of the ancient ballad, a jargon sustained by a rhapsodic and formulaic tradition that aligns itself easily with the replicative methods of the commonplace book and elite poetry (favored by Gray and his school). Radicalized conservative poets thus sought to render the vernacular in a way that replicates the insularity of classical languages—in essence, to turn the vernacular into a dead language (with all of its seductive opacities). Both of these poetic models (balladry and conservative lyric) are united by a common investment in reproducibility, which distills poetic language—a program of arresting poetry in the interests of imaginative, expressive, and social solidarity (within their respective classes). Fashionable and replicative devices such as the ballad *refrain* therefore acquire new significance within an elite tradition that finds itself promoting and sometimes mimicking, incongruously, an evolving aesthetic of kitsch.

Thinking about poetry's relation to kitsch thus highlights the intertextuality—the echolalia—characterizing the ballad tradition and its elite counterpart, the school of the commonplace book. This orientation—shared by poetic traditions at opposite ends of the social spectrum (and opposing the middle ground of literary values, which favor originality)—draws attention to the rich potential of the verbal cliché, or formula, as a basis of poetic composition. The denotative poverty of the cliché—it describes nothing accurately—yields a mode of anti-realism that depends almost entirely on the effects of reverberation and expression, on connotative meaning. The poetic cliché (or a poem made of clichés) reveals nothing about the natural world or about the psychology of its protagonists; instead, it *expresses* the truth, whether manifest or submerged, of the society in which it circulates. The poetic cliché is thus a prototype of the pop artifact.

In this sense, the poetics of the cliché—reflected in the intertextuality of the ballad and commonplace traditions—calls to mind the importance of the coterie as a social matrix of poetic kitsch. In fact, the prototypical artifacts of kitsch must be viewed—to grasp fully their social significance—as expressions of the social cliques that fostered them: the domestic circles of the female antiquarians of the Scottish Enlightenment, the homosocial connoisseurship of the Strawberry Hill Set, the "suicidal mimicry" of the New York school of poets. In this sense, these social and aesthetic formations may be described as *textual coteries*. Pound's sense of the correspondences between the poetic image conceived as a "vortex" and the social "vortex" of London in which such images were produced reveals an early construction of the textual coterie.

Approaching certain vanguard movements as textual coteries helps to explain why Pound's episodic and alienated indulgence in poetic kitsch in the *Cantos* (which stemmed from the unresolved paradigms of Imagism and Vorticism) inclined eventually towards the fabrication of social (and incidentally Fascist) totalities: an experiment revealing correspondences among the despised categories of kitsch, poetic diction, and totality. Social microcosms (and the artifacts they produce or promote) function—potentially—as models of social or cultural totality, as blueprints for more expansive forms of collaboration and solidarity. The reverberating substance of poetic kitsch thus models the intersubjective relations of the coterie or *tribe* (with common beliefs, goals, or interests), which may also be described as *fugitive* totalities (in part because of their ephemerality). In this sense, the poetics of kitsch tends at times toward collectivism in practice and toward a paradigm of relational aesthetics in which sociality becomes the substance of art.

Illustrating the mechanics of the textual coterie, the clichéd or borrowed language used by poets such as John Ashbery (whose early books show the influence of Dadaism) and Ted Berrigan (who repeatedly touts the example of Warhol's methods) reveals the need for a fundamental revision of Greenberg's iconic antithesis of avant-garde and kitsch. Overturning this opposition discloses a hitherto veiled correspondence between Dada's purely political sublimation of the cliché and what appears to be a purely aesthetic sublimation of clichés associated with kitsch (which yields an artifact consonant with the fluidity of mass culture). Judging from the frivolity and triviality of Ashbery's influential brand of poetry, one must acknowledge that the orientation of a dominant school of the poetic avant-garde has indeed migrated towards the condition of kitsch (without abandoning the procedures of Dadaism).

Negotiating a path between aesthetic and political sublimations of the cliché, the poetic vanguard has exploited the binding, synthetic powers of stereotypical language to cultivate new ways of verbally mapping solidarity and political will. Under these conditions, kitsch becomes an extension of the avant-garde, rather than its antithesis, redirecting the collectivist and libidinal dimensions of commercial language, for example, towards the synthesis of concrete totalities (just as advertising jingles help to produce volatile and fleeting collectivities).

Historically, the equation of Dada and kitsch, which arose defensively in the context of the emergence of pop art, and which implies the sacrifice of a purely critical and adversarial stance, has been judged in the harshest terms as a betrayal of the premises of the historical avant-garde (founded on a program of negation). Yet the imposition of an absolute choice between pure negation or pure pleasure, between opposition or affirmation, obscures an alternative paradigm of the avant-garde grounded in Baudelaire's lyrical program of "inventing clichés" and Benjamin's valorization of Baudelaire's "profound duplicity" as a poet. Rejecting the purely critical and destructive posture of Dadaist poetry (which appears to be extraneous to the temptations of consumerism), Benjamin chooses to focus instead on the fate of "the *lyric* poet in the era of high capitalism," on the inescapably symptomatic nature of Baudelaire's poetic practice. In contrast to the purely negative gesture of Dadaism and its legacy in twentieth-century poetry, Baudelaire's writing manipulates the lyric substance—the *"argot plastique"*—of poetry to produce artifacts rivaling the "profane halo" of the commodity. In this sense, his poems contest the "permanent catastrophe" of modern capitalism in part by documenting the poet's (and poetry's) abject relation to the marketplace.

Benjamin saw Baudelaire producing—as a critical gesture—poems that were intended to mimic, but also to dialectically overturn, the sensuous and imaginative pleasures of the commodity. These objectives identify the poetic artifact of the Baudelairean avant-garde as reliably symptomatic of the delirium of the marketplace (that is, helplessly polarized in its addictions to pleasure and illusion). At the same time, precisely because it distills and exploits aesthetic pleasure, the radicalized lyric poem is predisposed to circulate in a manner aping the transitivity of the pop artifact. That the libidinal and hedonistic properties of poetry are essential to its political efficacy is precisely the argument advanced by Ezra Pound in his defense of poetry as the appropriate medium for epic poetry committed to the reformation of society. Imagine if the formal and imaginative achievements of the *Cantos* had been placed in the service of progressive values! Producing pleasure and beauty in excess of the standards of prosaic verisimilitude (and good taste) thus becomes the prerequisite of a poetic artifact designed to circulate on the scale of a commodity, thereby enhancing the gesture of critical intervention (a power deliberately withheld from artifacts produced under the censorious regime of the historical avant-garde and its historical legacy). A similar—and thoroughly alienated—profile can be detected in the hyperlyrical and confessional poems of Sylvia Plath.

Based on these premises, an alternative paradigm of the avant-garde becomes visible, encompassing poets with an affinity for Baudelaire's alternately profane and auratic program, but also for Warhol's silver factory of
collaboration and dissolution, for the New Realism of pop art, for *plastic
poetry*. Founded on a platform of verbal and libidinal "duplicity," a critical poetics of kitsch thus offers a strategy for radicalizing lyric poetry by
exploiting its relation to the rhapsodic dimension of modern epic (without
requiring the scale of epic). As a means of replicating, but also contesting,
the "permanent catastrophe" of modern capitalism, the radicalized lyric (in
the form of kitsch) becomes what the French pop artist Daniel Spoerri calls
a "snare picture": a sensuous and imaginative trap luring the reader into a
disorienting space of indulgence, alienation, and critique—into "the poisonous candy factory" (to borrow a phrase from Jack Spicer) of poetic diction.
From this perspective, the poem's relation to consumerism and the marketplace may be described as *homeopathic*—the substance of the remedy being
an infinitesimal trace of the malady. The homeopathic poetics of kitsch thus
activates a disposition, a mode of critique, which is at once physically real
and undetectable, substantial and negligible, active and trivial.

It is not only the superficiality of the snare picture but the disabling effects of the pleasure it generates that allow it to circulate freely and widely,
to cross borders, to reach a mass audience. As a borderline phenomenon,
the transitivity of the snare picture enables it to accumulate meaning and
value as it passes through disparate communities, to harbor the ghost of
social capital that is the source of its allure, to begin to *reverberate*. And
it is precisely the promiscuity of the snare picture—an icon of counterfeit
capital—that exceeds the provisional negativity of Dadaism and its medusal
legacy. By proscribing sensuous, imaginative, and affective pleasures, even
as it retains incongruously an overdetermined conception of the artifact
(indebted to formalism), the historical avant-garde ensures the immobility,
the isolation, of its works. Unable to circulate beyond a community of like-
minded disciples, art that offers nothing more than anti-lyrical critique is
doomed to irrelevance as an instrument of cultural and political persuasion.

Only the homeopathic logic of kitsch, forswearing false immunity to the
libidinal currents of the marketplace, can put into circulation certain kinds
of artistic time bombs, snare pictures, stealth weapons. At the same time, a
critical poetics of kitsch calls for the deliberate and dialectical production of
aesthetic failures, for the invention of clichés. These riddling tasks recall the
paradoxical Romantic project of creating modern poetic fragments—a task

that the genealogy of kitsch reveals to be an act of imposture. What unites these puzzling endeavors—manufacturing fragments, crafting artistic failures, inventing clichés—is a conception of the aesthetic artifact that magically comprehends, at the very moment of its production, the history of its own reception. The poetics of kitsch offers a solution to the riddle posed by these aesthetic anomalies: a work of art that cannot be extracted—like a pop artifact—from its social substance, from its garbled history of transmission. Even art, it seems, can turn into kitsch—if word gets around.

Notes

Chapter 1. Arresting Poetry

1. Broch's earliest writing on kitsch appears in a section entitled "Der Kitsch" of a larger essay, "Das Böse in Wertsystem der Kunst" (Evil in the value system of art), published in the journal *Neue Rundschau* in August 1933. Broch revised these ideas for a lecture at Yale University in 1950, which was published as "Einege Bemerkungen zum Problem des Kitsches" (Notes on the Problem of Kitsch) in Hermann Broch, *Gesammelte Werke* (Zurich: Rhein-Verlag, 1955), 6:295-309. This essay appears in English as "Notes on the Problem of Kitsch," in *Kitsch: The World of Bad Taste*, ed. Gillo Dorfles (New York: Bell, 1969), p. 63.

2. T. W. Adorno, *Aesthetic Theory*, trans. C. Lenhardt (London: Routledge, 1984), pp. 340, 53. The etymology of the word "kitsch" comes from the German verb *kitschen*, "to smear or scrape together."

3. Clement Greenberg, "Avant-Garde and Kitsch" (1939), reprinted in Greenberg, *Art and Culture: Critical Essays* (Boston: Beacon Press, 1961), p. 11.

4. The latter phrase is Adorno's, *Aesthetic Theory*, p. 340; and the former appears in Broch's essay "Notes on Kitsch," p. 50.

5. On kitsch and fascism, see Broch, "Notes on Kitsch," pp. 63-66; and Greenberg, "Avant-Garde and Kitsch," pp. 19-21. See also Susan Sontag, "Fascinating Fascism," in *Under the Sign of Saturn* (New York: Farrar, Straus and Giroux, 1980), pp. 73-105. On kitsch representations of National Socialism in postwar culture, see Saul Friedlander, *Reflections of Nazism: An Essay on Kitsch and Death*, trans. Thomas Weyr (New York: Harper and Row, 1984).

6. Andrew Hewitt, *Political Inversions: Homosexuality, Fascism, and the Modernist Imaginary* (Stanford: Stanford University Press, 1996), p. 206. On historical constructions of homosexuality and the mimeticism of kitsch, see Eve Kosofsky Sedgwick, *Epistemology of the Closet* (Berkeley: University of California Press, 1990), pp. 141-146, 156-167.

7. Greenberg, "Avant-Garde and Kitsch," p. 15.

8. Ibid., p. 10.

9. Broch, "Notes on Kitsch," p. 49.

10. Clement Greenberg, "A Victorian Novel," in *Art and Culture*, p. 251.

11. Sedgwick, *Epistemology of the Closet*, p. 155. In full, Sedgwick's quote is "kitsch-man is never the person who uses the word 'kitsch.'" She is borrowing from Broch the term "kitsch-man," which he coined to designate the producer and consumer of kitsch. See Broch, "Notes on Kitsch" p. 49.

12. Sedgwick, *Epistemology of the Closet*, p. 156.

13. Svetlana Boym, *Commonplaces: Mythologies of Everyday Life* (Cambridge, MA: Harvard University Press, 1995). Danilo Kis, "The Gingerbread Heart, or Nationalism" (from *The Anatomy Lesson*), reprinted in Kis, *Homo Poeticus: Essays and Interviews*, ed. Susan Sontag (New York: Farrar, Straus and Giroux, 1995), pp. 15–35. Celeste Olalquiaga, *The Artificial Kingdom: On the Kitsch Experience* (Minneapolis: University of Minnesota Press, 2002). One could also include on this list of poetry's dispossessors Susan Sontag, "Notes on 'Camp,'" *Against Interpretation and Other Essays* (New York: Farrar, Straus and Giroux, 1966).

14. Broch, "Notes on Kitsch," p. 62. On the "danger" posed by kitsch, Broch remarks that it is "all the greater when at first glance the system and the anti-system appear to be identical" (p. 62).

15. I am thinking specifically of Ben Jonson's play *The Poetaster, or His Arraignment* (the first use of the word in English), which locates the bad poet verbally between various kinds of jargon (academic or criminal) and, dramatically, within the scandal of poetic exile (Ovid's exile from Rome).

16. Bürger refers to the "avant-gardist protest, whose aim it is to reintegrate art into the praxis of life." Peter Bürger, *Theory of the Avant-Garde*, trans. Michael Shaw (Minneapolis: University of Minnesota, 1984), p. 22.

17. Susan Stewart, *Crimes of Writing: Problems in the Containment of Representation* (Oxford: Oxford University Press, 1991), p. 92.

18. Dwight Macdonald, "Annals of Crime," cited in K. K. Ruthven, *Faking Literature* (Cambridge: Cambridge University Press, 2001), p. 53.

19. Greenberg states, "The precondition of kitsch, a condition without which kitsch would be impossible, is the availability close at hand of a fully matured cultural tradition. . . . It borrows from it devices, tricks, stratagems, rules of thumb, themes, converts them into a system, and discards the rest. It draws its life blood, so to speak, from this reservoir of accumulated experience." Greenberg, "Avant-Garde and Kitsch," p. 10.

20. Ibid.

21. Johann Gottfried von Herder, "Über Ossian und die Lieder alter Völker" (1773), *Werke*, vol. 2, ed. Regine Otto (Berlin: Aufbau-Verlag, 1982).

22. "The idealism of Schiller contrasts with the transcendental-critical language of Kant. Schiller appears as the ideology of Kant's Critical philosophy." Paul de Man,

"Kant and Schiller," *Aesthetic Ideology*, ed. Andrej Warminski (Minneapolis: University of Minnesota, 1996), p. 147.

23. See Bürger's subchapter "The Autonomy of Art in the Aesthetics of Kant and Schiller" in *Theory of the Avant-Garde*, pp. 41-46. Bürger, it should be noted, is less inclined than de Man to contrast Kant and Schiller.

24. In contrast to the principle of the sublime, which aspires to be transcendental, "the beautiful is a metaphysical and ideological principle." Paul de Man, "Phenomenality and Materiality in Kant," *Aesthetic Ideology*, p. 72.

25. Paul de Man, "Kant's Materialism," *Aesthetic Ideology*, p. 119.

26. Ibid., pp. 119-120.

27. From Schiller there emerges, according to de Man, "a way of setting up the aesthetic as exemplary, as an exemplary category, as a unifying category, as a model for education, as a model even for the state." De Man, "Kant and Schiller," p. 130. Elsewhere, citing a passage from a novel by Joseph Goebbels, de Man asserts, "As such the aesthetic belongs to the Masses . . . it belongs to culture, and as such it belongs to the state, to the aesthetic state" (p. 154).

28. Georges Bataille, "The Old Mole and the Prefix *Sur*," *Visions of Excess: Selected Writings, 1927-1939*, trans. Allan Stoekl (Minneapolis: University of Minnesota, 1985), p. 41.

29. Georges Bataille, "The Lugubrious Game," *Visions of Excess*, p. 29.

30. Lytle Shaw addresses the avant-gardist trivialization of poetry in reference to Frank O'Hara's poetry and criticism. Shaw, *Frank O'Hara: The Poetics of Coterie* (Iowa City: University of Iowa Press, 2006), pp. 11-15.

31. Broch, "Notes on Kitsch," p. 59.

32. Elaine Scarry, *On Beauty and Being Just* (Princeton: Princeton University Press, 2001), p. 3.

33. Ibid., p. 4.

34. Ibid., p. 6.

35. Poe spells out his doctrine of poetic effects by recounting the compositional method of his poem "The Raven." Edgar Allan Poe, "The Philosophy of Composition" (1846), reprinted in *The Raven, with The Philosophy of Composition* (Boston: Northeastern University Press, 1986). Poe begins his essay by noting that he was prompted to record his thoughts by a note from Charles Dickens indicating that William Godwin's gothic novel *Caleb Williams* (1804) was written backwards. Poe thus finds a correlation between his own poetics of effect and the inverted compositional methods of gothic fiction.

36. Sianne Ngai, "Literary Gimmicks," lecture delivered at a panel on the poetics of kitsch at Poets House, New York City, October 20, 2012. When I say poetic "procedures," I am referring to sampling techniques often associated with Conceptualism or "Flarf" in contemporary experimental poetry. On the trick of writing backwards, Poe begins his essay on composition by noting that he was prompted to write on

the subject by a letter from Charles Dickens indicating that William Godwin's gothic novel *Caleb Williams* (1804) was written backwards. Poe thus finds a correlation between his doctrine of calculated poetic effects and the inverted compositional methods of Gothic fiction.

37. Gilles Deleuze and Felix Guattari, *Kafka: Towards a Minor Literature*, trans. Dana Polan (Minneapolis: University of Minnesota Press, 1986), p. 18. References to "literature" in this case must be understood in reference to my thesis about militant poeticism.

38. Ezra Pound, *Selected Letters, 1907–1941*, ed. D. D. Paige (New York: New Directions, 1971), p. 296.

39. The phrase "arresting poetry" echoes the title of Peter Fenves's coruscating book, *Arresting Language: From Leibniz to Benjamin* (Stanford: Stanford University Press, 2001). While Fenves writes of linguistic events frequently evoking, or implying, a theological perspective on language, my use of the trope of *arresting*—certainly more modest in scope—is resolutely poetic and profane in its orientation.

40. John Keats, "Lamia," *Complete Poems and Selected Letters*, ed. Edward Hirsch (New York: Modern Library, 2001), p. 194 (part 1, line 196). As an emblem of the aesthetic category of kitsch, the phrase "my silver planet" resonates in fascinating ways with Timothy Morton's thinking about "ecology without nature" and, more specifically, with the concept of "ecological kitsch" (as a progressive principle). See Timothy Morton, *Ecology without Nature: Rethinking Environmental Aesthetics* (Cambridge: Harvard University Press, 2007).

41. Teskey's comments are made in reference to Milton's diction and its dependence on the classical tradition. Gordon Teskey, *Delirious Milton* (Cambridge: Harvard University Press, 2006), p. 127.

42. Greenberg, "Avant-Garde and Kitsch," p. 19.

43. On the concept of totality, Lukács writes, "It is not the primacy of economic motives in historical explanation that constitutes the decisive difference between Marxism and bourgeois thought, but the point of totality. The category, the all-pervasive supremacy of the whole over the parts, is the essence of the method which Marx took over from Hegel and brilliantly transformed into the foundations of a wholly new science. *The primacy of the category of totality is the bearer of the principle of revolution.*" Georg Lukács, *History and Class Consciousness: Studies in Marxist Dialectics* (1923), trans. Rodney Livingstone (Cambridge, MA: Harvard University Press, 1971), p. 27. In a less political vein, see Eric Hayot's *On Literary Worlds* (Oxford: Oxford University Press, 2012), which develops a non-Marxian model of literary totalities.

44. On the correlation of historical experience and tradition, Benjamin states, "Experience is indeed a matter of tradition, in collective existence as well as in private life. It is less the product of facts firmly rooted in memory than of a convergence in memory of accumulated and frequently unconscious data." Walter Benjamin, "On

Some Motifs in Baudelaire," reprinted in *Illuminations*, ed. Hannah Arendt, trans. Harry Zohn (New York: Schocken Books, 1969), p. 157. On Benjamin's conception of "kitsch as an organon of historical experience," see Winfried Menninghaus, "On the 'Vital Significance' of Kitsch: Walter Benjamin's Politics of 'Bad Taste,'" in *Walter Benjamin and the Architecture of Modernity*, ed. Andrew Benjamin and Charles Rice (Melbourne: Re-Press, 2009), pp. 39-57. Also available as open source text online. One may also consult a recent double issue of the journal *Neue Rundschau*, vols. 123-124 (2012), devoted to the topic of *Walter Benjamin: Traumkitsch*.

45. Eliot's revaluation of "minor poetry" begins to appear in his first collection of criticism, *The Sacred Wood* (1928), and later in essays on Dryden, Marvell, and Milton (two of them), and in "What Is Minor Poetry?"—the last reprinted in T. S. Eliot, *On Poetry and Poets* (New York: Farrar, Straus and Giroux, 1967).

46. T. S. Eliot, *John Dryden: The Poet, the Dramatist, the Critic* (New York: Terence and Elsa Holliday, 1932), pp. 22.

47. Ibid., p. 5.

48. Shaw, *Frank O'Hara*, p. 16.

49. The coterie, or expressive totality, in which the poetics of kitsch takes root anticipates the models of "relational aesthetics" articulated recently by Nicolas Bourriaud, who describes "an art taking as its theoretical horizon the realm of human interaction and its social context rather than the assertion of an independent and *private* symbolic space." Bourriaud, *Relational Aesthetics*, trans. Simon Pleasance and Fronza Woods (Dijon: les presses du réel, 2002), p. 14.

50. Deleuze and Guattari, *Towards a Minor Literature*, p. 23.

51. Broch refers to "a disastrous fall from the cosmic heights to kitsch." "Notes on Kitsch," p. 2.

52. On the expressive alienation of poetic kitsch, Adorno notes, "Its false glitter is the complement to the disenchanted world from which it extricates itself." Theodor W. Adorno, "On Lyric Poetry and Society," in *Notes on Literature*, trans. Shierry Weber Nicholsen (New York: Columbia University Press, 1991), p. 1:45.

53. See the special issue on "Surface Reading" of *Representations*, Vol. 8, No. 1 (Fall 2009). See also Franco Moretti, *Distant Learning* (London: Verso, 2013).

54. Siegfried Kracauer, "Cult of Distraction" (1926), reprinted in *The Mass Ornament*, trans. Thomas Y. Levin (Cambridge: Harvard University Press, 1995), p. 326.

55. John Guillory, *Cultural Capital: The Problem of Literary Canon Formation* (Chicago: University of Chicago Press, 1993), pp. 92-93.

56. Adorno, *Aesthetic Theory*, p. 435.

Chapter 2. Poetic Diction and the Substance of Kitsch

1. Robert Musil, "Black Magic," in *Posthumous Papers of a Living Author*, trans. Peter Wortsman (New York: Archipelago Books, 2006), p. 55. This essay, originally

published in 1923 as "Schwarze Magie," appears in Musil's *Gesammelte Werke*, ed. Adolf Frisé (Reinbek: Rowohlt, 1978-1982), 7:503.

2. Hermann Broch, "Notes on the Problem of Kitsch," reprinted in *Kitsch: The World of Bad Taste*, ed. Gillo Dorfles (New York: Bell, 1969), pp. 50, 56-59.

3. Clement Greenberg, "Avant-Garde and Kitsch," reprinted in Greenberg, *Art and Culture: Critical Essays* (Boston: Beacon Press, 1961), p. 15. One of Eddie Guest's many books of poetry is entitled *A Heap o' Livin'* (Chicago: Reilly and Lee, 1916), which sold more than a million copies.

4. Greenberg, "Avant-Garde and Kitsch," p. 3.

5. Walter Benjamin, "Dream Kitsch" (1927), trans. Stefan G. Rehm, *Sulfur* 32 (Spring 1993), p. 185. When this brief essay was first published in *Neue Rundschau* in January 1927, it appeared with the title "Gloss on Surrealism." Walter Benjamin, *Gesammelte Schriften*, ed. Rolf Tiedemann, and Hermann Schweppehäuser (Frankfurt: Suhrkamp, 1979-1989), pp. 2:620-622. Another English translation of this essay can be found in Walter Benjamin, *Selected Writings*, vol. 2, part 1, 1927-1930, ed. Michael W. Jennings, Howard Eiland, and Gary Smith (Cambridge, MA: Harvard University Press, 1999), pp. 3-5.

6. Benjamin, "Dream Kitsch," p. 186.

7. Ibid., p. 185.

8. On Benjamin's understanding of the correlation of kitsch, historical experience, and tradition, see Winfried Menninghaus, "On the 'Vital Significance' of Kitsch: Walter Benjamin's Politics of 'Bad Taste,'" in *Walter Benjamin and the Architecture of Modernity*, ed. Andrew Benjamin and Charles Rice (Melbourne: Re-Press, 2009), pp. 39-57. Also available as open source text online. And on the correlation between the "worlds of childhood" and kitsch—what Benjamin calls its "dream and child side"— see Menninghaus, p. 45 (including note 3). For a consideration of the relation between poetic diction and constructions of adolescence, see Stephen Burt, *The Forms of Youth: Twentieth-Century Poetry and Adolescence* (New York: Columbia University Press, 2007).

9. Benjamin, "Dream Kitsch," p. 185. Concerning Benjamin's preoccupation with aesthetic "insufficiency" and failure, see Menninghaus, "On the 'Vital Significance' of Kitsch," p. 48. In contrast to works associated with the fine arts, Menninghaus states, "The aesthetic imperfection of the dusty and outdated has the advantage of entailing less sublimation and self-sufficiency, and hence of allowing greater scope for everyday 'dream energies'" (p. 49).

10. Benjamin, cited in Menninghaus, "On the 'Vital Significance' of Kitsch," p. 46.

11. Peter Bürger. *Theory of the Avant-Garde*, trans. Michael Shaw (Minneapolis: University of Minnesota Press, 1984), pp. 22, 61-66, 91. Bürger, it should be noted, is generally hostile to the example of Surrealism.

12. Matei Călinescu, *Five Faces of Modernity: Modernism, Avant-Garde, Decadence, Kitsch, Postmodernism* (Durham, NC: Duke University Press, 1987).

13. In the preface to her *Selected Poems* (1970)—one of several documents where she addresses her abandonment of poetry in 1938-Riding states, "Truth begins where poetry ends." Laura (Riding) Jackson, *The Poems of Laura Riding* (1938; repr., New York: Persea, 1980), p. 416. Marianne Moore, "Poetry" (the longer version), *The Complete Poems of Marianne Moore* (New York: Macmillan, 1981), p. 266.

14. Charles Baudelaire, "Fusées," *Oeuvres completes*, ed. Claude Pichois (Paris: Gallimard, 1975), p. 662. Baudelaire writes, "Créer un poncif c'est le génie. Je dois créer un poncif."

15. Walter Benjamin, "Some Motifs on Baudelaire," in *Charles Baudelaire: A Lyric Poet in the Era of High Capitalism*, trans. Harry Zohn (London: Verso, 1970), p. 155.

16. Anton C. Zijderveld, *On Clichés* (London: Routledge and Kegan Paul, 1979), p. 98.

17. Ibid., p. 14. On the "social functionality" of clichés, see pp. 17-25.

18. Ibid., p. 16.

19. Ibid.

20. Ibid., p. 5. On the "genius" of inventing clichés, see the passage by Baudelaire cited in note 14 above. And, on the effects of poetic repetition, see Siobhan Phillips, *The Poetics of the Everyday: Creative Repetition in Modern American Verse* (New York: Columbia UP, 2009).

21. Broch, "Notes on Kitsch," pp. 52, 63.

22. Roland Barthes, cited in Mark Booth, "*Camp-toi!* On the Origins and Definitions of Camp," in *Camp: Queer Aesthetics and the Performing Subject*, ed. Fabio Cleto (Ann Arbor: University of Michigan Press, 1999), p. 70.

23. "Linguistic capital" is John Guillory's phrase for one of the two components (the other being "symbolic capital") composing what he calls "a form of capital which is specifically symbolic or cultural." Guillory, *Cultural Capital: The Problem of Literary Canon Formation* (Chicago: University of Chicago Press, 1993), pp. viii-ix.

24. Broch, "Notes on Kitsch," p. 51.

25. Francis Jeffrey, review of Walter Scott's *Lady of the Lake*, orig. pub. in the *Edinburgh Review* 16 (August 1810), reprinted in *Jeffrey's Criticism: A Selection*, ed. Peter F. Morgan (Edinburgh: Scottish Academic Press, 1983), p. 69.

26. Ibid.

27. Ibid.

28. Donald Davie, *Purity of Diction in English Verse* (New York: Schocken Books, 1967), p. 12.

29. Ibid., p. 119. See Owen Barfield's definition of poetic diction: "When words are selected and arranged in such a way that their meaning arouses, or is obviously intended to arouse, aesthetic imagination, the result may be described as *poetic diction*." Barfield, *Poetic Diction: A Study in Meaning* (1928; Middletown, CT: Wesleyan University Press, 1973), p. 41.

30. Fredric Jameson "Criticism in History," reprinted in Neil Larson, ed. *The Ideol-*

ogies of Theory: Essays, 1971–1986 (Minneapolis: University of Minnesota Press, 1988), pp. 119–136.

31. On the historical struggle to preserve the verbal and cultural distinctions of poetry in the late eighteenth century, see Guillory, *Cultural Capital*, p. 124.

32. On the historical tension between poetry and the emerging category of literature in the late eighteenth century, see Guillory, *Cultural Capital*, pp. 118–124.

33. On the correlation of literacy, canon formation, diction, and the evolution of literary genres, see, among many sources, Roy Porter, *English Society in the Eighteenth Century* (Harmondsworth, UK: Penguin Books, 1982); Jeffrey Kittay and Wlad Godzich, *The Emergence of Prose: An Essay in Prosaics* (Minneapolis: University of Minnesota Press, 1987); Thomas Sheridan, *British Education: On the Source of the Disorders of Great Britain* (New York: Garland, 1970); A. D. Harvey, *English Poetry in a Changing Society, 1780–1825* (London: Alison and Busby, 1980).

34. On the effects of the introduction of vernacular writing into English school curricula, see Guillory, *Cultural Capital*, pp. 77–80, 99–102.

35. On the shifting parameters of early formulations of literature (and the man of letters), see Guillory, *Cultural Capital*, pp. 122–123.

36. Wordsworth refers to "adulterated phraseology" in the 1802 appendix to the *Lyrical Ballads*, and to "inane phraseology" in the preface to the same volume. William Wordsworth and Samuel Taylor Coleridge, *Lyrical Ballads*, ed. Michael Mason (London: Longman, 1992), pp. 90, 34.

37. Wordsworth, preface to *Lyrical Ballads*, p. 61.

38. For a recent anthology including examples of what might conceivably be called experiments in diction—though without any reference to poetic kitsch—see Craig Dworkin and Kenneth Goldsmith, eds., *Against Expression: An Anthology of Conceptual Writing* (Evanston, IL: Northwestern University Press, 2010). The introduction to the volume is entitled "The Fate of Echo." One should pay close attention to Dworkin's superb annotations to individual entries in the anthology.

39. Marjorie Perloff, for example, argues that the practices and poetic value of textual sampling can be traced to modernist practices of citation to be found in Pound's *Cantos* and Eliot's *The Waste Land*. The formal resemblance of sampling and citation veils, however, their divergent perspectives and values. Perloff, *Unoriginal Genius: Poetry by Other Means in the New Century* (Chicago: University of Chicago Press, 2010), p. 12.

40. Aristotle, *Poetics*, p. 69.

41. Matthew Hart develops a theory of "synthetic vernacular writing" in the context of modernism in his book *Nations of Nothing but Poetry: Modernism, Transnationalism, and Synthetic Vernacular Writing* (Oxford: Oxford University Press, 2010).

42. K. K. Ruthven offers a polemical and theoretical approach to literary forgery, along with a comprehensive survey of its critical reception. Ruthven, *Faking Literature* (Cambridge: Cambridge University Press, 2001).

43. Jean-Jacques Rousseau, "Pygmalion," *Letter to D'Alembert and Other Writings for the Theater*, trans. Allan Bloom, Charles Butterworth, and Christopher Kelly (Lebanon, NH: University Press of New England, 2004), pp. 230-236.

44. Susan Stewart, *Crimes of Writing: Problems in the Containment of Representation* (Oxford: Oxford University Press, 1991), pp. 3-26.

45. On the implications of literary forgery for historiological models, see Ian Haywood, *The Making of History: A Study of the Literary Forgeries of James Macpherson and Thomas Chatterton in Relation to Eighteenth Century Ideas of History and Fiction* (Rutherford, NJ: Fairleigh Dickinson University Press, 1986).

46. Guillory, *Cultural Capital*, p. 88.

47. Wordsworth, appendix to *Lyrical Ballads*, p. 90.

48. Herrick's trope of the "tiffany" appears in at least three of the poems collected in *Hesperides*: "To Anthea Lying in Bed" (H 104); "The Parliament of Roses" (H 11); and "A Nuptial Song, or Epithalamie, on Sir Clipsy Crew and his Lady" (H 283). Robert Herrick, *The Poetical Works of Robert Herrick*, ed. George Saintsbury, 2 vols. (London: George Bell and Sons, 1893).

49. Keats's phrase "silver proxy" appears in line 267 of part 1 of "Lamia." John Keats, *Complete Poems and Selected Letters*, ed. Edward Hirsch (New York: Modern Library, 2001), p. 94.

50. Keats, "Lamia," p. 194 (part 1, line 196).

Chapter 3. Miscreant

1. Hermann Broch, "Notes on the Problem of Kitsch," reprinted in *Kitsch: The World of Bad Taste*, ed. Gillo Dorfles (New York: Bell, 1969), p. 62.

2. Francis Jeffrey, review of Walter Scott's *Lady of the Lake*, orig. pub. in the *Edinburgh Review* 16 (August 1810), reprinted in *Jeffrey' Criticism*, ed. Peter F. Morgan (Edinburgh: Scottish Academic Press, 1983), p. 65.

3. Broch, "Notes on Kitsch," p. 62. One should not overlook the fact that Broch *gothicizes* kitsch by describing it as "a foreign body lodged in the overall system of art." This startling image calls to mind Sedgwick's treatment of "live burial" in her analysis of the themes of the Gothic novel. Eve Kosofsky Sedgwick, *The Coherence of Gothic Conventions* (New York: Arno Press, 1980).

4. Broch, "Notes on Kitsch," p. 62.

5. On the common "beauty" of art and kitsch, see Broch, "Notes on Kitsch," pp. 61-64; and Jeffrey, review of Scott, pp. 68-69.

6. On Broch's rejection of the Marxist understanding of kitsch as "the full flowering of industrial capitalism," see "Notes on Kitsch," pp. 53, 61.

7. Jeffrey, review of Scott, p. 69.

8. Ibid.

9. Ibid., p. 73.

10. The phrase "nervous diction" is especially revealing as an index of the emerging discourse of kitsch, since the term "nervous" in the late eighteenth century conveyed antithetical meanings: it could signify (according to the *OED*) either "strong and vigorous" or "timid and agitated" (the former being the older definition). Ultimately, whether the term denotes weakness or vigor, it comes to be associated with the stereotypical diction of commonplace book—and the poetics of kitsch.

11. Aristotle, in section 22 of the *Poetics*, entitled "The Language of Poetry" (1458a), trans. James Hutton (New York: Norton, 1982), p. 69.

12. Ibid.

13. Jeffrey, review of Scott, p. 73. Jeffrey adds, "He has made more use of common topics, images, and expressions, than any original poet of later times; and, at the same time, displayed more genius and originality than any recent author who has worked in the same materials" (p. 72).

14. Dante, *De vulgari eloquentia*, trans. Steven Botterill (Cambridge: Cambridge University Press, 1996), Book One, section I, p. 3; Book One, section XVI, p. 69.

15. Ibid., Book One, section XVIII, p. 43; Book One, section XV, pp. 33, 37.

16. Ibid., Book One, section XVIII, p. 43.

17. William Wordsworth, preface (1802) to *Lyrical Ballads*, ed. Michael Mason (London: Longman, 1992), p. 57.

18. Ibid., pp. 57, 59.

19. Ben Jonson, *Timber or Discoveries Made upon Men and Matter*, ed. Felix E. Schelling (1641; Boston: Ginn, 1892), pp. 24–25.

20. Ibid.

21. Preface to Cleveland's poetry (1677), cited in Donald Davie, *Purity of Diction in English Verse* (New York: Schocken Books, 1967), p. 210. See Davie's discussion of "a balance to be struck between too much strength and too much ease," pp. 206–210.

22. John Dryden, *An Essay of Dramatic Poesy*, ed. Thomas Arnold (1665; Oxford: Clarendon Press, 1884), pp. 70–71.

23. Samuel Johnson, "Cowley" (1779), *The Lives of the Poets*, ed. Roger Lonsdale (Oxford: Oxford University Press, 2009), p. 33.

24. Ibid.

25. Douglas Bush, *English Literature in the Earlier Seventeenth Century* (New York: Oxford University Press, 1952), pp. 115–116.

26. Samuel Taylor Coleridge, *Biographia Literaria*, ed. George Watson (London: Dent, 1975), p. 191 (chap. 17).

27. Concerning Coleridge's views on his training in Latin, Patrick Cruttwell writes, "he certainly recognized that the traditional kind of classical education, with as its finest flower that absurd bi-lingual acrostic known as 'Latin verses,' was largely responsible for bad taste in English poetry; and *that* sort of education was the pedagogical infant of Roman and English Augustan Taste." Cruttwell, *The Shakespearean*

Moment and Its Place in the Poetry of the Seventeenth Century (New York: Columbia University Press, 1955), p. 221.

28. Wordsworth, preface to *Lyrical Ballads*, p. 71.

29. John Guillory, *Cultural Capital: The Problem of Literary Canon Formation* (Chicago: University of Chicago Press, 1993), p. 76. Similarly, he declares, "It is the emergence of vernacular literacy which brings the category of 'literature' to the forefront of the public sphere" (p. 123).

30. Ibid., p. 132.

31. Wordsworth, preface to *Lyrical Ballads*, p. 66.

32. Wordsworth, appendix to *Lyrical Ballads*, p. 89.

33. Ibid., p. 89.

34. Wordsworth, preface to *Lyrical Ballads*, p. 66.

35. Wordsworth, appendix to *Lyrical Ballads*, p. 90.

36. Ibid.

37. Coleridge, *Biographia Literaria*, pp. 199 (chap. 17), p. 223 (chap. 19).

38. Wordsworth, preface to *Lyrical Ballads*, pp.68–69.

39. Ibid., p. 70.

40. Ibid., pp. 80, 9 (Wordsworth's note). Elsewhere Wordsworth declares, "The language of a large portion of every good Poem, even of the most elevated character, must necessarily, except with reference to metre, in no respect differ from that of good Prose" (p. 67).

41. Ibid., pp. 56–57.

42. Ibid., p. 62.

43. Jean-Pierre Mileur, *Literary Revisionism and the Burden of Modernity* (Berkeley: University of California Press, 1985), p. 202.

44. Guillory, *Cultural Capital*, p. 129. Similarly, Mileur warns, "to remove the identity of the poet from its objective manifestation in having written is to move away from a visible canon or the source and shape of literary authority toward an altogether vaguer, internal standard." *Literary Revisionism*, p. 203.

45. Robert Heron, "A Critical Essay on the Seasons" (1793), cited in A. A. Mendilow, "Robert Heron and Wordsworth's Critical Essays," *Modern Language Review* 52 (1957), pp. 335–336.

46. Coleridge, *Biographia Literaria*, p. 212 (chap. 17). Elsewhere, Coleridge explains, "the very act of poetic composition is, and is allowed to imply and to produce, an unusual state of excitement, which of course justifies and demands a correspondent difference of language" (p. 211 [chap. 18]).

47. Ibid., p. 209 (chap. 18).

48. Francis Jeffrey, review of Wordsworth's poems, orig. pub. in the *Edinburgh Review* 11 (October 1807), reprinted in *Jeffrey's Criticism*, pp. 58, 56.

49. Oliver Goldsmith, "Poetry Distinguished from Other Writing," essay 15

(1765), reprinted in *Miscellaneous Works of Oliver Goldsmith*, ed. Washington Irving (Philadelphia: J. Crissy, 1834), p. 507.

50. Thomas Gray, *The Works of Thomas Gray*, ed. Edmund Gosse, 4 vols. (London: Macmillan, 1903), 2:108. Gerard Manley Hopkins echoes the view of Gray and Goldsmith in a letter to Robert Bridges: "the poetical language of an age should be the current language heightened, to any degree heightened and unlike itself." Hopkins, *The Letters of Gerard Manley Hopkins to Robert Bridges*, ed. Claude Colleer Abbott (London: Oxford University Press, 1955), p. 95.

51. Samuel Johnson, "Gray," *Lives of the Poets*, p. 458.

52. See Guillory's excellent discussion of the role of commonplacing in the composition of Gray's poetry, *Cultural Capital*, p. 88.

53. On the historical genealogy of the term "commonplace" (from Roman antiquity to the Romantic Revival), see Ernst Robert Curtius, *European Literature and the Latin Middle Ages*, trans. Willard R. Trask (London: Routledge, 1979), p. 70.

54. On the historical significance of poetry for commonplace books, see David Allan, *Commonplace Books and Reading in Georgian England* (Cambridge: Cambridge University Press, 2010), pp. 141, 259–260.

55. Ibid., p. 154.

56. Edward Young, *Conjectures on Original Composition*, ed. Edith J. Morley (1759; repr., Manchester: Manchester University Press, 1918), p. 9.

57. William Hazlitt, *Complete Works of William Hazlitt*, ed. P. P. Howe, 21 vols. (London: Dent, 1930–34), 17:209.

58. Wordsworth, preface to *Lyrical Ballads*, pp. 64, 67–68.

59. Ibid., 87.

60. On the role of class difference in Gray's relationship with Walpole, see Roger Lonsdale, ed., *The Poems of Thomas Gray, William Collins, and Oliver Goldsmith* (London: Longmans, 1969), p. 118. For a more detailed account of these tensions, see R. W. Ketton-Cremer, *Thomas Gray: A Biography* (Cambridge: Cambridge University Press, 1955), pp. 44–51.

61. Thomas Gray, "Elegy Written in a Country Church Yard," *The Complete Poems of Thomas Gray*, ed. H. W. Starr and J. R. Hendrickson (Oxford: Clarendon Press, 1966), p. 38.

62. Joshua Scodel, *The English Poetic Epitaph* (Ithaca: Cornell University Press, 1991), p. 357.

63. Davie, *Purity of Diction*, p. 25.

64. Ibid., pp. 24, 138.

65. Ibid., 130, 158.

66. Guillory, *Cultural Capital*, p. 88.

67. Ibid., 92, 87. Guillory's use of the term "literary" in these citations must be viewed with caution, since, strictly speaking, the clichés of Gray's rhapsody are explicitly *poetic*, in opposition to the rising tide of literary (i.e., prosaic) poetry.

68. Hazlitt, "On Shakespeare and Milton," cited in Gordon Teskey, *Delirious Milton* (Cambridge: Harvard University Press, 2006), p. 123.

69. Margaret Russett, *De Quincey's Romanticism: Canonical Minority and the Forms of Transmission* (Cambridge: Cambridge University Press, 1997), p. 18. Russett's comments pertain to De Quincey's appropriation of the "gross and violent stimulants" of poetic diction, yet she also reveals the degree to which Gray's commonplace methods haunt various Gothic themes: solipsism and the doppelgänger are functions of poetic inversion at the level of signifier.

70. William Hazlitt, *Lectures on the English Poets*, ed. A. R. Waller (London: Dent, 1916), p. 118.

71. Johnson, "Gray," cited by Guillory, *Cultural Capital*, pp. 90-91.

72. Teskey, *Delirious Milton*, p. 127.

73. Leslie Stephen, *Hours in a Library* (London: Smith, Elder, 1909), p. 97.

74. Jeffrey, review of Scott, p. 68.

75. Ezra Pound, *Selected Letters, 1907-1941*, ed. D. D. Paige (New York: New Directions, 1971), p. 296.

76. Pope's poem sometimes appears under the alternate title "Song, By a Person of Quality," which allows it to be confused at times with a poem of the same title by Jonathan Swift, which is cited by Jeffrey (though he may be confusing it with Pope's satire): "a selection of some of the most trite and well-sounding phrases and epithets in the poetical lexicon of the time, strung together without any kind of meaning or consistency." Jeffrey, review of Scott, pp. 69-70. The text of Pope's satire can be found in Alexander Pope, *The Works of Alexander Pope*, ed. Whitewell Elwin and William John Courthope (London: John Murray, 1882), 4:489-490.

77. See Vico's genealogy of "poetic wisdom" (and "poetic logic") in Giambattista Vico, *The New Science of Giambattista Vico*, trans. Thomas Goddard Bergin and Max Harold Fisch (1744; Ithaca: Cornell University Press, 1984), pp. 109-169.

78. Johann Wolfgang von Goethe, *The Sorrows of Young Werther*, trans. Elizabeth Mayer and Louise Bogan (1774; New York: Vintage, 1973), p. 110.

79. Roger Lonsdale, "The Poetry of Thomas Gray: Versions of the Self," in *Thomas Gray's "Elegy Written in a Country Churchyard,"* ed. Harold Bloom (New York: Chelsea House, 1987), p. 24.

80. Mileur, *Literary Revisionism*, p. 199.

81. Ibid., p. 196.

82. Gray, "Elegy Written in a Country Church Yard," p. 42.

83. Ibid., p. 40.

84. Gray, "The Bard," *Complete Poems*, p. 24.

85. Ibid., p. 23.

86. Gray, "The Progress of Poesy," *Complete Poems*, p. 16.

87. Laura Riding, introduction to the 1980 edition of *The Poems of Laura Riding* (1938; New York: Persea Books, 1980), p. 5.

88. Ibid., p. 4.

89. Ibid., p. 10.

90. Ibid., p. 3.

91. In 1768, Gray published translations of three ancient ballads, "The Fatal Sisters," "The Descent of Odin," and "The Triumphs of Owen, A Fragment." Since Gray had no knowledge of the original languages, he worked from Latin translations of the original Old Norse and Old Welsh. *Complete Poems*, pp. 27–36.

92. Wordsworth, preface to *Lyrical Ballads*, p. 62.

93. Guillory, *Cultural Capital*, p. 92.

94. Jeffrey, review of Wordsworth, p. 57.

95. Jeffrey, review of Byron's "Corsair," orig. pub. in the *Edinburgh Review* 23 (April 1814), reprinted in *Jeffrey's Criticism*, p. 79.

96. Davie, *Purity of Diction*, p. 26.

97. Guillory, *Cultural Capital*, p. 120.

98. Ibid., p. 124. Elsewhere, concerning the poetic project of vernacular estrangement, Guillory refers to "poetry as a distinct language, the vernacular's own Latin" (p. 131).

99. Samuel Johnson, essay no. 37 in *The Rambler*, cited in Guillory, *Cultural Capital*, p. 125. Jeffrey identifies a similar alloy of "elegance" and "coarseness" (a compound essential to kitsch) coined by the authors of "popular poetry," who seek "to write all the fine and strong feelings to which cultivation and reflection alone can give birth, with those manners and that condition of society, in which passions are uncontrolled, and their natural indications manifested without reserve. It was necessary, therefore, to write two things that did never exist together in any period of society; and the union, though it may startle sober thinkers a little, is perhaps within the legitimate prerogatives of poetry." Jeffrey, review of Byron's "Corsair," p. 81.

100. Guillory, *Cultural Capital*, p. 124.

101. Owen Barfield, *Poetic Diction: A Study in Meaning* (1928; Middletown: Wesleyan University Press, 1973), p. 163.

102. Barfield writes, "Properly understood, archaism chooses, not old words, but young ones" (p. 165).

Chapter 4. The Spurious Progeny of Bare Nature

1. Albert B. Friedman, *The Ballad Revival: Studies in the Influence of Popular on Sophisticated Poetry* (Chicago: University of Chicago Press, 1961), pp. 8, 9. Of the many fine studies of balladry and ballad culture I have consulted, Friedman's book combines familiarity with primary sources, a command of the intricate editorial and critical history of ballad poetry, and a lively sense of the ballad's relation to the lyric tradition. A superb and perhaps neglected study. The latest and most comprehensive collection of essays assessing the role of "song" in English poetry (from the

perspective of the eighteenth century) can be found in "Ballads and Songs in the Eighteenth Century," edited by Ruth Perry, special issue, *The Eighteenth Century: Theory and Interpretation*, 47, nos. 2–3 (2006).

2. Friedman, *Ballad Revival*, p. 9.

3. About the "Ballad of Chevy Chase," Sidney writes, "I must confess my own barbarousness, I never heard the old song of Percy and Douglas that I found not my heart moved more than a trumpet; and yet it is sung by some blind crowder, with no rougher voice than rude style." Philip Sidney, *A Defence of Poetry*, ed. Geoffrey Shepherd (New York: Harper and Row, 1973), p. 118.

4. *Ben Jonson: The Man and His Work*, ed. C. H. Herford and Perry Simpson, (Oxford: Clarendon Press, 1925), p. 1:145.

5. Friedman, summarizing the cultural changes associated with humanism between 1550 and 1700, observes, "Humanism is commonly said to have done most to undermine the ballad tradition." *Ballad Revival*, pp. 25–26.

6. Ibid., p. 24.

7. Michel de Certeau, *Heterologies: Discourse on the Other*, trans. Brian Massumi (Minneapolis: University of Minnesota Press, 1986), p. 121.

8. Friedman, *Ballad Revival*, p. 4.

9. Ibid., pp. 2, 6.

10. On the role of balladry in shaping the emergence of popular culture (and the lyric tradition), see Steve Newman, *Ballad Collection, Lyric, and the Canon: The Call of the Popular from Restoration through the New Criticism* (Philadelphia: University of Pennsylvania Press, 2007).

11. Samuel Johnson, *Lives of the English Poets*, ed. Arthur Waugh (Oxford: Oxford University Press, 1949), p. 2:90.

12. Francis Jeffrey, "The State of Modern Poetry," orig. pub. in the *Edinburgh Review* 48 (September 1828), reprinted in *Jeffrey's Criticism*, ed. Peter F. Morgan (Edinburgh: Scottish Academic Press, 1983), p. 96.

13. Francis Jeffrey, review of Walter Scott's *Lady of the Lake*, orig. pub. in the *Edinburgh Review* 16 (August 1810), reprinted in *Jeffrey's Criticism*, p. 70.

14. Theodor W. Adorno, "On Lyric Poetry and Society" (1957), reprinted in *Notes to Literature*, ed. Rolf Tiedemann, trans. Shierry Weber Nicholsen (New York: Columbia University Press, 1991), p. 1:53.

15. Susan Stewart, *Crimes of Writing: Problems in the Containment of Representation* (Oxford: Oxford University Press, 1991), p. 3.

16. Friedman, *Ballad Revival*, pp. 35, 64, 70, 57.

17. Scott, cited in Friedman, *Ballad Revival*, p. 181. Percy's phrase can be found in a letter to Thomas Birch, dated February 2, 1765. Cited in Nick Groom, *The Making of Percy's Reliques* (Oxford: Clarendon Press, 1999), p. 54.

18. Friedman, *Ballad Revival*, p. 5.

19. Ibid., p. 59.

20. Clement Greenberg, "Avant-Garde and Kitsch" (1939), reprinted in Greenberg, *Art and Culture: Critical Essays* (Boston: Beacon Press, 1961, p. 18, note 5.

21. Ibid.

22. Siegfried Kracauer, "The Mass Ornament" (1927), reprinted in *The Mass Ornament: Weimar Essays*, trans. Thomas Y. Levin (Cambridge: Harvard University Press, 1995), p. 76.

23. Ibid., p. 77.

24. Ibid., p. 82.

25. Ibid., p. 85. On the ambivalence of the mass ornament of kitsch, see p. 83.

26. Friedman, *The Ballad Revival*, p. 26.

27. Ibid., p. 4. On theories of the aristocratic origins of vernacular ballads, see p. 17, note 25.

28. Ibid., pp. 294–295.

29. Hermann Broch, "Notes on the Problem of Kitsch," reprinted in *Kitsch: The World of Bad Taste*, ed. Gillo Dorfles (New York: Bell, 1969), p. 62.

30. Theodor W. Adorno, *Aesthetic Theory*, trans. C. Lenhardt (London: Routledge, 1984), pp. 339–340.

31. Friedman, *Ballad Revival*, p. 6.

32. Adorno, *Aesthetic Theory*, p. 340.

33. Broch, "Notes on Kitsch," p. 56. Greenberg, "Avant-Garde and Kitsch," pp. 4, 8, 21.

34. Ezra Pound, *Selected Letters, 1907–1941*, ed. D. D. Paige (New York: New Directions, 1971), p. 296.

35. Eve Kosofsky Sedgwick, *The Coherence of Gothic Conventions* (New York: Methuen, 1986), pp. 86, 41–42.

36. Ibid., pp. 63, 95. Sedgwick sometimes refers to this structure as "X within and X without" or "an X within an X," p. 34.

37. Ibid., p. 38.

38. Ibid., pp. 48, 93.

39. Ibid., p. 49.

40. Ibid., pp. 5, 95, 20.

41. Broch, "Notes on Kitsch," p. 62.

42. Sedgwick, *Coherence of Gothic Conventions*, p. 87.

43. Ibid.

44. Ibid., p. 91.

Chapter 5. Illiterature

1. Albert B. Friedman, *The Ballad Revival: Studies in the Influence of Popular on Sophisticated Poetry* (Chicago: University of Chicago Press, 1961), p. 49.

2. Ibid., p. 60.

3. Ibid.

4. Ibid., p. 249. Herder's most important essay on folk poetry is "Über Ossian und die Lieder alter Völker" (1773), in Johann Gottfried von Herder, *Werke*, vol. 2, ed. Regine Otto (Berlin: Aufbau-Verlag, 1982).

5. Friedman, *Ballad Revival*, p. 75.

6. Ibid., pp. 66, 67.

7. Friedman discusses the earliest printings of "Chevy Chase" (and its appearance side-by-side with its Latin translation). Ibid., pp. 127-130.

8. Ibid., pp. 111, 128-129.

9. Ibid., p. 108. In *Guardian*, no. 40 (April 27, 1713), Pope published "A Pastoral Ballad," an essay satirizing the new antiquarian philology and its infatuation with "Doric" language.

10. Ibid., p. 152.

11. Gilles Deleuze and Felix Guattari, *A Thousand Plateaus: Capitalism and Schizophrenia*, trans. Brian Massumi (New York: Continuum Books, 1988), p. 331.

12. Ibid., p. 329.

13. Friedman, *Ballad Revival*, p. 3.

14. All ballads in this chapter are cited from historically significant and influential editions, such as Percy's *Reliques* (1765), and the anonymously edited *Collection of Old Ballads* (1723-1725). "Edward, Edward" published in Thomas Percy, *Reliques of Ancient English Poetry*, ed. Henry B. Wheatley (New York: Dover, 1966), p. 1:83.

15. Dante Gabriel Rossetti, "Sweet Helen," cited in Friedman, *Ballad Revival*, p. 323.

16. "Edom O'Gordon," published in Percy, *Reliques*, p. 1:144.

17. "In Spite of Everything," Frederick Seidel, *Life on Earth* (New York: Farrar, Straus and Giroux, 2001), p. 37.

18. Friedman, *Ballad Revival*, p. 320.

19. Anonymous, "The Cruel Brother," *English and Scottish Popular Ballads*, ed. F. J. Child (Boston: Houghton Mifflin, 1882-1898), p. 1:145.

20. William Morris, *The Defense of Guenevere* (London: Kelmscott Press, 1892), p. 161.

21. "Willow, Willow, Willow," published in Percy, *Reliques*, pp. 1:199, 200.

22. Kaja Silverman, *The Acoustic Mirror: The Female Voice in Psychoanalysis and Cinema (Theories of Representation and Difference)* (Bloomington: Indiana University Press, 1987). Silverman dubs this phenomenon "philosophy on the telephone"—a nice way of intimating, inadvertently, the perversity of the ballad tradition.

23. Friedman, *Ballad Revival*, p. 3.

24. "Willow, Willow, Willow," p. 200.

25. Refrains cited in Friedman, *Ballad Revival*, p. 3.

26. Lewis Carroll, "Jabberwocky," *The Complete Illustrated Lewis Carroll* (Ware: Wordsworth Editions, 1996), pp. 140-142.

27. Lewis Carroll, "King-Fisher Song," *Illustrated Carroll*, pp. 479-480.

28. The first edition of Mother Goose nursery rhymes, published (arguably) in 1765, is entitled *Mother Goose's Melody, or Sonnets for the Cradle* (London: John Newberry, 1765).

29. Federico Garcia Lorca, "Las nanas infantiles," *Obras completas* (Madrid: Aguilar, 1967), p. 1075. See Walter Benjamin's brief essay, "Dream Kitsch" (1925), republished in *Selected Writings*, vol. 2, part 1, 1927–1930, ed. Michael W. Jennings, Howard Eiland, and Gary Smith (Cambridge: Harvard University Press, 1999), pp. 3–5.

30. Marina Warner, *No Go the Bogeyman: Scaring, Lulling, and Making Mock* (New York: Farrar, Straus and Giroux, 1998), p. 200.

31. Friedman, *Ballad Revival*, p. 87.

32. Susan Sontag, "Notes on 'Camp,'" (1964), reprinted in *Against Interpretation and Other Essays* (New York: Farrar, Straus, and Giroux, 1966), p. 280.

33. Ibid., p. 281.

34. On Lady Wardlaw's role in the composition of "Hardyknute" and other ballads adopted by Percy, see Henry B. Wheatley, general Introduction to Percy, *Reliques*, pp. 1:xliv, l:lvii.

35. Although it traces principally the eighteenth-century dissemination of popular ballads about female heroines, Dianne Dugaw addresses as well the historical role of female antiquarians in her book, *Warrior Women and Popular Balladry, 1650–1850* (Chicago: University of Chicago Press, 1996).

36. Percy, *Reliques*, p. 1:105.

37. Susan Stewart, *Crimes of Writing: Problems in the Containment of Representation* (Oxford: Oxford University Press, 1991), p. 118.

38. Ibid.

39. For a diverse examination of eighteenth-century women poets, including the Scottish circle I have mentioned here, see Moira Ferguson, ed., *Eighteenth-Century Women Poets: Nation, Class and Gender* (Albany: State University of New York Press, 1995).

40. In fact, class tensions in the British circle contributed to an unpleasant scandal involving the commoner poet Anne Yearsley (known as the Bristol Milkwoman) and Elizabeth Montagu (along with Hannah More), who sought to control the proceeds from Yearsley's books. See Elizabeth Eger, *Bluestockings: Woman of Reason from Enlightenment to Romanticism* (London: Palgrave Macmillan, 2010), p. 83.

41. A superb overview of this context can be found online in Margery Palmer McCulloch's essay, "Women, Poetry, and Song in Eighteenth Century Lowland Scotland," *Scottish Corpus of Texts and Speech*, http://www.scottishcorpus.ac.uk/corpus/search/document.php?documentid=1437.

42. Poems by a number of these women (and the working-class poets they recommended) can be found in Catherine Kerrigan, ed., *An Anthology of Scottish Women Poets* (Edinburgh: Edinburgh University Press, 1991).

43. See Kerrigan's anthology for examples of work by these poets. See also Su-

sanne Kord, *Women Peasant Poets in Eighteenth-Century England, Scotland, and Germany* (Suffolk: Camden House, 2003).

44. Janet Little, *The Poetical Works of Janet Little, The Scottish Milkmaid* (Ayr, UK: Wilson and Peter, 1792).

45. On the history and poetics of the canting tradition, see Daniel Tiffany *Infidel Poetics: Riddles, Nightlife, Substance* (Chicago: University of Chicago Press, 2009).

46. Friedman, *Ballad Revival*, p. 65.

47. The details of Rousseau's employment in the Dupin household are recounted in Maurice Crauston, *Jean-Jacques: The Early Life and Work of Jean-Jacques Rousseau* (Chicago: University of Chicago Press, 1982), pp. 207–208.

48. It appears, since Bewick was born in 1753, that his woodcuts could not have been part of the 1765 Newbery edition (of which no copy survives). Blake contributed engravings to Ritson's *Select Collection of English Songs* (1783) and Bewick to his *Pieces of Ancient Popular Poetry* (1791).

49. Charlotte Bronte, *Jane Eyre* (Harmondsworth, UK: Penguin Books, 2006), p. 20.

50. Leigh Hunt, "The Feast of the Poets," *Poetical Works*, ed. H. S. Milford (Oxford: Oxford University Press, 1923), p. 152.

51. Percy, preface to *Reliques*, pp. 1:10, 14.

52. Ibid., pp. 1:13, 14.

53. Preface to *Mother Goose's Melody, or, Sonnets for the* Cradle (a facsimile), with an introduction by Nigel Tattersfield (Oxford: Bodleian Library, 2003), p. v. This facsimile reproduces the second edition (1780), published by John Marshall.

54. *Mother Goose's Melody*, pp. ii, 75.

55. Ibid., p. ii.

56. Ibid., p. 38.

57. Ibid., p. 68.

58. Iona Opie and Peter Opie, eds., *The Oxford Dictionary of Nursery Rhymes* (Oxford: Oxford University Press, 1997), pp. 257–258.

59. *Mother Goose's Melody*, p. 69.

60. On Percy's sense of the Gothic in relation to the ancient balladry he collected in his anthology, see Nick Groom, *The Making of Percy's "Reliques"* (Oxford: Oxford University Press, 1999), p. 98.

61. Aaron Hill, *Plain-Dealer*, no. 36 (1724).

62. Friedman, *Ballad Revival*, p. 177.

63. Joseph Addison, *Spectator*, no. 70 (1711).

64. Joseph Addison, *Spectator*, no. 74 (1711).

65. John Armstrong, "Taste: An Epistle to a Young Critic" (London: British Library, 2011), no pagination.

66. Joseph Addison, *Spectator*, no. 419 (1712).

67. Oliver Goldsmith, "The Hermit," *Gems of Goldsmith: The Traveller, The Deserted Village, The Hermit* (London: Brousson Press, 2010), p. 49.

68. *Mother Goose's Melody*, p. 28.

69. Ibid., p. 58.

70. Charles Welsh, introduction to *History of Goody Two-Shoes* (London: Griffith and Farrar, 1882), p. xv.

71. On the subject of British "peasant poets" of the eighteenth century, see Rayner Unwin, *The Rural Muse: Studies in the Peasant Poetry of England* (London: Allen and Unwin, 1954); and more recently, John Goodridge, *Rural Life in Eighteenth-Century English Poetry* (Cambridge: Cambridge University Press, 1995).

72. John Jones, "The Red-Breast," cited in Robert Southey, *The Lives and Works of the Uneducated Poets*, ed. J. S. Childers (1831; London: Humphrey Milford, 1925), pp. 4–5.

73. Southey, *Lives and Works of the Uneducated Poets*, p. 13.

74. Cited by J. S. Childers, in Southey, *Lives and Works of the Uneducated Poets*, p. 185.

75. Swift, correspondence, cited by J. S. Childers, in Southey, *Lives and Works of the Uneducated Poets*, p. 182.

76. For an especially subtle reading of the problem of "minority" in the relation between Wordsworth and Thomas de Quincy, see Margaret Russett, *De Quincy's Romanticism: Canonical Minority and the Forms of Transmission* (Cambridge: Cambridge University Press, 1998.)

77. On the role of shoemaker poets in "ultraradical" circles, see Iain McCalman, *Radical Underworld: Prophets, Revolutionaries, and Pornographers in London, 1795–1840* (Cambridge: Cambridge University Press, 1988). Writing by many of the poets I have mentioned here can be found in a superb anthology, John Goodbridge, ed., *Nineteenth Century English Labouring-Class Poets* (London: Chatto, 2005).

78. The writing of some of these poets appears in Southey's anthology, *Lives and Works of the Uneducated Poets*. See also S. McEathron, "Wordsworth, Lyrical Ballads, and the Problem of Peasant Poetry," *Nineteenth Century Literature* 54, no. 1 (1999).

79. Southey, *Lives and Works of the Uneducated Poets*, p. 114.

80. Ibid., pp. 114–115.

81. Walpole, cited by J. S. Childers in Southey, *Lives and Works of the Uneducated Poets*, p. 196

82. Friedman, *Ballad Revival*, p. 178.

83. Cited in Friedman, *Ballad Revival*, p. 180.

84. Friedman, *Ballad Revival*, p. 206.

85. William Shenstone, "Jemmy Dawson," *The Poetical Works of William Shenstone* (Edinburgh: Apollo Press, 1778), p. 2:58.

86. William Shenstone, "A Pastoral Ballad," *Poetical Works*, pp. 190–191.

87. Friedman, *Ballad Revival*, p. 180.

88. Ibid., p. 269.

89. Ibid., p. 178.

90. Thomas Gray, "Elegy Written in a Country Church-Yard," *The Complete Poems of Thomas Gray*, ed. H. W. Starr and J. R. Hendrickson (Oxford: Clarendon Press, 1966), p. 41.

91. Friedman, *Ballad Revival*, p. 270.

92. Lord George Gordon Byron, "Epitaph for Joseph Blacket, Late Poet and Shoemaker," *The Complete Poetical Works*, ed. Paul Elmer More (New York: Houghton Mifflin, 1905), p. 163.

93. Joshua Scodel, *The English Poetic Epitaph* (Ithaca, NY: Cornell University Press, 1991), p. 374.

94. Lord Byron, cited in N. B. Penny, "Dead Dogs and Englishman," *Connoisseur* 192 (1976): p. 301. Penny's essay offers a fine survey of eighteenth and nineteenth century British commemorations of dogs.

95. Penny, "Dead Dogs and Englishman," p. 302.

96. Ibid., p. 302.

97. Here are a few lines from Pope's poem about his dog, Bounce:

FOP! You can dance, and make a leg
Can fetch and carry, cringe and beg,
And (what's the top of all your tricks)
Can stoop to pick up Strings and Sticks.
We country dogs love nobler sport,
And scorn the Pranks of Dogs at Court

Alexander Pope, *The Poems of Alexander Pope*, ed. John Butt (London: Routledge, 1963), p. 824.

98. *Aeneid*, book 4, line 433. Horace Walpole, correspondence, cited in Christopher Frayling, *Horace Walpole's Cat* (New York: Thames and Hudson, 2009), p. 24.

99. Thomas Gray, "Ode on the Death of a Favourite Cat, Drowned in a Tub of Gold Fishes," *Complete Poems of Thomas Gray*, p. 5.

100. Frayling, *Horace Walpole's Cat*, p. 21.

101. Samuel Johnson, "Gray" (1759), *The Lives of the Poets*, ed. Roger Lonsdale (Oxford: Oxford University Press, 2009) p. 458.

102. Robert Dodsley, *The Toy-Shop: A Dramatick Satire* (London: Gilliver, 1735), p. 42.

103. Robert Dodsley, *Trifles* (London: Tully's Head, 1745).

104. Dodsley, *Toy-Shop*, pp. 10–13.

105. Ibid., p. 38.

106. Ibid., pp. 45, 12.

107. Ibid., p. 34.

108. Ibid., p. 9. On "Faeries" who converse with objects, see Addison, *Spectator* no. 429.

109. Caroline Franklin begins her essay on gothic verse by stating, "There has

been a marked reluctance to acknowledge the existence of a category such as 'Gothic verse.' . . . Most studies of Gothic literature barely mention poetry." Franklin, Introduction to *The Longman Anthology of Gothic Verse* (London: Longman, 2011), p. 1.

110. Hermann Broch, "Notes on the Problem of Kitsch," reprinted in Gillo Dorfles, ed., *The World of Bad Taste* (New York: Bell, 1969), p. 50.

111. Susan Stewart, *Crimes of Writing*, p. 122. Coleridge makes his comment about "homeliness" in reference to the ballad imitation he authored with Wordsworth, "The Three Graves." Samuel Taylor Coleridge, *Poetical Works*, ed. Ernest de Selincourt (Oxford: Oxford University Press, 1940), pp. 1:267–268.

112. Edward Young, *Conjectures on Original Composition*, ed. Edith J. Morley (1759; Manchester: University Press, 1918), p. 15. Young's figure of "infantine genius" should be seen as the "daemon" looming, unacknowledged, over attempts by contemporary critics to explain the poetics of unoriginality ("uncreative writing"). See, for example, Marjorie Perloff, *Unoriginal Genius: Poetry by Other Means in the New Century* (Chicago: University of Chicago, 2012).

113. Ibid., p. 3.

114. Ibid., p. 37. An "oylet-holed suit" is a garment embroidered with bits of seashell.

115. Ibid., p. 37.

116. Ibid., pp. 26–27.

117. Jonathan Culler, "Apostrophe," reprinted in *The Pursuit of Signs* (Ithaca: Cornell University Press, 1981), p. 138.

118. Edward Young, "The Complaint; Or Night Thoughts on Life, Death, and Immortality," *The Poetical Works of Edward Young* (Boston: Little, Brown, 1854), p. 263 (book 9, lines 90–113).

119. Culler, "Apostrophe," p. 137.

120. Friedman, *Ballad Revival*, p. 269.

121. William Shenstone, "The School-Mistress," *Poetical Works*, p. 2:182.

122. Geoffrey Hartmann, "Wordsworth, Inscriptions, and Romantic Nature Poetry," reprinted in *Beyond Formalism, Essays 1958–1970* (New Haven: Yale University Press, 1970), p. 208.

123. Mark Akenside, "Inscriptions," *The Poems of Mark Akenside, M.D.* (London: Bowyer and Nichols, 1772), pp. 388–393.

124. Culler, "Apostrophe," p. 153.

125. For a superb and well-illustrated essay (anonymously written), see "William Shenstone, the Leasowes, and Landscape Gardening," *Revolutionary Players*, n.d., http://www.search.revolutionaryplayers.org.uk/engine/resource/exhibition/standard/default.asp?resource=1345&offset=8.

126. Robert Dodsley, "A Description of The Leasowes," in Shenstone, *Poetical Works*, pp. 1:xlvii, xlii, xlv.

127. Ibid., p. 1:xl. Shenstone's "Ode to Indolence" (1750) can be found in *Poeti-*

cal Works, p. 1:98. Shenstone's poem follows James Thomson's "The Castle of Indolence" (1748).

128. Dodsley, "Description," p. 1:xxix.

129. Ibid., p. 1:xxiii.

130. Dodsley, "Verses by Mr. Dodsley, on his first arrival at The Leasowes, 1754," in Shenstone, *Poetical Works*, p. 1:lix.

131. Dodsley, "Description," p. 1:xlvi.

132. Ibid., pp. 1:xli, xxxiv, xliii.

133. Mary Shelley, *Frankenstein* (Mineola, NY: Dover Books, 1994), p. 152.

134. See Laurie Scheck's fascinating and heterogeneous work of poetry and prose, *A Monster's Notes* (New York: Alfred Knopf, 2009), which exploits hints of the creature's immortality and what Shelley calls its "powers of eloquence and persuasion." The book begins with the discovery of an "unbound manuscript," said to have been left behind (a common conceit of Gothic fiction) by the creature in an empty apartment on East Sixth Street in Manhattan.

135. Shelly, *Frankenstein*, p. 152.

136. Eve Kosofky Sedgwick, *The Coherence of Gothic Conventions* (London: Methuen, 1986), p. ix.

137. In his verse biography, Tom Clark twice indicates that Keats was dubbed a "pocket Apollo" by his friends. Clark, *Junkets on a Sad Planet: Scenes from the Life of John Keats* (Santa Barbara: Black Sparrow Press, 1994), pp. 96, 123.

138. John Keats, "Lamia," *Complete Poems and Selected Letters of John Keats*, ed. Jim Pollock (New York: Modern Library, 2001), p. 199 (part 2, line 19).

139. Ibid., pp. 192, 194, 199 (part 1, lines 196 and 267; part 2, line 48).

140. Ibid., pp. 202, 193; Keats, "Isabella, or the Pot of Basil," *Complete Poems*, p. 218. For an acute analysis of the philosophical project of "derealization" (in relation to Coleridge's "spectra" and other kinds of ephemera), see Rei Terada, *Looking Away: Phenomenality and Dissatisfaction, Kant to Adorno* (Cambridge: Harvard University Press, 2009).

141. Keats, "Isabella," p. 218.

142. Keats, "Lamia," p. 188.

143. Ibid., p. 452.

144. For a cursory discussion of the correlation of poetic kitsch and aesthetic ideology, see chapter 1 of the present volume. On de Man's concept of aesthetic ideology, see the essays in Paul de Man, *Aesthetic Ideology*, ed. Andrej Warminski (Minneapolis: University of Minnesota Press, 1996).

145. Paul de Man, "Sign and Symbol in Hegel's Aesthetics," *Aesthetic Ideology*, p. 100. De Man contrasts the "ideology of the symbol" with the uncompromising formalism of what he calls "poetics"—a conception guided inscrutably by the agenda of radical positivism.

146. I take the phrase "queer phenomenality" from Rei Terada's book, *Looking Away.*

147. On the correlation between "lyric substance" and the iconography of philosophical materialism, see Daniel Tiffany, *Toy Medium: Materialism and Modern Lyric* (Berkeley: University of California Press, 2000).

Chapter 6. Queer Idylls

1. Robert Dodsley, "A Description of The Leasowes," in William Shenstone, *The Poetical Works of William Shenstone* (Edinburgh: Apollo Press, 1778), p. 1:xxiii.

2. Ibid., p. 1:xxx.

3. The major scholar on Gray, Walpole, and their queer coterie is George E. Haggerty, with many articles on this and other related topics: to start, see Haggerty, *Queer Gothic* (Urbana: University of Illinois Press, 2006).

4. Walpole, cited in Timothy Mowl, *Horace Walpole: The Great Outsider* (London: John Murray, 1996), p. 10.

5. See Sean R. Silver, who notes that Walpole referred to Strawberry Hill as his own "little Gothic castle" but also, after the publication of his novel, as his "Otranto." Silver, "Visiting Strawberry Hill: Horace Walpole's Gothic Historiography," *Eighteenth-Century Fiction* 21, no. 4 (2009): p. 537.

6. Concerning the effects of the textual prompts framing the sights of Strawberry Hill, Walpole remarks, "Animated prospect is the theatre that will always be the most frequented." Walpole, "On Modern Gardening," *The Works Horatio Walpole, Earl of Oxford* (London: Robinson, 1798), p. 2:541.

7. James Thomson, *The Castle of Indolence: An Allegorical Poem. Written in Imitation of Spencer* (London: A. Millar, 1748), p. 1.

8. Thomas Gray, "The Bard," *The Complete Poems of Thomas Gray*, eds. H. W. Starr and J. R. Hendrickson (Oxford: Oxford University Press, 1966), p. 23.

9. Nick Groom calls his book on history of literary forgery *The Forger's Shadow* (London: Picador, 2002).

10. Horace Walpole, *The Yale Edition of Horace Walpole's Correspondence*, ed. W. S. Lewis, 48 vols. (New Haven: Yale University Press, 1948-1983). "Patapan" appears—for the first time—in appendix 1 of volume 30.

11. Ibid.

12. Ibid.

13. Ibid.

14. On the Strawberry Hill Set, see George E. Haggerty, "Queering Horace Walpole," *Studies in English Literature* 43, no. 3 (2006).

15. Mowl, *Horace Walpole*, p. 7.

16. Far less has been written about Shenstone, his poetry, or the circle at the Leasowes than about Gray, Walpole, and the Strawberry Hill Set. On same-sex

desire in the elegies of Shenstone (and other eighteenth-century poets), see Chris Mounsey, "Persona, Elegy, Desire," *Eighteenth Century Studies* 43, no. 3 (2006).

17. Eve Kosofsky Sedgwick, *Epistemology of the Closet* (Berkeley: University of California Press, 1990), p. 72.

18. Eve Kosofsky Sedgwick, *The Coherence of Gothic Conventions* (London: Methuen, 1986), p. 86. On the trope of live burial in Thomas de Quincey, see chapter 2.

19. Rei Terada, *Looking Away: Phenomenality and Dissatisfaction* (Cambridge: Harvard University Press, 2009), p. 97.

20. Mowl, *Horace Walpole,* p. 45.

21. In a letter to Horace Mann, Walpole describes the fake fretwork—a kind of wallpaper—at Strawberry Hill: "Imagine the walls covered with (I call it paper, but it is really paper painted in perspective to represent) Gothic fretwork." Cited in Silver, "Visiting Strawberry Hill," p. 554n39. Numerous descriptions of Strawberry Hill record, as well, its "cardboard battlements."

22. Sedgwick, *Epistemology of the Closet*, pp. 145, 77.

23. Thomas Gray, "Lines Spoken by the Ghost of John Dennis at the Devil Tavern," *Complete Poems of Thomas Gray*, pp. 71, 72. On the queerness of Gray's elegiac poetry, see George E. Haggerty, "The Voice of Nature in Gray's Elegy," *Journal of Homosexuality* 23, nos. 1-2 (1992).

24. Dodsley, "Description," p. 1:li.

25. Ibid., p. 1:xlviii.

26. Mowl, *Horace Walpole*, p. 101.

27. These observations are part of a lengthy verbal "portrait" of Walpole written by Mme. du Deffand in 1766, cited in Wilmarth S. Lewis, *Rescuing Horace Walpole* (New Haven, CT: Yale University Press, 1978), p. 151. It is Lewis who refers to this portrait of Walpole as "the most important summary of him ever written."

28. Mowl, *Horace Walpole*, p. 23.

29. Ibid., p. 7.

30. Horace Walpole, *A Description of the Villa of Mr. Horace Walpole*, 2nd ed. (Strawberry Hill: Thomas Kirgate, 1784), p. iii.

31. Anna Chalcraft and Judith Viscardi, *Visiting Strawberry Hill* (Wimbledon: Chalcraft and Viscardi, 2005), p. 11.

32. The ballad "Strawberry Hill" was composed by William Pulteney, Earl of Bath (1684-1764). See Walpole, *Description*, p. 118.

33. Mowl, *Horace Walpole*, p. 6.

34. William Hazlitt, commenting on Gray's odes, cited in Christopher Frayling, *Horace Walpole's Cat* (New York: Thames and Hudson, 2009), p. 41.

35. The melodramatic aspect of Holcroft's innovation can be detected in the numerous stage directions in the text, such as "*the stage dark: soft music, but expressing first pain and alarm; then the successive feelings of the scene.*" The expressive relation between the melodramatic elements (words and music) of the play becomes a kind

of literal reverberation at moments: "*the shrieks of Selima joining the music, which likewise shrieks.*" Thomas Holcroft, *A Tale of Mystery, A Melo-Drame in Three Acts*, 2nd ed. (New York: Longworth, 1808), pp. 15, 16.

36. Dwight Macdonald, "Annals of Crime," cited in K. K. Ruthven, *Faking Literature* (Cambridge: Cambridge University Press, 2001), p. 53.

37. Susan Stewart, *Crimes of Writing: Problems in the Containment of Representation* (Oxford: Oxford University Press, 1991), p. 108.

38. Ibid., p. 110.

39. Ibid., p. 109.

40. Nicholas Bourriaud, *Relational Aesthetics*, trans. Simon Pleasance and Fronza Woods (Dijon: les presses du réel, 2002), p. 33.

41. Ibid., p. 9.

42. Thomas Gray, *Correspondence of Thomas Gray*, ed. Paget Toynbee and Leonard Whibley (Oxford: Oxford University Press, 1935), p. 2:680.

43. Ibid.

44. A reprint of *A New Dictionary of Terms, Ancient and Modern, of the Canting Crew* (compiled by "B. F. Gentleman" in 1699) has recently appeared as *The First English Dictionary of Slang* (Chicago: University of Chicago Press, 2010). A literary and cultural analysis of the "quyre whiddes" of the canting crew can be found in Daniel Tiffany, *Infidel Poetics: Riddles, Nightlife, Substance* (Chicago: University of Chicago Press, 2009).

45. Ben Jonson, *Poetaster, or His Arraignment* (London: William Stansby, 1612), IV.iii, III.i.

46. Philip Stubbes, *The Anatomy of Abuses* (1583), cited in Bruce R. Smith, ed. *Twelfth Night: Texts and Contexts* (New York: Bedford St. Martins, 2001), p. 275.

47. John Rainolds, *The Overthrowe of Stage Playes* (1599), cited in Smith, *Twelfth Night*, p. 276.

48. Hermann Broch, "Notes on the Problem of Kitsch," reprinted in Gillo Dorfles, ed., *Kitsch: The World of Bad Taste* (New York: Bell, 1969), p. 49.

49. Ibid.

50. In his introduction to a five-hundred-page anthology of essays on camp and its relation to queer identity, Fabio Cleto writes, "We can draw an hypothesis in which the origins of camp and those, by way of the Wilde trials of 1895, of the homosexual as 'type,' identifiable because articulated on the effeminate Wildean theatricality, are inextricable." Cleto, *Camp: Queer Aesthetics and the Performing Subject* (Ann Arbor: University of Michigan Press, 1999), p. 21. Broch's and Greenberg's formulations of kitsch, by contrast, focus explicitly on bourgeois desires and consumption.

51. Susan Sontag, "Notes on 'Camp,'" reprinted in *Against Interpretation* (New York: Farrar, Straus and Giroux, 1966), p. 280. Mowl, *Horace Walpole*, p. 7.

52. The most extended and explicit treatment of the correlation of kitsch and

fascism (National Socialism, to be more precise) occurs in Saul Friedlander, *Reflections of Nazism: An Essay on Kitsch and Death*, trans. Thomas Weyr (New York: Harper and Row, 1984).

53. Sedgwick, *Epistemology of the Closet*, p. 156.

54. Lee Edelman, *No Future: Queer Theory and the Death Drive* (Durham, NC: Duke University Press, 2005), p. 6.

55. Andrew Hewitt, *Political Inversions: Homosexuality, Fascism, and the Modernist Imaginary* (Stanford, CA: Stanford University Press, 1996), p. 207.

56. Ibid., p. 206.

57. Ibid., pp. 207-208.

58. Ibid., p. 208.

59. *Hardyknute: A Fragment* (London: R. Dodsley, 1740), p. 4.

60. James Macpherson, *Fragments of Ancient Poetry* (Edinburgh: G. Hamilton and J. Balfour, 1760), p. iii.

61. Gray, *Correspondence*, p. 2:664.

62. Ibid., p. 2:665.

63. Horace Walpole, *Selected Letters of Horace Walpole*, ed. W. S. Lewis (New Haven: Yale University Press, 1973), p. 103.

64. William Shenstone to Percy, September 17, 1761, *Letters of William Shenstone*, ed. Duncan Mallam (Minneapolis: University of Minnesota Press, 1939), p. 421.

65. Shenstone to Percy, October 1, 1760, *Letters*, p. 399.

66. Thomas Percy, *Reliques of Ancient English Poetry*, ed. Henry B. Wheatley (New York: Dover, 1966), p. 1:12. Ian Haywood, *The Making of History* (Rutherford: Fairleigh Dickinson University Press, 1986), p. 101.

67. Percy, *Reliques*, p. 1:11.

68. Ibid.

69. In addition to Percy's account of the checkered history of Wardlaw's "Hardyknute," see his speculations about Wardlaw's "affectedly antique orthography" in dubious copies of the ballad "Edward, Edward." Percy, *Reliques*, p. 1:82.

70. On the larger dimensions of the ballad revival and the Ossianic controversy, especially in relation to fiction, see Katie Trumpener, *Bardic Nationalism* (Princeton: Princeton University Press, 1997).

71. Joseph Ritson, *Scottish Songs* (London: J. Johnson, 1794), p. 1:lxii.

72. Joseph Ritson, *Ancient English Metrical Romances* (London: G. and W. Nicol, 1802), p. 1:cix.

73. Ibid., p. 1:clxi.

74. Shenstone to Percy, cited in Irving R. Churchill, "William Shenstone's Share in the Preparation of Percy's *Reliques*," *PMLA* (1936): p. 968.

75. Percy, *Reliques*, p. 11.

76. Albert B. Friedman, *The Ballad Revival* (Chicago University of Chicago Press, 1961), p. 193.

77. On the details of Ritson's life, see Henry Alfred Burd, *Joseph Ritson, A Critical Biography* (Urbana: University of Illinois, 1916).

78. Ritson, *Scottish Songs*, p. 1:lxiii. John Pinkerton, *Ancient Scottish Poems* (London: C. Dilly, 1786), p. 1:xv.

79. Shenstone, cited in Churchill, "William Shenstone's Share," p. 971.

80. Thomas Percy, "An Essay on the Ancient Minstrels," *Reliques*, p. 380.

81. Shenstone to Percy, February 3, 1762, and November 10, 1760, *Letters*, pp. 439, 402.

82. Shenstone, cited in Churchill, "William Shenstone's Share," p. 469.

83. Shenstone to Percy, January 4, 1758, *Letters*, p. 346.

84. Ian Haywood, *Making of History*, p. 101. William Wordsworth, cited in Friedman, *Ballad Revival*, p. 212.

85. Friedman, *Ballad Revival*, p. 206. F. J. Furnival on Percy, cited in Friedman, *Ballad Revival*, p. 209.

86. Pat Rogers, "Chatterton and the Club," *Thomas Chatterton and Romantic Culture*, ed. Nick Groom (London: Macmillan, 1999), p. 133.

87. Claude Rawson, "Unparodying and Forgery: The Augustan Chatterton," in *Thomas Chatterton and Romantic Culture*, p. 28.

88. Grevell Lindop, introduction to Thomas Chatterton, *Selected Poems* (Manchester: Carcanet, 1972), p. 20.

89. Thomas Chatterton, "Aella," *Selected Poems*, p. 59, ll. 296–299.

90. Aristotle, *Poetics*, trans. James Hutton (New York: Norton Books, 1982), section 22, p. 69.

91. On Spence's "New Alphabet," see David Worrall, *Radical Culture: Discourse, Resistance, and Surveillance, 1790–1820* (Detroit, MI: Wayne State University Press, 1992), p. 78. Also, Iain McCalman, *Radical Underworld: Prophets, Revolutionaries, and Pornographers in London, 1795–1840* (Cambridge: Cambridge University Press, 1988), p. 92.

92. Keats's comment about Chatterton occurs in a letter to John Hamilton Reynolds, September 22, 1819, in John Keats, *The Poetical Works and Other Writings of John Keats*, ed. Harry Buxton Forman (London: Reeves and Turner, 1883), p. 2:329.

93. Chatterton, "Aella," p. 62, ll. 1044–1047.

94. Rogers, "Chatterton and the Club," p. 130. Percy, cited in Nick Groom, "Fragments, Reliques, & MSS: Chatterton and Percy," in *Thomas Chatterton and Romantic Culture*, p. 198.

95. Rogers, "Chatterton and the Club," p. 133.

96. Joseph Ritson, cited in Bertrand H. Bronson, *Joseph Ritson: Scholar at Arms* (Berkeley: University of California Press, 1938), p. 2:548.

97. Walpole, cited in Lewis, *Rescuing Horace Walpole*, p. 137.

98. Horace Walpole to William Cole, March 13, 1780, in *Selected Letters*, p. 234. Walpole, cited in Rawson, "Unparodying and Forgery," p. 16. Wordsworth's reference to Chatterton occurs in "Resolution and Independence": "I thought of Chat-

terton, the marvelous Boy,/The sleepless Soul that perished in his pride." William Wordsworth, *The Collected Poems of William Wordsworth* (Ware: Cumberland House, 1994), p. 195.

99. Walpole and Chatterton, letters, cited in Haywood, *Making of History*, pp. 150–151.

100. Thomas Chatterton, "To Horace Walpole," *Selected Poems*, pp. 26–27.

101. Walpole to Lady Ossary, August 11, 1778, cited in *Rescuing Horace Walpole*, p. 138.

102. Letitia Hawkins, cited in Lewis, *Rescuing Horace Walpole*, p. 136.

103. Theodor W. Adorno, *Aesthetic Theory*, trans. C. Lenhardt (London: Routledge, 1984), p. 340.

Chapter 7. Kitsching the *Cantos*

1. Ezra Pound, "A Retrospect," *Poetry*, March 1913, reprinted in *Literary Essays of Ezra Pound*, ed. T. S. Eliot (New York: New Directions, 1960), p. 5. Abbreviated hereafter in the text as *LE*.

2. Ezra Pound, "Ballad of the Goodly Fere," reprinted in *Collected Early Poems*, ed. Michael John King (New York: New Directions, 1976), p. 112. Abbreviated hereafter in the text as *CEP*.

3. Ezra Pound, correspondence, cited in K. K. Ruthven, *A Guide to Ezra Pound's "Personae"* (Berkeley: University of California Press, 1969), p. 41.

4. Ezra Pound, "In a Station of the Metro," *Gaudier-Brzeska: A Memoir* (New York: New Directions, 1971), p. 89. Abbreviated hereafter in the text as *GB*.

5. In addition to praising the "hardness and gauntness" of James Joyce's prose as a model for Imagism, Pound writes, "We can be thankful for clear, hard surfaces, for an escape from softness and mushiness." Ezra Pound, *Pound/Joyce: The Letters of Ezra Pound to James Joyce*, ed. Forrest Read (New York: New Directions, 1967), pp. 32, 33.

6. It is interesting to note that Thomas Percy preceded Pound in combining an interest in old ballads and ancient Chinese poetry. In 1761, four years before he published *Reliques of Ancient English Poetry*, Percy published a collection of "Fragments of Chinese Poetry" in *Hau Kiou Choaan or The Pleasing History: A Translation from the Chinese Language* (R. and J. Dodsley: London, 1761).

7. Ezra Pound, "The Jewel Stairs' Grievance," reprinted in Pound, *Personae*, ed. Lea Baechler and A. Walton Litz (New York: New Directions, 1990), p. 91. Abbreviated hereafter in the text as *P*.

8. Ezra Pound, "Laudantes Decem Pulchritudinis Johannae Templi," *Collected Early Poems*, p. 119.

9. Pound, from an early manuscript of Canto 4, cited in Christine Froula, *To Write Paradise: Style and Error in Pound's Cantos* (New Haven: Yale University Press, 1984), p. 40.

10. Ezra Pound, "To E.B.B.," *Collected Early Poems*, p. 262.

11. Ezra Pound, "Redondillas," *Collected Early Poems*, p. 218.

12. Ezra Pound, "Anima Sola," *Collected Early Poems*, p. 19.

13. Ezra Pound, correspondence, *Selected Letters, 1907–1941*, ed. D. D. Paige (New York: New Directions, 1971), p. 296. Abbreviated hereafter in the text as *L*.

14. Humphrey Carpenter, *A Serious Character: The Life of Ezra Pound* (Boston: Houghton Mifflin, 1988), p. 157.

15. Ezra Pound, *Ezra Pound and the Visual Arts*, ed. Harriet Zinnes (New York: New Directions, 1980), p. 151.

16. Hugh Witemeyer, *The Poetry of Ezra Pound: Forms and Revival, 1908–1920* (Berkeley: University of California Press, 1969), p. 162.

17. Ezra Pound, Canto 20, *Cantos* (New York: New Directions, 1987), p. 94. Abbreviated hereafter in the text as *C*.

18. The passages cited in this sentence appear, respectively, in Cantos 115, 107, and 115: Pound, *Cantos*, pp. 796, 762, 797.

19. Hermann Broch, "Notes on the Problem of Kitsch," reprinted in *Kitsch: The World of Bad Taste*, ed. Gillo Dorfles (New York: Bell, 1969), p. 58.

20. Saul Friedländer, "Kitsch and the Apocalyptic Imagination," *Salmagundi*, nos. 85–86 (Winter<N>Spring 1990), p. 206.

21. Saul Friedländer, *Reflections of Nazism: An Essay on Kitsch and Death*, trans. Thomas Weyr (Bloomington: Indiana University Press, 1993), p. 30.

22. My knowledge of the historical context of Cantos 72 and 73 depends on an article by Robert Casillo, "Fascists of the Final Hour: Pound's Italian Cantos," in *Fascism, Aesthetics, and Culture*, ed. Richard J. Golsan (Hanover: University Press of New England, 1992). Casillo provides a translation of the Italian cantos, which I cite here (with some variation).

23. Friedländer, "Kitsch and the Apocalyptic Imagination," p. 205.

24. Friedländer, *Reflections of Nazism*, pp. 52, 50.

25. Clement Greenberg describes a parasitic relation between kitsch and the avant-garde: "the old is looted for new 'twists,' which are then watered down and served up as kitsch." Greenberg, "Avant-Garde and Kitsch" (1939), reprinted in *Art and Culture: Critical Essays* (Boston: Beacon Press, 1961), pp. 10, 11.

26. All of these definitions are to be found under the entry for *epos* in the unabridged Liddell and Scott *Greek-English Dictionary*.

27. Ezra Pound, *Guide to Kulchur* (New York: New Directions, 1970), p. 194. Abbreviated hereafter in the text as *GK*. Pound, *Literary Essays*, p. 86. Pound, *The Spirit of Romance* (New York: New Directions, 1968), p. 161.

28. On the methods of the ancient paradigm of rhapsodic composition, see Alfred B. Lord, *The Singer of Tales* (Cambridge, MA: Harvard University Press, 2000).

29. On Brecht's concept of epic theater, see Bertolt Brecht, "A Short Organum

for the Theater," in *Brecht on Theater*, trans. and ed. John Willet (New York: Hill and Wang, 1964).

30. James Macpherson, "Comala," *The Poems of Ossian* (1765; London: Dewick and Clarke, 1806), p. 1:164.

31. Georg Lukács, *The Theory of the Novel*, trans. Anna Bostock (Cambridge, MA: MIT Press, 1971), p. 56.

32. Ezra Pound, *Ripostes* (London: Elkin Matthew, 1912), p. 59.

33. T. E. Hulme, "Romanticism and Classicism," in *Selected Writings*, ed. Patrick McGuiness (New York: Routledge, 2003), p. 48.

34. Before rejecting the influence of French vitalism, Hulme was the translator of Henri Bergson's *Introduction to Metaphysics* (1913). It was only after his rejection of Bergson and vitalism that Hulme asserted his doctrine of "classicism" and "hard" facts.

35. Hulme published his translation of Sorel's text a year later in a book: Georges Sorel, *Reflections on Violence*, trans. T. E. Hulme (1908; London: Allen and Unwin, 1916).

36. On Sorel's influence on Marxist theorists of totality, see Martin Jay, *Marxism and Totality: The Adventures of a Concept from Lukács to Habermas* (Berkeley: University of California Press, 1984), pp. 71, 154, 160.

37. Sorel describes the phenomenon of a "social myth" as follows: "when the masses are deeply moved, it then becomes possible to describe a picture which constitutes a social myth." Georges Sorel, *Reflections on Violence*, ed. and trans. Jeremy Jennings (Cambridge: Cambridge University Press, 1999), p. 27.

38. G. W. F. Hegel, cited in Jay, *Marxism and Totality*, p. 96.

39. Jay, *Marxism and Totality*, p. 63. My understanding of the history of the concept of totality, along with most of the sources I cite on the topic, derive from Jay's indispensable study.

40. Georg Lukács, *Theory of the Novel*, p. 147.

41. Georg Lukács, *History and Class Consciousness: Studies in Marxist Dialectics*, trans. Rodney Livingstone (Cambridge, MA: Harvard University Press, 1971), p. 27.

42. Jay, *Marxism and Totality*, p. 104.

43. Marx uses this phrase for the first time in the *Introduction to the Critique of Political Economy*. Cited in Jay, *Marxism and Totality*, p. 400.

44. Lukács, *History and Class Consciousness*, p. 8.

45. On the relevance of Vico's philosophy to the Marxist theories of totality, see Jay, *Marxism and Totality*, pp. 32-39.

46. Antonio Gramsci, *Selections from the Prison Notebooks*, ed. and trans. Quintin Hoare and Geoffrey Nowell-Smith (New York: International, 1971), p. 349. See also Jay's account of the role of linguistic intersubjectivity in Gramsci's theorization of totality, *Marxism and Totality*, pp. 159-162.

47. On Jürgen Habermas's integration of ordinary-language philosophy in his efforts to reground the concept of totality, see Jay, *Marxism and Totality*, pp. 494–495.

48. Lukács, *Theory of the Novel*, p. 127.

49. Fredric Jameson, *Marxism and Form: Twentieth-Century Dialectical Theories of Literature* (Princeton, NJ: Princeton University Press, 1971), p. 113.

50. Herbert Marcuse, *An Essay on Liberation* (Boston: Beacon Books, 1969), p. 90.

51. See Jay's discussion of Ernst Bloch's "idiosyncratic ontology of the 'not yet,' " *Marxism and Totality*, p. 238.

52. The best insight into Pound's conception of the Chinese ideogram can be gained from his annotations (begun in 1908) to Ernest Fenollosa's short treatise, *The Chinese Written Character as a Medium for Poetry* (San Francisco: City Lights, 2001). A great deal has been written on this subject, needless to say, in Pound scholarship.

53. Bernard Hart, cited in Martin Kayman, "A Context for Hart's 'Complex,' " *Paideuma*, 12, nos. 2–3 (Fall/Winter 1982–1983), p. 225. My knowledge of Hart's texts and their historical context is indebted to Kayman's fine article.

54. Ibid., p. 226.

55. Ezra Pound, "Affirmations: Vorticism," *Visual Arts*, pp. 7, 8. The metaphor of "the rose in the steel dust" later occurs in Pound's writings during his involvement with Fascism: in *Guide to Kulchur*, p. 152; and in Canto 74 of the Pisan cantos, *Cantos*, p. 449.

56. The concept of paideuma appears in one of Frobenius's first publications, *Ursprung der afrikanischen Kulturen* (1898).

57. Léopold Senghor summarizes Frobenius's concept of paideuma in his foreword to an anthology of writings by Frobenius: "Every race possesses its own *Paideuma*, that is, its own peculiar capacity for and manner of being moved: of being 'possessed.' " Leopold Senghor, foreword to *Leo Frobenius: An Anthology* (Wiesbaden: Franz Steiner Verlag, 1973), p. ix.

58. Fox's six-part article appears in the *New English Weekly* issues of September 3, 17, 21 and October 1, 8, 15 of 1936.

59. Douglas Fox, "Paideuma," *New English Weekly*, September 3, 1936.

60. Leo Frobenius, *Paideuma: Umrisse einer Kultur- und Seelenlehre* (Munich: Beck, 1921).

61. A superb monograph on Jünger's influential writings can be found in Marcus Paul Bullock, *The Violent Eye: Ernst Jünger's Visions and Revisions on the European Right* (Detroit: Wayne State University Press, 1992). It is worth noting that Walter Benjamin's famous dictum about fascism and the "aestheticization of politics" occurs in a review of Jünger's work entitled "Theories of German Fascism," published in 1930.

62. Martin Heidegger, "The Age of World-Picture," *The Question Concerning Technology and Other Essays*, trans. William Lovitt (New York: Harper, 1977). According to Michael Zimmerman, Spengler's influence is a problematic though unmistakable feature of Heidegger's thinking. Zimmerman, *Heidegger's Confrontation with Modernity, Technology, Politics, Art* (Bloomington: Indiana University Press, 1990), pp. 26–29.

63. Fox, "Paideuma," September 17, 1936.

64. T. W. Adorno, "Spengler after the Decline," *Prisms*, trans. Samuel Weber and Shierry Weber (Cambridge, MA: MIT Press, 1981), p. 69.

65. The phrase "family resemblance" is Wittgenstein's and is related to his earlier conception (articulated in the *Tractatus*) of the kind of resemblance that pertains between a word-picture (or hieroglyph) and a state or affairs in the world. It is also related, surprisingly, to the present discussion of Spengler and Frobenius, in that Wittgenstein offers the concept of "family resemblance" as a clarification of Spengler's concept of *Kulturseele*: "Spengler could be better understood if he said: I am *comparing* different cultural epochs with the lives of families; within a family there is a family resemblance." Ludwig Wittgenstein, *Culture and Value*, ed. G. H. von Wright, trans. Peter Winch (Oxford: Basil Blackwell, 1980), p. 14.

66. Forrest Read, *'76: One World and "The Cantos" of Ezra Pound* (Chapel Hill: University of North Carolina Press, 1981), p. 297.

67. Ezra Pound, "Totalitarian Scholarship and the New Paideuma," *Germany and You* (Berlin), April 25, 1937, p. 96.

Chapter 8. Junk

1. Gerard Malanga, *Chic Death* (Cambridge, MA: Pym-Randall, 1971).

2. Kenneth Koch, "A Note on This Issue," *Locus Solus* 2 (Summer 1961): p. 197.

3. John Ashbery, "Paris Notes," *Art International* 7 (June 25, 1963): p. 76.

4. Warhol, cited in Reva Wolf, *Andy Warhol, Poetry, and Gossip in the 1960s* (Chicago: University of Chicago Press, 1997), p. 90.

5. John Ashbery, "Andy Warhol in Paris," *New York Herald-Tribune*, May 17, 1965, reprinted in Ashbery, *Reported Sightings: Art Chronicles: 1957–1986*, ed. David Bergman (New York: Alfred Knopf, 1989), p. 120.

6. Jerome McGann, "Infatuated Worlds," *London Review of Books* 16, no. 18 (September 22, 1994): p. 7.

7. Serge Gainsbourg, "Chatterton," http://www.metrolyrics.com/chatterton-lyrics-gainsbourg-serge.html (my translation).

8. Michel Foucault, "What Is an Author?" (1969), trans. Josué V. Harari, in *Aesthetics, Method, and Epistemology: Essential Works of Michel Foucault*, ed. James D. Faubian (New York: New Press, 1998), p. 206. On the subject of "the art of suicide," I want to acknowledge a significant debt to an unpublished paper, "The Art of Suicide: Notes on Foucault and Warhol," by Christian Hite, part of whose title I have appropriated for this subchapter. Some of my sources, as indicated, were first cited by Hite in his essay.

9. Michel Foucault, "Theatrum Philosophicum" (1970), in *Aesthetics, Method, and Epistemology*, p. 362.

10. See Catherine Liu, "Lacan's Afterlife: Jacques Lacan Meets Andy Warhol," in

The Cambridge Companion to Lacan, ed. Jean-Michele Rabaté (Cambridge: Cambridge University Press, 2003), p. 354. Cited in Hite, "Art of Suicide."

11. Michel Foucault, "Un plaisir si simple," *Le Gai Pied* (April 1979), p. 10. Image reproduced in Hite, "Art of Suicide."

12. Yves-Alain Bois (with reference to Roger Caillois), "Camouflage as Hypertelia," in *Andy Warhol: The Late Work* (Munich: Prestel Verlag, 2004), p. 111. Cited in Hite, "Art of Suicide."

13. Warhol states, "In August '62, I started doing silkscreens . . . and then when Marilyn happened to die that month, I got the idea to make screens of her beautiful face. The first Marilyns." Andy Warhol and Pat Hackett, *POPism: The Warhol 60s* (New York: Harcourt Brace Jovanovich, 1980), p. 22. And in response to an interview question, "Why did you start these 'Death' pictures?" Warhol says, "I guess it was the big plane crash picture, the front page of a newspaper: 129 DIE. I was also painting the *Marilyns*." Warhol, interview with G. W. Swenson, "What is Pop Art? Part 1," *Art News* (November 1963), p. 25, reprinted in Steven Henry Madoff, ed., *Pop Art: A Critical History* (Berkeley: University of California Press, 1997), p. 104.

14. Andrew Ross, "Taking the Tennis Court Oath," in *The Tribe of John: Ashbery and Contemporary Poetry*, ed. Susan M. Schultz (Tuscaloosa: University of Alabama Press, 1995), p. 205.

15. Ibid.

16. Warhol made a number of statements about his interest in poetry and Malanga's influence in that respect: "In the fall of '63 I started going around more and more to poetry readings with Gerard. . . . Poets would just get up and read about their lives from stacks of paper that they had in front of them. I've always been fascinated by people who can put things down on paper and I liked to listen for new ways to say old things and old ways to say new things." Warhol and Hackett, *POPism*, p. 51.

17. In an interview with David Shapiro, Warhol muses, "I would like to be like Gerard. I think that I am fascinated by Gerard. I mean Gerard Malanga. How Gerard can write poetry, that is something I could never understand. I mean, can you understand it? I mean, the way he can write it. I'm in awe to see that he takes, let's say, a sentence here and another one there, and then he puts them together and it sounds real, and therefore is true. I mean, it is really fascinating." Cited in Wolf, *Andy Warhol, Poetry*, pp. 90-91.

18. The poster for Malanga's reading at the Leo Castelli Gallery is reproduced in Wolf, *Andy Warhol, Poetry*, p. 67.

19. Eugenia Shepherd, "Pop Art, Poetry, and Fashion," *New York Herald Tribune*, January 3, 1965, p. 10.

20. John Ashbery, untitled essay in *Warhol* (Paris: Galerie Ileana Sonnabend, 1964), cited in (and translated by) Wolf, *Andy Warhol, Poetry*, p. 86.

21. Gerard Malanga, "The Young Mod," in *Chic Death*, p. 131.

22. John Ashbery, *The New Realists*, exhibition catalog (New York: Sidney Janis Gallery, 1962), reprinted in Madoff, *Pop Art*, p. 81.

23. Ibid., p. 82.

24. Ibid.

25. John Ashbery, "The New Realism," in *The Tennis Court Oath* (Middletown: Wesleyan University Press, 1962), pp. 60, 61.

26. Wolf, *Andy Warhol, Poetry*, p. 81.

27. John Ashbery, "The Skaters," in *Rivers and Mountains* (New York: Ecco Press, 1966), p. 43.

28. Ted Berrigan, "Sonnet LXXVI," in *The Sonnets*, 2nd ed. (1964; New York: Penguin Putnam, 2000), p. 68.

29. Gerard Malanga, "Some Suicides," in *Chic Death*, p. 49.

30. David Lehman, "The Whole School," review of Malanga's *Chic Death*, Poetry (1972), cited in Wolf, *Andy Warhol, Poetry*, p. 43.

31. John Ashbery, "Le livre est sur la table," in *Some Trees* (New Haven: Yale University Press, 1956), p. 74.

32. Gerard Malanga, "A," in *Chic Death*, pp. 22, 23.

33. Jacques-Emile Blanche, cited in Robert Motherwell, introduction to *The Dada Painters and Poets*, ed. Robert Motherwell (1951; Cambridge, MA: Harvard University Press, 1982), p. xxxii. For a discussion of the suicidal impulse in Dada, see A. Alvarez, *The Savage God: A Study of Suicide* (New York: Norton, 2002), pp. 244-256. On the legacy of the emblematic suicide of the Dadaist Jacques Vaché, Alvarez contends, "art from the wilder shores of Pop descends directly from Vaché's suicide" (249). The phrase "allegorical suicides" is Christian Hite's, from his eassy, "The Art of Suicide."

34. Jacques Rigaut, cited in Motherwell's introduction to *Dada Painters and Poets*, pp. xxxi, 330n47. Rigaut, like several other members of the Dada group, did actually commit suicide. The writings of these emblematic suicides are collected in Roger Conover, Terry Hale, and Paul Lenti, eds., *Four Dada Suicides: Selected Texts of Arthur Graven, Jacques Rigaud, Julian Torma, and Jacques Vaché* (London: Atlas Press, 1971).

35. Frank O'Hara, cited in Wolf, *Andy Warhol, Poetry*, p. 75. Concerning the instability of terms, Peter Selz introduced a panel discussion on the new art in 1962 by noting, "We picked the term pop art. We might have called it New Realism, as they did in the Sidney Janis Gallery, or New Dada." *Arts* (April 1963), reprinted as "A Symposium on Pop Art," in Madoff, *Pop Art*, p. 79.

36. Barbara Rose, "Dada, Then and Now," *Art International* (January 1963), reprinted in Madoff, *Pop Art*, p. 57.

37. Andy Warhol, interview with G. W. Swenson, p. 105.

38. Ashbery, "New Realists," p. 82.

39. Rose, "Dada, Then and Now," p. 62.

40. Wolf, *Andy Warhol, Poetry*, p. 81.

41. Gerard Malanga, "All the Beautiful People," in Eugenia Shepherd, "Pop Art, Poetry, and Fashion," *New York Herald-Tribune*, January 3, 1965, p. 12. Reproduced in this article, Malanga's poem carries an asterisk directing the reader's attention to a note cribbing Tzara's directions for a cut-up: "The poem, an avant-garde form of poetry, was written, snipped apart, then put back together, the lines shuffled to fall into place at random."

42. Rose, "Dada, Then and Now," p. 62.

43. Gilbert Sorrentino, "Kitsch into 'Art': The New Realism," *Kulchur* (Winter 1962), reprinted in Madoff, *Pop Art*, pp. 47, 56. Sorrentino argues that the New Realism "is a depiction of certain things in the outer world which have heretofore found their objectification in that form of art which may be called *kitsch*," p. 50.

44. Hilton Kramer, "A Symposium on Pop Art" (1962), pp. 69, 68.

45. Max Kozloff, "'Pop' Culture, Metaphysical Disgust, and the New Vulgarians," *Art International* (March 1962), reprinted in Madoff, *Pop Art*, pp. 32, 30.

46. Clement Greenberg, "After Abstract Expressionism," *Art International* (October 1962), reprinted in Madoff, *Pop Art*, p. 13.

47. Ibid., p. 13.

48. Clement Greenberg, "How Art Writing Earned Its Bad Name" (1962), in *The Collected Essays and Criticism*, ed. John O'Brian (Chicago: University of Chicago Press, 1986), p. 4:144.

49. On Greenberg's (and other critics') reaction to the perceived corruption of art criticism by poetry, see Lytle Shaw, *Frank O'Hara: The Poetics of Coterie* (Iowa City: University of Iowa Press, 2006), pp. 151–160.

50. Greenberg's poem (from c. 1935), cited in Alice Goldfarb Marquis, *Art Czar: The Rise and Fall of Clement Greenberg* (Boston: Museum of Fine Art, 2006), p. 30.

51. Greenberg's poem (from c. 1930), cited in Marquis, *Art Czar*, p. 14.

52. Peter Bürger, *Theory of the Avant-Garde*, trans. Michael Shaw (Minneapolis: University of Minnesota, 1984), p. 22.

53. Ibid., p. 53.

54. Ibid., pp. 22, 49.

55. Ibid., p. 54.

56. Ibid., p. 54. Elsewhere Bürger states, "The culture industry has brought about the false elimination of the distance between art and life" (50). That is to say, popular culture produces a mere semblance, in Bürger's view, of what the avant-garde seeks to achieve authentically.

57. For Bürger, the future of the avant-garde depends on the work of iconoclastic figures such as Bertolt Brecht, whose poetry is nevertheless a product of high culture. Bürger, *Theory of the Avant-Garde*, pp. 88–89.

58. Max Kozloff, "'Pop' Culture, Metaphysical Disgust, and the New Vulgarians," op. cit., pp. 30, 31.

59. Gilbert Sorrentino, "Kitsch into 'Art,'" pp. 50, 48.

60. Stanley Kunitz, "A Symposium on Pop Art," p. 80.

61. Hilton Kramer, "A Symposium on Pop Art," p. 69.

62. Peter Selz and Leo Steinberg, "A Symposium on Pop Art," p. 80.

63. Leo Steinberg, "A Symposium on Pop Art," p. 30.

64. Bürger, *Theory of the Avant-Garde*, p. 58.

65. Ibid., p. 61.

66. Adorno, cited in Bürger, *Theory of the Avant-Garde*, p. 62. Adorno's statement, which appears in *Aesthetic Theory*, can be consulted in context: Theodor W. Adorno, *Aesthetic Theory*, trans. C. Lenhardt (London: Routledge, 1984), p. 171.

67. Francis Jeffrey, *Jeffrey's Criticism*, ed. Peter F. Morgan (Edinburgh: Scottish Academic Press, 1983), pp. 70, 96.

68. Isidore Ducasse (Comte de Lautréamont), "Poésies II," *Oeuvres complètes* (Paris: Flammarion, 1969), p. 287.

69. The historian of New York school poetry Mark Ford titled an essay devoted to the Ern Malley affair "Marvelous Boys"—an allusion to Wordsworth's reference to Chatterton as a "marvelous Boy." Ford, "Marvelous Boys," *London Review of Books* 15, no. 17 (September 9, 1993), pp. 17-18.

70. Maxwell Henley Harris, ed., *Ern Malley's Poems* (Melbourne: Landsdown Press, 1961).

71. John Tranter and Philip Mead, eds., *The Penguin Book of Modern Australian Poetry* (Harmondsworth: Penguin Books, 1991).

72. Mark Ford, "Marvelous Boys," p. 18.

73. Michael Heyward, *The Ern Malley Affair* (London: Faber and Faber, 1993), p. 137.

74. Herbert Read, correspondence, cited in Heyward, *Ern Malley Affair*, pp. 196-197. McAuley and Stewart, the forgers, were eventually tried—astonishingly—on Australian "obscenity" charges and fined a small amount of money.

75. McAuley and Stewart, cited in Heyward, *Ern Malley Affair*, p. 173.

76. Tristan Tzara, *The Dada Painters and Poets*, ed. Robert Motherwell (1951; Cambridge, MA: Harvard University Press, 1981), p. 92.

77. Ted Berrigan, notes to Ted Berrigan and Ron Padgett, *Bean Spasms*, 2nd ed. (1967; Gramercy Books, 2012), pp. 200, 201.

78. Ern Malley, "Sybilline," *Locus Solus* 2 (Summer 1961): p. 74.

79. Rimbaud, cited in John Ashbery, review of Joseph Cornell, *Art News* (Summer 1967), reprinted in Ashbery, *Reported Sightings*, p. 13.

80. John Ashbery, "Europe," in *Tennis Court Oath*, p. 64.

81. John Ashbery, cited in John Shoptaw, *On the Outside Looking Out: John Ashbery's Poetry* (Cambridge, MA: Harvard University Press, 1994), p. 57.

82. John Ashbery, "Into the Dark-Charged Air," in *Rivers and Mountains*, pp. 17, 18.

83. John Ashbery, "Daffy Duck in Hollywood," in *Houseboat Days* (New York: Viking, 1977), p. 31.

84. John Ashbery and Joe Brainard, *The Vermont Notebook* (Los Angeles: Black Sparrow Press, 1975), p. 13.

85. Ross, "Taking the Tennis Court Oath," pp. 199, 200.

86. Ibid., p. 198.

87. Alice Notley, introduction to Berrigan, *Sonnets*, p. x. One should consult Berrigan's "Cento: A Note on Philosophy," in his *Collected Poems*, ed. Alice Notley, with Anselm Berrigan and Edmund Berrigan (Berkeley: University of California Press, 2005), pp. 436-437.

88. The repetition of words functions prominently in some of the Koch/Ashbery collaborations from *Locus Solus* 2: the words "bumper" and "bonus" are repeated in every line, and the words "autumn" and "summer" are alternated in every line in "Gottlieb's Rainbow." Similarly, the word "button" is repeated in every line of "The Young Collectors" (a self-portrait of the young collaborators composing these poems). *Locus Solus* 2 (Summer 1961): pp. 165-166, 156-157.

89. Repetitions of the title of Ashbery's poem (*Tennis Court Oath*, p. 25), or variants of it, appear in Berrigan's "Sonnet II" (*Sonnets*, p. 2) and in Malanga's "A" (*Chic Death*, p. 24).

90. In the collaboration "New Year's Eve," for example, Ashbery wrote the odd lines and Koch the even ones. *Locus Solus* 2 (Summer 1961): pp. 166-168.

91. On the relaxation of poetic diction, David Lehman cites Allen Ginsberg (who is thinking of a remark of Frank O'Hara's): "Everybody had some reference to the transformation of the diction and the rhythms into vernacular rhythms and/or spoken cadences and idiomatic diction." Lehman, *The Last Avant-Garde: The Making of the New York School of Poets* (New York: Doubleday, 1998), p. 335.

92. John Ashbery, "Europe," p. 74.

93. Gerard Malanga, "The New Realism," in *Chic Death*, p. 56.

94. Ted Berrigan, "Sonnet LI," in *The Sonnets*, p. 48.

95. Frank O'Hara, "Poem in January," in *The Selected Poems of Frank O'Hara*, ed. Donald Allen (New York: Vintage Books, 1974), p. 83.

96. Shaw, *Frank O'Hara*, p. 119.

97. See the statements on poetics by a dozen or so American poets in Donald Allen, ed., *The New American Poetry, 1945-1960* (Berkeley: University of California Press, 1960).

98. Ted Berrigan and Ron Padgett, "Here Are Just a Few of the Ways This Book Will Help You," in Berrigan and Padgett, *Bean Spasms*, p. 195.

99. Ted Berrigan, notes to Berrigan and Padgett, *Bean Spasms*, p. 199.

100. Warhol and Hackett, *POPism*, p. 111.

101. Geoff Ward, *Statutes of Liberty*, 2nd ed. (New York: Palgrave, 2001), p. 40.

102. Daniel Kane, *All Poets Welcome: The Lower East Side Poetry Scene in the 1960s* (Berkeley: University of California Press, 2003), p. 113.

103. Berrigan, cited in David Kermani, *John Ashbery: A Comprehensive Bibliography,*

Including His Art Criticism, and with Selected Notes from Unpublished Materials (New York: Garland, 1976), p. 83.

104. John Ashbery, "Rivers and Mountains," in *Rivers and Mountains*, p. 10. Ted Berrigan, *So Going Around Cities: New & Selected Poems 1958-1979* (Berkeley: Blue Wind Press, 1980).

105. Ron Padgett, "A Note on *Bean Spasms*" (unpaginated preface), Padgett and Berrigan, *Bean Spasms*.

106. Ted Berrigan, in "Tom Clark Interviews Ted Berrigan" (1971), in *Nice to See You: Homage to Ted Berrigan*, ed. Anne Waldman (Minneapolis: Coffee House Press, 1991), p. 81. Alice Notley sees a correlation between Berrigan's use of lines by other poets and the "method rearrangement" guiding his composition of *The Sonnets*: "Some sonnets are composed of phrases, lines, or blocks of material from previous sonnets, exclusively or in combination with new material; . . . many are composed of lines or blocks of lines from older poems written before *The Sonnets*, or are simply older poems; some are composed of lines by other poets." Notley, introduction to Berrigan, *Sonnets*, p. xi.

107. Wolf, *Andy Warhol, Poetry*, p. 94.

108. Ted Berrigan and Ron Padgett, "An Interview with John Cage," *Bean Spasms*, p. 62.

109. When "An Interview with John Cage" was first published in Peter Schjeldahl's magazine, *Mother*, in 1966, the text contained no indication of its fraudulent status. Only after Cage and others complained did Berrigan append a statement, acknowledging, "The above interview is completely a product of its author. John Cage served neither as collaborator nor as an interviewee." Berrigan and Padgett, *Bean Spasms*, p. 67.

110. With regard to Ashbery's poetics of "misrepresentation," Shoptaw claims, "Crypt words or phrases must be hidden for their misrepresentative power to be released." Shoptaw, *On the Outside Looking Out*, p. 9. Shoptaw's conception of poetic cryptonymy is heavily dependent, it should be noted, on Nicolas Abraham and Maria Torok, *The Wolf Man's Magic Word: A Cryptonymy*, trans. Nicholas Rand (Minneapolis: University of Minnesota Press, 1986).

111. Shoptaw states, "Although, or rather because, Ashbery leaves himself and his homosexuality out of his poetry, his poems misrepresent in a particular way which I will call 'homotextual'." *On the Outside Looking Out*, p. 4.

112. Gerard Malanga, "The New Realism," in *Chic Death*, p. 56.

113. Shaw, *Frank O'Hara*, p. 6.

114. Ibid., p. 16.

115. Ward, *Statutes of Liberty*, p. 179.

116. Ibid., p. 61.

117. Shaw, *Frank O'Hara*, p. 16.

118. Ibid., p. 7.

119. Ibid., p. 4. The notion of a textual coterie—a paradigm, or trope, linking poetic and social practices—can be found as well in Ezra Pound's use of the term "vortex." He first used the word in 1914 as a metaphor for the poetic "image" but later also came to use it in reference to a social nexus of creative individuals (reflecting his experiences in London and Paris): a textual coterie.

120. Nicolas Bourriaud, *Relational Aesthetics*, trans. Simon Pleasance and Fronza Woods (Dijon: les presses du réel, 2002), p. 33.

121. Thomas Chatterton, "The Account of W. Canynges Feast," *Locus Solus* 2 (Summer 1961): p. 49.

122. Frank O'Hara (with Kenneth Koch and John Ashbery), "The Coronation Murder Mystery," in O'Hara, *Amorous Nightmares of Delay: Selected Plays,* with an Introduction by Joe LeSueur (Baltimore: Johns Hopkins University Press, 1997), p. 149.

123. O'Hara (with Bill Berkson), "Flight 115, a play, or Pas de Fumer sur la Piste," in O'Hara, *Amorous Nightmares of Delay*, p. 168.

124. Bill Berkson, cited in Joe LeSueur, Introduction to O'Hara, *Amorous Nightmares of Delay*, p. xxiii.

125. Frank O'Hara (with Frank Lima), "Love on the Hoof," in *Amorous Nightmares of Delay*, pp. 173-176.

126. Bourriaud, *Relational Aesthetics*, p. 22.

127. Frank O'Hara, "C Revisited, or the True Legend of Carole Lombard," in *Amorous Nightmares of Delay*, pp. 178, 183, 184.

128. Berrigan and Padgett, "Interview with John Cage," p. 62. Warhol's original interview with G. W. Swenson was published as "What is Pop Art? Part 1" (1963), reprinted in Madoff, *Pop Art*, p. 103.

129. LeSueur, Introduction to O'Hara, *Amorous Nightmares of Delay*, p. xx. Jonathan Flatley writes, "Warhol's emphasis on the connection between being alike and liking can be understood as an effort to make room for a conception of queer sexual attraction." Flatley, "Like: Collecting and Collectivity," *October* 132 (Spring 2010): p. 76.

130. The entirety of Warhol's statement involving Brecht and totality is as follows: "Someone said that Brecht wanted everyone to think alike. I want everybody to think alike. But Brecht wanted to do it through Communism, in a way. Russia is doing it under government. It's happening here all by itself without being under a strict government; so if it's working without trying, why can't it work without being Communist? Everybody looks alike and acts alike, and we're getting more and more that way." Warhol, interview with G. W. Swenson, in Madoff, *Pop Art*, p. 103.

131. Shaw, *Frank O'Hara*, p. 6.

132. Warhol and Hackett, *POPism*, p. 64.

133. Ibid., pp. 64-5.

134. Ibid., p. 65.

135. The phrase "silver tenement" is David Antin's, from his 1966 essay, "Warhol:

The Silver Tenement," reprinted in Madoff, *Pop Art*, pp. 287-291. Keats (as I have indicated in earlier chapters) calls the topos of poetic substance—a realm of special effects—"my silver planet." John Keats, "Lamia" (part 1, line 196), in Keats, *Complete Poems and Selected Letters*, ed. Edward Hirsch (New York: Modern Library, 2001), p. 194.

136. The posters for the first Velvet Underground shows announced:

> Come Blow Your Mind
> The Silver Dream Factory Presents The First
> ERUPTING PLASTIC INEVITABLE
> With
> Andy Warhol
> The Velvet Underground
> And
> Nico

Warhol and Hackett, *POPism*, p. 162.

137. Roland Barthes, "Plastic" (1957), in *Mythologies*, trans. Annette Lavers (New York: Hill and Wang, 1972), p. 97.

138. Ibid., p. 98.

139. Ibid., pp. 98, 97.

140. Ibid., p. 98.

141. Ibid., p. 98.

142. Warhol and Hackett, *POPism*, p. 40.

143. Ibid., p. 235.

144. Ibid., p. 91.

145. Barthes, "Plastic," p. 99.

Chapter 9. Inventing Clichés

1. Baudelaire, in Benjamin's view, is the central figure in what Franz Werfel calls "a dreamy epoch of bad taste," a figure whose "legend," according to Anatole France, "abounds in marks of bad taste." Walter Benjamin and Anatole France, cited in Winfried Menninghaus, "On the 'Vital Significance' of Kitsch: Walter Benjamin's Politics of 'Bad Taste,'" in *Walter Benjamin and the Architecture of Modernity*, ed. Andrew Benjamin and Charles Rice (Melbourne: Re-Press, 2009), pp. 39-57 Also available as open source text online.

2. Peter Bürger, *Theory of the Avant-Garde*, trans. Michael Shaw (Minneapolis: University of Minnesota Press, 1984), p. 70.

3. Walter Benjamin, "The Work of Art in the Age of Mechanical Reproduction," reprinted in *Illuminations*, ed. Hannah Arendt, trans. Harry Zohn (New York: Schocken Books, 1969), pp. 237-238.

4. Walter Benjamin, "Central Park," in *The Writer of Modern Life: Essays on Charles Baudelaire*, ed. Michael W. Jennings (Cambridge, MA: Harvard University Press, 2006), p. 135. On the significance of Leibniz's monadology for theories of lyric poetry, see the chapter entitled "Lyric Monadologies" in Daniel Tiffany, *Infidel Poetics: Riddles, Nightlife, Substance* (Chicago: University of Chicago Press, 2009), pp. 98–136.

5. Benjamin remarks, "Baudelaire was a secret agent—an agent of the secret discontent of his class with its own rule," cited in Michael W. Jennings, introduction to Benjamin, *Writer of Modern Life*, p. 16.

6. Benjamin, "Work of Art in the Age of Mechanical Reproduction," p. 237.

7. Walter Benjamin, "The Paris of the Second Empire in Baudelaire," in *Writer of Modern Life*, p. 126.

8. Ibid., p. 59.

9. On the correlation of historical experience and tradition, Benjamin states, "Experience is indeed a matter of tradition, in collective existence as well as in private life. It is less the product of facts firmly rooted in memory than of a convergence in memory of accumulated and frequently unconscious data." Benjamin, "On Some Motifs in Baudelaire," reprinted in *Illuminations*, p. 157.

10. Benjamin, "Central Park," p. 165. In the same vein, Benjamin states, "Allegorical emblems return as commodities," and, "the devaluation of the world of things in allegory is surpassed within the world of things itself by the commodity," in "Central Park," pp. 159, 138.

11. Jennifer Bajorek develops Benjamin's thesis that Baudelaire's poetry may be understood as an "ironic" commodity, in Bajorek, *Counterfeit Capital: Labor and Revolutionary Irony* (Stanford: Stanford University Press, 2009).

12. Ibid., p. 5.

13. Benjamin, "Central Park," p. 150.

14. Geoff Ward, *Statutes of Liberty*, 2nd ed. (New York: Palgrave, 2001), p. 144.

15. Leo Steinberg, "Symposium on Pop Art" (1962), reprinted in *Pop Art: A Critical History*, ed. Steven Henry Madoff (Berkeley: University of California Press, 1997) p. 72.

16. Ibid., p. 71.

17. Walter Benjamin, "Central Park," p. 165.

18. Anton C. Zijderveld, *On Clichés* (London: Routledge and Kegan Paul, 1979), pp. 5–6.

19. The comment about clichés ("things better left *unsaid*") appears on the back cover of Eric Partridge, *Dictionary of Clichés* (London: Routledge and Kegan Paul, 1978).

20. Zijderveld, *On Clichés*, p. 24.

21. Benjamin, "Central Park," p. 145.

22. Ibid., p. 137.

23. Ibid., p. 161.

24. Benjamin, "The Paris of the Second Empire in Baudelaire," p. 52.

25. Walter Benjamin, "The Work of Art in the Age of Its Technological Reproducibility," in *Selected Writings, Volume 3: 1935-1938* (Cambridge, MA: Harvard University Press, 2002), pp. 104-105.

26. On the comparable scale of the impact of the two books, Benjamin muses, "*Les Fleurs du mal* is the last book of poems to have had an impact throughout Europe. Before that, perhaps Ossian?" Benjamin, "Central Park," p. 159.

27. Charles Baudelaire, "Quelques caricaturistes Français," in *Oeuvres complètes de Charles Baudelaire*, ed. Jacques Crépet (Paris: L. Conard, 1922-1953), p. 2:550. On Baudelaire's concept of *"argot plastique"* and modern caricature, see Ainslie Armstrong McLees, *Baudelaire's "Argot Plastique": Poetic Caricature and Modernism* (Athens: University of Georgia Press, 2010).

28. Charles Baudelaire, "Lost Halo," in *Paris Spleen*, trans. Keith Waldrop (Middletown, CT: Wesleyan University Press, 2009), p. 88.

29. Benjamin, "On Some Motifs in Baudelaire," p. 192.

30. Benjamin, "Central Park," pp. 147, 148-149.

31. Giorgio Agamben, *The Coming Community*, trans. Michael Hardt (Minneapolis: University of Minnesota Press, 1993), pp. 50, 53-58.

32. Benjamin, "On Some Motifs in Baudelaire," p. 191.

33. These phrases from Baudelaire's *Salon of 1859* (a segment of which serves as the epigraph to the present chapter) are cited by Walter Benjamin in his essay, "On Some Motifs in Baudelaire," p. 191.

34. John Ashbery, "The Impossible," review of *Stanzas in Meditation*, by Gertrude Stein, *Poetry* 90, no. 4 (July 1957): p. 254. Ted Berrigan and Ron Padgett, "Interview with John Cage," in *Bean Spasms* (1967), 2nd ed. (Gramercy Books, 2012), p. 62.

35. John Wilkinson, "Chamber Attitudes," in *The Lyric Touch: Essays on the Poetry of Excess* (Cambridge: Salt Publishing, 2007), p. 215.

36. Frank O'Hara, "To a Poet," in *The Collected Poems of Frank O'Hara*, ed., Donald Allen (Berkeley: University of California Press, 1995), p. 185.

37. John Wieners, "Reading *Second Avenue*," in John Wieners, *Selected Poems, 1958-1984*, ed. Raymond Foye (Santa Barbara: Black Sparrow Press, 1986), pp. 220-221. This poem appears in a section entitled "Uncollected Poems, 1958-1975."

38. John Wilkinson, "A Poem for Liars," in *Lyric Touch*, p. 251.

39. John Wieners, "A Poem for Vipers," in *Selected Poems*, p. 28.

40. John Wilkinson, "A Poem for Liars," p. 252.

41. Ibid., p. 253.

42. Wilkinson, "Chamber Attitudes," pp. 233, 234.

43. John Wilkinson, "Too-Close Reading: Poetry and Schizophrenia," in *Lyric Touch*, p. 162.

44. Barbara Guest, *The Location of Things* (New York: Tibor de Nagy Gallery, 1960).

45. Barbara Guest, "The Hero Leaves His Ship," in *Collected Poems of Barbara*

Guest, ed. Hadley Haden Guest (Middletown: Wesleyan University Press, 2008), pp. 9, 10.

46. Barbara Guest, "Windy Afternoon," *Collected Poems*, p. 8.

47. Barbara Guest and Joe Brainard, "Joan and Ken," cited in Maggie Nelson, *Women, The New York School, and Other True Abstractions* (Iowa City: University of Iowa Press, 2007), p. 41.

48. Nelson, *Women, the New York School*, p. 41.

49. Barbara Guest, "Fan Poems," *Collected Poems*, p. 80.

50. Barbara Guest, "Knight of the Swan," *Collected Poems*, p. 111.

51. Marjorie Welish, "The Lyric Lately (a work-in-progress)," *Jacket*, no. 10 (October 1999), n.p. Web: www.jacketmagazine.com/10.

52. Ibid.

53. Frederick Seidel, "Poem by the Bridge at Ten-Shin," in *Poems, 1959–2009* (New York: Farrar Straus Giroux, 2009), p. 44. The title is lifted from Pound.

54. Frederick Seidel, "Barbados," in *Ooga-Booga* (New York: Farrar, Straus and Giroux, 2006), p. 63.

55. Frederick Seidel, "Another Muse," in *Going Fast* (New York: Farrar, Straus and Giroux, 1998), p. 44.

56. Frederick Seidel, "The New Frontier," in *Sunrise* (New York: Penguin Books, 1980), p. 52.

57. Frederick Seidel, "Going Fast," in *Going Fast*, p. 93.

58. Frederick Seidel, "Vermont," in *Going Fast*, p. 72.

59. Ange Mlinko, "With Mercy for the Greedy," *Nation*, July 13, 2009. Also available at www.thenation.com/article/mercy-greedy# (n.p.).

60. Frederick Seidel, "The Death of the Shah," in *Ooga-Booga*, p. 96.

61. Dr. Seuss, "Italy," cited in Mlinko, "With Mercy for the Greedy."

62. Djuna Barnes, unpublished (and untitled) poem, *Collected Poems*, eds. Phillip Herring and Osias Stutman (Madison: University of Wisconsin Press, 2005), p. 191.

63. Djuna Barnes, "Six Songs of Khalidine," *Collected Poems*, p. 86.

64. Djuna Barnes, "Shadows," *Collected Poems*, p. 63.

65. Djuna Barnes, "A Last Toast," *Collected Poems*, p. 61.

66. Djuna Barnes, "Suicide," *Collected Poems*, p. 55.

67. Djuna Barnes, "Vaudeville," *Collected Poems*, p. 76.

68. Djuna Barnes, "Seen from the 'L,'" *Collected Poems*, p. 49.

69. Baudelaire, cited in Walter Benjamin, "Paris of the Second Empire in Baudelaire," pp. 122, 119.

70. Djuna Barnes, "Twilight of the Illicit," *Collected Poems*, p. 51.

71. Peter Gizzi and Kevin Killian, Introduction to Jack Spicer, *My Vocabulary Did This to Me: The Collected Poetry of Jack Spicer*, eds. Peter Gizzi and Kevin Killian (Middletown: Wesleyan University Press, 2008), p. xxii.

72. Gizzi and Killian, Introduction to Spicer, *Collected Poetry*, p. xvii.

73. Jack Spicer, Vancouver Lecture 1 (June 13, 1965), in *The House That Jack Built: The Collected Lectures of Jack Spicer*, ed. Peter Gizzi (Hanover, NH: University Press of New England, 1998), p. 39. Spicer's most direct discussion of the principle of "dictation" occurs on pp. 4-17.

74. Spicer, *Collected Poetry*, pp. 110-111.

75. The editors of Spicer's *Collected Poetry* use the phrase "fake translations" to describe the texts in *After Lorca*. Gizzi and Killian, Introduction to Spicer, *Collected Poetry*, p. xxii.

76. Spicer, *Collected Poetry*, p. 123.

77. Ibid., pp. 163-164.

78. Ibid., p. 157.

79. In several of his letters to Lorca, Spicer develops a model of poetic "correspondences" to explain his theory of translation, including a striking reference to "Poe's mechanical chess player," which is manipulated by a man inside the automaton. Because the "fake translation" is thus a kind of toy, Spicer declares, "The analogy is false, of course, but it holds both a promise and a warning for each of us." Spicer, *Collected Poetry*, pp. 133-134, 153.

80. Jack Spicer, "For Jerry" (from *Admonitions*), *Collected Poetry*, p. 167.

81. Spicer, "A Poem for Dada Day at the Place, April 1, 1955," *Collected Poetry*, p. 46.

82. Ibid., pp. 46-47.

83. Ibid., p. 47.

Index

Spence, Joseph, 109
Spence, Thomas, 83
Spengler, Oswald, 164-65
Spenser, Edmund, 94
Spicer, Jack, 227-30, 241, 287n79; work:
    Admonitions, 229; After Lorca, 228, 229
Spoerri, Daniel, 185, 241
"Star-Spangled Banner, The," 153
Steinberg, Leo, 185, 214
Stephen, Leslie, 53-54
stereotype, 13, 50, 55, 72, 76, 239
Stewart, Harold, 188
Stewart, Susan, 9, 65-66, 82, 99, 115, 116
Strawberry Hill Set, 112, 123, 232, 266n6,
    267n21; as coterie, 202, 203, 238; homo-
    sexuality/queerness and, 6, 111, 113-14,
    120; Walpole and, 109, 266n5
Stubbes, Philip, 118
sublimation, 37, 93; political vs. aesthetic,
    185, 192, 200, 213, 214, 217, 239
sublime, 44, 245n24
suicide, 172, 175, 177, 186, 226, 238; of
    Chatterton, 56, 130-31, 133, 170, 172,
    173; Dadaism and, 179, 230, 277n34; and
    forgery, 131, 170, 172; Gray and, 56, 57, 58,
    173; poetics of, 173-74, 178-79; as Warhol
    theme, 172-73
superficiality, 16, 21, 68-69, 73, 214, 226, 241
surface reading, 17
Surrealism, 170, 204, 248n11; and kitsch, 19,
    20, 23; New Realism and, 177, 189, 190
Swift, Jonathan, 92
Symons, Arthur, 138
symptomatology, 166
syntax, 30, 195
synthesis, 14, 163, 169
synthesizing, 17, 59, 75, 99, 122, 145
synthetic vernaculars, 8, 36, 43-45, 90, 250n41

Tatersal, Robert, 91-92
Tavel, Ronnie, 209
Tennis Court Oath, The (Ashbery), 171, 172-73,
    174, 176, 192, 205
Terada, Rei, 111
Teskey, Gordon, 13, 53
textual coteries, 203, 238-39, 282n119
Thermofax, 175-76
Thomson, James, 109
Tickell, Thomas, 65, 93

Tin Pan Alley, 18
topography, 70, 111
topology, 117, 141, 175; of privacy, 111, 113
totalitarianism, 14, 155, 158, 165, 167; kitsch
    and, 146-47, 150
totality: coterie as, 16, 247n49; cultural, 135,
    153, 169; epics and, 154-55, 161; and kitsch,
    13-14, 153, 158, 161; Marxism and, 14, 156,
    157-59, 160, 161, 162, 246n43; and memory,
    161-62; poetic, 157, 161, 167; political, 155,
    168; Pound and, 155-56, 158, 160; queer,
    123; social, 14, 23, 31, 69, 72, 74, 153,
    160-61, 207, 239; and solidarity, 13, 239;
    as synthetic, 14, 153, 160
toys, 27, 97-98, 103; kitsch as, 4; Mother
    Goose as toy-book, 86-87
traditionalism, 213, 224, 234, 235
transitivity, 122, 240, 241
translation, 45, 137; Spicer theory of, 228,
    229, 287n79
Tranter, John, 187
trash, 66, 118; artistic, 1; poetic, 85
trifles, 87, 97-98, 101, 104, 194, 214
triviality, 120, 224, 235; kitsch and, 3, 16,
    21, 148
twice made, 13-14, 53, 206
Twombly, Cy, 202
Tzara, Tristan, 180, 182, 189, 278n41

unoriginality, 34, 99, 174, 187, 232

Velvet Underground, 208, 209, 282-83n136
vernacular language, 61, 75, 196, 198, 201,
    232, 238; ballads and, 75, 234; Dada and,
    182; definition of, 237; elite culture and,
    2, 8, 12, 15, 28, 81, 231, 233; Guillory on,
    46, 253n29; kitsch and, 12, 15, 36, 63;
    and poetic diction, 8, 9, 32, 36, 43, 60;
    and poetry, 2, 8, 33, 50-51, 60, 81, 82,
    86, 237-38, 256n98; prose and, 42, 60;
    synthetic, 44, 45, 90, 237; writing in, 32,
    33, 46, 47, 50
Vico, Giambattista, 56, 160
vocabulary, 34-35, 229; and poetic diction,
    31, 43, 196
Volkslieder, 74
von Ofterdingen, Henrich, 19
vortex and Vorticism, 224, 238, 239; Pound
    and, 140, 155, 156-57, 238-39, 282n119